Convergence of Digitalization, Innovation, and Sustainable Development in Business

Alper Erturk
Australian University, Kuwait

Stephen Edward Colbran
Central Queensland University, Australia

Erman Coşkun
Izmir Bakircay University, Turkey

Faidon Theofanidis
Australian University, Kuwait

Oualid Abidi
Australian University, Kuwait

IGI Global
PUBLISHER of TIMELY KNOWLEDGE

A volume in the Advances in Business Strategy and Competitive Advantage (ABSCA) Book Series

Published in the United States of America by
IGI Global
Business Science Reference (an imprint of IGI Global)
701 E. Chocolate Avenue
Hershey PA, USA 17033
Tel: 717-533-8845
Fax: 717-533-8661
E-mail: cust@igi-global.com
Web site: http://www.igi-global.com

Library of Congress Cataloging-in-Publication Data

Names: Erturk, Alper, editor.
Title: Convergence of digitalization, innovation, and sustainable development in business / edited by Alper Erturk, Stephen Colbran, Erman Coskun, Faidon Theofanidis, Oualid Abidi.
Description: Hershey, PA : Business Science Reference, [2024] | Includes bibliographical references and index. | Summary: "This book covers digital transformation from several different perspectives related to sustainable development, and provide organizations a variety of digital innovative solutions and strategies, from which they can choose the ones that best suit their own requirements and sustainability strategies"-- Provided by publisher.
Identifiers: LCCN 2023052957 (print) | LCCN 2023052958 (ebook) | ISBN 9798369307984 (hardcover) | ISBN 9798369307991 (ebook)
Subjects: LCSH: Sustainable development--Technological innovations. | Information technology--Environmental aspects.
Classification: LCC HC79.E5 C636 2024 (print) | LCC HC79.E5 (ebook) | DDC 338.9/27--dc23/eng/20231207
LC record available at https://lccn.loc.gov/2023052957
LC ebook record available at https://lccn.loc.gov/2023052958

This book is published in the IGI Global book series Advances in Business Strategy and Competitive Advantage (ABSCA) (ISSN: 2327-3429; eISSN: 2327-3437)

British Cataloguing in Publication Data
A Cataloguing in Publication record for this book is available from the British Library.

Advances in Business Strategy and Competitive Advantage (ABSCA) Book Series

Patricia Ordóñez de Pablos
Universidad de Oviedo, Spain

ISSN:2327-3429
EISSN:2327-3437

Mission

Business entities are constantly seeking new ways through which to gain advantage over their competitors and strengthen their position within the business environment. With competition at an all-time high due to technological advancements allowing for competition on a global scale, firms continue to seek new ways through which to improve and strengthen their business processes, procedures, and profitability.

The **Advances in Business Strategy and Competitive Advantage (ABSCA) Book Series** is a timely series responding to the high demand for state-of-the-art research on how business strategies are created, implemented and re-designed to meet the demands of globalized competitive markets. With a focus on local and global challenges, business opportunities and the needs of society, the **ABSCA** encourages scientific discourse on doing business and managing information technologies for the creation of sustainable competitive advantage.

Coverage

- Competitive Strategy
- Strategic Management
- Foreign Investment Decision Process
- Ethics and Business Strategy
- Tacit Knowledge
- Innovation Strategy
- Business Models
- Balanced Scorecard
- Core Competencies
- Small and Medium Enterprises

IGI Global is currently accepting manuscripts for publication within this series. To submit a proposal for a volume in this series, please contact our Acquisition Editors at Acquisitions@igi-global.com or visit: http://www.igi-global.com/publish/.

The Advances in Business Strategy and Competitive Advantage (ABSCA) Book Series (ISSN 2327-3429) is published by IGI Global, 701 E. Chocolate Avenue, Hershey, PA 17033-1240, USA, www.igi-global.com. This series is composed of titles available for purchase individually; each title is edited to be contextually exclusive from any other title within the series. For pricing and ordering information please visit http://www.igi-global.com/book-series/advances-business-strategy-competitive-advantage/73672. Postmaster: Send all address changes to above address.

Titles in this Series

For a list of additional titles in this series, please visit: http://www.igi-global.com/book-series/advances-business-strategy-competitive-advantage/73672

Trends, Challenges, and Practices in Contemporary Strategic Management
Filiz Mızrak (Beykoz University, Turkey)
Business Science Reference • © 2024 • 355pp • H/C (ISBN: 9798369311554) • US $275.00

Fostering Global Entrepreneurship Through Business Model Innovation
Varun Gupta (Multidisciplinary Research Centre for Innovations in SMEs, Gisma University of Applied Sciences, Potsdam, Germany & Department of Economics and Business Administration, Universidad de Alcalá, Alcalá de Henares (Madrid), Spain)
Business Science Reference • © 2024 • 293pp • H/C (ISBN: 9781668469750) • US $275.00

Sustainable Consumption Experience and Business Models in the Modern World
Maria Amélia Machado Carvalho (Business School, Polytechnic Institute of Porto, Portugal) and Maria Antónia Rodrigues (CEOS, Business School, Polytechnic Institute of Porto, Portugal)
Business Science Reference • © 2024 • 257pp • H/C (ISBN: 9781668492772) • US $240.00

Ecosystem Dynamics and Strategies for Startups Scalability
Neeta Baporikar (Namibia University of Science and Technology, Namibia & SP Pune University, India)
Business Science Reference • © 2024 • 333pp • H/C (ISBN: 9798369305270) • US $275.00

Smart Strategies and Societal Solutions for Sustainable International Business
Abdelkader Mohamed Sghaier Derbali (Taibah University, Saudi Arabia)
Business Science Reference • © 2024 • 228pp • H/C (ISBN: 9798369305324) • US $275.00

Applying Interdisciplinarity to Globalization, Management, Marketing, and Accountancy Science
Vladislav Pavlát (The University of Finance and Administration, Czech Republic) Ladislava Knihová (The University of Finance and Administration, Czech Republic) Lubomír Civín (AMBIS, Czech Republic) Jaroslav Halík (Metropolitan University, Prague, Czech Republic) and Radka MacGregor Pelikánová (University of New York in Prague, Czech Republic)
Business Science Reference • © 2023 • 310pp • H/C (ISBN: 9781799886693) • US $240.00

Transformational Interventions for Business, Technology, and Healthcare
Darrell Norman Burrell (Marymount University, USA)
Business Science Reference • © 2023 • 584pp • H/C (ISBN: 9798369316344) • US $295.00

IGI Global
PUBLISHER of TIMELY KNOWLEDGE

701 East Chocolate Avenue, Hershey, PA 17033, USA
Tel: 717-533-8845 x100 • Fax: 717-533-8661
E-Mail: cust@igi-global.com • www.igi-global.com

Table of Contents

Detailed Table of Contents

Urban development literature has gained great traction due to the unprecedent challenges that cities face, and digitalization has been signaled as a game-changer against these challenges. However, the effects that urban digitalization might have on the economic prosperity at city-level remain unexplored. This research analyzes the bidirectional relationship between the digitalization degree and the economic situation of a city, based on a sample of 404 cities. The analysis resulted in confirming the positive bidirectional relationship between digitalization levels and the city's economic condition. If the economic prosperity of a city increases, so does its level of digitalization and if cities embrace and integrate digitalization, there is a positive impact on their economic growth. Thus, economic development and technological advancement mutually reinforce each other in urban contexts. This study not only aims to nurture the urban literature, but also to shed light on the shift towards the cities of the future.

Digital maturity, which emerges as evaluating the digitalization level of businesses and municipalities and guiding them for the digital transformation process, is a very comprehensive concept that has been emphasized in the literature recently. This study provides a conceptual model for assessing the digital maturity of a municipality and analyzing the relationship between digital maturity and the sustainability of the municipality. The study proposes parameters from literature and customizes them based on specifications to determine different dimensions of municipality digital maturity and develops hypotheses to assess digital maturity dimensions and sustainability relations for a city or municipality. The study is also aiming to create a reliable and tested conceptual framework for the assessment of municipal digital maturity and the relationship between this maturity level and the sustainability of the municipality.

This chapter is centered on investigating the usability of process modeling tools, which are fundamental components of business process management (BPM). It is structured into two main sections. The first part offers a theoretical overview of the lifecycle of business process management, the concept of business process modeling, and various notations for process modeling. Furthermore, the chapter presents the key knowledge of BPMN and the tools for business process modeling, along with a comparative analysis of the investigated tools. The second part of the chapter is dedicated to evaluating the usability, focusing on

The primary objective of this chapter is to offer readers a thorough grasp of the intricate relationships that exist between organizational policies, digital tools, and the impacts that technology has on people and the natural world. Today's businesses profit from having easy access to a plethora of online resources and tools that promote improved communication, openness, gathering and interpreting information, and the spurring of innovation. These capabilities have allowed for the integration of CSR and SD principles into major company planning, promoting long-term sustainability and beneficial social results. The chapter examines how CSR and SD practices have grown as a result of digital technology, highlighting both the challenges and the new potential. Businesses that use the digital era for CSR and SD could open the door to a more prosperous and ecologically conscious future for humanity.

The literature on continuous mobile banking use lacks research on cross-cultural variations and comparisons between countries at different levels of economic and technological development. These differences can lead to varying perceptions and attitudes among residents. This study aimed to identify significant differences between Kuwaiti and Serbian university students in their use of mobile banking applications and their perceptions of factors influencing such usage. The data on eight constructs that have been hypothesized in previous literature to impact continuous mobile banking app use were collected: perceived usefulness, perceived ease of use, confirmation, perceived trust, compatibility, privacy, environmental awareness, and satisfaction. The Mann-Whitney U-test was employed to test for differences in perceptions between the two groups. The findings suggest that differences in perceptions between the two countries are influenced by cultural backgrounds, development levels, user habits, mobile banking app characteristics, and socio-economic factors.

This study conducts a systematic literature review to identify forms of user behavioral bias, affecting the generation of content, evaluation patterns, and the impact of online reviews. Furthermore, it indicates the resulting implications for organizations' management of customer knowledge. The authors collected studies dating from 2009 to 2023 in Scopus, where a high dimensionality of bias definitions is observed. As a result of this review, a series of thematic distinctions is proposed, distinguishing sentiment and

Preface

In the current landscape of rapid technological advancement and ever-evolving business paradigms, the fusion of digitalization, innovation, and sustainable development has emerged as a cornerstone in shaping the future of global enterprises. This convergence represents a pivotal juncture wherein digital transformation not only revolutionizes operational methodologies but also becomes integral to fostering sustainability across various sectors. We, the editors – Alper Erturk, Stephen Colbran, Erman Coskun, Faidon Theofanidis, and Oualid Abidi – are honored to present *Convergence of Digitalization, Innovation, and Sustainable Development in Business.*

In an era defined by ceaseless change, the integration of diverse digital technologies into organizational frameworks marks a significant paradigm shift. This transformation encompasses multifaceted components, spanning from data analytics and artificial intelligence to simulation, virtual/augmented reality, process automation, and novel product development. Regardless of the business domain, the ultimate aim of digital transformation is to fortify competitiveness, endorse sustainability, and augment overall efficiency by embracing digital technologies across the spectrum.

Simultaneously, sustainable development has rightfully assumed a paramount role, compelling organizations and global entities alike to prioritize preserving natural resources, nurturing the environment, and ensuring the availability of essential resources for future generations. It necessitates a progressive alteration in technology development and utilization, emphasizing the crucial role that digital technologies play in sustainable development endeavors.

Convergence of Digitalization, Innovation, and Sustainable Development in Business represents a comprehensive exploration delving into the interrelationships between digitalization, innovation, and sustainable development within the contemporary business landscape. Mainly derived from a selection of papers presented at the International Conference on Digitalization, Innovations, and Sustainable Development, this compilation endeavors to amalgamate insights from leading scholars, researchers, and practitioners across diverse fields, elucidating the latest trends and business perspectives pertinent to this nexus.

The primary essence and significance of this book lies in the convergence of digital transformation and sustainable development and how their symbiotic relationship operates. Our foremost objective is to furnish organizations with a spectrum of digital innovative solutions and strategies, tailored to align with their specific requirements and sustainability agendas.

Encompassing a vast array of technologies and tools, the impact of this book is poised to reverberate through academic literature and practical applications across varied industries, spanning healthcare, tourism, banking, education, aviation, logistics, and more. This technology-driven approach towards sustainable development is poised to unlock new vistas of opportunities for industries and academia, while simultaneously presenting challenges that necessitate adaptive strategies to avoid disruption.

Our envisioned audience comprises university professors, researchers, students, and industry practitioners deeply vested in comprehending digital transformation and its contextual nuances. The amalgamation of findings within this book holds the potential to steer future research trajectories in the realm of digital transformation while guiding practical decision-making within industry settings.

The chapters encapsulated within this compendium encompass a diverse spectrum of themes, including digitalization's role in sustainable development, innovations in circular economies, smart cities, supply chain sustainability, renewable energy, agriculture, transportation, corporate social responsibility, sustainable finance, business models, public policy, digital marketing technologies, and forecasting the future trajectory of digitalization and sustainable development.

ORGANIZATION OF THE BOOK

Chapter 1

This chapter investigates the correlation between a nation's digital readiness, international trade openness, and innovation potential. By analyzing data from 115 countries, the study establishes a positive connection between a country's digital readiness and innovation index. However, it uncovers that increased trade openness negatively mediates the relationship between digitalization and innovation, possibly due to challenges in absorptive capacity and cross-border collaboration.

Chapter 2

Focusing on Bhutan's traditional trade methods and the rise of digital technologies and e-commerce, this chapter explores opportunities and challenges in Bhutan's international trade. It delves into the potential benefits and hurdles of digital entrepreneurship and e-commerce, offering insights for policymakers and stakeholders shaping Bhutan's international trade strategies.

Chapter 3

Examining the relationship between urban digitalization and a city's economic condition based on 404 cities, this study establishes a positive bidirectional link. It highlights how economic development and technological advancement mutually reinforce each other in urban contexts, shedding light on the trajectory of future cities.

Chapter 4

This chapter introduces a conceptual model to assess municipal digital maturity and its relationship with sustainability. By proposing parameters and hypotheses, the study aims to create a reliable framework for evaluating digital maturity and its impact on municipal sustainability.

Chapter 5

Focusing on Business Process Management, this chapter evaluates the usability of process modeling tools like Camunda Web, SAP Signavio, and Camunda Desktop. It concludes that Camunda Web received the highest scores in usability, usefulness, and ease of use, establishing itself as a preferred choice among participants.

Chapter 6

By incorporating sustainability into the evaluation of platform business models, this study proposes a framework using the Analytical Hierarchy Process. It emphasizes product innovation, customer relationships, and financial aspects, indicating the importance of considering sustainability in decision-making processes.

Chapter 7

Focusing on logistics firms in Turkiye, this chapter establishes that high levels of digital transformation strongly predict the adoption of sustainability innovations in logistics. It contributes valuable insights to supply chain sustainability and the digitalization of environmental sustainability.

Chapter 8

This chapter explores how digital technology facilitates the integration of Corporate Social Responsibility (CSR) and Sustainable Development (SD) principles into company planning. It examines the challenges and potential in using the digital era to promote CSR and SD, envisioning a more sustainable future for businesses and society.

Chapter 9

Comparing Kuwaiti and Serbian university students' perceptions of mobile banking apps, this study identifies differences influenced by cultural backgrounds, technological development levels, and user habits. It highlights how cultural variations impact mobile banking app perceptions.

Chapter 10

This chapter conducts a systematic review of user behavioral biases in online reviews, presenting thematic distinctions and analogies with cognitive bias literature. It offers insights into understanding and mitigating biases in online review platforms, proposing methods for bias-centered management.

Chapter 11

Utilizing data visualization tools, this chapter assesses cancer incidence in Jordan from 2012 to 2018. It reveals demographic patterns and incidence rates, emphasizing the need for proactive healthcare strategies and the potential of digital tools in early detection and proactive healthcare planning.

These chapters collectively provide a comprehensive exploration of digital transformation's multifaceted impacts across various domains, offering insights, frameworks, and empirical findings to guide stakeholders, policymakers, and researchers navigating the intersection of digitalization, innovation, and sustainability in the contemporary business landscape.

In conclusion, we extend our gratitude to the esteemed contributors for their invaluable insights and endeavors, hoping that this edited reference book serves as a cornerstone for deeper explorations and informed actions, contributing significantly to the ongoing discourse on the convergence of digitalization, innovation, and sustainable development in contemporary business.

Chapter 1
Country Digitalization, Trade Openness, and Innovation:
Is There a Symbiosis?

Oualid Abidi
https://orcid.org/0000-0002-0099-889X
Australian University, Kuwait

Vladimir Dzenopoljac
https://orcid.org/0000-0003-2974-6466
Zayed University, UAE

Aleksandra Dzenopoljac
SP Jain School of Global Management, UAE

ABSTRACT

Digital transformation programs at the national level had a significant impact on innovation. However, there is a lack of understanding as to whether this dynamic is compounded by the higher exposure to international trade, thanks to digitalization. Thus, the objective of this chapter is to demonstrate that a nation's spending on digital transformation may encourage local organizations to expand their business beyond national borders, which could enhance their innovation potential. Drawing on recent secondary data compiled for 115 countries, the effect of digital readiness on a country's innovation index was tested with path analysis using AMOS software. The findings confirm the positive and significant effect of country digital readiness on both, trade openness and innovation. However, these results show that trade openness negatively mediates the relationship between a country's digitalization and innovation capacity. This result may be explained by the insufficient absorptive capacity of newly internationalized firms and the cultural hindrance in cross-border collaborations.

DOI: 10.4018/979-8-3693-0798-4.ch001

INTRODUCTION

Digital transformation programs aimed at improving digital platforms and infrastructure at the national level have had a significant impact on innovation and entrepreneurial activity in general (Myovella et al., 2020). Digital transformation is a growing phenomenon in organizations that is characterized by substantive business model transformations driven by innovative digital technologies (Zhang & Chen, 2023). The modernization of digital conditions is key to economic prosperity, as it directly affects the quality of the business environment. Different countries have been making significant efforts to ensure the effectiveness and affordability of digital platforms, including mobile technologies, cloud computing, and the Internet of Things (Gurbaxani & Dunkle, 2018). As a result, digital transformation has a positive impact on economic development and other indicators, such as employment and labor productivity (Aly, 2022). In the same sense, digitalization accelerated the decentralization of governmental decision-making which facilitated the achievement of sustainability development goals (ElMassah & Mohieldin, 2020).

Despite growing interest in understanding the effects of digital transformation on the innovative capacity of local organizations, it is unclear whether this dynamic is exacerbated by another effect associated with increased exposure to international trade as a result of digitalizationEvidence shows that digital transformation allowed major shifts in trade modes and the related business models including the distribution channels. It disrupted the old trade traditions as digital forms of products are replacing the physically embodied ones (Ciuriak & Ptashkina, 2018). Furthermore, digitalization has generated opportunities for international business and digital commerce (Ahmedov, 2020). Therefore, the present chapter will attempt to address the following research question: Does a country's digitalization boost its innovation capabilities by promoting trade openness? The latter is defined as a country's exposure to international trade, materialized in terms of exporting and importing activities (Afesorgbor & Demena, 2022).

Our objective is to demonstrate that a country's investment in digital transformation can encourage local organizations to expand beyond national borders, which can help them increase their scope, diversify their operations, and expand their product markets through sustained innovation efforts. Indeed, trade openness benefits nations by contributing to economic growth (Intisar et al., 2020; Kong et al., 2021) and innovation in particular (Galbreath, 2019). By examining the impact of nationwide digital transformation efforts on imports and exports, this chapter aims to shed light on how these initiatives can contribute to enhancing the overall innovation potential of the local economy. Furthermore, understanding the relationship between digital transformation and international trade can provide valuable insights for policymakers seeking to foster economic growth through technological advancements.

To our knowledge, no study had focused on the interplay between those three dimensions, namely country digital readiness, trade openness and innovation capacity. Filling this gap represents the main contribution of the present manuscript. If the findings support the hypothesized model, this would be insightful for policy makers at state level. Their attention would need to focus on imparting technological updates that support the exposure and accessibility of local organizations to partnering opportunities abroad, e.g., outsourcing, simplified digital monetary transfers. Changes could also concern the development of e-government services destined to foreign companies, with the aim of facilitating the paperwork and procedures necessary to invest in local collaborations with domestic firms.

This chapter is organized as follows: The first section provides an overview of the literature on digital transformation and states the three research hypotheses. Then, the methodology applied is explained, followed by the research results and discussion. Finally, the conclusion presents the significant contributions, as well as future research directions.

LITERATURE REVIEW AND HYPOTHESES

The literature is abundant with definitions of digital transformation, which mainly revolve around the concept being defined at the national level and at the organizational level. A conceptual definition of digital transformation points to it as "a process that aims to improve an entity by triggering significant changes to its properties through combinations of information, computing, communication, and connectivity technologies" (Vial, 2021, p. 13). Another comprehensive definition of digital transformation sees it as "a fundamental change process, enabled by the innovative use of digital technologies accompanied by the strategic leverage of key resources and capabilities, aiming to radically improve an entity and redefine its value proposition for its stakeholders" (Gong & Ribiere, 2021). The latter definition defines "entity" as an organization, a business network, an industry, or an entire society. The focus of the current chapter is on digital transformation at the national level, which is fostered through the cumulative effect of digital transformation achieved at organizational levels.

Investment in new information technologies and infrastructure has been argued to be a driver of economic growth (Habibi & Zabardast, 2020). Digital transformation is seen in developing countries as a fundamental means for wealth creation and prosperity. Those countries aim for the achievement of structural change with the newly implemented technologies and platforms in terms of productivity, sectoral employment shifts, and trade (Matthess & Kunkel, 2020). Investing in network readiness, for example, supports the impact of public digitalization on economic growth and social progress (Silva et al., 2022). The digitalization of governance systems helps in creating effective crisis management capabilities and alleviates the societal repercussions of crises, as was the case with the South-Korean response to the COVID-19 pandemic (Lee-Geiller & Lee, 2022).

The achievement of higher levels of technological and digital readiness supports the creation and development of efficient logistic systems in the economy. In this sense, efforts should be made to enhance digital connectivity (Moldabekova et al., 2021). Nonetheless, digital transformation builds on national intellectual capital, essentially social capital and working skills. The differentials registered across countries in terms of national intellectual capital are responsible for the digital divide that separates them (Švarc et al., 2021). Furthermore, the growth of developed economies is primarily driven by national human and renewal capital, which are the primary carriers of knowledge and future investment in their growth (Dženopoljac et al., 2022).

Despite the concerns raised about the risks and limitations associated with digitalization, such as digital skills bias (Matthess & Kunkel, 2020) and the ineffective role in combating poverty and social exclusion in well-established economies (Kwilinski et al., 2020), it remains a primary choice for many countries for the next decades. In this regard, digital transformation can support local organizations through three categories of digital facilitators, namely e-commerce (online transactions), e-marketing (communication and promotion), and e-business (supply chain and business internal configuration) (Dethine et al., 2020). In terms of business activity, digital transformation at country level promotes firms' competitiveness in all possible aspects, i.e., innovation, cost structure, and global value chain management (Leão & da Silva, 2021). It supports the creation of competitive advantages, as well as supply chain procurement (Alabdali et al., 2022). Evidence shows that country digitalization has a positive effect on the level of economic development (Androniceanu et al., 2022). Businesses being affected by digital transformation capitalize on their digital competence, which comprises three sub-factors: digital infrastructure, digital integration, and digital management (Yu & Moon, 2021).

Digital transformation increased firms' innovation performance as it enabled them to apply collaborative value creation models, that involve heterogeneous agents (Gao et al., 2023). It also helped manufacturers meet the net-zero emissions and circular economy objectives, which results in a sustainable competitive edge (Okorie et al., 2023). For instance, digital transformation enabled Chinese firms fostering their green innovation performance (Feng et al., 2022). Digital transformation is more successful when it targets efficiency objectives (Shen et al., 2022). Hence, a new concept appeared in recent literature, i.e., digital entrepreneurship. The latter reflects the firm's inclination to seize new business opportunities, by leveraging digital platforms as well as information and communication technologies (Hervé et al., 2020).

In sum, digitalization promoted at country level is likely to facilitate innovation in different competitive aspects (supply chain, logistics, green management, etc.). Through developed digital platforms and networks offered by governments, local organizations can more easily access invaluable knowledge sources and build on advanced production conditions to expand their innovation potential. As a matter of fact, Jiao et al. (2022) demonstrated that when the institutional context supports firms' access to digital platforms, this is likely to promote technology-based entrepreneurial innovations. Huang et al. (2023) found that e-government services, that aim to support information and communication, is strongly impacting talent competitiveness. As a result, we believe that country digitalization increases business connectivity, which enables local stakeholders to more easily engage in rewarding collaborations. Additionally, country digitalization allows local organizations to access information and develop more efficient solutions. As they become more efficient, local organizations may allocate more resources to research and development, which is likely to result in highly innovative activity. Thus, the following hypothesis is formulated:

Hypothesis 1: Country digitalization has a positive influence on its innovation capabilities.

Recent research has started to emphasize the effects of digital transformation on firms' international expansion that essentially concern their production activities and sales distribution (Strange et al., 2022). Digital transformation, e.g., e-commerce, business intelligence, cloud solutions, and big data, is regarded as a prerequisite for successful firm internationalization (Dethine et al., 2020; Pereira et al., 2022). Access to digital solutions among small-and medium-sized firms results in the adoption of more innovative, proactive, and risk-taking entrepreneurial behaviors, which support strategic decision-making processes in international markets. More specifically, the availability of advanced technologies allows organizations to undertake more fluid and nonlinear entrepreneurial initiatives that transcend the constraints of time and geography (Hervé et al., 2020). Countries at high levels of digital readiness are more effective in transferring national research and development resources to entrepreneurial ventures and small businesses, which accentuates their global competitiveness (Moeini Gharagozloo et al., 2022). Furthermore, e-business digital facilitators are the most powerful in promoting global expansion (Dethine et al., 2020). Digital transformation allows organizations to enter new markets and maintain close relationships with foreign customers at lower costs (Pereira et al., 2022).

Overall, digital transformation seems to play a crucial role in expanding international exposure for businesses in today's globalized world. The ability to export and import goods and services across borders has become easier than ever before, thanks to advancements in technology. The importance of digital transformation lies in its ability to break down geographical barriers and connect businesses with customers on a global scale. It enables companies to leverage technology to improve efficiency, increase productivity, and explore new avenues for growth. Hence, the following hypothesis is argued:

Hypothesis 2: Country digitalization has a positive influence on its trade openness.

The expansion into foreign markets has become an important innovation channel for organizations. Growing beyond home-country markets, offers a vast array of learning opportunities. One of the key advantages of engagement in a dynamic international exchange is the exposure to different markets and new customer segments. Exporting to other countries allows firms to acquire a deeper familiarity with different consumer preferences and demands. This proximity results in innovation as it encourages organizations to develop and adapt existing products and offerings to fit diverse market needs. Therefore, the higher exposure to technical spillovers and to different demand profiles in international markets supports the development of new innovation capabilities in organizations (Fassio, 2018). Such consumer-driven innovation forces companies to adopt creative thinking to find novel solutions that match the needs of the target market (Branstad & Solem, 2020). For instance, export intensity is positively related to green innovations. This relationship is stronger among firms with higher absorptive capacity (Galbreath, 2019). Innovations tailored for foreign markets can then be applied back to the home market, further enhancing innovation capabilities (Hitt et al., 2005).

In summary, and as illustrated in figure 1 below, international trade is essential for fostering innovation within firms, as it exposes businesses to challenging consumer needs and facilitates knowledge sharing with foreign partners. This may encourage organizations to opt for creative problem-solving models aimed at achieving successful product adaptations. Therefore, embracing global trade opportunities with the support of advanced digital infrastructure could allow companies to propel their innovative undertakings forward. This relationship is hence hypothesized:

Hypothesis 3: Trade openness has a positive influence on country innovation capabilities.

Figure 1. Conceptual model

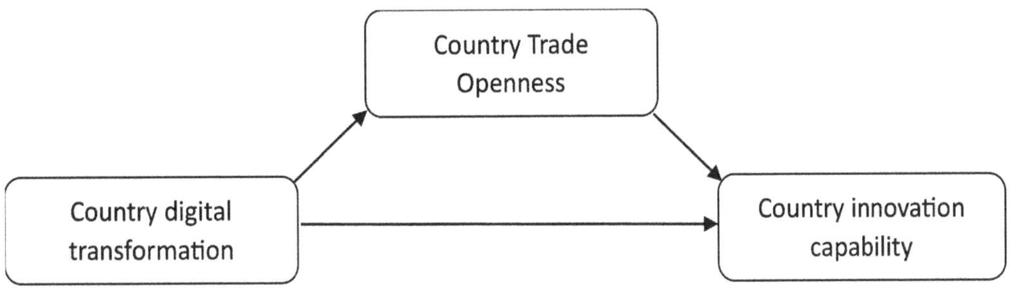

METHODOLOGY

The impact of digital readiness on a country's innovation score was investigated using path analysis method, drawing on recent secondary data compiled for 115 nations from all continents. Countries were selected based on data availability for all three model variables. Countries with missing values were excluded from the analysis. The model, executed with the aid of the AMOS 21 for Windows software, also examined how trade openness might mediate this relationship.

Country digital readiness is captured using the *Cisco digital readiness index* for the latest year available, which is 2021. The underlying approach defines digital readiness using a holistic model with seven core components, including technology infrastructure and technology adoption, ease of doing business, human capital development, business and government investment, basic human needs, and the start-up environment. The seven components are standardized and aggregated to generate the overall score for each country (Cisco, 2023). However, we changed the range of the original scores, which varied from -2.5 to 2.5, into a 0–5 interval. For instance, the neutral score in the initial range (zero) was changed to 2.5. By removing the negative score indications, this transformation tries to make data analysis more straightforward. To have a broader representation of country digital transformation, we included three potential drivers of digital readiness, namely government digitalization, business digitalization, and people digitalization. The data for these three antecedents was obtained from the World Bank digital adoption index for the latest year available: 2016. Each of these indicators focus on the supply of technologies required for the respective agent to promote its digital development. Business Digital Adoption Index (DAI Business) refers to technologies affecting business productivity and broad-based growth. People Digital Adoption Index (DAI People) deals with the technologies supporting individual's welfare and their exposure to opportunities. Finally, government Digital Adoption Index (DAI Government) includes the technologies that serve the objectives of public administration efficiency and accountability (The World Bank, 2016).

Trade openness is assessed in terms of exports and imports as a percentage of the gross domestic product. Data were retrieved from *The World Bank* online databank for the year 2021, which is comprehensive for more countries than the data available for 2022 (The World Bank, 2021). The year 2021 was intentionally selected to match the data with the availability of the *Cisco digital readiness index.*

Finally, the *Global Innovation Index* developed by *The World Intellectual Property Organization* (WIPO) was used to evaluate a country's innovation capability. The information included in this index covers the year 2022. The *Global Innovation Index* has two sub-indices: the innovation input and the innovation output. Institutions, human capital and research, infrastructure, market sophistication, and business sophistication serve as the foundation for the first sub-index. The knowledge and technology outputs and creative outputs are the two pillars on which the second sub-index is built. Each pillar is further subdivided into sub-pillars, each of which is made up of distinct indicators (The World Intellectual Property Organization, 2022).

RESULTS

The model-fit indicators were generated to evaluate the overall fit of the path analysis model, i.e., chi-square to degrees of freedom ratio, normed fit index (NFI), comparative fit index (CFI), goodness-of-fit index (GFI), incremental fit index (IFI), and root mean square error of approximation (RMSEA). According to a review of the model scores reported in Table 1, the indicators show a very satisfactory level of fit between the sample data and the hypothesized model.

Table 1. Model-fit indicators (default model)

Model	Chi-Square (χ^2)	χ^2/df	NFI	CFI	GFI	IFI	RMSEA
Structural model	χ^2: 6.493 Degrees of freedom (*df*): 6 p: 0.339	6.493/6 =1.08	0.991	0.999	0.982	0.999	0.027
Recommended values	p>0.05	$1<\chi^2/df<2$	>0.95	>0.95	>0.95	>0.95	<0.08

As shown in Table 2 and illustrated in Figure 2, our findings confirm the positive and significant effect of country digital readiness on both trade openness and innovation. The country digital readiness stems mainly from the technologies that support the digital adoption efforts by people and businesses. As per our results, the availability of modern conditions for governmental digital upgrade does not yield significant outcomes in terms of digital readiness (*p*-value: 0.99).

However, our results show that trade openness negatively mediates the relationship between country digitalization and innovation capacity. Although the effect is weakly significant at the 90% confidence level (*p*-value: 0.051), the trade openness negative effect on innovation deserves to be carefully examined in order to determine the potential reasons.

Table 2. Regression weights: (Group number one: Default model)

			Estimate	S.E.	C.R.	P	Label
Digitalreadiness2021	<---	DAI Government	.003	.216	.012	.990	
Digitalreadiness2021	<---	DAI Business	1.541	.357	4.313	***	
Digitalreadiness2021	<---	DAI People	2.561	.300	8.537	***	
Tradeopenness2021	<---	Digitalreadiness2021	29.532	5.353	5.517	***	
Innovationindex2022	<---	Digitalreadiness2021	14.221	.623	22.842	***	
Innovationindex2022	<---	Tradeopenness2021	-.019	.010	-1.949	.051	

Figure 2. Results

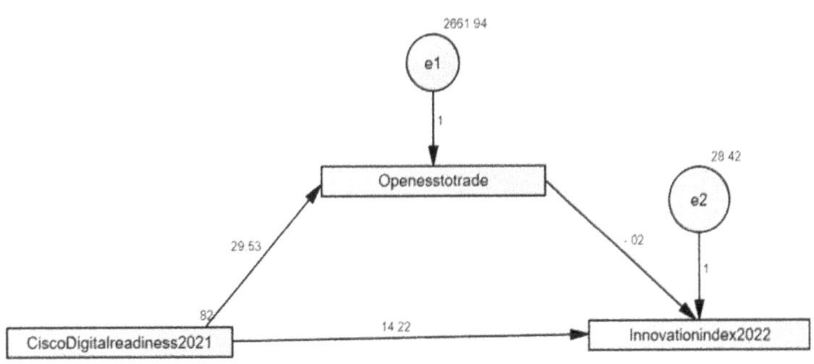

DISCUSSION

The present study confirms that national digitalization plays a positive role in developing a country's innovation capability, through the creation of a stimulating environment where local organizations benefit from advanced and integrated technological infrastructure. Countries offering high-speed connectivity and integrated data sources enable local organizations to produce creative solutions (e-estonia.com, 2023; Falcon, 2023). This research also confirms the positive influence of country digitalization on its prospects of international involvement. Countries that significantly improved their service digitalization have attained higher levels of digital service exports (Jiang & Jia, 2022).

The study's findings regarding the positive effect of country digitalization on trade openness and innovation are in accordance with Jafari-Sadeghi et al. (2021), who assessed whether digital transformation impacts technology entrepreneurship and technological market expansion in 28 European countries. Similarly, Shreyasee & Varun (2023) asserted that the digital readiness of India, together with its population size and political ecosystem, has a significant and positive impact on the country's export preparedness. More indirectly, a study undertaken by Moeini Gharagozloo et al. (2021) investigated the effect of digital readiness on how international capital markets react to announced mergers and acquisitions. The study revealed that financial markets perform better when it comes to investors' reactions to these announcements in cases where the company that initiates the merger or acquisition originates from a country that shows higher digital readiness. On a firm level, digital transformation has a positive impact on innovation capabilities. For example, Chen & Kim (2023) confirmed this relationship among the Chinese manufacturing firms. As it was mentioned before, digital transformation on a national level can be seen as a synergistic cumulation of organizational-level digital transformation. In line with this, a study done by Li et al. (2022) concluded that digital economy development was positively associated with enterprise innovation. Apart from this, the authors asserted that the digital economy has a positive impact on the digital transformation of companies, which yields in turn a significant positive effect on enterprise innovation. This is further confirmed by Niu et al. (2023) who investigated Chinese listed firms in a period between 2007 and 2019 and found that digital transformation positively impacts corporate innovation. Additionally, the authors found that digital transformation improves corporate governance. Finally, it was revealed that digital transformation has a more emphasized effect within high-tech industries. On a national level, digital transformation has been proven to improve the performance of companies, while at the same time stimulating the momentum of innovation (Peng & Tao, 2022).

The unexpected negative mediating effect of trade openness into the digitalization-innovation relationship could be attributed to the rationale put forward by authors like González & Ferencz (2018), who claim that digital transformation does not impact all industries in the same way. For example, in more complex manufacturing and industries that provide digital products, this impact is more significant. Another possible explanation points to the insufficient absorptive capacity of newly internationalized firms. Indeed, recent research found that absorptive capacity is associated with small and medium-sized firms' speed of internationalization in a reversed U-shape relationship (Kang et al., 2022). Furthermore, a study implemented by Bakari et al. (2022) found that digital transformation and trade openness are significant drivers of economic growth, but mainly for the richest countries in terms of natural and human resources. As a result, organizations from developing economies may choose to relocate their innovation efforts to more developed countries to benefit from technological spillovers. Such relocations may have had a negative impact on the home country innovation capacity. For instance, the increasing importance of new mobility-focused technologies in the automotive industry is significantly affecting the business location choices of European car manufacturers (Turienzo & Lampón, 2023).

It is also possible that other factors, such as cultural disparities or a lack of collaboration between domestic and international partners, may hinder them from tapping into learning opportunities and attaining high levels of knowledge transfer that result in tangible innovative outcomes. Despite recent evidence pointing at the decreasing effect of cultural distance on international research collaborations (Viera et al., 2022), the challenging impact of cultural diversity in cross-border partnerships should not be underestimated by decision-makers who should be also mindful of context-specific conditions (Elia et al., 2019).

In sum, digital transformation creates a vicious circle for countries that fail to capitalize on it properly. If digital transformation is implemented poorly, the countries lose various important benefits that include opportunities for technology transfer, human expertise acquisition, access to a wider array of international markets, and spillover effects from collaborating with international partners. An especially important, often hidden, but present barrier to the successful implementation of digital transformation is the "unseen dynamic of pervasive mindsets" (Jones et al., 2021, p. 936) that exist both within organizations and societies engaged in digital transformation. This means that internal subtle forces may inhibit the genuine aims pursed through digital transformation. Some groups have preconceived beliefs and assumptions about digitalization that do not necessarily relate with its merits. This concerns more specifically the tendency of some influential stakeholders to protect their interests that may be threatened if digitalization plans are brought into execution. Moreover, power struggles are being witnessed across the globe between different parties that are competing to dominate the emerging technologies, such as artificial intelligence applications (UNCTAD, 2019).

More generally, Vogelsang et al. (2019) conducted a qualitative study that aimed at identifying the main barriers to digital transformation. The main identified barriers to digital transformation were categorized into missing skills, technical barriers (e.g., current infrastructure or security), individual barriers (like fear of job loss or fear of acceptance), organizational and cultural barriers (e.g., risk aversion, lack of financial resources, or lack of time), and environmental barriers (e.g., lack of standards or lack of appropriate laws). The combination of all those barriers to digital transformation can ultimately affect the relationship between digital transformation and innovation.

CONCLUSION

This study broadens the analysis of the implications of nationwide digital transformation efforts to include possible import and export stimulation, which may increase national innovation capacity. The study utilizes the *Cisco digital readiness index* as a proxy for the level of digital transformation in a country. The reason for using this index is the fact that it comprises the main components of digital transformation at national and organizational levels, including technology infrastructure and technology adoption, business and government investment, and start-up environment. Our findings show that firms that use home country digital platforms to build strong ties with overseas partners are not achieving a knowledge transfer that may be transformed into innovative production within home country economy. In other words, the empirical results of the present study show two divergent effects of country digital readiness on country innovation index.

Several examples of successful national digitalization endeavors could be mentioned in this sense. The Estonian digital governance experience focused on connected different databases which increased information accessibility and transparency (e-estonia.com, 2023). Additionally, South-Korea upgraded its broadband infrastructure which significantly increased connectivity levels and results in large-scale innovations (Falcon, 2023). Nonetheless, developing countries in particular are dealing with barriers slowing down their digitalization efforts, such as the underdeveloped regulatory framework, the lack of concerted action among key local actors (Raj et al., 2020), and the incapacity of local organizations in defining a digital strategy that aligns with national digital transformation plans (Senna et al., 2023).

The present study builds on a relevant intersection between two streams of literature, namely digitalization and international trade. This is particularly important since digitalization has become a key area of international trade, given that the global economy and digitalization are growing rapidly. Furthermore, digitalization significantly alters the conditions of global competition, which is reflected in the intensification of global competition, shifting focus towards intangible assets, the emergence of new opportunities in international markets, and the expansion of commerce that crosses country borders, to name a few (Ahmedov, 2020). In line with this, the *World Trade Organization* (WTO) member states recognized the growing importance of digitalization and invested significant efforts into developing digital trade (Malkawi, 2019).

In terms of practical implications, policymakers in organizations, particularly those with less international experience, should adapt their internal innovation systems and develop their absorptive capacity to embrace the learning opportunities that may arise from import and export activities. This is especially relevant knowing that research conducted by Kastelli et al. (2022) showed a positive and direct impact of digitalization on innovation performance. Furthermore, this relationship is augmented in the presence of absorptive capacity as a mediator.

Finally, this research has some limitations. Firstly, the study could have been enriched if firm-level data was used. We opted for readily available country-level information due to time constraints and data accuracy. Using firm-level data would have implied the dissemination of questionnaires and the use of perceptive measurements provided by representatives from the firms. Furthermore, the lack of available data for 2022 (for all model variables) forced the authors to use datasets from different years (namely 2021 and 2022), which might be considered as a limitation due to time inconsistency. Another limitation pertains to the method used. Using panel data that reflect the longitudinal evolution of the dependent variables could have provided stronger conclusions. Nonetheless, those missing aspects represent future avenues of research. In this sense, researchers could focus on conducting a large-scale empirical survey with validated metrics to capture and test the hypothesized relationships between the model dimensions (digital readiness at firm level, percentage of international sales, and innovation capacity).

REFERENCES

Afesorgbor, S. K., & Demena, B. A. (2022). Trade openness and environmental emissions: Evidence from a meta-analysis. *Environmental and Resource Economics*, *81*(2), 287–321. doi:10.1007/s10640-021-00627-0

Ahmedov, I. (2020). The Impact Of Digital Economy On International Trade. *European Journal of Business and Management Research*, *5*(4). doi:10.24018/ejbmr.2020.5.4.389

Alabdali, M. A., Salam, M. A., Mangla, S., Li, G., Sun, J., Wu, H., Alabdali, M. A., & Salam, M. A. (2022). The Impact of Digital Transformation on Supply Chain Procurement for Creating Competitive Advantage: An Empirical Study. *Sustainability, 14*(19), 12269. https://doi. doi:org/10.3390/SU141912269

Aly, H. (2022). Digital transformation, development and productivity in developing countries: Is artificial intelligence a curse or a blessing? *Review of Economics and Political Science*, *7*(4), 238–256. doi:10.1108/REPS-11-2019-0145

Androniceanu, A., Georgescu, I., & Sabie, O. M. (2022). The impact of digitalization on public administration, economic development, and well-being in the EU countries. *Central European Public Administration Review*, *20*(2), 9–31. doi:10.17573/cepar.2022.2.01

Bakari, S., & El Weriemmi, M. (2022). The Impact of Digitalization and Trade Openness on Economic Growth: New Evidence from Richest Asian Countries. *Journal of Research. Innovation and Technologies*, *I*(2(2)), 95–106. doi:10.57017/jorit.v1.2(2).01

Branstad, A., & Solem, B. A. (2020). Emerging theories of consumer-driven market innovation, adoption, and diffusion: A selective review of consumer-oriented studies. *Journal of Business Research, 116*, 561–571. doi:10.1016/j.jbusres.2020.01.028

Chen, P., & Kim, S. (2023). The impact of digital transformation on innovation performance – The mediating role of innovation factors. *Heliyon*, *9*(3), e13916. doi:10.1016/j.heliyon.2023.e13916 PMID:36895347

Cisco. (2023). *Digital readiness index: World distribution for 2021*. Cisco. https://www.cisco.com/c/m/en_us/about/corporate-social-responsibility/research-resources/digital-readiness-index.html#/

Ciuriak, D., & Ptashkina, M. (2018). *The Digital Transformation and the Transformation of International Trade*. SSRN. https://papers.ssrn.com/abstract=3107811

Dethine, B., Enjolras, M., & Monticolo, D. (2020). Digitalization and SMEs' export management: Impacts on resources and capabilities. *Technology Innovation Management Review*, *10*(4), 18–34. doi:10.22215/timreview/1344

Dženopoljac, V., Georgievski, B., Cavagnetto, S., & Abidi, O. (2022). National intellectual capital: A comparative longitudinal study. *Ekonomika Preduzeca*, *70*(3–4), 147–160. doi:10.5937/EKOPRE2204147D

e-estonia.com. (2023). *Government cloud*. e-estonia. https://e-estonia.com/solutions/e-governance/government-cloud/

Elia, S., Petruzzelli, A. M., & Piscitello, L. (2019). The impact of cultural diversity on innovation performance of MNC subsidiaries in strategic alliances. *Journal of Business Research*, *98*, 204–213. doi:10.1016/j.jbusres.2019.01.062

ElMassah, S., & Mohieldin, M. (2020). Digital transformation and localizing the Sustainable Development Goals (SDGs). *Ecological Economics*, *169*, 106490. doi:10.1016/j.ecolecon.2019.106490

Falcon, E. (2023). *Why Is South Korea a Global Broadband Leader?* Electronic Frontier Foundation. https://www.eff.org/deeplinks/2020/02/why-south-korea-global-broadband-leader

Fassio, C. (2018). Export-led innovation: The role of export destinations. *Industrial and Corporate Change, 27*(1), 149–171. doi:10.1093/icc/dtx028

Feng, H., Wang, F., Song, G., & Liu, L. (2022). Digital Transformation on Enterprise Green Innovation: Effect and Transmission Mechanism. *International Journal of Environmental Research and Public Health, 19*(17), 10614. https://doi. doi:org/10.3390/IJERPH191710614

Galbreath, J. (2019). Drivers of Green Innovations: The Impact of Export Intensity, Women Leaders, and Absorptive Capacity. *Journal of Business Ethics, 158*(1), 47–61. doi:10.1007/s10551-017-3715-z

Gao, J., Zhang, W., Guan, T., Feng, Q., & Mardani, A. (2023). The effect of manufacturing agent heterogeneity on enterprise innovation performance and competitive advantage in the era of digital transformation. *Journal of Business Research, 155*, 113387. doi:10.1016/j.jbusres.2022.113387

Gong, C., & Ribiere, V. (2021). Developing a unified definition of digital transformation. *Technovation, 102*, 102217. doi:10.1016/j.technovation.2020.102217

González, J. L., & Ferencz, J. (2018, October 29). *Digital Trade and Market Openness | Documents de travail de l'OCDE sur la politique commercial.* (OECD Trade Policy Papers). OECD. https://www.oecd-ilibrary.org/trade/digital-trade-and-market-openness_1bd89c9a-en

Gurbaxani, V., & Dunkle, D. (2018). *Gearing Up for Successful Digital Transformation Center for Digital Transformation.* Center for Digital Transformations. http://www.centerfordigitaltransformation.org/assets/APC-Report-Digital-Transformation_18_r2-merged.pdf

Habibi, F., & Zabardast, M. A. (2020). Digitalization, education and economic growth: A comparative analysis of Middle East and OECD countries. *Technology in Society, 63*, 101370. doi:10.1016/j.techsoc.2020.101370

Hervé, A., Schmitt, C., & Baldegger, R. (2020). Digitalization, entrepreneurial orientation and internationalization of micro-, small- And medium-sized enterprises. *Technology Innovation Management Review, 10*(4), 5–17. doi:10.22215/timreview/1343

Hitt, M. A., Worthington, W. J. IV, & Li, H. (2005). Emerging Markets as Learning Laboratories: Learning Behaviors ofLocal Firms and Foreign Entrants in Different InstitutionalContexts. *Management and Organization Review, 1*(3), 353–380. doi:10.1111/j.1740-8784.2005.0019a.x

Huang, Y., Li, K., & Li, P. (2023). Innovation ecosystems and national talent competitiveness: A country-based comparison using fsQCA. *Technological Forecasting and Social Change, 194*, 122733. doi:10.1016/j.techfore.2023.122733

Intisar, R. A., Yaseen, M. R., Kousar, R., Usman, M., & Amjad Makhdum, M. S. (2020). Impact of Trade Openness and Human Capital on Economic Growth: A Comparative Investigation of Asian Countries. *Sustainability, 12*(7), 2930. https://doi. doi:org/10.3390/SU12072930

Jafari-Sadeghi, V., Garcia-Perez, A., Candelo, E., & Couturier, J. (2021). Exploring the impact of digital transformation on technology entrepreneurship and technological market expansion: The role of technology readiness, exploration and exploitation. *Journal of Business Research, 124*, 100–111. doi:10.1016/j.jbusres.2020.11.020

Jiang, M., & Jia, P. (2022). Does the level of digitalized service drive the global export of digital service trade? Evidence from global perspective. *Telematics and Informatics*, *72*, 101853. doi:10.1016/j.tele.2022.101853

Jiao, H., Wang, L., & Shi, Y. (2022). How does institutional environment in the digital context affect technology entrepreneurship? The moderating roles of government digitalization and gender. *Journal of Organizational Change Management*, *35*(7), 1089–1112. doi:10.1108/JOCM-10-2021-0321

Jones, M. D., Hutcheson, S., & Camba, J. D. (2021). Past, present, and future barriers to digital transformation in manufacturing: A review. *Journal of Manufacturing Systems*, *60*, 936–948. doi:10.1016/j.jmsy.2021.03.006

Kang, Y., Zhao, C., & Battisti, M. (2022). Organizational learning in SMEs' internationalization: A moderated mediating effect of absorptive capacity. *Long Range Planning*, *55*(4), 102220. doi:10.1016/j.lrp.2022.102220

Kastelli, I., Dimas, P., Stamopoulos, D., & Tsakanikas, A. (2022). Linking Digital Capacity to Innovation Performance: The Mediating Role of Absorptive Capacity. *Journal of the Knowledge Economy*. doi:10.1007/s13132-022-01092-w

Kong, Q., Peng, D., Ni, Y., Jiang, X., & Wang, Z. (2021). Trade openness and economic growth quality of China: Empirical analysis using ARDL model. *Finance Research Letters*, *38*, 101488. doi:10.1016/j.frl.2020.101488

Kwilinski, A., Vyshnevskyi, O., & Dzwigol, H. (2020). Digitalization of the EU Economies and People at Risk of Poverty or Social Exclusion. *Journal of Risk and Financial Management, 13*(7), 142. https://doi. doi:org/10.3390/JRFM13070142

Leão, P., & da Silva, M. M. (2021). Impacts of digital transformation on firms' competitive advantages: A systematic literature review. *Strategic Change*, *30*(5), 421–441. doi:10.1002/jsc.2459

Lee-Geiller, S., & Lee, T. (2022). How Does Digital Governance Contribute to Effective Crisis Management? A Case Study of Korea's Response to COVID-19. *Public Performance & Management Review*, *45*(4), 860–893. doi:10.1080/15309576.2022.2054434

Li, R., Rao, J., & Wan, L. (2022). The digital economy, enterprise digital transformation, and enterprise innovation. *MDE. Managerial and Decision Economics*, *43*(7), 2875–2886. doi:10.1002/mde.3569

Malkawi, B. H. (2019). Digitalization of International Trade. *The Journal of Law and Technology*, *23*. https://philpapers.org/rec/MALDOI

Matthess, M., & Kunkel, S. (2020). Structural change and digitalization in developing countries: Conceptually linking the two transformations. *Technology in Society*, *63*, 101428. doi:10.1016/j.techsoc.2020.101428

Moeini Gharagozloo, M. M., Askarzadeh, F., & Moeini Gharagozloo, A. (2021). More power for international entrepreneurs: The effect of digital readiness of economies on channeling national R&D resources to entrepreneurship. *Journal of International Entrepreneurship*, *20*(3), 474–502. doi:10.1007/s10843-021-00296-6

Moeini Gharagozloo, M. M., Askarzadeh, F., & Moeini Gharagozloo, A. (2022). More power for international entrepreneurs: The effect of digital readiness of economies on channeling national R&D resources to entrepreneurship. *Journal of International Entrepreneurship*, *20*(3), 474–502. doi:10.1007/s10843-021-00296-6

Moldabekova, A., Philipp, R., Reimers, H.-E., & Alikozhayev, B. (2021). Digital Technologies for Improving Logistics Performance of Countries. *Transport and Telecommunication Journal*, *22*(2), 207–216. doi:10.2478/ttj-2021-0016

Myovella, G., Karacuka, M., & Haucap, J. (2020). Digitalization and economic growth: A comparative analysis of Sub-Saharan Africa and OECD economies. *Telecommunications Policy*, *44*(2), 101856. doi:10.1016/j.telpol.2019.101856

Niu, Y., Wen, W., Wang, S., & Li, S. (2023). Breaking barriers to innovation: The power of digital transformation. *Finance Research Letters*, *51*, 103457. doi:10.1016/j.frl.2022.103457

Okorie, O., Russell, J., Cherrington, R., Fisher, O., & Charnley, F. (2023). Digital transformation and the circular economy: Creating a competitive advantage from the transition towards Net Zero Manufacturing. *Resources, Conservation and Recycling*, *189*, 106756. doi:10.1016/j.resconrec.2022.106756

Peng, Y., & Tao, C. (2022). Can digital transformation promote enterprise performance?—From the perspective of public policy and innovation. *Journal of Innovation & Knowledge*, *7*(3), 100198. doi:10.1016/j.jik.2022.100198

Pereira, C. S., Durão, N., Moreira, F., & Veloso, B. (2022). The Importance of Digital Transformation in International Business. *Sustainability, 14*(2), 834. https://doi. doi:org/10.3390/SU14020834

Raj, A., Dwivedi, G., Sharma, A., de Sousa Jabbour, A. B. L., & Rajak, S. (2020). Barriers to the adoption of industry 4.0 technologies in the manufacturing sector: An inter-country comparative perspective. *International Journal of Production Economics*, *224*, 107546. doi:10.1016/j.ijpe.2019.107546

Senna, P. P., Roca, J. B., & Barros, A. C. (2023). Overcoming barriers to manufacturing digitalization: Policies across EU countries. *Technological Forecasting and Social Change*, *196*, 122822. doi:10.1016/j.techfore.2023.122822

Shen, L., Zhang, X., & Liu, H. (2022). Digital technology adoption, digital dynamic capability, and digital transformation performance of textile industry: Moderating role of digital innovation orientation. *MDE. Managerial and Decision Economics*, *43*(6), 2038–2054. doi:10.1002/mde.3507

Shreyasee, K., & Varun, R. T. (2023). Effect of Digital Readiness on the Export Preparedness in India. *Prajnan (Pune)*, *51*(4), 323–339.

Silva, D. S., Yamashita, G. H., Cortimiglia, M. N., Brust-Renck, P. G., & ten Caten, C. S. (2022). Are we ready to assess digital readiness? Exploring digital implications for social progress from the Network Readiness Index. *Technology in Society*, *68*, 101875. doi:10.1016/j.techsoc.2022.101875

Strange, R., Chen, L., & Fleury, M. T. L. (2022). Digital Transformation and International Strategies. *Journal of International Management*, *28*(4), 100968. doi:10.1016/j.intman.2022.100968

Švarc, J., Lažnjak, J., & Dabić, M. (2021). The role of national intellectual capital in the digital transformation of EU countries. Another digital divide? *Journal of Intellectual Capital*, *22*(4), 768–791. doi:10.1108/JIC-02-2020-0024

The World Bank. (2016). *Digital Adoption Index.* World Bank. https://www.worldbank.org/en/publication/wdr2016/Digital-Adoption-Index

The World Bank. (2021). *Gross Domestic Product by country.* Databank: World Development Indicators. https://databank.worldbank.org/reports.aspx?source=2&series=NY.GDP.MKTP.CD&country

The World Intellectual Property Organization. (2022). *Global innovation index 2022: What is the future of innovation-driven growth?* Global Innovation Index. https://www.globalinnovationindex.org/gii-2022-report

Turienzo, J., & Lampón, J. F. (2023). New mobility technologies as incentive to location decisions: Relocation strategy in the automotive industry. *Kybernetes*, *52*(11), 5444–5459. doi:10.1108/K-03-2022-0317

UNCTAD. (2019). *Digital Economy Report 2019: Value Creation and Capture - Implications for Developing Countries.* UNCTAD. https://unctad.org/publication/digital-economy-report-2019.

Vial, G. (2021). Understanding digital transformation: A review and a research agenda. *Managing Digital Transformation*, 13–66. doi:10.4324/9781003008637-4

Vieira, E. S., Cerdeira, J., & Teixeira, A. A. (2022). Which distance dimensions matter in international research collaboration? A cross-country analysis by scientific domain. *Journal of Informetrics*, *16*(2), 101259. doi:10.1016/j.joi.2022.101259

Vogelsang, K., Liere-Netheler, K., Packmohr, S., & Hoppe, U. (2019, January 8). Barriers to Digital Transformation in Manufacturing: Development of a Research Agenda. *Hawaii International Conference on System Sciences 2019 (HICSS-52).* AISEL. https://aisel.aisnet.org/hicss-52/in/digital_transformation/3

Yu, J., & Moon, T. (2021). Impact of Digital Strategic Orientation on Organizational Performance through Digital Competence. *Sustainability, 13*(17), 9766. doi:10.3390/su13179766

Zhang, J., & Chen, Z. (2023). Exploring Human Resource Management Digital Transformation in the Digital Age. *Journal of the Knowledge Economy*. doi:10.1007/s13132-023-01214-y

Chapter 2
Digital Entrepreneurship and E-Commerce:
Opportunities and Challenges for Bhutan's International Trade

Bhuwan Shrivastava
https://orcid.org/0009-0004-2114-3606
Royal Thimphu College, Thimphu, Bhutan

Madhav Verma
Royal Thimphu College, Thimphu, Bhutan

Sumita Dave
Amity University, Raipur, India

ABSTRACT

This research chapter explores the opportunities and challenges presented by digital entrepreneurship and e-commerce for Bhutan's international trade. Bhutan, a small landlocked country in South Asia, has traditionally relied on traditional trade methods. However, with the advent of digital technologies and the growth of e-commerce, new avenues for international trade have emerged. This chapter examines the potential benefits of digital entrepreneurship and e-commerce for Bhutan, while also addressing the challenges that need to be overcome for successful integration into the global digital economy. By analyzing the current state of digital entrepreneurship and e-commerce in Bhutan, this research aims to provide valuable insights for policymakers, entrepreneurs, and stakeholders involved in shaping Bhutan's international trade strategies.

DOI: 10.4018/979-8-3693-0798-4.ch002

INTRODUCTION

E–commerce or internet sales have shown a remarkable increment over the years. It is estimated that by the year 2026, out of total retail sales worldwide, approximately 24% of retail sales will be done over online platforms (Daniela Coppola, 2023). With its growth rate of approximately 2% (Daniela Coppola, 2023), online sales and e-commerce are surely going to play a very crucial role in the development of any economy across the world. None of the countries can keep itself aloof from this e–commerce wave. At least, looking at the volume of online trade happening across the world no country can have doubt in this regard. This is very much evident from the fact that the total volume of e-commerce is expected to touch approximately $ 8 trillion (Baluch, 2023). If we further go with data then, country wise China is the biggest market for e–commerce with a total size of approximately $ 1500 Billion followed by the USA with approximately $ 800 billion and Japan with approximately $ 240 billion as of 2022 (Cox, 2023).

E–Commerce plays a crucial role in adding value to the total GDP of a country. Bigger economies of the world have significant contributions to their GDP from sales over online platforms, viz. China's e–commerce share to GDP is 6% whereas for America it is 3% (Dykes, 2022). This clearly signifies the importance of e-commerce to any country's growth and its economic health.

Looking at the importance and contribution of the digital revolution and its contribution to the economy, governments all over the world promote and develop such environments which are conducive for the digital economy and infrastructure to flourish (Chen et al., 2021). This rise and dependency on digital technology is relatively a recent phenomenon. Since only last decade the digital technology has emerged to such an extent that it has propelled various digital technologies and supporting infrastructure to develop and has further changed the way we have worked, dealt and transacted over various platforms (Jafari-Sadeghi et al., 2021). Especially during the years of 2020 and 2021 when the whole world was gripped under the clutches of COVID–19, there was emergence and increment in the speed and how we do our business. This was a period when digital transformation and technology took a new stride and reached another level (SECUNDO et al., 2021). The digital revolution which happened during the period of COVID – 19 brought a new approach to doing business. The whole of the business process saw a shift from a more traditional way of doing business to a more technology-driven way. It provided an altogether new approach to delivering the product as well as services. In other words, there was an altogether new concept and understanding of business and its process (Jafari-Sadeghi et al., 2021). Thus, with all these opportunities and possibilities which this digital transformation has brought, i.e., shifting from more of an offline format to online/digital mode, has led to a new form of activity which can be called as "digital entrepreneurship".

Since every economy across the globe is trying their best to get perfect utilisation of this digital wave to benefit their country's economic health and in turn also bring employment benefits to the country, this article attempts to understand the status and level of digital entrepreneurship in Himalayan nation of Bhutan. While doing so, it will fathom the policies and regulations which the Royal Government of Bhutan has, pertaining to nurturing, development and growth of a conducive environment for digital entrepreneurship in the country. Further, this article will also understand the initiatives taken by entrepreneurs to enter this area of digital entrepreneurship, their current status and their future prospects by taking the case study of an organisation already working in the digital domain. To set the background for this research chapter an attempt has been made to understand Bhutan's international trade scenarios and the contribution of e-commerce.

By understanding the important aspect of digital entrepreneurship and its effect on Bhutan's international trade and entrepreneurship scenario, this research chapter will serve as a guiding torch to policymakers, business houses and other stakeholders to nurture and develop the digital entrepreneurship and e-commerce scenario in Bhutan.

RESEARCH OBJECTIVE

The objective of this research article:

- To understand the landscape of Bhutan's international trade scenarios.
- To understand the e-commerce and digital entrepreneurship environment in Bhutan by taking into consideration the unique socio–cultural fabric of the country and also its effect on the international trade scenario.
- To understand and explore the status quo of Bhutan's e-commerce and digital entrepreneurship scenario.
- To identify the shortcomings and limitations, if any, for the effective and efficient utilisation and implementation of the digital revolution in Bhutan's entrepreneurial scenario.

RESEARCH METHODOLOGY

The nature of the study will be exploratory study. It will also involve a case study method to study and understand further the issues involved in this area. The source of information employed here is a secondary source. Various research papers, articles, and government publications were considered while collecting the data. To prepare the case study we employed the interview method of data collection.

Bhutan's Economic Health and International Trade Scenario

Bhutan's stance with respect to its country's economy is unique. The country emphasizes "Gross National Happiness (GNH)" and not GDP. The concept of GNH was given by the fourth king His Majesty King Jigme Singye Wangchuk in the year 1972. GNH is based on 4 pillars. These four principles are based on the philosophy of good governance, protection of the environment, protection and promotion of cultural ethos and sustainable and equitable economic development. Bhutan's economic and political policies are guided by these pillars only. It pursues the policies that place people's well-being at its centre.

Bhutan follows the five-year plan pattern. In the beginning, the focus was more on infrastructural development. In one of his addresses, the fifth king, His Majesty The King Jigme Khesar Namgyel Wangchuk, laid importance on the technological advancement of current times by focusing more on Artificial Intelligence, Blockchain technology, quantum computers, digital wallets and digital banking to accelerate the economic growth.

As it is quite evident from Table 1, the economic growth of Bhutan is driven majorly by its hydropower projects and services, of which the major portion is of tourism.

Table 1. Bhutan development indicators, 2020

Indicator	2012	2018
Agriculture, forestry and fishing, value added (% of GDP)	13.96	15.89
Bank liquid reserves to bank assets ratio (%)	24.23	18.82
Bank nonperforming loans to total gross loans (%)	5.44	7.03
Charges for the use of intellectual property, payments (BoP, current USD)	65332.23	304211.00
Charges for the use of intellectual property, receipts (BoP, current USD)	14886.99	11086.66
Current account balance (% of GDP)	-21.17	-20.34
Expense (% of GDP)	20.92	20.42
Exports of goods and services (% of GDP)	39.65	30.82
External balance on goods and services (% of GDP)	-24.89	-25.07
Fixed broadband subscriptions	15766	10802
Fixed telephone subscriptions	27005	22015
Fixed telephone subscriptions (per 100 people)	3.85	2.92
Foreign direct investment, net inflows (% of GDP)	1.37	0.11
GDP (current billion USD)	1.78	2.45
GDP growth (annual %)	5.12	3.03
GDP per capita, PPP (current international USD)	7912.13	11613.16
GNI (constant 2010 billion USD)	1.62	2.15
GNI growth (annual %)	3.38	2.70
GNI per capita (constant 2010 USD)	2305.73	2850.03
Gross national expenditure (% of GDP)	124.89	125.07
Gross savings (% of GDP)	48.74	21.60
Imports of goods and services (% of GDP)	64.54	55.89
Industry (including construction), value added (% of GDP)	42.61	38.30
Inflation, consumer prices (annual %)	10.92	2.72
International tourism, receipts (% of total exports)	12.76	15.54
International tourism, receipts (current USD million)	93	121
International tourism, receipts for travel items (current USD million)	61	103
Manufacturing, value added (% of GDP)	9.06	7.53
Merchandise trade (% of GDP)	85.67	67.60
Net ODA received per capita (current USD)	230.41	133.18
Personal remittances, received (% of GDP)	1.02	2.38
Personal remittances, received (current USD million)	18.14	58.15
Rural population (% of total population)	63.63	59.11
Start-up procedures to register a business (number)	8	8
Tax revenue (% of GDP)	15.05	16.02
Time required to start a business (days)	35	12
Total reserves (% of total external debt)	65.86	38.73
Total reserves (includes gold, current USD million)	954.68	987.25
Trade (% of GDP)	104.19	86.71
Trade in services (% of GDP)	16.71	17.28
Vulnerable employment, female (% of female employment) (modelled ILO estimate)	85.48	84.15
Vulnerable employment, male (% of male employment) (modelled ILO estimate)	58.62	63.43

Source: Diagnostic Trade Integration Update, The Ministry of Economic Affairs, RGoB Publication

Figure 1. Sectoral contribution to GDP, Bhutan's economy
Source: Diagnostic Trade Integration Update, The Ministry of Economic Affairs, RGoB, Publication

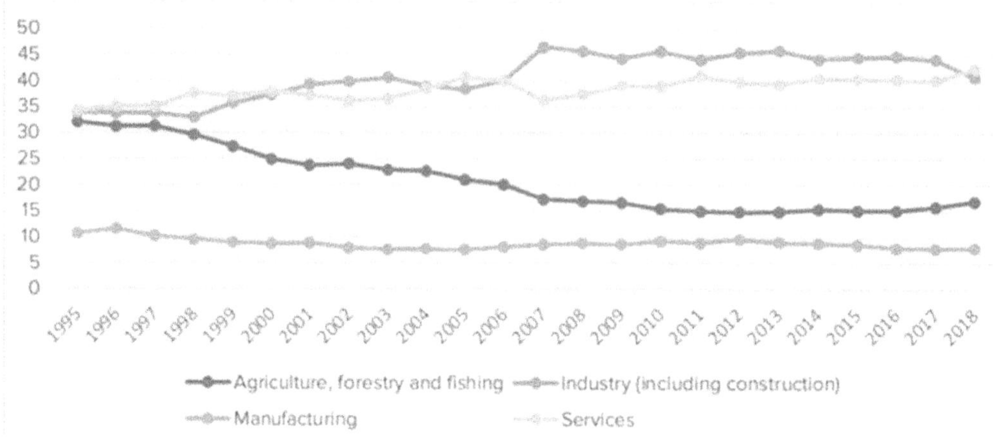

As it is clear from the above figure, it is the industrial sector that has contributed maximum to the Bhutanese economy, whereas the contribution from the manufacturing sector has remained constant and stagnant over the period. The contribution from the industrial sector comes mainly from electricity production and also from mining and construction. Industrial contribution roughly accounts for 82% of the GDP of the Bhutanese economy.

Figure 2. Sectoral contribution to employment, Bhutan's economy
Source: Diagnostic Trade Integration Update, The Ministry of Economic Affairs, RGoB Publication

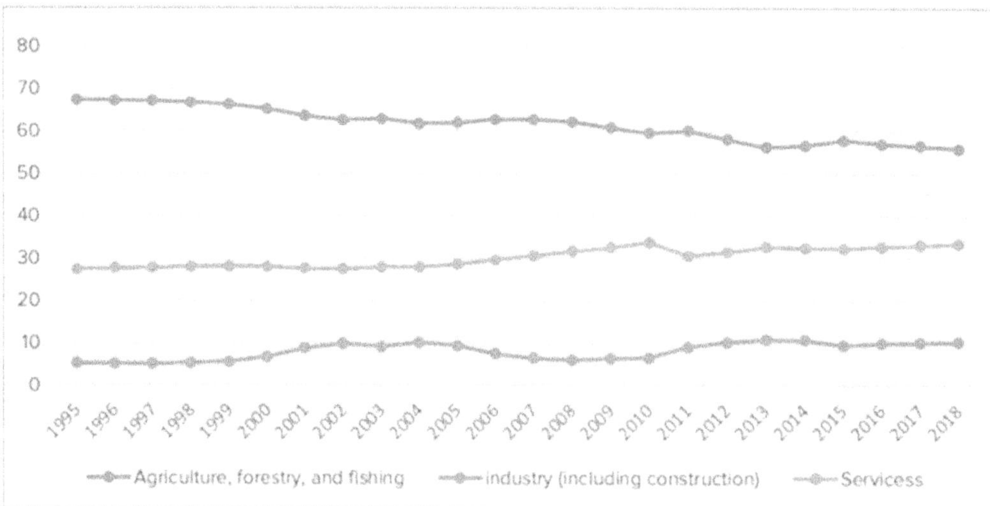

In contrast, we see the contribution of agriculture to the Bhutanese economy is around 16% as in 2018 whereas the total labour or employment contribution is around 58% for the same period. This data clearly indicates the lower labour productivity in agriculture. Whereas in the case of industry, the productivity is highest, which can be clearly inferred from the figure above while looking at the contribution of industry to employment vis – a – vis contribution of the same to the GDP.

The twelfth five-year plan (2018-2023) has directed all its policies intending to join WTO by the end of 2023 and attain the Sustainable Development Goals Agenda 2030, which is clear from some of its economic indicators like growth in GDP from USD 1.5 Bn in 2010 to approx. USD 2.5 Bn in 2018, life expectancy has increased from 68 (2010) to 74 (2018) etc.

Figure 3. Indicators to growth, Bhutan's economy
Source: Diagnostic Trade Integration Update, The Ministry of Economic Affairs, RGoB Publication

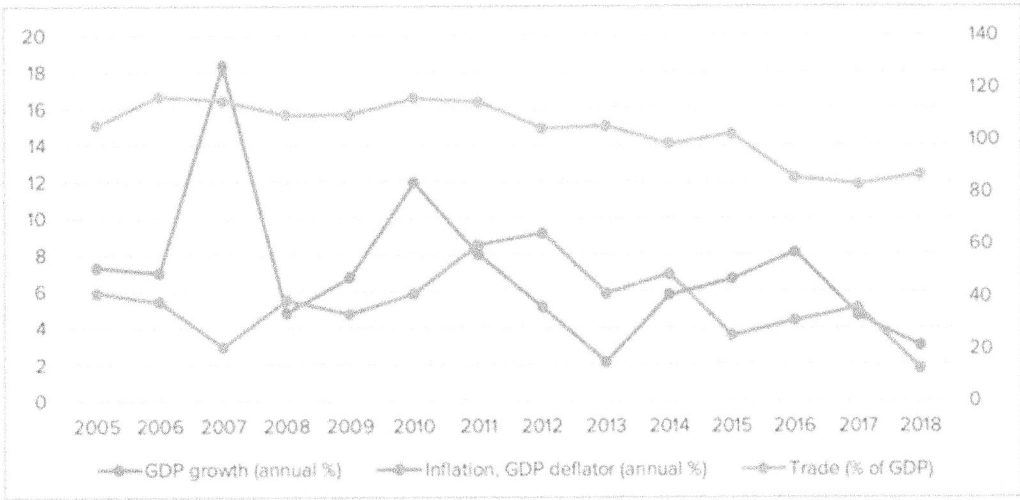

As it is clear from Figure 3, trade has the maximum share in GDP, but the trade deficit has continuously increased since 2014 (ESCAP). The reasons are many but the prominent one is low productivity and production capacity, especially, as far as the domestic market is concerned. Being majorly an importing economy, even the exports to neighbouring countries like India, Bangladesh etc. are not sufficient to bring a balance to high import volume. Looking at the data more closely, by the year 2018-19, the total import value accounted for approximately 50% of GDP of which approximately 82% of import is for goods and services is approximately 18%, which according to RGoB has declined by almost 7% as compared to 2017-18 data. But in 2020, in contrast to general perception (being the year of COVID-19), the Bhutanese economy showed a negative trend towards the import figure and rather, their export rose. The import figure went down to almost BTN 2 Bn for the first quarter as compared to that of the previous year in the same quarter, this was as a result of the decline in industrial and commercial activities. For example, in the year 2020 the import of smartphones was almost nil along with other industrial raw-materials such as ferrous and allied products (Department of Revenue and Customs, 2021). Whereas exports went up by BTN 5 Bn in the same period. The reason for the same, according to RGoB, is the commissioning and starting of the Mangdechhu hydroelectric project in the year 2019. But, in a country which depends on imports, the situation of international trade went down in the later part of the year during the pandemic. The pandemic had adverse effects on almost each and every portion of the economy. The result was a negative 6.3% growth rate for the year 2020-21. The country had the projection that it would bounce back for the year 2021-22 with a 4.2% growth rate (Report on Bhutan's External Trade, 2021).

As far as trade and export are concerned, India and Bangladesh have occupied a prominent position in overall export value and percentage from Bhutan. As of 2020, there are a total of 105 countries with which Bhutan does international trade. Its international trade has majorly been concentrated or confined to two of its neighbouring countries, i.e., India and Bangladesh which jointly account for 82% of total trade, as it is clear from Figures shown below.

Figure 4. Export Market, 2020
Source: Data Source: Bhutan Trade Statistics 2020, DRC, Ministry of Finance.

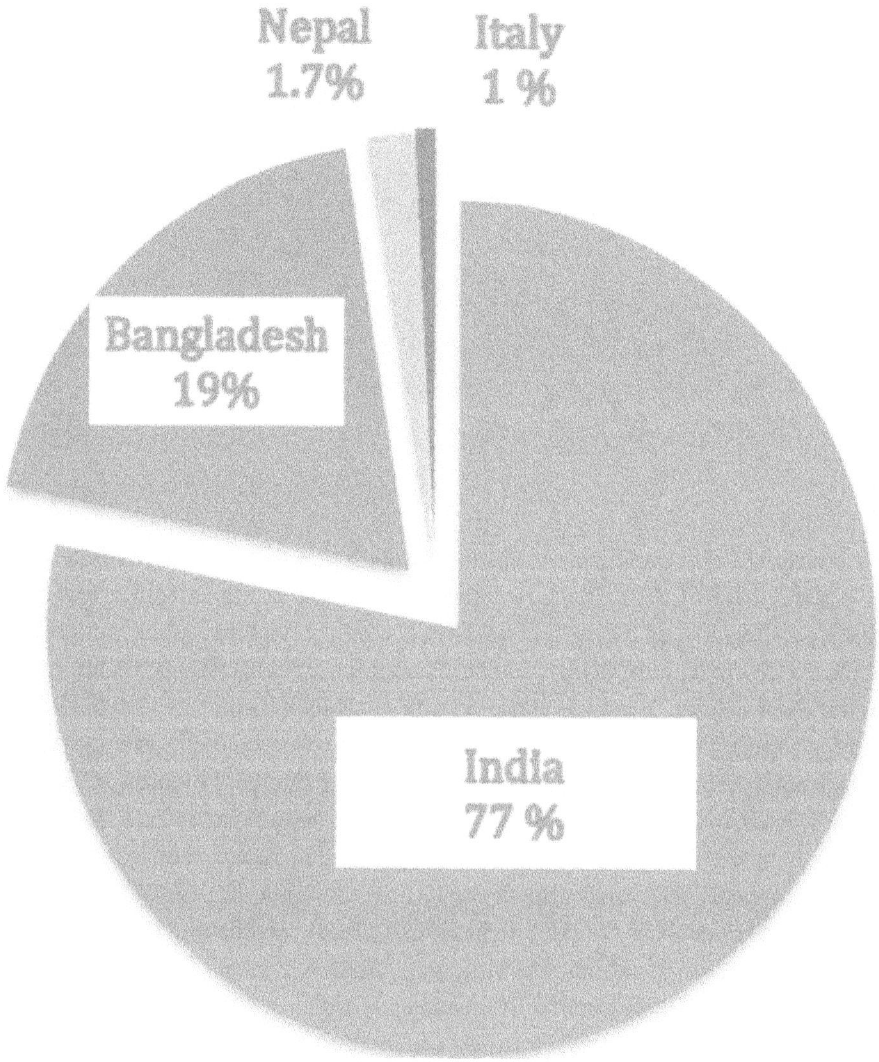

Figure 5. Source of Import, 2020
Source: Data Source: Bhutan Trade Statistics 2020, DRC, Ministry of Finance.

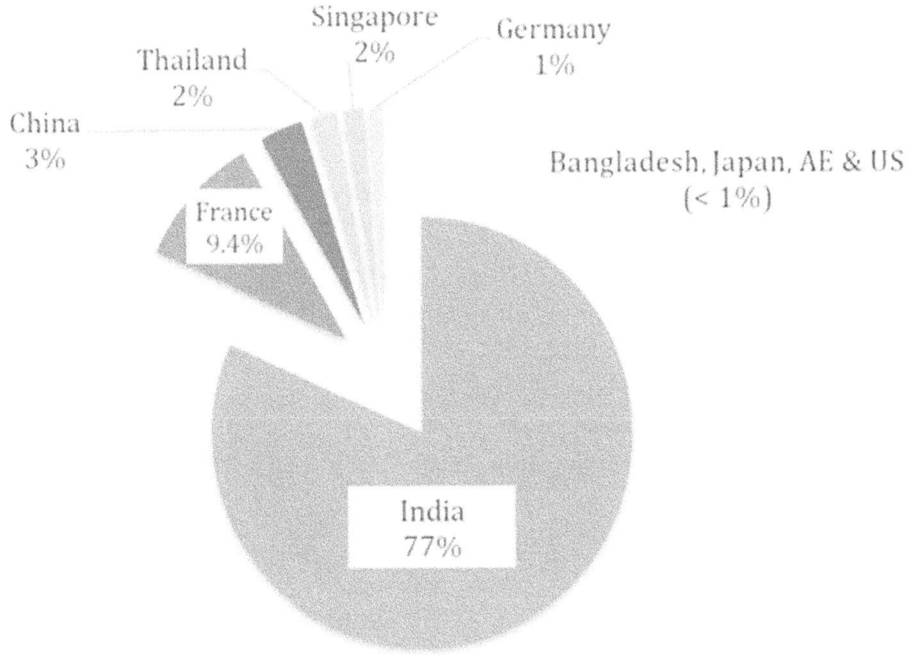

This can be attributed to the agreement which Bhutan has with these two countries separately in the nature of the Free Trade Agreement (FTA) with India and the Bilateral Trade Agreement (BTA) with Bangladesh. There has been a trend of diversification in trading partners. Now Bhutan imports from almost 61 countries from 43, which was a decade ago. As far as export is concerned it has risen to 44 countries from just 16 within a decade. In this regard, the trade value with Nepal cannot be ignored. As per the data from the Ministry of Finance, Royal Government of Bhutan, trade with Nepal has increased by almost BTN 400 mn during the period from 2010 to 2019.

Trade With India

The trade with India and Bhutan dates back to 1947 with the signing of the treaty between the Government of India and the Royal Government of Bhutan in the year 1947 (Joseph, 2007). The more formal and clear understanding and agreement was signed in 1972. Till then this agreement has undergone five revisions in the years 1983, 1990, 1995, 2006 and 2016. The current agreement will undergo further revision in the year 2026. To facilitate Bhutan in furtherance of its trade ties, India has agreed to the free transit of goods from within its territory to other countries. One such example is the instance where the Government of India has entered into a trilateral agreement with Bhutan and Bangladesh to facilitate the export of electricity from Bhutan to Bangladesh. (Dolkar, 2023).

Figure 6. Top ten commodities exported to India, 2020
Source: Report on Bhutan's External Trade, Department of Trade, Ministry of Economic Affairs, 2021

Sl. No.	BTC Code	Commodity Description	Value in million Nu.
1	2716.00.00	Electricity	27,523.03
2	7202.21.00	Ferro -silicon	7,232.17
3	7207.19.00	Semi-finished products of iron or non-alloy steel	1,820.47
4	2523.29.30	Portland pozzolana cement	1,214.22
5	0908.31.00	Cardamoms (Neither crushed nor ground)	354.00
6	2517.10.00	Pebbles, gravel, broken or crushed	113.49
7	2520.10.00	Gypsum, anhydrite	271.61
8	2523.29.10	Ordinary portland cement	564.41
9	2849.20.00	Silicon Carbide	397.03
10	2518.10.30	Dolomite lumps and slabs	322.29
		Other commodities	3,699.86
		Total	**43,512.58**

Figure 7. Top ten commodities imported from India, 2020
Source: Report on Bhutan's External Trade, Department of Trade, Ministry of Economic Affairs, 2021

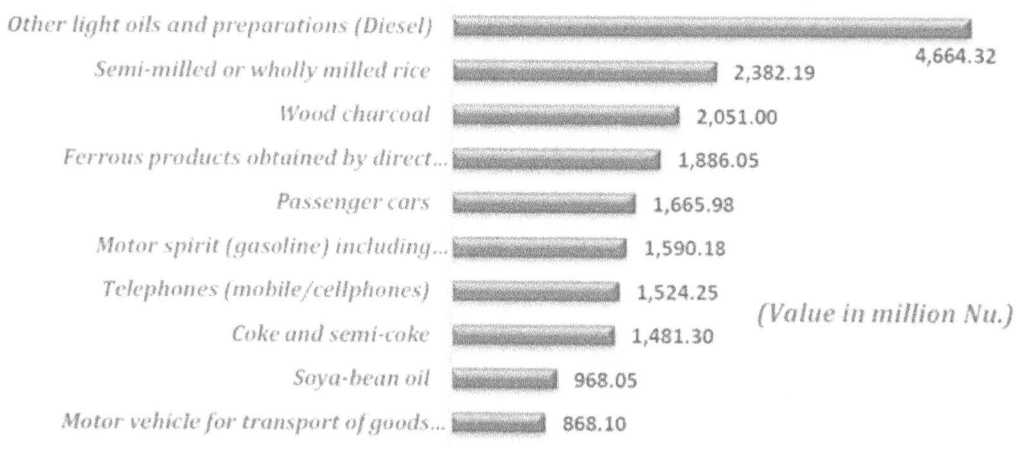

Trade With Bangladesh

Whereas trade with Bangladesh formally started in 1978. Hence in the year 1980, Bhutan and Bangladesh entered into an agreement which was formally signed in the year 1984 by giving MFN (most favoured nation) status to Bhutan. With this, the trade with Bangladesh has risen considerably over the years. The details of which are shown in above figures.

Figure 8. Top ten commodities exported to Bangladesh, 2020
Source: Report on Bhutan's External Trade, Department of Trade, Ministry of Economic Affairs, 2021

Sl. No.	BTC Code	Commodity Description	Value in million Nu.
1	2516.90.10	Boulders	1,848.56
2	2517.10.00	Pebbles and gravels	783.67
3	0908.31.00	Cardamom	657.55
4	0805.10.00	Oranges	279.85
5	2521.00.00	Limestone flux & calcareous stone	253.88
6	2518.10.10	Dolomite (powdered)	63.94
7	2836.50.00	Calcium carbonate	20.08
8	2009.00.00	Fruit juice	10.57
9	2520.20.00	Gypsum anhydrite plaster	6.97
10	2202.99.90	Mineral water	8.32
		Other commodities	21.63
		Total	**3,955.02**

Figure 9. Top ten commodities imported from Bangladesh, 2020
Source: Report on Bhutan's External Trade, Department of Trade, Ministry of Economic Affairs, 2021

Sl. No.	BTC Code	Commodity Description	Value in million Nu.
1	2619.00.00	Slag, dross, scaling, etc. from manufacture of iron	115.84
2	6100 to 6200	Readymade Garments	73.85
3	1905.00.00	Sweet biscuits, cakes & pastry	64.83
4	2009.00.00	Fruit Juices (mango & litchi)	38.14
5	3003 to 3004	Medicaments	30.44
6	3924.10.00	Tableware and kitchenware of plastic	19.48
7	9403.00.00	Other furniture (wood & plastic)	19.07
8	7615.10.00	Tableware and kitchenware of aluminum	14.71
9	3401.11.00	Soaps (for toilet use)	12.71
10	1704.90.00	Sugar confectionery (sweets)	8.59
		Other commodities	42.80
		Total	**440.46**

Figure 10. Comparison of sectoral shares for trade in services (2010 and 2018) (in USD million), The Ministry of Economic Affairs, RGoB Publication

Sector	Export 2010	Export 2018	Import 2010	Import 2018
Travel	40.15	1 102.95	41.39	78
Transport	23.64	71.67	51.57	53
Insurance and pension services	1.50	2.71	4.62	4
Financial services	0.95	2.05	0.07	6
Telecommunications, computer and information services	0.64	0.43	2.23	4
Charges for the use of intellectual property not included elsewhere	0.01	0.01	0.17	0.304
Other business services	0.00	0.00	12.90	20
Construction (not including employment of expatriates)			22.19	63
Maintenance and repair services not included elsewhere			0.12	6

Trade in Services

Bhutan is known to the outside world as a model for sustainable tourism model with a major focus on its rich cultural heritage and at the same time preserving and conserving the nature. The Green Destinations Gold Award by ITB Berlin is evidence of its efforts towards this direction.

Being a tourism-dominated country, it is obvious that total trade in services will be dominated by tourism-related industries. If we go by the data of 2018 the travel and transport-related services accounted for 99% and 97% of total export and import of total services.

As discussed above, the pandemic had a severe impact on the Bhutanese economy, since this economy is majorly dependent on tourism and travel services. It was in the years 2020 and 2021 when tourists' arrival was banned and thus, the country did not receive any tourists. The pandemic, further, had a severe impact on the tourism-related industry as well which in turn resulted in the loss of jobs and hence an increase in high unemployment across industries like hotels, transportation and restaurants.

FDI and Bhutan

For the development of any economy, foreign investment plays a very important role (Anuradha, J. et al., 2014). Bhutan opened itself to FDI in 2002 with the adoption of the FDI Policy 2002; since then, the policy has been revised in 2010, 2014, and 2019 (Dr Tshering Cigay, 2022). In Bhutan, foreign direct investment (FDI) must align with the country's distinctive development philosophy centred around Gross National Happiness. Since its inception, Bhutan has attracted a relatively small portion of foreign investment due to factors such as country size, location, population, and growth rate (Sultan, Mohammad et al., 2023). Nevertheless, Bhutan has implemented various promotional measures to attract foreign investment.

According to the Ministry of Economic Affairs' FDI Report 2022, the total number of FDI companies in Bhutan stood at 101. The hotel sector received the highest FDI (36%), followed by IT/ITES (ITES = IT-enabled services) with 22%, and Agro-dairy at 10%. Notably, the share of the hotel sector in overall

FDI has declined from 42% in 2019 to 36% in 2022, while the share of IT/ITES increased from 19% in 2019 to 22% in 2022. This shift indicates a diversification of FDI across sectors, moving away from hotels to other sectors. Further, most of the FDI IT companies earn almost all their revenue from exports and employ 100% of the Bhutanese workforce. (Dr Tshering Cigay, 2022).

The importance of international trade and foreign direct investment (FDI) can be clearly understood by the fact that FDI not only brings business to the economy but also enables the country to be more cost-effective than others. This is more applicable to the landlocked economy like Bhutan. The importance of FDI is more in this case, as Bhutan is surrounded by two economic superpowers i.e., India and China on the one hand and other hand, the world's budding manufacturing hub i.e. Bangladesh (Business Post, 2023). It becomes imperative for Bhutan to focus on importing more knowledge and technological know-how from neighbours that would promote local industries which in times would contribute to its international trade.

Bhutan Entrepreneurial Environment: Issues/Challenges

The World over almost every economy is dominated by the presence of small and micro enterprises, hence their importance and contribution to their respective GDP cannot be ignored.

Figure 11. Contribution of SMEs in GDP of respective economies
Source: Marzban, Shehab, et al, 2015

Figure 11 clearly shows the contribution of SMEs to the GDP of major economies of the world. The same case is with the economies of Asian countries, where SMEs have contributed 53.8%, 40%, and 30.9% to the economies of Japan, India and the Republic of Korea respectively (Abdullah, Moha, et al., 2020). Bhutan's scenario is no different. Out of the total licenses allotted to businesses across Bhutan, 98% have been allotted to SMEs. But there is a difference here with the world's counterpart. SMEs in Bhutan contribute to only 5% of the country's GDP (Moktan, S., 2007). The reason for this is discussed in the later part of this chapter. The importance of SMEs extends beyond numbers. Its importance lies in the number of employment it generates and hence contributes to the growth of the economy.

In Bhutan, SME is known as Cottage and Small-Scale Industries (CSI). As per the Department of Cottage and Small Industry (DCSI), "cottage industries" are those employing 1-4 people with less than Nu.1 million as investment whereas "small industries" employ 5-14 people with more than Nu. 1 million but less than Nu. 10 million as investment (RMA, 2017). Hence, the distinction of CSI from other forms of business is made by initial investment and workers employed (size) in the business.

The nature of doing business in Bhutan is different from other nations, because of its location and topography which makes it difficult to access the outside world. During COVID–19 and its aftermath, the whole industrial scenario in Bhutan saw a negative turn. And tourism was not untouched from this effect. The revenue from tourism fell from USD 225 million to USD 19 million (Rinzin, 2021). In the same period, the unemployment rate of the youth rose from approx. 12% to 23% (National Statistics Bureau, 2020). The Royal Government of Bhutan has various policies in force to take out the struggling small and micro enterprises sector from this trouble. Since this sector comprises over 95% of the total unit strength in the country, a separate CSI scheme has been set up for the promotion and development of micro-enterprises. Most of these small-scale enterprises are engaged in trading or other such kinds of retail, which are mostly imported goods.

The Ministry of Economic Affairs, through its publication "DIAGNOSTIC TRADE INTEGRATION STRATEGY UPDATE 2020", has identified certain issues which are hampering the growth and contribution of SMEs to the economy. Not having proper certifying authority and any regulation to keep a check on the standard of products being exported outside Bhutan, the high cost of transportation and the lack of electronic or digital platform opportunities to expand to overseas markets, are some of the reasons identified. The publication further suggested that there should be a robust electronic platform and a digital environment that can let Bhutan's products reach a wider market across the globe.

Further, in the same line ADBI's case study "Promoting Entrepreneurship in Bhutan" published in 2022, has pointed out the challenges/obstacles faced by entrepreneurs in Bhutan:

- Complex administrative procedures
- Government officials' lack of understanding of the clearance procedure especially for new business ideas
- Lack of entrepreneurial culture
- Difficulty in accessing finance

Complex administrative procedure: To initiate a venture, an entrepreneur has to undergo various clearances and certificate/licensing procedures. This procedure includes from land clearance to religious/societal. Below is the figure which highlights the number of clearances a person has to take before venturing into real business.

Figure 12. Procedure for starting a pig farm in Bhutan
Source: ADB I's case study "Promoting Entrepreneurship in Bhutan", 2022

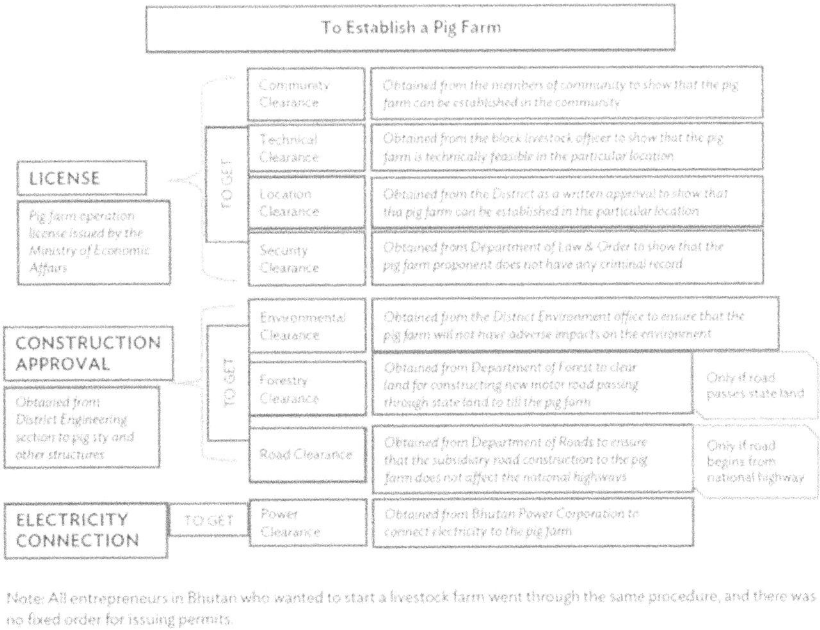

This is just an illustrative procedure. In actuality, it is depicting the number of steps a business has to take before seeing the light of the day.

Government officials' lack of understanding: There is a second issue that is somewhat peculiar in nature. It is the lack of Government official's understanding of the business. It may be due to a lack of training or positioning the wrong person at the wrong place. They sometimes perceive the problems differently which may not be the actual problem. They don't have proper training to handle the issues raised by budding entrepreneurs.

Lack of entrepreneurial culture: Entrepreneurship in Bhutan is not perceived as the best choice for one's career. It is not taken as a sign of high education and reputation in the society of Bhutan. There is a tendency of the youth to join government jobs rather than having an entrepreneurial venture.

Difficulty in accessing finance: Getting finance for business is another arduous task for an entrepreneur to initiate the process. There is a mandatory requirement of collateral or guarantee for budding businessmen, which sometimes becomes difficult for them. Moreover, there are other options like getting a loan from NGOs but they are not that attractive since the interest rates are high.

Further, in a report titled "Status-Quo Analysis of the Status of Entrepreneurship Efforts in Bhutan, Nepal and Lao PDR" published by an Erasmus+ co-funded project, ENCORE. Have pointed out the following challenges:

- The Government policies are not recent enough to accommodate new business ideas and this poses challenges for any new innovative business ideas to launch. Also, there is a huge gap in terms of implementation and interpretation of the policies.
- Lack of funding support for businesses that are ready to scale up.

- Lack of support in areas such as access to market, storage, copyrights & protection, certification of local products, technical know-how and others.
- Limited support like to entrepreneurs who have crossed their start-up phase and are ready to scale up.
- Lack of access to skilled HR especially in the areas of IT and R&D.
- The lack of coordination and sharing of information between various stakeholders in the ecosystem has resulted in duplicated efforts and support.

All of the above listed are the broad issues/challenges faced by entrepreneurs when embarking on a business venture, which clearly indicates the entrepreneurship ecosystem in Bhutan is still developed to support the needs of the entrepreneurs.

The Royal Government of Bhutan through the Ministry of Economic Affairs has initiated various schemes and procedures to facilitate the growth of CSIs. The intention to introduce these measures was to address the concern pointed out by various agencies. One such development is the establishment of "Industrial Infrastructure Development Division (IIDD)". The objective with which IIDD has been established is to develop the industrial scenario across the country, viz. setting up of industrial parks/estates in every district.

Figure 13. Industrial estates, techparks, incubation centres, and start-up centres setup by IIDD
Source: Information gathered from IIDD and DCSI, MoEA

Name	Location	Size	Industry Type/ Size	Status
Jigmeling Industrial Estate	Sarpang (South-Central)	729 acres	Any	Under construction
Dhamdum Industrial Estate	Samtse (South-West)	349.07 acres	Green and non-polluting	Under construction
Motanga Industrial Estate	S/Jongkhar (South-East)	155.56 acres	Any	Under construction
Bondeyma Industrial Estate	Mongar (East)	110.35 acres	Any	Under construction
Pasakha Industrial Estate	Chukha (South-West)	188 acres	Any	Operational
Bjemina Industrial Estate	Thimphu	32 acres	Non-polluting	Operational
Thimphu TechPark 1	Thimphu	18 acres with Lower Ground Fl + Ground Fl + 2 Upper Floors	ICT, business incubators, shared technology, data centre	Operational
Thimphu TechPark 2	Thimphu	20,000 sq. ft	ICT, business incubators, shared technology, data centre	Operational
Start-up Centre	Thimphu	30 start-ups	Any	Operational
Start-up Centre	Monger	30 to 50 start-ups	Any	Under construction
Start-up Centre	Samste	30 to 50 start-ups	Any	Under construction
CSI Estate	Tsirang	12 CSI	Any	Under construction

The table in Figure 13 shows industrial estates, techparks, incubation centres as established by IIDD under their CSI/industrial development plan.

While going through various documents and other sources, we have identified certain shortcomings in the industrial development scenario of the country. Some of which are discussed below:

- There is a major lack of data pertaining to the CSI sector which in turn hampers the development of policies and regulations which can facilitate further the development of CSI as a whole.
- Since women have a considerable share in Bhutan's entrepreneurial environment, there are no proper schemes/policies for having a maximum contribution from this section of the country's demography.
- The digital economy and digital way of doing business is the way companies across the globe perform their operation and transactions. In Bhutan, there is no such specific policy which can facilitate the growth of digital infrastructure like e -e-payments which are indeed an important element in the development of digital infrastructure.

There is an urgent need to move towards a digital way of doing business. This will not only help the companies to move further ahead in the market but also this will help them to reduce costs and be competitive in the global market. In this regard, the Royal Government of Bhutan has initiated the Digital Drukyul Flagship programme. The objective of this programme is to create an online platform that can facilitate documentation and clearances. This programme has a plan to process import and export clearance online expanding further to public service which includes health and education as well.

In the coming section, we will be dealing with digital business / entrepreneurship issues and challenges in great detail.

Digital Business/Entrepreneurship: Issues and Challenges

In recent times, information technology-enabled services (ITES) have emerged as one of the important tools for giving the country's economy a required boost. We have the example of major economies like the USA, China and India benefiting from the ITES wave. It is evident that, with emphasis on information technology and other allied sectors these economies have shown positive signs towards growth (PANAGARIYA, 2023). The data and figures shared in the initial paragraphs of this chapter highlight and support this fact and the importance of digital business to the overall economy.

There are many factors which help the digital revolution to flourish and develop further. With the recent developments in mobile technologies, big data technologies, and cloud computing etc have created an atmosphere which is conducive for the digital economy and digital entrepreneurship to develop. These technologies are a must for any economy to develop in the international platform. (Pereira, C.S, et al, 2022).

It is established that in order to have a wider reach to the international market Hervé, et al, 2022 have proposed factors which is important for the internationalisation of the market. They are cost, accessibility, resources, competencies, knowledge of the market, distance and location of the market.

Digitalisation has changed the way business is done globally. The emergence of digitally powered global companies like Uber, and Airbnb has put pressure on domestic businesses to work more on their business model which should be necessarily directed towards some digital innovation.

Further, Muthuraman, S., 2020, have emphasises the importance of digital innovation and digitalisation as a whole for business growth and sustainable development.

The digital revolution has brought so much impact to the whole of business that it is now been replaced with the term "digital disruption". This word is used to describe the impact of digital technologies and infrastructure on how business, economy and society operate. This digital disruption brings opportunities and paves the way for the growth of enterprises especially the smaller ones to grow and internationalise. The impact is so strong that if they fail to catch the revolution they may be thrown out of the business. (Huckstep, R, 2016).

Though a formal definition of Digital entrepreneurship is not available, some scholars have defined the terms to include the following; use of technological advancement, and selling of goods and services across automated networks. (Baig et al., 2022)

There are many factors that have affected the growth of the digital business or digital entrepreneurship in recent years. The informal institution is supposed to be the first such factor which affects the growth of the digital entrepreneurial domain. Informal institutions are defined as an unwritten set of rules or norms which affect or guide society's behaviour (Dau, L., et al., 2022). These informal institutions include important elements like norms, culture, traditions, practices etc. (Helmke, G, et al., 2004). Informal institution serves as important guide for society to bind, move in a direction and behave to an instance in a particular manner. (Dau, L., et al., 2022). These informal institutions have put pressure on digital business / digital entrepreneurship to behave and develop the model according to their environment. The best example is TikTok. Their version which works well in the US however does not work well in their home country China. (Klaus E. Meyer et al., 2023). One such element of informal institutions is the attitude of society towards new technologies. It means how fast a society is open to change and adapt the new technology. How fast a society is absorbing the latest development in this field is directly proportional to the degree of uncertainty avoidance which in turn influences the growth in the area of digital entrepreneurship. (Park, C. et al, 2003). Such factors in turn affect the growth of digital entrepreneurship in a particular economy.

Just opposite to the informal institution, is the formal institution which includes the laws, rules and regulations prevailing in an economy. Many firms view the existence and intensity of formal institutions as hindrances to their growth (Cusumano, 2014). The laws pertaining to consumer protection, privacy laws, National security, intellectual property rights, taxes and employment laws are such examples of formal institutions which affect the growth of digital entrepreneurship in an economy.

Figure 14. Formal institution affecting the growth of digital entrepreneurship
Source: Meyer, Klaus E., et al.

Sphere of formal institutions	Concerns	Examples
Employment	When is a contractor an employee? What are the minimum standards (work hours, pay, etc.) for employees?	Employment status of delivery drivers for online shopping sites (Amazon, T-Mall), car sharing (Uber, Lyft) and food delivery platforms (DoorDash, Deliveroo)
Consumer protection	What is the liability of the platform operator for faulty products delivered via the platform, or for outright fraud by platform users?	Fake brands sold via Alibaba Express or Amazon Sexual harassment by drivers using ride sharing platforms Rules aimed at preventing addiction to gambling
Taxation	Where is corporate tax due for services delivered across borders? Do platforms have to ensure platform users pay taxes they are liable for?	Amazon warehouses serving multiple countries License fees paid to Regional HQ in low-tax location
Privacy	What rights do individuals have on their personal data? What are companies allowed to do with data collected from consumers?	Facebook collecting user data and using them for third party targeted advertising (incl. political)
National security	What spheres of the economy does the government consider national security?	TikTok access to data of US-based users Geographic data in China – car navi system must license from local partner
Censorship	What is illegal to say in public? What is illegal to promote?	Historical reports and political opinions (Facebook, Google and others in China) Advertisement for harmful substances or activities (alcohol, gambling, pornography, guns)
Competition policy	What criteria apply to M&A of digital firms? What practices of dominant platforms represent abuse of market power?	Approval of acquisition of start-ups by big-5 digital firms Google search prioritizing services of associated firms
Intellectual property rights	How can we globally utilize IP rights that are defined nationally and owned by different rights holders?	Spotify and Netflix streaming music or videos need to negotiate with rights holders in each country

According to Klaus E. Meyer et al., 2023, business in the digital domain, pays little emphasis on conventional business infrastructure, but instead, they focus more on technological infrastructure such as the availability of high-speed internet facilities and entrepreneurship ecosystem, to name a few. However, there are companies in the digital domain which has to depend on conventional infrastructure especially those who is selling physical products over online platform. This conventional infrastructure includes the transport facility, availability of consumers, proper banking and payment systems etc. Business aspiring to enter or start in a new market, therefore, has to access and identify the quality of resource available for them to grow.

Susan. F., et al. 2017, have identified the local entrepreneurial ecosystem as an important element and factor in the development of digital entrepreneurship. Ecosystem here means knowledge clusters which helps in sharing and developing of new ideas, recruiting and retaining new talents and acquiring new innovative resources. Economies with appropriate ecosystems serve as important catalysts for the growth of digital businesses.

Sometimes the new entrant into the digital domain has to face competition from already existing players, which are not in this area of operation. The result is the improvement in services and products and their delivery too. This brings a new dimension of competition for the digital entrepreneurs. For example, when Airbnb moved into Taiwan market, the market moved to such a level which was not anticipated by any of the markets to respond. In general, when a digital disruptor enters the market, the already existing competitors who are majorly into conventional business models, tend to react in a negative way. Either they choose to move out of the market or they lower down the offering price. The reverse was the case in Taiwan. The hotel industry went to increase the prices, rather than lowering down. The further aftereffect was that the quality of service was improved with the entry into the next higher segment. (Chang, H. H., et al. 2022). The effect of the digital revolution is obviously felt all across the world. The same effect is felt in Bhutan as well.

Status Quo of Digital Business/Entrepreneurship in Bhutan

With the latest technologies pouring in and with the COVID-19 pandemic, Bhutan's industrial scenario specifically small and micro enterprises was left in shock. There were disruptions in the supply chain, liquidity shortages, sudden fall in demand, and market and customer reach. Against these setbacks The stage was set for a substantial digital revolution to take root in this Himalayan kingdom, facilitated by an impressive 100% mobile penetration rate as of 2023, almost all households (99.60%) in the country have an internet connection (the National Statistical Bureau's (NSB) Bhutan Living Standard Survey-2022), there are 625,905 total active mobile banking app users, (Royal Monetary Authority, Annual payment System Report 2022) and the country witness an increase in other related services like OR code usage, internet banking, domestic and international payment and e-wallet.

To promote and nurture the digital environment in the country. The Royal Government of Bhutan developed certain key objectives and plans, some of the prominent ones among them are:

- **Digital Drukyul:** As discussed earlier, the idea and objective of floating this programme is to develop a proper all-round environment that can facilitate the digital revolution to reach almost every citizen of the country.
- With three basic objectives of creating almost 2600 jobs in this sector, increasing the revenue from this domain to almost BTN 6.5 billion and supporting more than 5000 businesses to develop and flourish further in digital entrepreneurship, the programme called **iDzodrak** was launched by RGoB in the year 2015 with a five-year horizon of 2016-2020.
- One of the major steps taken by RGoB was its 21st century economic roadmap which lays emphasis on the development of policies which can set Bhutan's development at par with other countries of the world, guided by the philosophy of Gross National Happiness at its core. One of the important key drivers which were identified for this economic roadmap was digital transformation, ie. equipping business houses with the digital tool so that they can stand in line with their global counterparts in terms of development and cost-effectiveness.

Despite the Royal Government of Bhutan's efforts to propel the nation toward a digital revolution, aiming to maximize opportunities and cultivate a considerable number of digital entrepreneurs, the programs and policies have encountered specific drawbacks and limitations.

Ministry of Economic Affairs, through its publication "DIAGNOSTIC TRADE INTEGRATION STRATEGY UPDATE 2020", has identified certain challenges which are impediments to the growth of a proper digital environment in the country, they are:

Lack of connectivity: There is a lack of access to information technology tools for many small enterprises, especially those who are located in rural areas. Also, these enterprises which are located in far-flung areas are more of informal in nature which poses another issue in implementing the proper scheme/policies for the development of digital space in the country. Due to its informal structure, policy-makers are not aware of their status/numbers and thus, they are not able to frame any policies which can motivate these enterprises to explore more with the digital environment. Thereby limiting their ability to utilise the incentives framed by the government.

Lack of digital awareness and trust: Even though the Royal Government of Bhutan has invested hugely in making enterprises aware of the benefits/advantages of moving towards the digital domain, there is still much work left to be done to create awareness.

Lack of proper digital skills: Due to a lack of appropriate digital skills amongst the entrepreneurs. They are not able to capitalise on digital opportunities.

As we know the growth of the digital environment leads to the overall development of the economy, which is reflected in the growth of GDP. Not only this, it further leads to the development of various participants of the economy like entrepreneurs, government and private employees etc.

In Bhutan, there are 129 licensed E-commerce operators, as reported by the Department of Trade. Additionally, a considerable number operate informally through free social media platforms like Facebook and Instagram. Although concrete data on the expansion of informal e-commerce is lacking, the prevalence of advertisements on social media suggests rapid growth and popularity in conducting business through this channel. Further, A vast majority (74%) of Bhutanese e-commerce consumers use unregistered online agents that advertise their products through free social media platforms such as Facebook and Instagram. Only 26% of the purchases come from the registered local, regional and global e-commerce companies. (Market Analysis Division, Office of Consumer Protection, Bhutan, 2022).

Additionally, the Royal Government of Bhutan issued a circular through the Department of Trade, Ministry of Economic Affairs on September 7, 2022. These circular mandates all unlicensed individuals and entities involved in online business without obtaining an e-commerce license to acquire one; otherwise, they may be subjected. This further validates the growth of e-commerce business in Bhutan.

Keeping in line with the requirements of the digital revolution sweeping all across the globe, there are certain developments/enterprises in this domain in Bhutan that are worth mentioning:

DrukRide: Just as other countries like the US have Uber, India has Ola, Bhutan developed its own ride-sharing app called "DrukRide" in the year 2017. This was made possible because of assistance from the Bhutan Taxi Association's, almost, 7000 taxi/cabs.

Housing.bt: This is another interesting development in this domain, "Housing. bt". The business offers real estate management over an online platform. Offering buying and selling of real estate property over their digital platform, the company was funded by the initial support from Loden Foundation. The idea was initially pitched at the Global Entrepreneurship Summit at Silicon Valley in the year 2016 and received additional funding in the year 2018 under the "Jab-chor" initiative of the Royal Monetary Authority, Bhutan and by Yarkay Group.

Zheygo and MyChharo: App-based food delivery service.

Medhey: Online shopping app.

AB Ventures: AB Ventures is a new Bhutanese customer interaction service established in collaboration with the Australian company Workforce BluePrint, which specializes in providing tailored workforce solutions for its Australian clients.

To gain a better understanding and clarity on the challenges faced by entrepreneurs involved in digital business, we interviewed one of Bhutan's prominent digital entrepreneurs.

Case of Mr. Sonam Chopel: Finding the Ground and Struggle with Internationalisation

Introduction

Bhutan, a small kingdom nested in the heart of the Himalayas, which is known for its breathtaking landscapes, rich cultural heritage and pioneer of the alternative measurement of economic growth Gross National Happiness. In recent times the country has seen some remarkable emergence of entrepreneurship. Among the pioneering figures in the Bhutanese business landscape is Mr. Sonam Chophel, the founder of Druksell, an online platform dedicated to promoting and selling Bhutanese handcrafted products to the global market.

In this case study an attempt has been made to explore Mr. Chophel's background, the journey of establishing the Druksell and CSI market, the challenges faced, and the impact of his business on Bhutan's artisan community and international trade.

A Brief Background of Mr. Sonam Chopel

Mr Sonam Chophel was born and raised in Bhutan and possessed a deep appreciation for his country's unique culture and craftsmanship. After completing his schooling in Bhutan, he did his Bachelor's degree in Science from Narsuan University, Thailand. He then did his Master of Business Administration from Canberra University. He is a strong advocate of being a lifelong learner. And thus, he went ahead and honed his skills in branding, digital marketing, and e-commerce. Which has helped him in the entrepreneurial journey that lay ahead. (Chophel, 2023)

Early in his career, Mr. Chophel worked as a digital specialist with Terton Travel Bhutan and later as a digital marketing manager at Keystobhutan. His entrepreneurial spirit led him to establish Bhutan's first branding and design firm, SC Branding, where he served as the creative director, design consultant, and branding advisor. His diverse experiences also included roles as a financial/economics specialist at APECS Consultancy. He has also served as a national consultant for product design and packaging specialist for the International Trade Centre. (Chophel, 2023)

In 2014, Mr. Chopel embarked on a ground-breaking venture by founding Druksell. Which is an e-commerce platform to connect Bhutanese artisans and products to the international market. And in 2020 Mr Chopel established The CSI Market in collaboration with the Department of Cottage and Small Industry and Entrepreneurs. (MoICE, 2023). The main idea behind this was to provide a unique hybrid marketplace that blends the attributes of both online and physical marketplace, which would give customers the unique opportunity to physically experience the locally made and grown products in Bhutan.

Formation of Druksell and CSI Market

Mr. Chopel's inspiration for Druksell stemmed from a profound belief in the power of locally made products to enrich lives and communities. He wanted to showcase Bhutanese artisanal products to the international market and to provide a gateway for local artists to enter the international market. His ardent aim was not only to introduce authentic Bhutanese products to the world but also to narrate the personal stories of the artisans behind each creation. (Yeewong Magazine, 2018, p. 55)

Recognizing the need for technology to scale up businesses and the limited scope of the domestic market, Mr. Chopel identified a niche in connecting Bhutanese artisans with global consumers. With these beliefs, he later laid the foundation for the CSI market, in Thimphu with the help and support from flagship program initiated by the Department of Cottage and Small Industry Ministry of Economic Affairs.

The Journey

Mr. Chopel's journey was not without its hurdles. Bhutan's e-commerce landscape presented challenges, including limited access to technology, capital and resources. Regulatory and legal complexities and the absence of standard payment gateways hindered transactions. (S. Chophel, personal communication, August 25, 2023)

Despite the challenges, Mr. Chopel has been successful in building a robust system for his business. He was able to do this with his sheer dedication, experience, and meticulously using the limited resources and infrastructure to the fullest. Early marketing strategies focused on showcasing the authenticity of Bhutanese products and creating a bridge between artisans and consumers helped him gain market tractions. Druksell's dedication to quality, cultural authenticity and fair trade set it apart in the global marketplace.

Challenges Faced by Mr. Sonam Chopel

Druksell faced numerous challenges. Navigating regulatory and legal hurdles demanded innovation and adaptability. Competition from larger international players was fierce, and the absence of standardized payment gateways posed challenges in online transactions. Certifying products in Bhutan was limited, affecting exports, and logistics costs were exponentially high. Further, Limited access to capital in Bhutan to scale up his business has been a major challenge all of which has hampered the growth potential of Druksell. (S.Chophel, personal communication, August,25, 2023)

Despite these challenges, Druksell's CSI Market has successfully positioned itself as an exclusive destination for a wide range of high-quality local products and has seen a growth of 25% in walk-in traffic in the CSI Market store. Today the CSI market in Thimphu has about 600 producers supplying more than 1200 products. (MoICE, 2023). Catering to the demand of both locals and international visitors. Recently, on 9th May 2023, the second CSI market was inaugurated in Paro, Bhutan. The work is on to establish more such markets all across 20 Dzongkha in Bhutan. (MoICE, 2023). The opening of several CSI markets will work as a catalyst and enhance market access for local producers, improve inter-business linkages and exchange business information, enhance visibility and garner patronage from customers for local products. (Wangmo, Choki, 2023)

International Business Strategies and Challenges

Mr. Chopel's internationalization strategies included expanding Druksell's presence beyond Bhutan and adapting to global competition. He was successful in opening CSI outlets in the USA, Thailand and Australia. In an interview given to Kuensel on May 10th 2023, he shared that by 2024, he plans to open similar CSI outlets in Bangladesh United States, Europe, and India. With the support from the Department of Industry and also aspires to open outlets in (Wangmo, Choki, 2023)

At present he shared that Druksell has about 10,000 dedicated international customers. (S.Chophel, personal communication, August,25, 2023)

Some of the challenges he has faced apart from fierce competition is the lack of internationally recognised lab certification for the local product. Due to the strict certification requirements, the store in Thailand has to be closed. Mr Chopel mentioned that the country has limited facilities. Moreover, the cost of certifying the products are expensive and the local manufacturers are not able to afford it, thereby limiting their chances to venture into international business. Further, the exponential logistic cost makes the product expensive and thus, loses competitive advantage over its competitors. (S.Chophel, personal communication, August,25, 2023)

Despite these challenges, Druksell has used its strategic partnerships and has been successful in exporting some of its products.

The Future of Bhutan's Online Business Landscape

Mr. Chopel has emerged as a pioneer and influencer in Bhutan's entrepreneurial scene. His success with Druksell has demonstrated the potential for further growth and innovation in Bhutan's e-commerce sector. We see some similar businesses emerging, in the country such as Zala.bt, Azhapasa. bt and many others.

The Druksell story is a testament to the entrepreneurial spirit thriving in Bhutan. Through Mr. Sonam Chopel's remarkable journey, the Bhutanese business landscape has undergone a transformative shift, serving as a guiding light for aspiring entrepreneurs seeking to harness the advantages of the digital wave. Druksell's success story not only highlights its individual achievements but also demonstrates how it has become a source of inspiration, providing valuable insights for other entrepreneurs on navigating and leveraging technology in their ventures.

RECOMMENDATION

With the issues and challenges discussed above, the following recommendation can be made:

- As identified in RGoB publication "DTIS update2020" as well, Bhutan can leverage the benefit of being a neighbour of one the world's software hub, ie. India and have valuable inputs from another neighbour, Bangladesh, in terms of industrial viability. In that publication, it was highlighted that collaboration could be in terms of spectrum sharing across the borders. Another point which was mentioned in the document was to explore the internet protocol interconnection agreements between the network providers of countries.
- Specialised support to digital entrepreneurs: There is a need to create specialized support in terms of infrastructure development, training, specialised mentors, technical know-how, testing and certifying agencies and R& D support that would support budding digital entrepreneurs of Bhutan. The country needs to strengthen its entrepreneurial eco-system which would make the environment more conducive for entrepreneurs to grow and develop.
- Increase Access to the Market. To overcome this, the Bhutanese government can enter into pact/ agreement with its partner agency to promote Bhutan as another destination for their digital offering. The benefit could be, that the companies in Bhutan who are looking for the global market can have access and on the other hand, companies outside Bhutan looking for the market can enter Bhutan to market their product.

- International payment gateway was one such issue highlighted in the discussion above. RMA along with RGoB needs to address this issue to facilitate the smooth transition to a digital entrepreneurship environment.

CONCLUSION

The Bhutanese international business scenario has evolved over the years and is changing especially in the times when the Bhutanese economy is in the phase of transition. The country is witnessing growth in the digital entrepreneurship, though in small numbers. The growth and shift which digital entrepreneurship has shown over the years in Bhutan will have a positive impact on the international business scenario of the country and it is expected that its contribution to the GDP will improve. According to the findings of this study, it may be inferred that the country's long-standing traditional business techniques may now be supplemented, if not completely replaced, by the power of digital technologies.

It is imperative for the country to accept its challenges and obstacles on the road to achieving the complete integration into the global digital economy. And work towards developing capacities to overcome these challenges so that it fully realises the potential of digital entrepreneurship and e-commerce.

REFERENCES

Abdullah, M., & Akhbar, T. (2020). Capacity building for SMEs: Realising training gap amongst SMEs in Malaysia, In M.A.Abdullah, R.Yayla, & D.Abdulrazak (Eds.) Cross Border SMEs: Malaysia & Indonesia (pp.107-131), UMY Press.

Anuradha, J., & Samy, G. (2014). The role of foreign direct investment in India. *International Journal of Current Research*, *6*(9), 8897–8901.

Baig, U., Hussain, B. M., Meidute-Kavaliauskiene, I., & Davidavicius, S. (2022). Digital entrepreneurship: Future research directions and opportunities for new business model. *Sustainability (Basel)*, *14*(9), 5004. doi:10.3390/su14095004

Baluch, A. (2023). E-Commerce Statistics of 2023. *Forbes Advisor*. www.forbes.com/advisor/business/ecommerce-statistics/

Businesspostbd.com (2023). *Bangladesh's potential as a manufacturing hub*. Business Post BD. businesspostbd.com/editorial/2023-03-12/bangladeshs-potential-as-a-manufacturing-hub-2023-03-12.

Chang, H. H., & Sokol, D. D. (2022). How incumbents respond to competition from innovative disruptors in the sharing economy— The impact of Airbnb on hotel performance. *Strategic Management Journal*, *43*(3), 425–446. doi:10.1002/smj.3201

Chen, C., Lin, Y., Chen, W., Chao, C., & Pandia, H. (2021). Role of government to enhance digital transformation in small service business. *Sustainability (Basel)*, *13*(3), 1028. doi:10.3390/su13031028

Coppola, D. (2020) Global e-commerce share of retail sales 2026. *Statista*. https://www.statista.com/statistics/534123/e-commerce-share-of-retail-sales-worldwide/#statisticContainer

Cox, B. (2023). *Ecommerce statistics to get you ahead in 2022*. Dash. dash.app/blog/ecommerce-statistics.

Cusumano, M. A. (2014). How traditional firms must compete in the sharing economy. *Communications of the ACM*, *58*(1), 32–34. doi:10.1145/2688487

Dau, L., Chacar, A., Lyles, M., & Li, J. (2022). Informal institutions and international business: Toward an integrative research agenda. *Journal of International Business Studies*, *53*(6), 985–1010. doi:10.1057/s41267-022-00527-5

Department of Revenue and Customs. (2021). Bhutan Trade Statistics 2021. Department of Revenue and Customs. [https://www.mof.gov.bt/wp-content/uploads/2022/04/BhutanTradeStatistics2021.pdf]

Dolkar, D. (2023). GoI to facilitate Bhutan-Bangladesh electricity trade." *Kuensel Online*. kuenselonline.com/goi-to-facilitate-bhutan-bangladesh-electricity-trade/.

Dykes, T. (2022). *China E-Commerce: Is it time to look beyond regulatory pressures?* Schroders. www.schroders.com/en-us/us/individual/insights/china-e-commerce-is-it-time-to-look-beyond-regulatory-pressures/

ENCORE. (2021). Status-Quo Analysis of the Status of Entrepreneurship Efforts in Bhutan, Nepal and Lao PDR. ENCORE. ENCORE. https://encore.fh-joanneum.at/wp-content/uploads/2022/08/ENCORE_Status-Quo_WEB.pdf

Fujita, A., Lhendup, J., & Thinley, S. (2022). *Promoting Entrepreneurship in Bhutan*. Asian Development Bank Institute. doi:10.56506/USDA5186

Helmke, G., & Levitsky, S. (2004). Informal institutions and comparative politics: A research agenda. *Perspectives on Politics*, *2*(4), 725–740. doi:10.1017/S1537592704040472

Hervé, A., Schmitt, C., & Baldegger, R. (2020). Internationalization and digitalization: Applying digital technologies to the internationalization process of small and medium-sized enterprises. *Technology Innovation Management Review*, *10*(7), 28–40. doi:10.22215/timreview/1373

Huckstep, R. (2016). Insurance of Things–How IoT shows prevention is better than cure for insurers. *InsurTech Weekly*, *39*. https://www.the-digital-insurer.com/blog/insurtech-insurance-of-things-how-iot-shows-prevention-isbetter-than-cure-for-insurers/.

Jafari-Sadeghi, V., Garcia-Perez, A., Candelo, E., & Couturier, J. (2021). Exploring the impact of digital transformation on technology entrepreneurship and technological market expansion: The role of technology readiness, exploration and exploitation. *Journal of Business Research*, *124*, 100–111. doi:10.1016/j.jbusres.2020.11.020

Joseph, C. M. (2007). India-Bhutan relations: An overview. *Indian Foreign Affairs Journal*, *2*(1), 88–101. https://www.jstor.org/stable/45340648

Market Analysis Division, Office of Consumer Protection, Department of Trade. (2022). Econpmic Research. Market Analysis Division, Office of Consumer Protection. [https://www.moice.gov.bt/wp-content/uploads/2023/04/ Ecommerce-Research-MAD.pdf]

Marzban, S., & Asutay, M. (2015). Alternative ways of developing GCC Islamic funds industry: Entrepreneurial development. In M. Asutay & A. Turkistani (Eds.), *Islamic Finance: Political Economy Perspectives*. Gerlach.

Meyer, K., Li, J., Brouthers, K. D., & Jean, R. B. (2023). International business in the digital age: Global strategies in a World of National Institutions. *Journal of International Business Studies*, *54*(4), 577–598. doi:10.1057/s41267-023-00618-x PMID:37305175

Modgil, S., Dwivedi, Y. K., Rana, N., Gupta, S., & Kamble, S. (2021). Has Covid-19 accelerated opportunities for digital entrepreneurship? An Indian perspective. *Technological Forecasting and Social Change*, *175*(6), 121415. doi:10.1016/j.techfore.2021.121415 PMID:36536802

Moktan, S. (2007). Development of small and medium enterprises in Bhutan: Analysing constraints to growth. *South Asian Survey*, *14*(2), 251–282. doi:10.1177/097152310701400205

Muthuraman, S. (2020). Digital business models for sustainability. *Gedrag Organizational Review*, *33*, 1095–1102.

National Statistical Bureau. (2022). *Bhutan Living Standard Survey-2022*. NSB. https://www.nsb.gov.bt/wp-content/uploads/ dlm_uploads/2022/12/Updated-BLSS-2022.pdf

National Statistics Bureau. (2020a). *2020 Labour Force Survey Report*. NSB. https://www.nsb.gov.bt/wp-content/uploads/dlm_uploads/2021/04/2020-Labour-Force-Survey-Report.pdf

Opening of Cottage and Small Industry (CSI) Market. (2023). *Paro* | *MoICE* | བཟོ་གྲྭ་ཚོང་ལས་དང་ལཱ་གཡོག་ལྷན་ཁག།. Ministry of Industry, Commerce and Employment. www.moice.gov.bt/?p=265901. Accessed 16 Sept. 2023.

Panagariya, A. (2023, July). How India's economy will overtake the US.'s. *Time*, *28*. time.com/6297539/how-india-economy-will-surpass-us/

Park, C., & Jun, J. (2003). A cross-cultural comparison of Internet buying behavior: Effects of Internet usage, perceived risks, and innovativeness. *International Marketing Review*, *20*(5), 534–553. doi:10.1108/02651330310498771

Pereira, C. S., Durão, N., Moreira, F., & Veloso, B. (2022). The importance of digital transformation in international business. *Sustainability (Basel)*, *14*(2), 834. doi:10.3390/su14020834

Report on Bhutan's External Trade. (2021). Royal Government of Bhutan.

Rinzin, Y. (2021). A cursed year for the tourism sector. *Kuensel Online*. https://kuenselonline.com/a-cursed-year-for-the-tourism-sector/

Royal Monetary Authority. (2022). *Annual Payment System Report 2022*. RMA. https://www.rma.org.bt/RMA%20Publication/DPSS/2023%20Q2.pdf

Secundo, G., Mele, G., Del Vecchio, P., Elia, G., Margherita, A., & Ndou, V. (2021). Threat or opportunity? A case study of digital-enabled redesign of entrepreneurship education in the COVID-19 emergency. *Technological Forecasting and Social Change*, *166*, 120565. doi:10.1016/j.techfore.2020.120565 PMID:33518821

Sultan, M., & Khan, S. A. (2023). FDI, disinvestment and growth: An appraisal of Bhutanese economy. *Journal of Chinese Economic and Foreign Trade Studies*, *16*(1), 64–82. doi:10.1108/JCEFTS-05-2022-0031

Sussan, F., & Acs, Z. J. (2017). The digital entrepreneurial ecosystem. *Small Business Economics*, *49*(1), 55–73. doi:10.1007/s11187-017-9867-5

Tshering Cigay, D. (2022). *Which are the main FDI companies in the IT Sector, and how have they brought socio-economic benefits to Bhutan?* Wordpress. https://tcdorji.wordpress.com/2021/11/24/the-role-of-fdi-in-technological-and-economic-advancement-of-a-country-a-brief-look-at-fdi-in-bhutan/

Wangmo, C. (2023). *CSI aims to be part of global supply chain*. Kuensel Online. kuenselonline.com/csi-aims-to-be-part-of-global-supply-chain.

World Bank. (2019). *Bhutan's Integration with the Global Economy: International Investment Treaties and Conventions*. World Bank.

Yeewong Magazine. (2018, December). Read the stories of 50 entrepreneurs in Bhutan. *Yeewong Magazine.*

Chapter 3
Affluent Cities and Digitalization:
A Bidirectional Approach in 404 Cities

María del Mar Martínez-Bravo
https://orcid.org/0000-0002-4236-6444
University of Almería, Spain

Ana Labella-Fernández
https://orcid.org/0000-0002-8136-2614
University of Almería, Spain

ABSTRACT

Urban development literature has gained great traction due to the unprecedent challenges that cities face, and digitalization has been signaled as a game-changer against these challenges. However, the effects that urban digitalization might have on the economic prosperity at city-level remain unexplored. This research analyzes the bidirectional relationship between the digitalization degree and the economic situation of a city, based on a sample of 404 cities. The analysis resulted in confirming the positive bidirectional relationship between digitalization levels and the city's economic condition. If the economic prosperity of a city increases, so does its level of digitalization and if cities embrace and integrate digitalization, there is a positive impact on their economic growth. Thus, economic development and technological advancement mutually reinforce each other in urban contexts. This study not only aims to nurture the urban literature, but also to shed light on the shift towards the cities of the future.

DOI: 10.4018/979-8-3693-0798-4.ch003

INTRODUCTION

Cities are experimenting huge tensions due to the unprecedent population growth and its consequences in the urban contexts (Vardoulakis & Kinney, 2019). The urban population growth pushes cities to the limit (Marans, 2015) as it generally involves higher population concentration which might be translated into resources collapse and sustainability-related issues (Sodiq et al., 2019). Indeed, research highlights that these issues are likely to involve negative impacts on urban features such as the environment degradation, worse quality of life, or citizens or place health menaces (Gupta et al., 2019; Martínez-Bravo & Martínez-del-Río, 2019; Paiva-Vianna et al., 2015). For instance, population concentration in cities and the consequent economic activities are associated with air quality degradation which is highly related to health issues (Díaz et al., 2020; Di et al., 2017) because air pollution causes approximately seven million deaths per year and is responsible of one third of stroke, lung cancer, and heart disease related deaths (WHO, 2020). In this context, urban sustainability and city livability have been signaled as two of the grand societal challenges of the current century (e.g., Vardoulakis and Kinney, 2019). Governments aim to address those pressing issues through different strategies among which digitalization stands out because it has the potential of positively enhancing sustainability (Helbing, 2012, Heemsbergen, 2016, Seele & Lock, 2017) and importantly rising efficiency (Sodiq et al., 2019). Not only are policy and decision makers increasingly been interested in digitalization, but also a growing stream of research is advocating the digitalization of cities as the solution for the current urban challenges (e.g., Bibri & Krogstie, 2017).

Digitalization has the ability of changing peoples' lifestyles and the way cities are governed (Seele & Lock, 2017) and has been associated with a myriad of benefits for urban contexts such as prosperity, effectiveness, and competitiveness (e.g., Ahvenniemi et al., 2017). First, scholars have outlined digitalization as a tool for optimizing urban planning and architectural design (Fertner et al., 2019) which might lead to better connectivity infrastructure and efficiency gains in terms of building management or resource use (Balogun et al., 2020). Second, research highlights that proper digitalization levels entail the possibility of gathering higher-quality data (Balogun et al., 2020) that could be afterwards used for governance purposes in terms of policy or decision-making. For example, Balogun et al. (2020) highlighted the possibility of using the data gathered thanks to digitalization for improving cities resiliency and diminishing their vulnerability against climate risks. Third, scholars also highlighted benefits for citizens because, thanks to effective digitalization, they might be offered greater possibilities of spatial and temporal conditions for engaging in urban activities (Lyons et al., 2018) because digitalization offers greater flexibility (Seele & Lock, 2017). For instance, they could take advantage of digital connectivity for socially and economically engage in society's life (Alexander et al, 2011).

Indeed, recent research discusses the emergence of digitalization-related advancements that cities could benefit from. On the one hand, Song et al. (2022) analyzed the concept of digital economy development and its beneficial effects on urban air quality, which leads to sustainable economic development and to improvements in citizens' quality of life. More specifically, this effect has been highlighted to be stronger in large and eastern coastal areas, showing an important potential for leveraging environmental sustainability (Bai et al., 2022). In a similar vein, urban digitalization and smartness have been pointed out as promoters of improvements such as urban resilience, sustainable economic growth and high-quality economic development (Apostu et al., 2022; Cong et al., 2022; Wang et al., 2022). On the other hand, digitalization might enhance opportunities of circularity based on its potential for promoting and supporting reduced consumption and increased awareness (Balogun et al., 2020). In other words, digital technologies have the potential to transform urban contexts to be more inclusive and diverse due to the enhanced reuse, repair, and recycling possibilities and infrastructures which might result in economic inclusivity and ecological sustainability (Lekan and Rogers, 2020).

Sustainability has been specially discussed by urban researchers in terms of its relationship with digitalization (e.g., Bibri & Krogstic, 2017). For instance, Ahvenniemi et al. (2017) defend that the deployment of technology might be a crucial factor in addressing air-pollutant emissions or in maximizing efficiency in cities, Stuermer et al. (2017) discuss that digitalization might tend to optimize processes, resulting in natural resources savings, and Balogun et al. (2020) associated digitalization with climate change adaptation successful initiatives in diverse projects all around the world such as the Blue Link project in Australia, which addressed dangerous local beach conditions such as the rise of the sea level (Hughes, 2003). Even digitalization has been overall said to be able to address the current and urgent sustainability challenges in cities (e.g., Martin et al., 2018), researchers claim that sustainability targets are not effectively addressed in cities which aim to deploy smart technologies (e.g., Yigitcanlar et al., 2019). Thus, published works present a debate on the effectiveness of digitalization in terms of addressing sustainability challenges (e.g., Ahvenniemi et al., 2017) while some of them are certain that digitalization has the potential to achieve sustainability in cities (e.g., Sodiq et al., 2019).

Not only sustainability, but also quality of life and well-being have been discussed by researchers as potential benefits of digitalization (e.g., Balogun et al., 2020). First, a stream of research argues that the deployment of technology should benefit not only cities' environmental and financial sustainability, but also dwellers well-being (Ahvenniemi et al., 2017). Other scholars defend that urban contexts supported by ICT systems may be able to offer citizens specific services that are more advanced and with higher standards of innovation, which in turn may enhance their global quality of life (Bibri & Krogstie, 2017). Second, another stream of research also suggests that technology deployment might facilitate citizens participation and open government' points of view towards e-participation and governance (He et al., 2016), where digitalization might enable the possibility of attaining the "information civilization" (Seele & Lock, 2017, p. 183) Besides, ICT implementation might foster citizens' participation and might influence overall governance (He et al., 2016) as digitalization has been set as an effective tool for shaping, monitoring, and communicating governance in urban environments (Heemsbergen, 2016). In this line, overall well-being is likely to be improved because citizens' participation and engagement are key determinants of enhanced quality of life (Jenks & Jones, 2010).

In a context where urban scenarios are facing great challenges, the digitalization of cities could generate a wide variety of solutions (e.g., Lyons et al., 2018). However, research falls short in the study of solutions in terms of digitalization initiatives for several reasons. First, there is a call for empirical research on the relationship and trade-offs among digitalization and urban dynamics (Lyons et al., 2018, Seele & Lock, 2012, Stuermer et al., 2017). In addition, already published research mainly addresses urban digitalization from a theoretical perspective (e.g., Stuermer et al., 2017) or based on empirical studies at country-level (e.g., Billon et al., 2010) – instead of empirically analyzing the issue at the city-level – which may involve misunderstandings of the urban dynamics. Thus, this study aims to develop a theoretical framework based on empirical evidence at the city-level and to focus on understanding how digitalization influences the economic development of a city and, simultaneously, how the city's level of economic development impacts the effective implementation of digital technologies in these urban contexts. In other words, this study aims to analyze the bidirectional relationship between urban digitalization and a city's economic situation.

This manuscript is structured as follows. First, in the following section we develop the theoretical background on urban dynamics in terms of the relationship between urban digitalization and the economic situation of a city, and we argue the reason why this relationship might present a bidirectional effect. Second, in the methodology and analysis sections we define and present our sample, variables, and the empirical analysis that we carried out. Then, we present and discuss the results derived from the empirical analysis, we illustrate the findings obtained, and we explain the implications for urban planners and decision makers, for business managers and entrepreneurs, and for citizens. We then discuss the limitations and the further research agenda derived from the findings of the study and which might help to address the existing limitations. Finally, we end up with the concluding remarks of our study on digitalization and the economic situation of cities.

THEORETICAL BACKGROUND AND HYPOTHESES

Urban digitalization means including ICT in cities and households' daily lives (Lyons et al., 2018). However, the high related costs of implementing ICT (Ashrafi & Murtaza, 2008, Harindranath et al., 2008) might chase away governments to make use of them. For instance, corporate research already defined two specific barriers to ICT adoption within community contexts such as small and medium enterprises. First, the great operationalization costs of those technologies and, second, the high wages of staff with specific technology skills (Harindranath et al., 2008). Not only the high costs associated with ICT implementation, but also the emerging concern on the cooling requirements that the extensive technology deployment needs in a context of water scarcity. However, digitalization initiatives are related with huge efficiency gains that might be translated into enhanced prosperity, effectiveness, and competitiveness (e.g., Ahvenniemi et al., 2017). These gains are associated with economic resources efficiency and savings.

Research addressing the relationships between digitalization levels and the economic situation of territorial contexts already deployed a route (e.g., Billon et al., 2010; Kiiski & Pohjola, 2002) in which scholars have mainly addressed how economic factors condition the adoption and diffusion of ICT (e.g., Kiiski & Pohjola, 2002) while, to the best of our knowledge, little research has analyzed the effects of digitalization on the economic features of specific contexts. Besides, extant research analyzes the effect of economic factors on ICT implementation from a theoretical perspective (e.g., Stuermer et a., 217) or from an empirical perspective at the country-level (e.g., Billon et al., 2010) instead of at the city-level. We argue that they may fall short in understanding the urban dynamics. First, it is needed to empirically analyze more type of contexts and, more specifically, the urban contexts. Second, it is also needed to study the effects of proper digitalization levels on the city's economic situation. Third, it is necessary to observe the possible emergence of feedback loops. The feedback loops might help to understand the dynamic interconnection among variables and to observe if the change of one variable might have and effect that feed each other or other variables. In other words, to observe if dynamic cycles emerge and if they can amplify variables effects over time.

The Bidirectional Relationship Between the Economic Situation of Cities and Their Digitalization Levels

In terms of the impact of the economic situation on digitalization levels, there are many factors that might be involved. First, cities with a proper economic situation might be more likely to invest in the needed and high economic resources related to the implementation of ICT (Ashrafi & Murtaza, 2008;

Billon et al., 2010; Harindranath et al., 2008). Not only are they more likely to invest in ICT, but they may also operate in wealthier contexts with more developed infrastructures which might strengthen the effects of ICT investing (Dewan & Kraemer, 2000) because contexts with better networks provide greater opportunities for enhanced digital innovation (Myovella et al., 2020). For instance, wealthier cities are more likely to hold physical infrastructure and labor force that can be devoted to implementing or adapting to new digital demands, new internet infrastructures, or new digital industries. Not only may these cities be better prepared, but they may also evolve more rapidly if they are suggested to host enhanced digital innovations.

Besides, cities attract highly educated people due to, among other, economic opportunities (Betz et al., 2016). Higher levels of education have been associated with greater innovativeness (Kiiski & Pohjola, 2002) and enhanced development of digital skills (Billon et al., 2010). Also, the fact of concentrating different economic actors in cities tends to create contexts of trust and openness, which may result in innovations (Betz et al., 2016). Indeed, cities with good economic situations are more likely to concentrate innovative and successful companies with a talented workforce (Florida, 2003). In this line, more educated people are likely to faster adopt new innovations than people with less education (Kiiski & Pohjola, 2002). Cities are likely to be scenarios with highly educated and talented workers with proper digital knowledge, which might favor ideal conditions for innovation and, thus, enhance cities' competitiveness. Thus, cities are the ideal environment for fostering economic resources allocation on the adequate implementation of technology and overall digitalization (Betz et al., 2016).

Overall, an urban strong economic situation has been considered by previous research as a requirement for digitalization at different levels such as the country-level (e.g., Billon et al., 2010). Thus, in relation with this impact at the city-level, we suggest:

H1: Better economic situations in cities are related to higher levels of urban digitalization.

In terms of the impacts of digitalization levels on the cities' economic situation, there might exist different reasons causing the effect. First, some scholars claimed that a better management of the complicated urban contexts should be based on ICT use for achieving resources consumption minimization and efficiency (e.g., Alusi et al., 2011). Besides, the application of technology for minimizing urban issues, might have an impact not only on sustainability and well-being improvements, but also on financial viability (Ahvenniemi et al., 2017) due to efficiency gains related to digitalization (Sodiq et al., 2019). Thus, theoretical research suggests that digitalization might be a source of efficiency and, consequently, economic saving.

Second, digitalization might have a two-fold effect on information spreading. On the one hand, the quantity and quality of the information generated due to proper digitalization and adequate connectivity might be a source of innovation (Sodiq et al., 2019). For example, the innovation as a consequence of urban digitalization might foster efficiency in terms of raw materials use (United Nations, 2015). On the other hand, ICT increases information accessibility and availability, which can result in an easy way of promoting or rising individuals' awareness in relation to urban issues (Stuermer et al., 2017). In this line, different studies suggest that digitalization is high likely able to prevent or reduce urban problems (e.g., Helbin, 2012) such as environmental degradation (Seele & Lock, 2017). For example, digitalization has successfully addressed urban issues in terms of climate change adaptation, such as the Blue Link project in Australia, which is related to minimizing the dangers of the sea level rise on local beaches (Balogun et al., 2020).

Third, digitalization might also have consequences for the human capital. From one angle, digital urban contexts might attract, or retain, citizens due not only to better work opportunities in terms of job offer and diversity (Betz, 2015), but also to social opportunities associated with better-connected communities (Balongun et al., 2020). For example, these digital assets could be used to distribute information about events or to search for real-time information in specific situations, such as finding parking or available events on the go. From the other angle, digital cities might be ideal scenarios for citizens to thrive because of the offer of greater opportunities. For instance, data and connectivity could contribute to the urban space design where citizens participate and report information that can be integrated based on an iterative approach to improve urban contexts (Lindkvist et al., 2021). This kind of civic participation might imply achieving personal fulfilment and developing the human capital (Thite, 2011). In these contexts, digitalization involves new approaches for shaping, monitoring, and communicating governance (Heemsbergen, 2016). In fact, ICTs might foster citizens' participations and might support governance from decision makers (He et al., 2016), that can suppose a vehicle for shifts, such as, for example, a shift towards sustainable development (Stuermer et al., 2017; Melville, 2010; Elliot, 2011; Seele, 2014); which is also related to efficiency and economic improvements.

Overall, digitalization has been theoretically suggested as a means for enhancing efficiency and increasing economic savings. In this line, associated with empirically testing this impact at the city-level, we suggest:

H2: Higher levels of urban digitalization are related to better economic situations of cities.

METHODOLOGY

Sample Selection

This study addresses the proposed relationship with objective data on urban digitalization levels and the city's economic condition from the OECD Metropolitan areas Database[1]. The OECD Metropolitan Database applies a methodology which enables comparison at the city-level among the 27 OECD countries (OECD, 2012). The data included in the OECD Database are calculated differently. Specifically, the indicators might be modelled by, for instance, adjusting indicators available at slightly different geographic scale using population grid (OECD, 2012). Specifically, we analyzed the functional urban areas (FUAs) because they encompass the economic and functional extent of cities based on the scope of daily people's movements (OECD, 2012). The FUAs provide information about the cities and their area of influence and allow comparability among countries all over the world because the FUAs classification goes further by applying a common territorial approach rather than just considering administrative boundaries. We added digitalization data to the economic data and also retrieved data for constructing different control variables. The combination of the retrieved data for those variables resulted in a sample of 404 cities.

Measures

In order to develop our empirical analysis, we used objective data on urban digitalization, the city's economic condition and several control variables at the city-level that allow the comparison across cities. We merged information on all those variables for the year 2020. Table 1 summarizes the information of the variables name and their operationalization.

Variable One: Urban Digitalization

Digitalization rates are measured through the share of households having quality access to certain technology. Specifically, the first variable of this study was operationalized using data on average download speed, measured based on the city's percentage deviation from the national average. We measured the digitalization levels based on the quality of the broadband because a direct, high-speed internet connection might represent the enabler for a context of digital dominance (Etezadzadeh, 2016) and because greater networks provide better opportunities for enhanced digital innovations (Myovella et al., 2020). Indeed, a growing number of people is shifting a big amount of the interactions into a more digital style (Etezadzadeh, 2016).

Variable Two: Economic Situation

The economic situation of cities is related to the standard of living in terms of economic well-being. In that line, we gathered data on the cities' economic output divided by its population, that is, this variable was through the Gross Domestic Product (GDP) per capita. The database gathers the GDP per capita data on USD with 2015 as the base year. We measured the city's economic situation based on the GDP per capita because this variable defines not only the citizens' standard of living, but also the context wealth (Morais & Camanho, 2011).

Control Variables

We introduced control variables from the OECD Metropolitan areas database in order to eliminate alternative explanations of the research findings. In order to add them, we followed two steps. First, we analyzed the possibility of adding four control variables to the research study: population, population density, employment rates and labor force. We preliminary analyzed their adequacy and multicollinearity of the cases that they consider and, based on the obtained values for their variance inflation indicators (VIF), we discarded the variable that measured the labor force. Second, we retained the other three control variables and merged them with the data un urban digitalization and on GDP per capita.

The control variables included data on population of all ages, on population density, (measured in inhabitants per square kilometer), and on urban employment rates (measured as the ratio of employed persons aged 15-64 to the total population aged 15-64).

Table 1. Variables and operationalization

Variables	Mean	Std. dev.	Operationalization
Digitalization level	2.99	18.32	Average downloading speed (deviation in % of the city compared to the national average)
Economic situation	35426.12	18449.68	GDP per capita in USD with 2015 as a base year
Population	1118168.89	2069761.76	Population of all ages
Population density	621.62	696.74	Population per square kilometer
Employment rate	64.80	14.06	Ratio of employment of persons aged 15-64 to the total population aged 14-64

Source: self-elaboration

The cities included in the study and the country to which they belong can be consulted in Appendix 1.

Analysis

In order to test the sample adequacy, we proceed as follows. First, we run the Durbin-Watson for analyzing the autocorrelation, which showed values nearer to 2 than to 0, indicating an adequate weak correlation among the error terms. With regards to heteroscedasticity, the results for the Breusch-Pagan test indicated sample adequacy. Second, we eliminate the outliers based on if their residuals were far from zero in more than 3 times the standard deviation. The authors reported standardized coefficients to convey the relative magnitude of individual variables. Third, based on the correlation matrix, the variance inflation factors (VIFs) and the tolerance values, no multicollinearity in the preliminary regressions was detected. For instance, VIFs were below 2, considerably below the critical threshold of 10 (Hair et al., 2014). We tested the suggested hypotheses (H1 and H2) with linear regression models with the software IBM SPSS Statistics version 28.0.

RESULTS

Table 2 shows the correlations between the two main variables – urban digitalization and the city's economic situation – and the control variables (population, population density, and urban employment rate). As expected, the two main variables present a significant and positive correlation. Besides, digitalization is significantly and positively correlated with population and with population density, while the economic situation is significantly and positively correlated with the urban employment rate. In terms of the correlation among control variables, there is a significant and positive correlation among population and population density while there is a significant and negative correlation between population density and urban employment rate.

Table 2. Correlations among variables and control variables

	Variables	1	2	3	4	5
1	Digitalization	1				
2	Economic situation	.255***	1			
3	Population	.215***	.078	1		
4	Population density	.225***	.005	.597***	1	
5	Employment	.016	.371***	-.042	-.109*	1
*p<.05; **p<.01; ***p<.001						

Source: self-elaboration

Table 3 presents the results associated with the linear regression analysis. We differentiate between Model 1 and Model 2 in which we tested Hypothesis 1 and 2, respectively. Model 1 tests H1 showing a significant and positive effect of the economic situation of a city on its digitalization level. Model 2 tests H2 presenting a significant and positive effect of digitalization on the economic situation of a city.

However, based on the R^2 and the adjusted R^2 obtained in both regressions, we cannot conclude that the influences are strong, which might mean that other variables would be needed for entirely understanding these urban interactions. Nevertheless, the models explain 12.4% and 20.3% of the variance of the dependent variable, respectively. The control variables helped to deeper understand the determinants of the dependent variables. For Model 1, higher population and higher population density are positively related with a more important improvement of the digitalization levels in cities that hold a better economic situation. For Model 2, proper urban employment rates might positively influence a greater increase in the economic situation of cities that present good digitalization levels.

Table 3. Regression analysis

Model	**1**			**2**		
Depend. var.	**Digitalization**			**Economic situation**		
		Coeff.	VIF		Coeff.	VIF
Independ. var.	Economic sit.	.270***	1.172	Digitalization	.246***	1.066
	Population	.096†	1.568	Population	.073	1.572
	Population dens.	.160**	1.572	Population dens.	-.054	1.597
	Employment	-.063	1.177	Employment	.365***	1.014
	R	.353		R	.451	
	R^2	.124		R^2	.203	
	Adjusted R^2	.116		Adjusted R^2	.195	
	Durbin-Watson	1.325		Durbin-Watson	1.080	
	Breusch-Pagan	✓		Breusch-Pagan	✓	

†p<.1; *p<.05; **p<.01; ***p<.001

Source: self-elaboration

The results obtained for Model 1, which test the first hypothesis (H1), suggest that the economic situation of a city has a significant and positive impact on the digitalization levels of a city. In other words, a strong economy of a city may influence its technology deployment and result in higher digitalization levels. In terms of the results regarding the control variables, we observe that higher population density is related with an enhanced improvement of the digitalization levels in cities that hold a better economic situation. More specifically, cities with higher population density are more likely to translate increases of GDP pc into effective digitalization improvements.

Regarding the results for Model 2, which test the second hypothesis (H2), we observe that the digitalization level of a city has a significant and positive impact on the urban economic situation. If the digitalization levels of a city increase, the economic situation of a city improves. In terms of the control variables outcomes in the model, we observe that proper urban employment rates might foster a greater increase in the economic situation of cities that hold good digitalization levels. In other words, cities with higher urban employment rates are more likely to translate digitalization improvements into effective GDP pc increases.

DISCUSSION

This study tests the two suggested hypotheses based on a sample of 404 cities with 2020 data on urban digitalization levels, urban economic situations, and control variables at city-level such as population, population density, and urban employment rate. We used linear regression models to test if a city's economic situation has an impact on the city's digitalization levels and to test if the urban digitalization levels of a city have an impact on the urban economic situation. We found both relationships to be significant and positive, resulting in a significant and positive bidirectional effect.

Previous research has addressed the effect of cities wealth on digitalization in territorial contexts such as countries (e.g., Billon et al., 2010; Kiiski & Pohjola, 2002), that mainly analyzed unidirectional effects. For example, extant publications addressed how economic conditions impact the adoption and diffusion of ICT (e.g., Kiiski and Pohjola, 2002) while the effect of digitalization on the economic features of specific contexts remains unexplored. Also, existing research analyzes these dynamics from a theoretical perspective (e.g., Stuermer et al., 2017) or from an empirical perspective at the country-level (e.g., Billon et al., 2010). Thus, we nurture extant research on urban dynamics with theoretically based empirical tests at the city-level on the bidirectional relationship suggested.

Researchers have claimed that digitalization implies high economic costs related to the implementation of ICT (e.g., Ashrafi & Murtaza, 2008, Harindranath et al., 2008) while other argue that cities face more urgent challenges such as sustainability-related issues (e.g., Martin et al., 2018). However, this study takes the literature a step beyond defending, first, that a city holding a strong economic situation may witness a greater impact on the digitalization deployment and, second, that digitalization needs to be considered as a source of wealth and a means to address urban challenges.

The findings of our study might have implications for the different urban stakeholders. We discuss the implications for urban planners and decision makers, for business managers and entrepreneurs, and for citizens.

Implications for Urban Planners and Decision Makers

Urban planners and decision makers might benefit from the conclusions of this study in a myriad of ways. First, in cities with strong economic situations, planners and decision makers might take advantage of the already wealth contexts and better-developed infrastructures in order to achieve greater levels of urban digitalization. Second, wealthy cities attract high-educated people which are more likely to engage in innovation and competitiveness, features that might lead to greater achievements in digitalization. Third, economic wealth has been confirmed as a city-level prerequisite for digitalization success.

Moreover, digitalization might serve not only to minimize resources use leading to economic savings, but also to favor the information spreading resulting in maximizing awareness of urban issues, which could help governors and citizens address them. Finally, another takeaway for urban planners and decision-makers is related to human capital. Digitalization might attract workers because of the growing number of digital jobs and the needs of connectivity for professional purposes. Workers in digital cities might also benefit from the enhancement of social connectivity that digitalization allows, which might result in overall improvements of their living contexts. These effects positively impact the economic situations of cities.

In a nutshell, this study provides guidance for urban planners and decision-makers by confirming at the city-level that better economic situations positively impact digitalization levels and that investments on digitalization can have a true and significant positive impact on urban wealth.

Implications for Business Managers and Entrepreneurs

This research offers valuable insights for business managers and entrepreneurs, shedding light on strategic implications that can significantly impact their decision-making processes. One crucial implication derived from our findings is the positive correlation between successful ICT investments and the economic affluence of cities. Firms venturing into Information and Communication Technology (ICT) initiatives in affluent urban settings tend to thrive due to the conducive environment provided by well-developed infrastructure and a pool of highly educated workers. This suggests that companies seeking optimal outcomes from their ICT investments should consider operating in cities characterized by robust economic conditions.

Furthermore, the study underscores the importance of location when searching for highly educated individuals with exceptional digital skills. Businesses aiming to attract and retain a workforce with advanced qualifications may find it advantageous to explore cities with favorable economic situations. This dual consideration of economic prosperity and digital proficiency ensures that companies tap into talent pools that align with their specific requirements.

Additionally, for enterprises focused on addressing urban challenges and fostering citizens' engagement, understanding the informational dynamics of affluent and digital cities is crucial. The research suggests that human capital originating from such cities may possess heightened awareness of urban issues due to the pervasive effects of digitalization. Leveraging this awareness can contribute to more effective initiatives that efficiently tackle urban problems.

Overall, this study provides actionable insights for business managers and entrepreneurs, emphasizing the interconnectedness of successful ICT investments, economic conditions, and the availability of a skilled workforce. By strategically aligning their initiatives with these findings, companies can enhance their likelihood of success in navigating the complexities of today's dynamic urban and business landscape.

Implications for Citizens

This study unfolds implications that extend beyond the realm of urban planning and decision making, and businesses and entrepreneurs, offering also valuable insights for citizens dwelling urban environments. The findings contribute to the understanding of how economic prosperity in cities can serve as a catalyst for digitalization. This fact highlights the notion that cities with robust economic situations are more likely to embrace and enhance digital technologies. Consequently, citizens in such urban contexts may witness a surge in digitalization initiatives, impacting various aspects of their daily lives.

The second takeaway highlights that digital cities, with their emphasis on technological advancement, tend to provide enhanced economic prospects. This, in turn, is associated with an improved quality of life for citizens. As cities invest in digital infrastructure, the ensuing economic growth contributes to a higher standard of living, creating a positive ripple effect on the overall well-being of urban dwellers.

The third implication builds upon the direct benefits that citizens can derive from residing in digital cities. The study suggests that digital environments maximize individuals' awareness of urban issues, facilitated by the widespread dissemination of information. This heightened awareness, in turn, positions digital cities as more adept at addressing and resolving urban challenges. Consequently, citizens in such digitalized urban settings are likely to experience improvements in well-being and overall quality of life, driven by the effectiveness of urban issue resolution strategies.

Besides, citizens dwelling wealthy or affluent cities might have the potential to exert certain pressures on governments decisions because those urban contexts are more likely to witness greater effects on investments on urban digitalization improvements.

Citizens stand to gain significantly from the implications drawn in this study, as it emphasizes the symbiotic relationship between economic prosperity, digitalization, and improved living standards. Understanding these dynamics can empower residents to actively engage with and benefit from the transformative effects of digital cities on their urban experiences.

Limitations and Future Research Lines

While this research contributes valuable insights, it is essential to acknowledge and address certain limitations inherent in the study. These limitations, rather than detracting from the research, open avenues for future investigations to build upon and refine the understanding of the relationships examined.

Firstly, one of the limitations stems from the use of one-year data for the variables, restricting the exploration of dynamic effects over time. A potential direction for future research involves adopting a longitudinal approach to capture the evolving nature of these relationships. By analyzing data across multiple years, researchers can gain a more nuanced understanding of how the variables interact and change over time, offering a more comprehensive view of the dynamic effects associated.

Secondly, while this study delves into bidirectional relationships between variables and identifies the possibility of feedback loops existence, it does not analyze the causality of these relationships. Future research endeavors could delve deeper into understanding the causal links between variables, identifying which factors influence each other first. Unraveling causality might be useful for a more in-depth comprehension of the mechanisms driving the observed relationships, and it opens avenues for exploring the existence of feedback loops that may amplify the impact of the variables among each other.

Thirdly, the study incorporates information on three control variables, providing a foundation for understanding the complexity of the relationships under examination. However, there remains room for expansion in terms of control variables. Future research could extend its scope by introducing additional control variables at either the city or country level. This expansion would enhance the robustness of the analysis, considering a broader range of factors that may influence the dynamics between the variables studied.

Fourth, in terms of the specific data that we analyzed, we only could retrieve data from some OECD countries, which may impede generalization to countries not pertaining to organization, and we measured urban digitalization and the city's economic situation based on one-variable data, which may fall short in the understanding of urban interactions. Forthcoming research could amplify this feature by adding information of different regions and measuring variables based on data corresponding to several variables, or even constructing factors based on, for example, factor analysis.

In conclusion, this research not only contributes valuable insights but also lays the groundwork for future investigations. By acknowledging and addressing the limitations identified, future research can refine the methodologies used and contribute to a more nuanced understanding of the intricate relationships between urban digitalization, a city's economic situation, and urban dynamics. Future studies can build upon these insights, adopting longitudinal approaches, exploring causality, and incorporating a more comprehensive set of control variables.

CONCLUSION

This paper delves into the intricate interplay between the levels of urban digitalization and the economic situation of a city, revealing a mutually reinforcing relationship. The study draws insights from a sample of 404 cities, utilizing data from the OECD Metropolitan database. The study suggests that cities with stronger economic foundations tend to exhibit higher levels of digitalization, and conversely, those with advanced digitalization often boast better economic conditions. Moreover, the research indicates that cities with increased population density experience more significant improvements in digitalization when already positioned in a favorable economic context. Additionally, our findings suggest that proper urban employment rates might increase the impact on the economic situation of cities that adopt digitalization strategies.

The implications of this research extend beyond a mere understanding of urban dynamics. Not only does it elucidate the impact of a city's robust economic standing on digitalization levels, but it also emphasizes the reciprocal relationship, highlighting how the process of urban digitalization can shape and enhance a city's economic situation. This chapter contributes to the existing body of literature by asserting that cities with a strong economic foundation are likely to witness more pronounced impacts from digitalization improvements. Furthermore, it advocates for the strategic implementation of digitalization as not only a source of wealth but also a potent means to address the myriad of challenges that urban areas are witnessing.

Overall, this work explores urban features that intricately interact within the dynamics of cities, serving as antecedents not only for urban sustainability but also for the enhancement of quality of life and overall well-being. By establishing these connections, the research provides a foundational understanding that can inform urban planning strategies, leading cities towards becoming prosperous, digitally empowered, sustainability-focused, and resilient urban environments.

REFERENCES

Ahvenniemi, H., Huovila, A., Pinto-Seppä, I., & Airaksinen, M. (2017). What are the differences between sustainable and smart cities? *Cities (London, England)*, *60*, 234–245. doi:10.1016/j.cities.2016.09.009

Alexander, B., Hubers, C., Schwanen, T., Dijst, M., & Ettema, D. (2011). Anything, anywhere, anytime? Developing indicators to assess the spatial and temporal fragmentation of activities. *Environment and Planning. B, Planning & Design*, *38*(4), 678–705. doi:10.1068/b35132

Alusi, A., Eccles, R. G., Edmondson, A. C., & Zuzul, T. (2011). Sustainable cities: oxymoron or the shape of the future? *Harvard Business School Organizational Behavior Unit Working Paper*, (11-062), 11-062.

Apostu, S. A., Vasile, V., Vasile, R., & Rosak-Szyrocka, J. (2022). Do Smart Cities Represent the Key to Urban Resilience? Rethinking Urban Resilience. *International Journal of Environmental Research and Public Health*, *19*(22), 15410. doi:10.3390/ijerph192215410 PMID:36430131

Ashrafi, R., & Murtaza, M. (2008). Use and impact of ICT on SMEs in Oman. *Electronic Journal of Information Systems Evaluation, 11*(3).

Bai, F., Huang, Y., Shang, M., & Ahmad, M. (2022). Modeling the impact of digital economy on urban environmental pollution: Empirical evidence from 277 prefecture-level cities in China. *Frontiers in Environmental Science, 10*, 991022. doi:10.3389/fenvs.2022.991022

Balogun, A. L., Marks, D., Sharma, R., Shekhar, H., Balmes, C., Maheng, D., Arshad, A., & Salehi, P. (2020). Assessing the potentials of digitalization as a tool for climate change adaptation and sustainable development in urban centres. *Sustainable Cities and Society, 53*, 101888. doi:10.1016/j.scs.2019.101888

Betz, M. R., Partridge, M. D., & Fallah, B. (2016). Smart cities and attracting knowledge workers: Which cities attract highly-educated workers in the 21st century? *Papers in Regional Science, 95*(4), 819–841. doi:10.1111/pirs.12163

Bibri, S. E., & Krogstie, J. (2017). Smart sustainable cities of the future: An extensive interdisciplinary literature review. *Sustainable Cities and Society, 31*, 183–212. doi:10.1016/j.scs.2017.02.016

Billon, M., Lera-Lopez, F., & Marco, R. (2010). Differences in digitalization levels: A multivariate analysis studying the global digital divide. *Review of World Economics, 146*(1), 39–73. doi:10.1007/s10290-009-0045-y

Cong, X., Wang, S., Wang, L., Qi, Z., & Skibniewski, M. J. (2023). New smart city clusters' construction level evaluation under economic circles: The case of Shandong, China. *Technological and Economic Development of Economy, 29*(3), 949–980. doi:10.3846/tede.2023.18792

Dewan, S., & Kraemer, K. (2000). Information technology and productivity: Evidence from country-level data. *Management Science, 46*(4), 548–562. doi:10.1287/mnsc.46.4.548.12057

Di, Q., Wang, Y., Zanobetti, A., Wang, Y., Koutrakis, P., Choirat, C., Dominici, F., & Schwartz, J. D. (2017). Air pollution and mortality in the Medicare population. *The New England Journal of Medicine, 376*(26), 2513–2522. doi:10.1056/NEJMoa1702747 PMID:28657878

Díaz, S., Settele, J., Brondízio, E., Ngo, H., Guèze, M., Agard, J., & Chan, K. (2020). *Summary for policymakers of the global assessment report on biodiversity and ecosystem services of the Intergovernmental Science-Policy Platform on Biodiversity and Ecosystem Services.*

Elliot, S. (2011). Transdisciplinary perspectives on environmental sustainability: A resource base and framework for IT-enabled business transformation. *Management Information Systems Quarterly, 35*(1), 197–236. doi:10.2307/23043495

Etezadzadeh, C. (2016). Digitalization. *Smart City–Future City? Smart City 2.0 as a Livable City and Future Market*, 37-45.

Fertner, C., Christensen, A. A., Andersen, P. S., Olafsson, A. S., Caspersen, S. P. O. H., & Grunfelder, J. (2019). Emerging digital plan data – New research perspectives on planning practice and evaluation. *Geografisk Tidskrift, 119*(1), 6–16. doi:10.1080/00167223.2018.1528555

Gupta, J., Hurley, F., Grobicki, A., Keating, T., Stoett, P., Baker, E., Guhl, A., Davies, J., & Ekins, P. (2019). Communicating the health of the planet and its links to human health. *The Lancet. Planetary Health, 3*(5), e204–e206. doi:10.1016/S2542-5196(19)30040-3 PMID:30876842

Hair, J. F., Black, W. C., Babin, B. J., & Anderson, R. E. (2014). *Multivariate data analysis: Pearson new international edition*. Pearson Education Limited.

Harindranath, G., Dyerson, R., & Barnes, D. (2008). ICT adoption and use in UK SMEs: a failure of initiatives? *Electronic Journal of Information Systems Evaluation, 11*(2).

He, G., Boas, I., Mol, A. P., & Lu, Y. (2016). E-participation for environmental sustainability in transitional urban China. *Sustainability Science, 12*(2), 187–202. doi:10.1007/s11625-016-0403-3

Heemsbergen, L. (2016). From radical transparency to radical disclosure: Reconfiguring (in) voluntary transparency through the management of visibilities. *International Journal of Communication, 10*, 138–151.

Helbing, D. (2012). Introduction: The FuturICT knowledge accelerator towards a more resilient and sustainable future. In P. Ball (Ed.), *Why society is a complex matter* (pp. 55–60). Springer. doi:10.1007/978-3-642-29000-8_12

Hughes, L. (2003). Climate change and Australia: Trends, projections and impacts. *Austral Ecology, 28*(4), 423–443. doi:10.1046/j.1442-9993.2003.01300.x

Jenks, M., & Jones, C. (Eds.). (2010). *Dimensions of the sustainable city* (Vol. 2). Springer Science & Business Media.

Kiiski, S., & Pohjola, M. (2002). Cross-country diffusion of the Internet. *Information Economics and Policy, 14*(2), 297–310. doi:10.1016/S0167-6245(01)00071-3

Lekan, M., & Rogers, H. A. (2020). Digitally enabled diverse economies: Exploring socially inclusive access to the circular economy in the city. *Urban Geography, 41*(6), 898–901. doi:10.1080/02723638.2020.1796097

Lindkvist, C., Temeljotov Salaj, A., Collins, D., Bjørberg, S., & Haugen, T. B. (2021). Exploring urban facilities management approaches to increase connectivity in smart cities. *Facilities, 39*(1/2), 96–112. doi:10.1108/F-08-2019-0095

Lyons, G., Mokhtarian, P., Dijst, M., & Böcker, L. (2018). The dynamics of urban metabolism in the face of digitalization and changing lifestyles: Understanding and influencing our cities. *Resources, Conservation and Recycling, 132*, 246–257. doi:10.1016/j.resconrec.2017.07.032

Marans, R. W. (2015). Quality of urban life & environmental sustainability studies: Future linkage opportunities. *Habitat International, 45*, 47–52. doi:10.1016/j.habitatint.2014.06.019

Martin, C. J., Evans, J., & Karvonen, A. (2018). Smart and sustainable? Five tensions in the visions and practices of the smart-sustainable city in Europe and North America. *Technological Forecasting and Social Change, 133*, 269–278. doi:10.1016/j.techfore.2018.01.005

Martínez-Bravo, M., & Martínez-del-Río, J. (2019). Urban pollution and emission reduction. Sustainable Cities and Communities. Encyclopedia of the UN Sustainable Development Goals, 1-11.

Melville, N. P. (2010). Information systems innovation for environmental sustainability. *Management Information Systems Quarterly, 34*(1), 1–21. doi:10.2307/20721412

Morais, P., & Camanho, A. S. (2011). Evaluation of performance of European cities with the aim to promote quality of life improvements. [Elsevier.]. *Omega, 39*(4), 398–409. doi:10.1016/j.omega.2010.09.003

Myovella, G., Karacuka, M., & Haucap, J. (2020). Digitalization and economic growth: A comparative analysis of Sub-Saharan Africa and OECD economies. *Telecommunications Policy, 44*(2), 101856. doi:10.1016/j.telpol.2019.101856

OECD. (2012). Redefining urban: A new way to measure metropolitan areas. Organisation for Economic Cooperation and Development (OECD).

Paiva Vianna, K. M., Cardoso, M. R. A., & Rodrigues, R. M. C. (2015). Noise pollution and annoyance: An urban soundscapes study. *Noise & Health, 17*(76), 125. doi:10.4103/1463-1741.155833 PMID:25913551

Seele, P. (2014). Unified reporting: integrating XBRL data repositories into sustainability reporting. *EMAN 2014.4. Presented at the 17th Environmental and Sustainability Management Accounting Network (EMAN): from sustainability reporting to sustainability management control.* EMAN.

Seele, P., & Lock, I. (2017). The game-changing potential of digitalization for sustainability: Possibilities, perils, and pathways. *Sustainability Science, 12*(2), 183–185. doi:10.1007/s11625-017-0426-4

Sodiq, A., Baloch, A. A., Khan, S. A., Sezer, N., Mahmoud, S., Jama, M., & Abdelaal, A. (2019). Towards modern sustainable cities: Review of sustainability principles and trends. *Journal of Cleaner Production, 227*, 972–1001. doi:10.1016/j.jclepro.2019.04.106

Song, B., Shi, H., Wang, M., & Gu, R. (2022). The research on the effect of digital economy development on urban air quality. *Frontiers in Environmental Science, 10*, 993353. doi:10.3389/fenvs.2022.993353

Stuermer, M., Abu-Tayeh, G., & Myrach, T. (2017). Digital sustainability: Basic conditions for sustainable digital artifacts and their ecosystems. *Sustainability Science, 12*(2), 247–262. doi:10.1007/s11625-016-0412-2 PMID:30174752

Thite, M. (2011). Smart cities: Implications of urban planning for human resource development. *Human Resource Development International, 14*(5), 623–631. doi:10.1080/13678868.2011.618349

Vardoulakis, S., & Kinney, P. (2019). Grand challenges in sustainable cities and health. *Frontiers in Sustainable Cities, 1*, 7. doi:10.3389/frsc.2019.00007

Wang, J., Wang, W., Ran, Q., Irfan, M., Ren, S., Yang, X., Wu, H., & Ahmad, M. (2022). Analysis of the mechanism of the impact of internet development on green economic growth: Evidence from 269 prefecture cities in China. *Environmental Science and Pollution Research International, 29*(7), 1–15. doi:10.1007/s11356-021-16381-1 PMID:34510353

WHO. (2020). *Q&A on Climate Change and COVID-19.* WHO. https://www.who.int/news-room/q-a-detail/q-a-on-climate-change-and-covid-19.

Yigitcanlar, T., Kamruzzaman, M., Foth, M., Sabatini-Marques, J., Da Costa, E., & Ioppolo, G. (2019). Can cities become smart without being sustainable? A systematic review of the literature. *Sustainable Cities and Society*, *45*, 348–365. doi:10.1016/j.scs.2018.11.033

KEY TERMS AND DEFINITIONS

Affluent Cities: human wealthy settlements characterized by high population density, where diverse economic and social activities take place based on urban institutions and infrastructure.

Digitalization: incorporating digital technologies to transform analog or manual processes into digital formats, enabling efficient data storage, retrieval, and analysis.

ICT (Information and Communication Technology): refers to the broad spectrum of technologies used for information handling, storage, retrieval, communication, and transmission. It encompasses computers, networks, software, and other digital tools.

Policy and Decision-making: formulation, evaluation, and implementation of courses of action by governments, resulting in leading to the achievement of specific goals, considering available information, resources, and objectives.

Smart Cities: urban settings that function based on technology integration through intelligent management.

Sustainable Development: development that meets the needs of the present generations without compromising future generations to meet their own needs.

Urban Digitalization: integration of advanced technology on urban contexts to enhance urban efficiency and minimize resources consumption.

Urban Management: management of the physical, social, and cultural surroundings within a city, which considers the built environment, the social dynamics, the economic activities, and the overall lifestyle of dwellers.

ENDNOTE

1 https://stats.oecd.org/Index.aspx?DataSetCode=CITIES

APPENDIXES

Table 4. Analyzed cities by country

Australia	Greater Sydney
	Greater Melbourne
	Greater Brisbane
	Greater Perth
	Greater Adelaide
	Gold Coast
	Canberra
	Newcastle
	Wollongong
Austria	Wien
	Graz
	Linz
	Salzburg
	Innsbruck
	Klagenfurt
Bulgaria	Sofia
	Plovdiv
	Varna
	Burgas
Canada	Toronto
	Montreal
	Vancouver
	Ottawa
	Calgary
	Edmonton
	Quebec
	Winnipeg
	Hamilton
	London
	Kitchener
	Halifax
	Victoria
	Windsor
	Saskatoon
	Sherbrooke
Switzerland	Bern
	Zürich
	Genève
	Basel
	Lausanne

Continued on following page

Table 4. Continued

Chile	Antofagasta
	Coquimbo-La Serena
	Rancagua
	Talca
	Concepcion
	Temuco
	Puerto Montt
Colombia	Bogota D.C.
	Medellin
	Cali
	Barranquilla
	Cartagena
	Bucaramanga
	Cucuta
	Pereira
	Ibague
	Manizales
	Santa Marta
	Pasto
	Armenia
	Villavicencio
	Monteria
	Valledupar
	Buenaventura
	Neiva
	Palmira
	Popayan
	Sincelejo
	Riohacha
Czech Republic	Praha
	Brno
	Ostrava
	Plzen
Germany	Berlin
	Hamburg
	München
	Köln
	Frankfurt am Main
	Ruhrgebiet
	Stuttgart
	Leipzig
	Dresden

Continued on following page

Table 4. Continued

	Düsseldorf
	Bremen
	Hannover
	Nürnberg
	Bielefeld
	Halle an der Saale
	Magdeburg
	Wiesbaden
	Göttingen
	Darmstadt
	Trier
	Freiburg im Breisgau
	Regensburg
	Erfurt
	Augsburg
	Bonn
	Karlsruhe
	Mönchengladbach
	Mainz
	Kiel
	Saarbrücken
	Koblenz
	Rostock
	Kaiserslautern
	Mannheim-Ludwigshafen
	Münster
	Chemnitz
	Braunschweig-Salzgitter
	Aachen
	Krefeld
	Lübeck
	Kassel
	Osnabrück
	Oldenburg (Oldenburg)
	Heidelberg
	Paderborn
	Würzburg
	Wolfsburg
	Heilbronn
	Ulm
	Pforzheim
	Ingolstadt

Continued on following page

Table 4. Continued

	Siegen
	Erlangen
	Wuppertal
Spain	Madrid
	Barcelona
	Valencia
	Sevilla
	Zaragoza
	Málaga
	Murcia
	Valladolid
	Vitoria/Gasteiz
	Oviedo
	Pamplona/Iruña
	Santander
	Bilbao
	Córdoba
	Alicante/Alacant
	Vigo
	Gijón
	A Coruña
	Granada
	Elche/Elx
	San Sebastián/Donostia
	Castellón de la Plana/Castelló de la Plana
	Cádiz
	Tarragona
	Marbella
Estonia	Tallinn
Finland	Helsinki/Helsingfors
	Tampere/Tammerfors
	Turku/Åbo
	Oulu/Uleåborg
United Kingdom	London
	West Midlands urban area
	Leeds
	Glasgow
	Liverpool
	Edinburgh
	Manchester

Continued on following page

Table 4. Continued

	Cardiff
	Sheffield
	Bristol
	Newcastle upon Tyne
	Leicester
	Aberdeen
	Cambridge
	Exeter
	Lincoln
	Portsmouth
	Coventry
	Kingston upon Hull
	Stoke-on-Trent
	Nottingham
	Guildford
	Doncaster
	Sunderland
	Medway
	Brighton and Hove
	Plymouth
	Swansea
	Derby
	Southampton
	Milton Keynes
	Northampton
	Bournemouth
	Colchester
	Dundee City
	Reading
	Blackpool
	Blackburn with Darwen
	Middlesbrough
	Oxford
	Preston
	Norwich
	Cheshire West and Chester
	Ipswich

Continued on following page

Table 4. Continued

Greece	Athina
	Thessaloniki
	Budapest
	Miskolc
	Nyíregyháza
	Pécs
	Debrecen
Ireland	Dublin
	Cork
	Limerick
	Galway
Italy	Roma
	Milano
	Napoli
	Torino
	Palermo
	Genova
	Firenze
	Bari
	Bologna
	Catania
	Venezia
	Verona
	Cagliari
	Padova
	Brescia
	Modena
	Salerno
	Messina
	Prato
	Parma
	Reggio nell'Emilia
	Rimini
	Bergamo

Continued on following page

Table 4. Continued

Korea	Seoul
	Gimhae
	Dalseong
	Gwangsan
	Seo
	Seongsan
	Ulsan
	Heungdeok
	Deokjin
	Sebuk
	Gyeongsan
	Pohan
	Gumi
	Jeju
	Jinju
	Wonju
	Iksan
	Chuncheon
	Gunsan
	Suncheon
Lithuania	Vilnius
	Kaunas
Luxembourg	Luxembourg
Latvia	Riga

Continued on following page

Table 4. Continued

Mexico	Mexico City
	Guadalajara
	Monterrey
	Puebla
	Toluca
	Tijuana
	Leon
	Queretaro
	Merida
	Juarez
	San Luis Potosi
	Torreon
	Mexicali
	Cuernavaca
	Villahermosa
	Culiacan
	Morelia
	Chihuahua
	Veracruz
	Hermosillo
	Aguascalientes
	Acapulco de Juarez
	Tampico
	Oaxaca de Juarez
	Reynosa
	Xalapa
	Saltillo
	Benito Juarez
	Celaya
	Durango
	Tuxtla Gutierrez
	Pachuca de Soto
	Irapuato
	Ahome
	Matamoros
	Ensenada
	Poza Rica de Hidalgo
	Tepic
	Orizaba
	Mazatlan
	Cajeme

Continued on following page

Table 4. Continued

	Nuevo Laredo
	Guadalupe
	Coatzacoalcos
	Tapachula
	Victoria
	Tlaxcala
	Cordoba
	Uruapan
	Tehuacan
	Minatitlan
	Cuautla
	Chilpancingo de los Bravo
	Monclova
	Los Cabos
	Colima
	La Paz
	Campeche
	Puerto Vallarta
	Salamanca
	San Juan del Rio
	Zamora
	Tulancingo de Bravo
	Carmen
	Nogales
Malta	Malta
Netherlands	Amsterdam
	Alkmaar
	Apeldoorn
	Arnhem
	Breda
	Eindhoven
	Enschede
	‘s-Gravenhage
	Groningen
	Heerlen
	‘s-Hertogenbosch
	Leiden
	Nijmegen
	Rotterdam
	Tilburg
	Utrecht
	Zwolle

Continued on following page

Table 4. Continued

Poland	Warszawa
	Lódz
	Kraków
	Wroclaw
	Poznan
	Gdansk
	Szczecin
	Bydgoszcz
	Lublin
	Katowice
	Bialystok
	Kielce
	Torun
	Olsztyn
	Rzeszów
	Opole
	Nowy Sacz
	Czestochowa
	Radom
	Bielsko-Biala
	Walbrzych
	Tarnów
Portugal	Lisboa
	Porto
	Braga
	Coimbra
Romania	Bucuresti
	Cluj-Napoca
	Timisoara
	Craiova
	Calarasi
	Constanta
	Iasi
	Brasov
Slovak Republic	Bratislava
	Košice
Slovenia	Osrednjeslovenska
	Podravska
Sweden	Stockholm
	Göteborg
	Malmö
	Uppsala

Continued on following page

Table 4. Continued

Türkiye	Ankara
	Adana
	Antalya
	Balikesir
	Bursa
	Denizli
	Diyarbakir
	Erzurum
	Gaziantep
	Hatay
	Istanbul
	Izmir
	Kayseri
	Kocaeli
	Konya
	Malatya
	Manisa
	Samsun
	Trabzon
	Van

Chapter 4
A Conceptual Framework Proposal for Digital Maturity Assessment and Sustainability for Municipalities

Gizem Turcan
https://orcid.org/0000-0002-5530-7777
İzmir Bakırçay University, Turkey

Erman Coşkun
İzmir Bakırçay University, Turkey

Mehtap Özşahin
Gebze Technical University, Turkey

ABSTRACT

Digital maturity, which emerges as evaluating the digitalization level of businesses and municipalities and guiding them for the digital transformation process, is a very comprehensive concept that has been emphasized in the literature recently. This study provides a conceptual model for assessing the digital maturity of a municipality and analyzing the relationship between digital maturity and the sustainability of the municipality. The study proposes parameters from literature and customizes them based on specifications to determine different dimensions of municipality digital maturity and develops hypotheses to assess digital maturity dimensions and sustainability relations for a city or municipality. The study is also aiming to create a reliable and tested conceptual framework for the assessment of municipal digital maturity and the relationship between this maturity level and the sustainability of the municipality.

DOI: 10.4018/979-8-3693-0798-4.ch004

INTRODUCTION

In the wake of an unprecedented digital revolution, municipalities worldwide are facing the significant consequences of embracing technology in the pursuit of not only operational efficiency but also sustainable urban development. The integration of digital technologies into the fabric of municipal governance has become a crucial element in effectively managing the complexities of modern urban landscapes. However, the prevailing challenge bases not only in the adoption of these technologies but in effectively coordinating an integration between digital maturity and sustainability imperatives.

This paper presents a conceptual framework for assessing digital transformation that goes beyond conventional boundaries. We contend that a municipality's digital maturity should not be limited to the technology alone; it should involve a comprehensive assessment of organizational adaptability, citizen engagement, and a strong commitment to environmental sustainability. By affording due consideration to these multi-faceted dimensions, our framework aims to provide municipalities with a comprehensive set of tools to navigate the evolving landscape of digital transformation and urban governance. At the heart of this proposal lies the recognition that sustainable urban development is associated with digital maturity. The strategic utilization of digital technologies becomes crucial in the pursuit of efficient resource allocation, robust infrastructure, and equal accessibility to services as urban areas see rapid growth in population and complexity. Moreover, the demands of sustainability are significant, necessitating a collective effort to integrate digital solutions that not only enhance efficiency but also minimize ecological footprints and improving social sustainability in the city.

Sustainability is the ability of an organization to maintain its operations and success over time while decreasing negative impacts on the environment, society, and economy. It involves equipping organizations with the management, skills, global perspectives, and strategies necessary to the unique challenges facing organizations (Goodland, 1995; Kupilas et al., 2023). The scope of sustainability extends beyond the implementation of measures that yield economic and cultural advantages by promoting environmental responsibility. Instead, sustainability can also be an end in itself without further justifications. In order to attain organizational sustainability, organizations must integrate sustainability into the core of their operations in order to get the necessary knowledge and capabilities to implement sustainable practices on a large scale. Organizational sustainability refers to the ability of an organization to maintain its operations and success over time while minimizing negative impacts on the environment, society, and economy (Linnenluecke & Griffiths, 2010).

Municipalities are local governments that possess legal recognition and possess the authority for self-governance or jurisdiction, as granted by national and regional laws to which they are subordinate. Municipalities are usually a single administrative division, such as towns, villages, or other local government units. These divisions are established as municipal corporations through the issue of a municipal charter by the state. Digital maturity assessment of municipalities is similar to the assessment of organizations. Digital maturity assessments are widely regarded as valuable tools for gaining insight into an organization's existing degree of maturity in the digital realm, as well as for identifying strategies to advance and accelerate digital transformation efforts. The assessment of digital maturity in municipalities is based on the same principles as the assessment of digital maturity in organizations. The assessment aims to evaluate the degree of digital transformation and identify areas for improvement. The proposed framework for digital maturity assessment and sustainability for municipalities will be developed based on existing models such as the Digital Transformation Maturity Model, Digital Maturity Index for local governments, and the Best-Worst Method. The framework will offer precise methodologies and evaluation criteria to assist local governments in effectively tackling the obstacles associated with digital transformation and sustainability. By using this framework, municipalities can evaluate their digital maturity and sustainability and make informed decisions to foster their digital transformation.

Digital maturity, measured in order to improve municipalities' decision-making and city life and to enable them to see their own maturity status, is directly or indirectly related to sustainability. Therefore, creating a framework that covers digital maturity components and sustainability dimensions can be a very useful reference for developing digital maturity under the umbrella of sustainability. This paper develops a framework that proposes different components of the digital maturity of municipalities, as well as metrics and parameters from literature to assess digital maturity level. Then it relates them to different dimensions of sustainability. The conceptualized framework consists of 5 components for digital maturity and relates them to 3 dimensions of sustainability.

The first part of this study, the literature review, consists of two parts: digital maturity in smart cities and digital maturity and sustainability. The literature review is followed by the proposed framework obtained and presented as a result of the literature research. The methodology section that follows includes the research objectives, research design, and operationalization of constructs for further. The discussion section discussing the outcomes of the study is followed by the conclusion section.

LITERATURE REVIEW

Digital Maturity for Smart Cities

Digital maturity refers to the level of an organization's capability to efficiently and strategically employ digital technologies and processes to drive business growth and innovation (Teichert, 2019; Aslanova & Kulichkina, 2020). This includes aligning organizational processes, human resources, and other assets with the digital environment to drive business growth and innovation. Westerman et al. (2014) introduced the idea as well and identified nine key components that affect an organization's digital maturity: digital strategy and leadership, digitally empowered employees, digital operations, customer experience, business model innovation, data and analytics, technology platform, external partnerships, and digital governance.

According to Haryanti et al. (2023), digital maturity is perceived as a comprehensive notion encompassing various aspects. This notion comprises the company's ability to effectively execute tasks and regulate the stream of information through information technology (IT). Additionally, it encompasses the company's accomplishments in terms of implementing digital transformation initiatives, which may involve modifications in products and services. Digital maturity models have a crucial role in assessing the level of digital maturity in various contexts (Ochoa-Urrego & Peña-Reyes, 2021; Hägg & Sandhu, 2017). These models provide a structured approach to understanding the current state of digital maturity and identifying areas for improvement. Haryanti et al. (2023) also state that digital maturity models often include dimensions and levels that explain the activities that signify an evolution toward digital maturity. These dimensions are organization and structure, culture, technology, customer, strategy, employee, and process transformation/business process.

Valdez-de-Leon (2016) mentioned 7 dimensions and 5 levels that determine digital maturity in his study. In the study, a digital maturity model consisting of strategy, organization, customer, technology, operations, ecosystem, and innovation dimensions was developed for telecommunication services.

Teichert (2019), on the other hand, made a comprehensive literature review in his study and touched upon 22 different digital maturity models. Looking at the findings of the study, it is emphasized that the dimensions applied in various maturity models may differ. According to Teichert's sample, the areas where digital maturity is most important are technology, digital capabilities, operations and processes, products and services, digital culture, compliance and security, digital strategy and organization.

After a systematic analysis of the literature on digital maturity models and frameworks, Bumann and Peter (2019) identified six sub-dimensions of digital maturity and proposed a digital maturity framework with the sub-dimensions of strategy, organization, culture, technology, customer and people. The digital maturity model by Anderson and Ellerby (2018) includes strategy, technology, operations, organization, and culture, as well as the customer dimensions, to assess the digital capabilities and create a broader view of digital maturity in the context of an organization.

Since digital maturity is an area studied to monitor and improve the digital infrastructure developments of organizations before cities, it is seen that in the literature there are dimensions and parameters of different organizational structures and inferences. Therefore, in the development of smart cities or the digitalization of cities, it is of great importance to first measure the digital maturity of municipalities.

A smart city refers to a local government that leverages information and communication technologies (ICT) to enhance operational effectiveness, facilitate public information sharing, and enhance the provision of government services and citizen well-being (Kummitha & Crutzen, 2017). Smart cities are characterized by their intelligent utilization of technology by the government, as well as their effective monitoring, analysis, planning, and governance of urban areas. The principal objective of a smart city is to establish an urban setting that fosters a superior standard of living for its inhabitants, concurrently stimulating comprehensive economic advancement. Smart cities employ interconnected digital technology, commonly referred to as the 'internet of things' (IoT), optimize the efficiency of the various systems that facilitate urban living (Kim et al., 2021).

According to the Nam and Pardo (2011), smart cities consist of three main dimensions (technology, people, community). While technology dimension is related with digital city, information city, intelligent city etc., people dimension is related with creative, learning, humane city, and the community dimension includes the smart community and smart growth concepts. From another perspective, Albino et al. (2015) suggest that the dimensions of a smart city are smart economy, people, governance, mobility, environment, and living. Similarly, Monzon (2015)'s study which bases the smart city assessment, also use the same parameters as Albino et al. (2015).

The concepts of digital maturity and the evolution of smart cities have emerged as crucial subjects within the realm of urban planning and administration. Smart cities leverage digital technology, communication technologies, and data analytics to create service environments that are characterized by increasing efficiency and effectiveness, hence improving the overall quality of life for its residents (Gracias, et al., 2023). As cities strive to become smarter, understanding their level of digital maturity becomes essential for effective planning and decision-making (Ghazinoory et al., 2023).

Digital maturity for cities refers to the level of digital transformation and adoption of digital technologies and solutions in the economy, society, and governance of a city (Kapkaev & Kadyrov, 2021). Municipalities play a crucial role in driving digital maturity in cities, as they are responsible for providing services and infrastructure to citizens (Holzer et al., 2010). The effects of municipalities on digital maturity can be positive or negative, depending on their level of commitment and investment in digital transformation. Municipalities that invest in digital transformation can improve the quality of life of citizens, enhance the efficiency of public services, and attract businesses and talent to the city (Fesenko

& Fesenko, 2017). On the other hand, municipalities that do not invest in digital transformation can lag behind in terms of economic growth, social inclusion, and environmental sustainability (Fesenko & Fesenko, 2017).

In the context of smart cities, digital maturity assessment can help identify the strengths and weaknesses of a city's digital infrastructure and services. The aforementioned data can then be utilized to generate strategies intended for expanding the digital maturity of the city and strengthening its smart city capabilities. (Aljowder, et al., 2019). Additionally, digital maturity assessments can help cities benchmark their progress against other cities and learn from best practices (Aljowder, et al., 2019). In addition, smart cities dedicate resources towards the execution of digital transformation strategies to enhance their intelligence, sustainability, and resilience. A smart sustainable city can be defined as a city that utilizes ICTs and other strategies to improve the overall quality of life, optimize city operations and services, and encourage competitiveness. It is crucial for such a city to effectively address the requirements of both current and future generations in terms of economic, social, environmental, and cultural dimensions (Bibri & Krogstie, 2017).

There are several bodies of literature emerged on the topic of smart city and digital maturity models, which assess the level of maturity for especially smart city projects. These models offer a conceptual structure for assessing the present condition and future potential of intelligent urban areas, while also examining the obstacles and possibilities they encounter (Aljowder, et al., 2019; Gracias, et al., 2023). However, there is still a need for flexible models that can be applied to measure and assess digital maturity of cities in different cultures and in different real-life conditions (Ghazinoory et al., 2023).

João et al. (2020) have conducted systematic literature reviews to gain insights into the current state of smart cities and the Internet of Things (IoT). This study provides a comprehensive overview of the research conducted between 2000 and 2019, highlighting the key trends and challenges in the field (Zhao, et al., 2021). The bibliometric analysis results of this study indicate that smart cities and IoT are rapidly growing in developed economies, including Spain, China, the USA, the United Kingdom, and Korea. However, in developing countries as Turkey, Romania, Saudi Arabia, reality, and new ideas can be very different from those in developed countries. João et al. (2020) indicate that the perception of smart cities in developing countries is quite limited, and more research is required to increase the practices of smart cities and IoT phenomena on a wider range of social and organizational aspects. This study aiming to specify the components of digital maturity and sustainability of municipalities in a developing country, Turkey, in context of smart cities and to examine the relations among components of those concepts (digital maturity and sustainability) conceptually is expected to address this need.

When examining municipal practices in cities, it is observed that 6 components are mostly come forward reflecting the digital maturity for cities as been depicted on Table 1.

Table 1. Digital maturity dimensions based on the literature

<table>
<tr><th>Study</th><th>Dimensions</th><th>Number</th><th>Repeated (>4)</th></tr>
<tr><td>Westerman et al. (2014)</td><td>digital strategy and leadership, digitally empowered employees, digital operations, customer experience, business model innovation, data and analytics, technology platforms, external partnerships, digital governance</td><td>9</td><td rowspan="6">Customer
Culture
Digital/Technology
Operations
Organization
Strategy</td></tr>
<tr><td>Valdez-de-Leon (2016)</td><td>strategy, organization, customer, technology, operations, ecosystem innovation</td><td>6</td></tr>
<tr><td>Anderson and Ellerby (2018)</td><td>strategy, technology, operations, organization, culture, customer</td><td>6</td></tr>
<tr><td>Bumann and Peter (2019)</td><td>strategy, organization, culture, technology, customer, people</td><td>6</td></tr>
<tr><td>Teichert (2019)</td><td>technology, digital capabilities, operations and processes, products and services, digital culture, compliance and security, digital strategy, organization</td><td>8</td></tr>
<tr><td>Haryanti et al. (2023)</td><td>organization and structure, technology, strategy, customer, employee, culture, process transformation/ business process</td><td>7</td></tr>
</table>

The *customer* dimension of digital maturity refers to organizations' ability to ensure a consistently designed customer experience (Berghaus et al., 2017; Peter, 2017). Valdez-de-Leon (2016) describes this dimension as focusing on customer engagement and authorization, as well as new benefits created in the customer experience. To bridge the digital and real worlds by providing continuous hybrid interaction channels, due to changing customer behaviour and the growing digital channel popularity, it is progressively necessary for organizations (Gasser et al., 2018; Nüesch et al., 2015; Puschmann, 2017; Bumann & Peter, 2019). Bumann and Peter (2019) suggest that digital technologies can help organizations collect and use client data. This enables the prediction of customer behaviour and the provision of personalised goods and services, resulting in an enhanced customer experience. In context of smart cities, citizens are considered as customers. Thus, municipalities are expected to ensure digital contents and channels to provide better service to their citizens in context of *customer* dimension of digital maturity. Since, providing service is part of main operations of municipalities, customer dimension will not be handled as a separate component, instead it will be examined as a part of operation dimension of digital maturity.

Organizational *culture,* defined by Hofstede (2010) as "*the collective programming of the mind that distinguishes the members of an organization from others*", has an important role in successful digital transformation. After stating that digitally mature businesses have common cultural characteristics such as the tendency to take risks, rapid experiments, and investing in talent, Kane et al. (2017) claim that these businesses value the social skills of leaders more than their technical strengths. The term digital cultural maturity, identified as the attitudes of leaders and employees towards digital interaction and their preferences for digital solutions by Gollhardt (2022:100), is one of the most difficult concepts to define because it is a part of people's perceptions and behaviors. As can be understood from the definition, the digitalization perspectives, attitudes and behaviors of leaders/managers, who have an important place in a successful digital transformation, are indispensable elements of digital cultural maturity. On the other hand, VanBoskirk (2017) also define culture as a company's digitally focused strategy for innovation and how it supports its employees with digital technology, which indicate importance of the digital skills of employees. However, the digital skills of employees and attitudes of employees to digitalization are different concepts. Thus, digital skill of employees should be examined as a different dimension rather than as part of culture. In this context, *human/people* factor will be handled as a separate component of digital maturity in this study, which refers to "*the employee with their skills and capabilities in digitalization*" (Bumann & Peter, 2019). Andersson et al. (2018) suggest that prospering digital transformation needs not only technological resources but also new personal skills with different digital technologies. Allam and Newman (2018) says that culture is one of the dimensions of three important dimensions (culture, metabolism, governance) of smart cities. In the context of urban settings, culture encompasses various aspects such as urban cultural legacy, urban creative industries, and coordinated efforts to prioritize the well-being of citizens by fostering livability inside cities. Lara et al. (2016) express that investing in human capital, involving citizens in governance processes, and establishing partnerships between the public and private sectors to facilitate activities are the foundation of the human infrastructure in smart cities. ICT alone cannot contribute to succession the expected improvements in living standards, and there is a need to increase human capital development among citizens. It takes the issue to the culture dimension of digital maturity.

Hess et al. (2016) supported the idea that a crucial aspect of digital transformation is an organization's ability to utilise new technologies. *Technology* dimension of digital maturity, in other words ICT infrastructure is defined as "the organization's use and adoption of developing technologies" (Bumann & Peter, 2019:28). According to the Yeh's (2017) study, ICT-based smart city services improve the comprehensive quality of life of citizens, and the more ICT-based smart city services are used, the higher the quality of life will be. Most of the application areas of smart cities include ICT infrastructure (transportation, urban infrastructure, coherency etc.) (Anthopoulos, 2015).

The *strategy* dimension of digital strategic maturity is defined as "incorporating digital transformation into business strategy" (Gollhardt, 2022:100). Researchers working on digital transformation point out that organizations that have successfully implemented digital transformation not only document the digital strategy, but also ensure that this documented strategy is communicated to employees at all levels, adopted and internalized (Kane et al., 2017; Bumann & Peter, 2019; Schumacher et al., 2016). Therefore, vision and mission statements, which are important tools in communicating and internalizing strategies, are main indicators reflecting the digital maturity of organizations, besides strategic plans. According to the Janurova et al. (2020) the integration of the Smart City concept into the urban ecology is achieved by the implementation of strategic plans or visions commonly known as "smart strategies" (Janurova et al., 2020). Smart cities require a clear strategy for investing in digital technologies to enable service reform and partner collaboration. This dimension ensures that the city's digital maturity efforts are directed towards achieving its long-term goals and objectives (Angelidou, 2016)

The *operation* dimension of digital maturity refers to emphasizing the abilities that facilitate providing services, and more development within this aspect indicates greater digitization, automation, and adaptability in operations (Valdez-de-Leon, 2016). Gollhardt (2022) explains the operation dimension as internal processes integrating the presence and degree of process standardization and automatization, checking for process improvements, and service launches based on technologies. Haryanti et al. (2023) also define this dimension as the extent to which processes are integrated through technology for efficiency. In context of smart cities, operation dimension of digital maturity can be defined as digitalized activities and services of municipalities for efficiency. The increased number of services and activities in municipalities emphasize the coordination and planning challenges of operations in the city as a result of urban sprawl. Talking about the digital maturity; efficient, quality and systematic operations can solve the problems efficiently (Zhuhadar et al., 2017).

The *organization* dimension of digital maturity is defined as "a collaborative approach by actively engaging relationships with different stakeholders" (Dintrans et al.,2017) for digital transformation of organization. According to Gimpel et al. (2018), this dimension also covers the organization's fast response capability to changes. Bumann and Peter (2019) argue that partnerships and ecosystems, which are considered as important element of organization dimension by Berghaus et al., (2017) and Schlaepfer et al., (2017), are part of strategy dimension. VanBoskirk (2017) also describe organization dimension as "*how aligned a company is to support digital strategy, governance, and execution*", which lead researchers to conclude that strategy and organization is closely aligned. Thus, in this study organization and strategy are handled as one dimension with the name of *strategy*.

In summary, considering the Table 1, most frequently used dimensions in the literature are taken into account for the framework. Despite different numbers of dimensions are included and studied and various researchers discussed many dimensions of digital maturity, in the literature, the five dimensions (*ICT infrastructure, human, culture, strategy, operations*) have been utilized in this study based on smart city and municipalities characteristics and found to be well representing the city digital maturity domain. The selected dimensions are also value-added factors for digital maturity and sustainability assessment.

Digital Maturity and Sustainability

The concept of sustainability can be described as the capability of a system to recover from disturbances and adapt to maintain stability (Kuhlman & Farrington, 2010). The explanation emphasizes the importance of a system's ability to withstand difficulties and maintain stability. This description aligns with the principle of sustainable development, which seeks to meet present demands without affecting the ability of future generations to meet their own needs (Scoones, 2007). Sustainability consists of 3 main dimensions: economic, social and environmental sustainability (Scoones, 2007). Environmental sustainability refers to the capacity to maintain the desirable attributes of the natural environment. Sutton (2004) argues that it is imperative to sustain components such as renewable resources, the quality of life for all individuals, and the livability of the environment. Eizenberg and Jabareen (2017) argue that social sustainability encompasses a range of methods that are focused towards addressing significant societal challenges in order to effectively manage the risks associated with climate change and environmental hazards. In other words, social sustainability endeavors to effectively address social concerns while also mitigating associated risks. According to Navarro-Galera et al. (2016), financial sustainability refers to the capacity to fulfill present and future service delivery and financial obligations by adhering to existing policies and avoiding a continuing increase in debt.

According to the study of Broccardo et al. (2023), there is a significant positive relationship between digitalization, sustainability, and profitability performance. The study proposes that the utilization of digital technology plays a pivotal role in facilitating the implementation and transformation of sustainability efforts. Furthermore, the relationship between digitalization and sustainability has the capacity to uncover greater potential. The study of Broccardo et al. (2023) demonstrates a correlation between digital maturity and sustainability, indicating that digital technologies have enabled companies to practice sustainability by changing the way they approach creating, innovating, running business and interacting with stakeholders. This, consequently, can result in improved economic performance.

The study by Ionaşcu et al. (2022) analyzes the relationship between digital transformation, financial performance, and sustainability in European Union-listed companies. The study found that digitalization supports sustainable development goals. The study suggests that technology can contribute to the accomplishment of sustainable development goals in the UN 2030 Agenda. Moreover, the study of Ionaşcu et al. (2022) titled as "An Innovative Digital Maturity Assessment Model for Smart Cities" proposes a digital maturity model for municipalities to assess the level of intelligence exhibited by their cities and fulfill the requirements of the concept of "smart city" in their cities. The model provides a frame of basis for the current state of digitalization and renewal in the organization (Ionaşcu et al., 2022).

Korachi and Bounabat (2018) proposes a model to evaluate the maturity of a smart city based on the quality of produced and consumed data. The study does not explicitly analyze aspects of sustainability, but it can be argued that the model proposed in the study can contribute to the sustainability of smart cities. By assessing the maturity of smart cities, the proposed model has the capacity to identify specific domains that require development and provide guidance for decision-making processes that prioritize the adoption of sustainable practices. For example, a smart city that scores low in environmental sustainability can use the model to identify data-driven solutions to reduce its carbon footprint. Similarly, a smart city that scores low in social sustainability can use the model to identify data-driven solutions to improve the quality of life of its citizens. Overall, the model proposed in the study can be a useful tool for smart cities to achieve sustainability goals.

Even though some studies have been conducted on digital maturity- sustainability relation in recent years, those studies are limited, and the current literature exhibits a lack of empirical research on that issue. This suggests a need for further research and collaboration between academia and industry to develop and refine digital maturity models that are applicable to the sustainable smart city ideas and practices, and unique challenges and opportunities of smart cities.

PROPOSED FRAMEWORK

Proposed framework is based on the extended literature review. Table 2 depicts the intersection between digital maturity dimensions and sustainability dimensions with a conceptual literature review. The table includes the positive relationship between digital maturity dimensions and sustainability.

The table illustrates how different components of digital maturity (ICT Infrastructure, Human, Culture, Strategy, Operation) are interconnected with various sustainability dimensions (Environmental, Social, Financial). For each intersection of digital maturity and sustainability, the table provides specific practices and applications. For instance, under ICT Infrastructure and Environmental, it mentions practices like Green ICT and reducing CO_2 emissions. The table supports its information with references to relevant literature, citing specific studies that have explored the relationship between digital maturity and sustainability in each dimension. This adds credibility and allows for further exploration of the discussed topics.

For this study, the table ensures that the framework provides a consistent and broad framework, taking into account the scope of the actual study.

Table 2. The intersection between digital maturity and sustainability

Digital Maturity Dimensions	Sustainability Dimensions	Practices and Applications	In Literature
ICT Infrastructure	Environmental	Green ICT, Human-Computer Interaction (HCI), Environmental Informatics, Reducing CO_2 emissions	Hilty et al., 2011; Higón et al., 2017; Aleksic, 2014; Elliot, 2011; Watson et al., 2012; Majeed, 2018; N'dri et al., 2021; Asongu et al., 2018; Khan et al., 2020; Lennerfors et al., 2015
	Social	Citizen Engagement	Bouzguenda et al., 2019; Ochara & Mawela, 2015; Bekaroo et al., 2016
	Financial	Cost-saving, long-term investment, public value assessment, cost-benefit opportunities, Reducing transaction costs and customer enhancement	Kariuki, 2021; Puron-Cid & Gil-Garcia, 2022; Mathison, 2005
Human	Environmental	Controlling consumerism and waste, relying on renewable energy, human support on environmental issues, avoiding strong changes in environment, environmental awareness	Arora, 2018; Sutton, 2004; Sarkodie et al., 2020
	Social	Increased social equity, reduced poverty, Corporate social sustainability, safety, eco-prosumption, urban forms, wellbeing, quality of work life, halting human population growth, understanding human behavior, and developing interventions	Rogers et al., 2012; Amrutha & Geetha, 2020; Roca-Puig, 2019; Vallance et al., 2011; Eizenberg & Jabareen, 2017; Pinzone et al., 2020; Zink, 2013, Šlaus & Jacobs, 2011; Arora et al., 2018; Clayton et al., 2015
	Financial	Human capital	Šlaus & Jacobs, 2011
Culture	Environmental	Managerial-level attitudes, promoting sustainability by policy makers, nature conservation	Isensee et al., 2020; Husted, 2005; Soini & Dessein, 2016
	Social	Creating sustainability-based organizational culture, promote sustainable behaviors and practices by creating social norms	Schönborn et al., 2019; Kashima, 2020
	Financial	High level individualism, uncertainty avoidance, stakeholder engagement	Adedeji et al., 2017; Salvioni & Almici, 2020
Strategy	Environmental	Infrastructure and equipment strategy, operational strategy, image improvement, sustainability strategies and environmental innovations	Yaakub et al., 2015; Hermundsdottir & Aspelund, 2022
	Social	Systems-based approach to the social system, identifying the social issues, developing principles, creating a shared vision	Missimer et al., 2017; Missimer 2015
	Financial	Management efficiency and portfolio at risk, reducing loans intensity, corporate sustainability management, creating unique products or services, corporate financial performance, incorporate a sustainability strategy into daily operations	Tehulu, 2013; Qiu et al., 2016; Epstein et al., 2010
Operation	Environmental	Consuming natural resources at an inferior pace, operationally efficient, energy awareness operations, environmentally friendly processes	Magon et al., 2018; Kwon & Lee, 2019; Kleindorfer et al., 2005
	Social	Capability-oriented strategies, quality process design, operating for public, connectivity, and openness in operations	Longoni & Cagliano, 2015; Lee, 2021; Currie et al., 2018; Akcali & Ispalar Cahantimur, 2023
	Financial	Activities considering financial conditions, optimizing the operations	Puron-Cid & Gil-Garcia, 2022; Breukelman et al., 2019

For the proposed framework have been grounded on the three dimensions(themes) -environmental, social, financial- of sustainability (Portney, 2015). The Figure 1 shows the comprehensive picture of the relationship between digital maturity and sustainability. The Figure 1 highlights the significance of the concepts and the wide range of practices and applications associated with digital maturity and sustainability, as indicated by the varying thickness of the arrows.

Figure 1. The association of digital maturity and sustainability

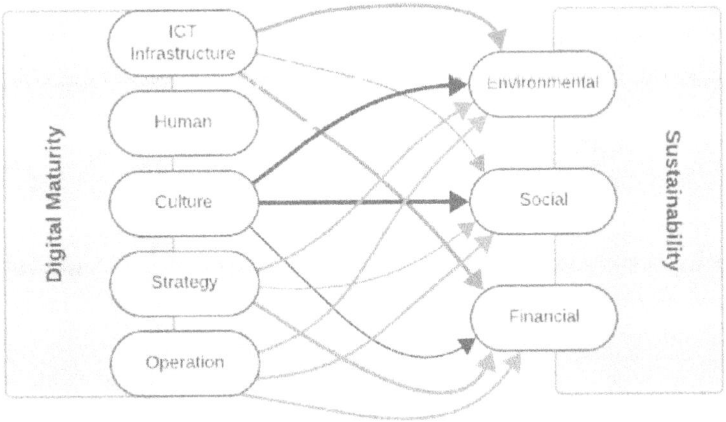

Figure 2 shows the relationships between digital maturity and sustainability. The thickness of the circles in the Figure 2 emphasizes the relevance of the concepts and the diversity of the related practices and applications (managerial practices or activities conducted by the municipalities and the society) of the digital maturity and sustainability. Colors are also indicating the level of relations of the dimensions. The thicker circle, the more impact and material in the literature. The remarkable insight of this framework is the green parameters that have strong relationship between digital maturity dimensions and sustainability (ICT infrastructure-environmental, financial; human-social; strategy-financial).

Figure 2. The relationships between digital maturity and sustainability

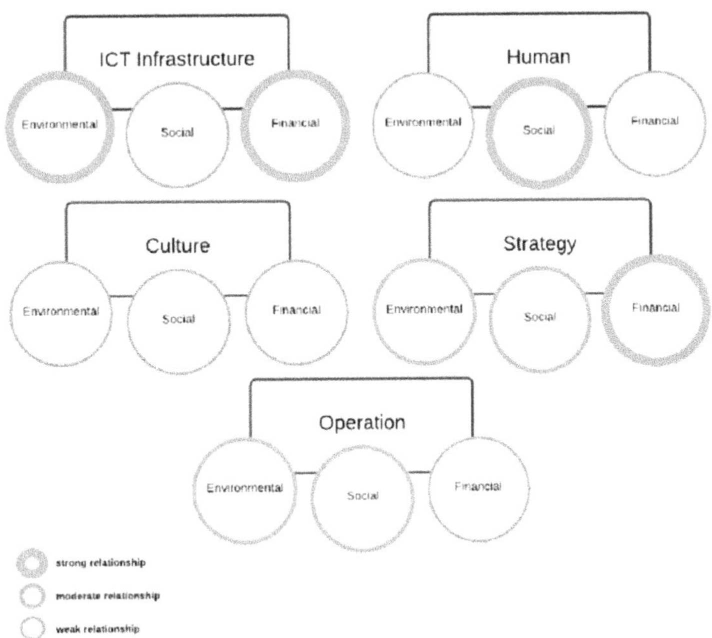

Digital maturity in *ICT infrastructure* can support environmental sustainability by reducing CO2 emissions and relying on renewable energy. By leveraging ICT, municipalities can reduce CO2 emissions, rely on renewable energy, and optimize operations, leading to cost savings and long-term investment opportunities. Additionally, ICT infrastructure can enable the monitoring, modeling, and management of environmental resources, contributing to more effective and sustainable environmental management. ICTs are used in smart sustainable cities to enhance the life quality of citizens, increase the efficiency of operational urban processes and services, and promote environmental sustainability. In terms of financial sustainability, digital maturity in ICT infrastructure can lead to cost-saving and long-term investment opportunities by optimizing operations, reducing costs associated with physical infrastructure, and enabling efficient resource allocation for sustainable urban development (Pérez González & Díaz Díaz, 2015).

Similarly, digital maturity in the human category is related to environmental sustainability by controlling consumerism and waste and relying on renewable energy. It is also associated with social sustainability by promoting increased social equity and reduced poverty for the municipalities. Human actions can improve the well-being and safety of individuals in society. It can be achieved through measures like workplace safety standards, digital literacy, fundamental digital proficiency and initiatives that enhance the overall quality of life. Furthermore, by equipping individuals with the necessary digital skills and knowledge, municipalities can harness the potential of their citizens to contribute to environmental, social, and financial sustainability, ultimately leading to the overall well-being and development of the community (Caetano et al., 2020). In terms of financial sustainability, digital maturity in the human category leads to human capital development.

In the context of *strategy*, the emphasis is on aligning organizational goals with environmental, social, and financial sustainability. This involves developing infrastructure and equipment strategies, operational strategies, and sustainability strategies and innovations to minimize negative environmental impacts and promote eco-friendly practices. Municipalities are strategically positioned to influence citizens and lead communities towards sustainability by providing services, building infrastructure, and formulating policies and regulations that promote sustainability (Hermundsdottir & Aspelund, 2022). The social aspect of the strategy dimension underscores the importance of taking a holistic view of the social system when formulating sustainability strategies. This involves identifying social issues, developing guiding principles, and fostering a shared vision, recognizing that addressing social challenges requires a comprehensive understanding of the interplay between various social factors (Missimer et al., 2017). Municipalities can play a crucial role in integrating social, political, and material aspects of sustainable urban transformations at the local level. Within the strategy dimension, there is a strong emphasis on financial management and performance, which involves practices like managing efficiency and portfolio risk, reducing loans intensity, and incorporating sustainability into daily operations (Tehulu, 2013). This underscores the notion that sustainable practices should not compromise financial viability but rather enhance it. Municipalities can strategically plan for a sustainable future by aligning with Sustainable Development Goals, enabling innovative change, building partnerships, and adopting best reporting practices to attract investment and promote sustainable urbanization.

Digital maturity in the *culture* category can be related to environmental sustainability by promoting nature conservation and managerial-level attitudes. The tendency of municipalities to embrace digitalization is essential for addressing current challenges, ensuring long-term resilience, and positively impacting environmental, economic, and social aspects of sustainable community life. When managers prioritize and advocate for sustainability policies, it sets the tone for the entire organization to adopt and implement environmentally friendly practices (Soini & Dessein, 2016). Social sustainability by creating a sustainability-based organizational culture can also promote the sustainable behaviors and practices. A culture that promotes sustainable behaviors can lead to positive social outcomes, including increased awareness of social issues, improved cooperation, and a shared commitment to societal well-being (Kashima, 2020). In terms of financial sustainability, digital maturity in the culture category can lead to high-level individualism (Adedeji et al., 2017). For instance, a culture that values individual initiative and empowerment may prioritize the innovative financial strategies. Moreover, digital literacy and proficiency of employees and managers can play a crucial role in promoting sustainability within municipalities. By developing a culture of digital maturity that prioritizes sustainability, municipalities can foster environmentally friendly practices, promote social equity, and enhance financial viability. Digital literacy and proficiency can enable employees to engage in sustainable practices, contribute to the development of a sustainable organizational culture, and promote innovative financial strategies that align with sustainability goals.

The *operation* dimension focuses on optimizing resource utilization. It includes strategies for consuming natural resources at a sustainable pace and implementing operationally efficient processes (Kleindorfer et al., 2005). Energy awareness operations and environmentally friendly practices are integral to this dimension. Social aspect of operations highlights the importance of designing operations with a focus on social benefits (Lee, 2021). It involves capabilities-oriented strategies, quality process design, and operating for the public good. This approach recognizes that operations have a direct impact on society and should be designed to create positive outcomes. Financial considerations are integrated into operational decisions (Breukelman et al., 2019). This includes activities that take into account a municipality's financial conditions and optimize operations accordingly. Digitalization of municipal activities can increase energy and resource efficiency in environmental sustainability while strengthening citizen participation and transparency in social sustainability. It also increases operational efficiency and supports economic growth by optimizing financial sustainability.

METHODOLOGY

Research Objective

This study aims to identify the components of digital maturity and sustainability for smart cities and investigate the relationship among those components. In this context, this study proposed a conceptual model to assess the digital maturity and sustainability of municipalities and examine the relations between these two constructs (digital maturity and sustainability) in context of smart cities. Based on literature review, the components of digital maturity and their impacts on sustainability are identified. This study aims to identify the components of digital maturity and sustainability for smart cities and investigate the relationship among those components. In this context, this study proposed a conceptual model to assess the digital maturity and sustainability of municipalities and examine the relations between these two constructs (digital maturity and sustainability) in context of smart cities. Based on literature review, the components of digital maturity and their impacts on sustainability are identified.

Research Design

This literature review was conducted solely through the Google Scholar search engine, with a specific set of keywords. The primary phrase utilized was "impact on sustainability". The keyword was integrated with the digital maturity dimensions outlined in Table 1. Studies published between 2000 and 2023 were examined to determine the digital maturity dimensions and their impacts on sustainability by searching. For each keyword combination (ex. 'ICT' impact on 'social' sustainability), 158 studies ranked by relevance in Google Scholar were examined. Studies that were highly relevant to digital maturity dimensions were separated by reading the abstracts. Screening was completed when studies began to become irrelevant depending on the context. A conceptual framework was created according to the list of 53 studies in total (Table 2). In this direction, *operational maturity (digital maturity of activities), cultural maturity, strategic maturity, ICT infrastructure (technological maturity) and human (digitally competent peopl*e) have come to the fore as components of digital maturity for municipalities.

Further Issues in Operationalization of Constructs

After identifying the components of digital maturity and sustainability constructs for cities, next step will be operationalization of these concepts and investigation of proposed relations by the conceptual framework empirically. For this purpose, a mixed methods approach, combining both qualitative and quantitative research methodologies can be used.

For example, in order to measure the operational digital maturity, it is necessary to determine the digitalization level of basic activity and service areas of the municipalities. In this context, the web pages of municipalities can be scanned and subjected to content analysis, so digitalization level of municipal services and activities can be assessed. Then digitalization level of those activities and services can be evaluated by using Likert scale (e.g. information about relevant activity/service on the web page - Level 1, execution of the entire process of relevant activity/service digitally on the web page - Level 5, etc.). for each municipality. In addition, digitalization of other city related authorities can be assessed as well with the same approach and total operational digital maturity level can be determined.

For operationalization of cultural digital maturity, a survey method, which is generally used to measure the concept of culture at macro and micro levels, can be used, and digital literacy (Gilster & Glister, 1997), digital awareness (Karakuş & Kılıç, 2022) and openness to innovation (Laursen & Salter, 2006) of staff of the municipalities can be assessed through that survey. At the city level, ratio of computer ownership, internet subscription, e-city service usage rates, education level, and similar parameters can be utilized.

Although the *human* factor, one of the important dimensions of digital maturity, is considered as a part of digital cultural maturity in some studies (Williams et al. 2019); within the scope of this study, the *human* component is handled as a separate dimension in determining the digital maturity level of municipality employees. In order to measure the digital maturity of municipalities in the context of *human* component, secondary data such as the number of employees in the IT department, the IT literacy levels, the education level of these people, as well as primary data collection tools such as assessment surveys can be utilized.

Furthermore, in order to evaluate digital maturity of municipalities in context of *strategy,* besides strategic plans, the vision and mission statements of the Municipalities can be analyzed with the help of the software programs, such as MAXQDA, and frequency of the words related to digitalization in those statements can be assessed. According to frequency level of those words in the vision, mission and strategic plan statements, the digital strategic maturity level of municipalities can be measured.

To operationalize the *technological maturity* (ICT infrastructure), which is defined as "*the organization's use and adoption of developing technologies*" (Bumann & Peter, 2019:28), secondary sources can be used and factors such as municipalities' information infrastructures, internet speed, number of computers per employee, etc. can be evaluated.

In summary, by utilizing different methods, including qualitative and quantitative techniques, digital maturity level of municipalities can be measured in the context of operation, strategy, culture, technology (ICT infrastructure) dimensions.

On the other hand, to assesses sustainability, different approaches, models and methods are proposed in literature. Székely and Knirsch (2005) present the approaches that measure, monitor and assess the sustainability. The mentioned approaches include surveys, award schemes, investors' criteria, benchmarking, sustainability indexes, external communication instruments, accreditation operations, standards and codes, indicators of sustainability, metrics for sustainability performance, and non-quantifiable sustainability initiatives. Sala et al. (2015) proposes a systemic framework to assess the sustainability to support decision-making. This framework includes the procedural methods in the literature and draw a comprehensive scope for assessment. Kaklauskas and Kaklauskiene (2020) conducted a study that presents the association between countries' success and sustainability dimensions by using Country Success and Sustainability (CSS) Maps and regression models. In the research, a quantitative study was conducted in 173 countries examining how national success affects 12 indicators regarding three dimensions of sustainability.

In the context of city sustainability, some indices are developed by researchers or some organizations to assess sustainability of cities in terms of environmental sustainability, social sustainability and economic (financial) sustainability. For example, Zhang (2002) developed The Urban Sustainability Index (USI) as a tool for measuring and comparing urban sustainability across China. The USI is derived from a sustainability indicator database by selecting 22 different indicators through extensive expert consultation. The Urban Sustainability Index (USI) comprises three components: urban status, urban coordination, and urban potential. The USI score is the addition of the weighted index component scores. The urban sustainability index score has been standardized on a scale ranging from 0 to 1 (Singh et al., 2012). The City Development Index (CDI), developed by the United Nations Centre for Human Settlements (HABITAT), consists of two indices and four sub-indices. The infrastructure index is subdivided into four equal indicators: the percentage of households connecting to clean water, canalization, electricity, and phone network access. The waste index is classified into two weighted indicators: the percentage of untreated sewage in total wastewater and the percentage of solid waste disposal. These sub-indices capture key aspects of urban development, such as infrastructure and waste management (Singh et al., 2012). LEED (Leadership in Energy and Environmental Design) is another tool to assess sustainability and the indicators for LEED-CCE (LEED-Cities and Communities: Existing) and LEED-CCPD (LEED-Cities and Communities: Plan and Design) cover nine themes: integrative process, natural systems, transportation, water efficiency, greenhouse gas emissions, resources, life quality, innovation, and regional focus (Sharifi et al., 2020). CASBEE (Comprehensive Assessment System for Built Environment Efficiency), a green building certification program used in Japan, has been designed to both enhance the quality of people's lives (social) and to reduce the life-cycle resource use (economic-financial) and environmental loads associated with the built environment (environmental), from a single home to a whole city (CASBEE, 2023). The CASBEE family comprises multiple assessment tools tailored to different project scales. Some members of this family, such as CASBEE-UD (CASBEE for Urban Development) and CASBEE-C (CASBEE for Cities) are used to assess the cities' sustainability (Sharifi et al., 2020). CASBEE assesses four fields: energy efficiency, resource efficiency, local environment, and indoor environment (Sharifi et al., 2020).

For operationalization of sustainability, CASBEE seems better tool to be used as it assesses the cities in environmental, economic, and social context, which are associated to digital maturity components as the dimensions of sustainability considered in this study. However, some indicators or sub-indices of the sustainability indices mentioned above can be chosen and adopted to measure environmental (e.g. waste sub-index of CDI), social (e.g. quality of life indicator of LEED) and economic-financial (e.g. resource efficiency sub-index of CASBEE) sustainability dimensions, and a new index can be constituted to measure sustainability of cities. In order to investigate the conceptually proposed relations among digital maturity components and sustainability components, some statistical analyses, such as correlation analysis, regression analysis, can be conducted.

DISCUSSION

This study proposed a framework that

a) Determines the components of digital maturity of municipalities
b) Determined the components of sustainability for municipalities
c) Associates' municipality digital maturity dimensions with municipality sustainability themes.

The proposed framework was created based on literature review on municipality digital maturity, municipality sustainability, and possible interaction among digital maturity level and 3 dimensions of sustainability. At the last part of the paper, operationalization of the proposed framework is also discussed and possible metrics and measures which can be utilized for the assessment are provided. Of course, further metrics can be provided by more detailed literature.

Our proposed framework can be used in various ways to support decision-making and policy making in cities for assessment of digital maturity level, assessment of sustainability dimensions, and assessment of interaction among maturity level and sustainability dimensions such as environmental, economic, and social sustainability. Since the study uses the framework to assess the level of digital maturity and sustainability across the five dimensions and three themes, firstly, the framework could be used as a basis for a comprehensive analysis that evaluates the digital maturity and sustainability level of municipalities. Secondly, after detailed analysis of digital maturity levels and sustainability, city decision maker can identify areas for improvement and what is missing in their city in terms of digital maturity. Once the operationalization of the framework is realized, a municipality can measure their level of digital maturity and can identify their weak or strong areas and can develop plans for improvement. One of the most important contributions of the proposed framework is looking at relationship and interactions between digital maturity components and different sustainability types. This may also help cities to develop digital strategies for more sustainable cities in terms of different sustainability dimensions.

From another aspect, in this digital era, all cities must use digital means for the economic, operational, and service efficiency and for the welfare of the city and citizens. At the same time sustainability is becoming a significant and urgent issue for organizations, societies, countries, and businesses. The proposed framework can be used by policymakers to develop policies and strategies that promote digital maturity and sustainability by providing a comprehensive and integrated approach. The relationship between digital maturity and sustainability can facilitate policymakers to identify the key areas that need to be addressed to achieve digital maturity and sustainability goals together. In the context of smart cities, it also can be operationalized by municipalities to take an action for their digital maturity and sustainability.

The framework is based on the understanding that digital maturity and sustainability are interconnected, and that the successful implementation of digital technologies can lead to improved sustainability outcomes. The framework is designed to be flexible and adaptable, allowing it to be applied in various contexts and organizations related to municipalities, and can be used to support decision-making at various managerial levels of municipalities.

Finally, municipalities or cities can also use the framework measurements for benchmarking with similar cities or other cities in general and identify their strengths, weaknesses, improvement areas in terms of digital maturity and sustainability, and they can improve their services to provide better living for citizens living in that municipality.

This study proposes the theoretical framework, and the next step should be operationalization of the framework further. The study already proposes metrics and measures for the data collection, data analysis and developing an index based on these measurements should be next steps.

CONCLUSION

In conclusion, this paper presents a comprehensive overview of the concept of municipality digital maturity and its relationship with municipality sustainability in the smart city context. The proposed framework emphasizes the significance of digital maturity in facilitating the implementation and transformation of sustainability efforts in various dimensions, such as ICT infrastructure, human resources, culture, strategy, and operations. The paper discusses the significance of digital maturity in achieving sustainability goals and the potential impact of digital technologies on various angles of sustainability.

This research contributes to current literature by proposing a novel framework for assessing the digital maturity of municipalities within the context of smart cities, with a distinct focus on sustainability. Notably, the study contributes to the field by assessing several digital maturity models, emphasizing the importance of sustainability in smart city development.

Although the proposed framework provides a valuable tool for municipalities to navigate the evolving landscape of digital transformation and urban governance, it is important to consider its limitations. One of the limitations of the proposed framework is the absence of empirical studies to support it. Future research could validate the proposed framework and gain insights into the relationship between digital maturity and sustainability by collecting data from real-world examples of smart cities or municipalities. The impact of digital maturity on different types of cities, such as small, medium, or large-scaled cities, was not considered in this paper. Future research could also explore how the proposed framework can be adapted to evaluate the digital maturity and sustainability of cities with varying sizes and characteristics. Despite its limitations, the framework offers a valuable contribution to the literature on digital maturity and sustainability in the context of smart cities.

Future research could focus on collecting data from real-world examples of smart cities or municipalities to validate the proposed framework and gain insights into the relationship between digital maturity and sustainability. Furthermore, it may be beneficial to conduct additional research on the relationship between digital maturity and sustainability in specific smart city applications or use cases to gain a better understanding of how the proposed framework can be practically applied. Additionally, future research could investigate how the proposed framework can be updated to reflect the ongoing changes in the digital landscape and sustainability goals, given their dynamic nature.

REFERENCES

Adedeji, B. S., Popoola, O. M. J., & Tze, S. O. (2017). National culture and sustainability disclosure practices: A literature review. [IPJAF]. *Indian-Pacific Journal of Accounting and Finance*, *1*(1), 26–50. doi:10.52962/ipjaf.2017.1.1.6

Akcali, S., & Ispalar Cahantimur, A. (2023). How socio-spatial aspects of urban space influence social sustainability: A case study. *Journal of Housing and the Built Environment*, *38*(4), 1–33. doi:10.1007/s10901-023-10052-y

Albino, V., Berardi, U., & Dangelico, R. M. (2015). Smart cities: Definitions, dimensions, performance, and initiatives. *Journal of Urban Technology*, *22*(1), 3–21. doi:10.1080/10630732.2014.942092

Aleksic, S. (2014, May). Green ICT for sustainability: A holistic approach. In *2014 37th International Convention on Information and Communication Technology, Electronics and Microelectronics (MIPRO)* (pp. 426-431). IEEE. 10.1109/MIPRO.2014.6859604

Aljowder, T., Ali, M., & Kurnia, S. (2019, September). Systematic literature review of the smart city maturity model. In *2019 International Conference on Innovation and Intelligence for Informatics, Computing, and Technologies (3ICT)* (pp. 1-9). IEEE. 10.1109/3ICT.2019.8910321

Allam, Z., & Newman, P. (2018). Redefining the smart city: Culture, metabolism and governance. *Smart Cities*, *1*(1), 4–25. doi:10.3390/smartcities1010002

Amrutha, V. N., & Geetha, S. N. (2020). A systematic review on green human resource management: Implications for social sustainability. *Journal of Cleaner Production*, *247*, 119131. doi:10.1016/j.jclepro.2019.119131

Anderson, C., & Ellerby, W. (2018). Digital maturity model. *Achieving digital maturity to drive growth.* Deloitte. https://www2.deloitte.com/content/dam/Deloitte/global/Documents/ Technology-Media-Telecommunications/deloitte-digital-maturity-model.pdf

Angelidou, M. (2016). Four European smart city strategies. *International Journal of Social Science Studies*, *4*(4), 18. doi:10.11114/ijsss.v4i4.1364

Anthopoulos, L. G. (2015). Understanding the smart city domain: A literature review. *Transforming city governments for successful smart cities*, 9-21.

Arora, N. K. (2018). Environmental Sustainability—Necessary for survival. *Environmental Sustainability*, *1*(1), 1–2. doi:10.1007/s42398-018-0013-3

Arora, N. K., Fatima, T., Mishra, I., Verma, M., Mishra, J., & Mishra, V. (2018). Environmental sustainability: Challenges and viable solutions. *Environmental Sustainability*, *1*(4), 309–340. doi:10.1007/s42398-018-00038-w

Aslanova, I. V., & Kulichkina, A. I. (2020, May). Digital maturity: Definition and model. In *2nd International Scientific and Practical Conference "Modern Management Trends and the Digital Economy: from Regional Development to Global Economic Growth" (MTDE 2020)* (pp. 443-449). Atlantis Press.

Asongu, S. A., Le Roux, S., & Biekpe, N. (2018). Enhancing ICT for environmental sustainability in sub-Saharan Africa. *Technological Forecasting and Social Change*, *127*, 209–216. doi:10.1016/j.techfore.2017.09.022

Baumgartner, R. J., & Rauter, R. (2017). Strategic perspectives of corporate sustainability management to develop a sustainable organization. *Journal of Cleaner Production*, *140*, 81–92. doi:10.1016/j.jclepro.2016.04.146

Bekaroo, G., Bokhoree, C., & Pattinson, C. (2016). Impacts of ICT on the natural ecosystem: A grassroot analysis for promoting socio-environmental sustainability. *Renewable & Sustainable Energy Reviews*, *57*, 1580–1595. doi:10.1016/j.rser.2015.12.147

Berghaus, S., Back, A., & Kaltenrieder, B. (2017). *Digital Maturity & Transformation Report 2017.* St.Gallen. Crosswlk. www.crosswalk.ch/dmcheck

Bibri, S. E., & Krogstie, J. (2017). Smart sustainable cities of the future: An extensive interdisciplinary literature review. *Sustainable Cities and Society*, *31*, 183–212. doi:10.1016/j.scs.2017.02.016

Bouzguenda, I., Alalouch, C., & Fava, N. (2019). Towards smart sustainable cities: A review of the role digital citizen participation could play in advancing social sustainability. *Sustainable Cities and Society*, *50*, 101627. doi:10.1016/j.scs.2019.101627

Breukelman, H., Krikke, H., & Löhr, A. (2019). Failing services on urban waste management in developing countries: A review on symptoms, diagnoses, and interventions. *Sustainability (Basel)*, *11*(24), 6977. doi:10.3390/su11246977

Broccardo, L., Truant, E., & Dana, L. P. (2023). The interlink between digitalization, sustainability, and performance: An Italian context. *Journal of Business Research*, *158*, 113621. doi:10.1016/j.jbusres.2022.113621

Bumann, J., & Peter, M. (2019). Action fields of digital transformation–a review and comparative analysis of digital transformation maturity models and frameworks. *Digitalisierung und andere Innovationsformen im Management. Innovation und Unternehmertum*, *2*, 13–40.

Caetano, L., Crespo, J., & Paraizo, R. (2020). Digital Governance and Digital Literacy: examining the Portuguese case. *Emergent technologies, New media and the Cities: Shifting Paradigms in Urban Communication. Capítulo*, *9*, 135–152.

CASBEE. (2023). *Index.* CASBE. https://www.ibec.or.jp/CASBEE/english/index.htm.

Clayton, S., Litchfield, C., & Geller, E. S. (2013). Psychological science, conservation, and environmental sustainability. *Frontiers in Ecology and the Environment*, *11*(7), 377–382. doi:10.1890/120351

Currie, G., Truong, L., & De Gruyter, C. (2018). Regulatory structures and their impact on the sustainability performance of public transport in world cities. *Research in Transportation Economics, 69*, 494–500. doi:10.1016/j.retrec.2018.02.001

Dintrans, P., Anand, A., Ponnuveetil, M., Acharya, A., & Chardukian, A. (2017). Why Banks Must Become Smart Aggregators in the Financial Services Digital Ecosystem. Technology Solutions, Cognizant. Retrieved from Bumann, J., & Peter, M. (2019). Action fields of digital transformation–a review and comparative analysis of digital transformation maturity models and frameworks. Digitalisierung und andere Innovationsformen im Management. *Innovation und Unternehmertum, 2*, 13–40.

Eizenberg, E., & Jabareen, Y. (2017). Social sustainability: A new conceptual framework. *Sustainability (Basel), 9*(1), 68. doi:10.3390/su9010068

Elliot, S. (2011). Transdisciplinary perspectives on environmental sustainability: A resource base and framework for IT-enabled business transformation. *Management Information Systems Quarterly, 35*(1), 197–236. doi:10.2307/23043495

Epstein, M. J., Buhovac, A. R., & Yuthas, K. (2010). Implementing sustainability: The role of leadership and organizational culture. *Strategic finance, 91*(10), 41.

Farias-Gaytan, S., Aguaded, I., & Ramirez-Montoya, M. S. (2022). Transformation and digital literacy: Systematic literature mapping. *Education and Information Technologies, 27*(2), 1417–1437. doi:10.1007/s10639-021-10624-x

Fesenko, T., & Fesenko, G. (2017). City-Governance: Conceptualizing digital maturity model. *SOCRATES, 5*(2), 106–122. doi:10.5958/2347-6869.2017.00016.4

Gasser, U., Gassmann, O., Hens, T., Leifer, L., Puschmann, T., & Zhao, L. (2018). Digital Banking 2025. FinTech. https://www.fintech.uzh.ch/dam/jcr: 2ef31105-1a60-43da-a657-8b140e47b3b4/Digital Banking 2025 FINAL.pdf

Ghazinoory, S., Roshandel, J., Parvin, F., Nasri, S., & Fatemi, M. (2023). Smart city maturity models: A multidimensional synthesized approach. *Wiley Interdisciplinary Reviews. Data Mining and Knowledge Discovery*, 1516.

Gilster, P., & Glister, P. (1997). *Digital literacy*. Wiley Computer Pub.

Gimpel, H., Hosseini, S., Xaver, R., Huber, R., Probst, L., Röglinger, M., & Faisst, U. (2018). Structuring Digital Transformation: A Framework of Action Fields and its Application at ZEISS. *Journal of Information Technology, 19*(1), 31–54. https://aisel.aisnet.org/cgi/viewcontent.cgi?article =1726&context=jitta

Gollhardt, T. (2022). *Towards Business Model Tools for SMEs–Knowledge Boundaries in Business Model Innovation Projects*.

Goodland, R. (1995). The concept of environmental sustainability. *Annual Review of Ecology and Systematics, 26*(1), 1–24. doi:10.1146/annurev.es.26.110195.000245

Gracias, J. S., Parnell, G. S., Specking, E., Pohl, E. A., & Buchanan, R. (2023). Smart Cities—A Structured Literature Review. *Smart Cities, 6*(4), 1719–1743. doi:10.3390/smartcities6040080

Hägg, J., & Sandhu, S. (2017). *Do or Die: How large organizations can reach a higher level of digital maturity*.

Haryanti, T., Rakhmawati, N. A., & Subriadi, A. P. (2023). The extended digital maturity model. *Big Data and Cognitive Computing*, *7*(1), 17. doi:10.3390/bdcc7010017

Hermundsdottir, F., & Aspelund, A. (2022). Competitive sustainable manufacturing-Sustainability strategies, environmental and social innovations, and their effects on firm performance. *Journal of Cleaner Production*, *370*, 133474. doi:10.1016/j.jclepro.2022.133474

Hess, T., Matt, C., Benlian, A., & Wiesböck, F. (2016). Options for Formulating a Digital Transformation Strategy. *MIS Quarterly Executive*, *15*(2), 123139.

Higón, D. A., Gholami, R., & Shirazi, F. (2017). ICT and environmental sustainability: A global perspective. *Telematics and Informatics*, *34*(4), 85–95. doi:10.1016/j.tele.2017.01.001

Hilty, L., Lohmann, W., & Huang, E. M. (2011). Sustainability and ICT-an overview of the field. *Notizie di Politeia*, *27*(104), 13–28.

Hofstede, G. (2010). Geert hofstede. *National cultural dimensions*, 2-7.

Holzer, M., Manoharan, A., & Van Ryzin, G. (2010). Global cities on the web: An empirical typology of municipal websites. *International Public Management Review*, *11*(3), 104–121.

Hortovanyi, L., Morgan, R. E., Herceg, I. V., Djuricin, D., Hanak, R., Horvath, D., Mocan, M. L., Romanova, A., & Szabo, R. Z. (2023). Assessment of digital maturity: The role of resources and capabilities in digital transformation in B2B firms. *International Journal of Production Research*, *61*(23), 1–19. doi:10.1080/00207543.2022.2164087

Husted, B. W. (2005). Culture and ecology: A cross-national study of the determinants of environmental sustainability. *MIR. Management International Review*, 349–371.

Ionaşcu, I., Ionaşcu, M., Nechita, E., Săcărin, M., & Minu, M. (2022). Digital transformation, financial performance and sustainability: Evidence for European Union listed companies. *Amfiteatru Economic*, *24*(59), 94–109. doi:10.24818/EA/2022/59/94

Isensee, C., Teuteberg, F., Griese, K. M., & Topi, C. (2020). The relationship between organizational culture, sustainability, and digitalization in SMEs: A systematic review. *Journal of Cleaner Production*, *275*, 122944. doi:10.1016/j.jclepro.2020.122944

Janurova, M., Chaloupkova, M., & Kunc, J. (2020). Smart city strategy and its implementation barriers: Czech experience. *Theoretical and Empirical Researches in Urban Management*, *15*(2), 5–21.

João, B., Nascimento, D., Souza, C. L. D., & Serralvo, F. A. (2020). A systematic review of smart cities and the internet of things as a research topic. *Cadernos EBAPE.BR*, *17*(4), 1115–1130. doi:10.1590/1679-395174442x

Kaklauskas, A., & Kaklauskiene, L. (2022). Analysis of the impact of success on three dimensions of sustainability in 173 countries. *Scientific Reports*, *12*(1), 14719. doi:10.1038/s41598-022-19131-6 PMID:36042278

Kane, G. C., Palmer, D., & Phillips, A. N. (2017). Achieving digital maturity. *MIT Sloan Management Review*.

Kapkaev, Y., & Kadyrov, P. (2021). Digital maturity of territories during digital transformation. In *E3S Web of Conferences* (Vol. 258, p. 01001). EDP Sciences. doi:10.1051/e3sconf/202125801001

Karakuş, İ., & Kılıç, F. (2022). 'digital'Overview At The Profiles Of Pre-Service Teachers: Digital Awareness, Competence And Fluency. *Problems of Education in the 21st Century, 80*(2), 324.

Kariuki, D. W. (2021). ICT for Sustainability or Sustainability in ICT? A Review of the Role of ICT in Enhancing Sustainability versus the Need to Enhance Sustainability in ICT. *East African Journal of Information Technology*, *3*(1), 7–21. doi:10.37284/eajit.3.1.333

Kashima, Y. (2020). Cultural dynamics for sustainability: How can humanity craft cultures of sustainability? *Current Directions in Psychological Science*, *29*(6), 538–544. doi:10.1177/0963721420949516

Khan, F. N., Sana, A., & Arif, U. (2020). Information and communication technology (ICT) and environmental sustainability: A panel data analysis. *Environmental Science and Pollution Research International*, *27*(29), 36718–36731. doi:10.1007/s11356-020-09704-1 PMID:32566985

Kim, H. M., Sabri, S., & Kent, A. (2021). Smart cities as a platform for technological and social innovation in productivity, sustainability, and livability: A conceptual framework. In *Smart cities for technological and social innovation* (pp. 9–28). Academic Press. doi:10.1016/B978-0-12-818886-6.00002-2

Kleindorfer, P. R., Singhal, K., & Van Wassenhove, L. N. (2005). Sustainable operations management. *Production and Operations Management*, *14*(4), 482–492. doi:10.1111/j.1937-5956.2005.tb00235.x

Korachi, Z., & Bounabat, B. (2018, October). Data driven maturity model for assessing smart cities. In *Proceedings of the 2nd International Conference on Smart Digital Environment* (pp. 140-147). ACM. 10.1145/3289100.3289123

Kuhlman, T., & Farrington, J. (2010). What is sustainability? *Sustainability (Basel)*, *2*(11), 3436–3448. doi:10.3390/su2113436

Kummitha, R. K. R., & Crutzen, N. (2017). How do we understand smart cities? An evolutionary perspective. *Cities (London, England)*, *67*, 43–52. doi:10.1016/j.cities.2017.04.010

Kupilas, K. J., Montequin, V. R., González, J. G., & Iglesias, G. A. (2023). Digital maturity model for research and development organization with the aspect of sustainability. *Procedia Computer Science*, *219*, 1583–1590. doi:10.1016/j.procs.2023.01.450

Kwon, H. B., & Lee, J. (2019). Exploring the differential impact of environmental sustainability, operational efficiency, and corporate reputation on market valuation in high-tech-oriented firms. *International Journal of Production Economics*, *211*, 1–14. doi:10.1016/j.ijpe.2019.01.034

Lara, A. P., Da Costa, E. M., Furlani, T. Z., & Yigitcanlar, T. (2016). Smartness that matters: Towards a comprehensive and human-centred characterisation of smart cities. *Journal of Open Innovation*, *2*(2), 1–13. doi:10.1186/s40852-016-0034-z

Laursen, K., & Salter, A. (2006). Open for innovation: The role of openness in explaining innovation performance among UK manufacturing firms. *Strategic Management Journal*, *27*(2), 131–150. doi:10.1002/smj.507

Lee, K. (2021). A systematic review on social sustainability of artificial intelligence in product design. *Sustainability (Basel)*, *13*(5), 2668. doi:10.3390/su13052668

Lennerfors, T. T., Fors, P., & van Rooijen, J. (2015). ICT and environmental sustainability in a changing society: The view of ecological World Systems Theory. *Information Technology & People*, *28*(4), 758–774. doi:10.1108/ITP-09-2014-0219

Linnenluecke, M. K., & Griffiths, A. (2010). Corporate sustainability and organizational culture. *Journal of World Business*, *45*(4), 357–366. doi:10.1016/j.jwb.2009.08.006

Longoni, A., & Cagliano, R. (2015). Environmental and social sustainability priorities: Their integration in operations strategies. *International Journal of Operations & Production Management*, *35*(2), 216–245. doi:10.1108/IJOPM-04-2013-0182

Magon, R. B., Thomé, A. M. T., Ferrer, A. L. C., & Scavarda, L. F. (2018). Sustainability and performance in operations management research. *Journal of Cleaner Production*, *190*, 104–117. doi:10.1016/j.jclepro.2018.04.140

Majeed, M. T. (2018). Information and communication technology (ICT) and environmental sustainability in developed and developing countries. *Pakistan Journal of Commerce and Social Sciences*, *12*(3), 758–783.

Mathison, S. (2005). *Increasing the outreach and sustainability of microfinance through ICT innovation*. Electronic Banking with the Poor, The Foundation for Development Cooperation.

Missimer, M. (2015). *Social sustainability within the framework for strategic sustainable development* [Doctoral dissertation, Blekinge Tekniska Högskola].

Missimer, M., Robèrt, K. H., & Broman, G. (2017). A strategic approach to social sustainability–Part 1: Exploring the social system. *Journal of Cleaner Production*, *140*, 32–41. doi:10.1016/j.jclepro.2016.03.170

Monzon, A. (2015, May). Smart cities concept and challenges: Bases for the assessment of smart city projects. In 2015 international conference on smart cities and green ICT systems (SMARTGREENS) (pp. 1-11). IEEE.

N'dri, L. M., Islam, M., & Kakinaka, M. (2021). ICT and environmental sustainability: Any differences in developing countries? *Journal of Cleaner Production*, *297*, 126642. doi:10.1016/j.jclepro.2021.126642

Nam, T., & Pardo, T. A. (2011, June). Conceptualizing smart city with dimensions of technology, people, and institutions. In *Proceedings of the 12th annual international digital government research conference: digital government innovation in challenging times* (pp. 282-291). ACM. 10.1145/2037556.2037602

Navarro-Galera, A., Rodríguez-Bolívar, M. P., Alcaide-Muñoz, L., & López-Subires, M. D. (2016). Measuring the financial sustainability and its influential factors in local governments. *Applied Economics*, *48*(41), 3961–3975. doi:10.1080/00036846.2016.1148260

Nüesch, R., Alt, R., & Puschmann, T. (2015). Hybrid customer interaction. *Business & Information Systems Engineering*, *57*(1), 73–78. doi:10.1007/s12599-014-0366-9

Ochara, N. M., & Mawela, T. (2015). Enabling social sustainability of e-participation through mobile technology. *Information Technology for Development*, *21*(2), 205–228. doi:10.1080/02681102.2013.833888

Ochoa-Urrego, R. L., & Peña-Reyes, J. I. (2021). Digital maturity models: a systematic literature review. *Digitalization: Approaches, Case Studies, and Tools for Strategy, Transformation and Implementation*, 71-85.

Pérez González, D., & Díaz Díaz, R. (2015). *Public services provided with ICT in the smart city environment: the case of spanish cities.*

Peter, M. K. (Ed.). (2017). *SME transformation. Successfully implement digital transformation as an SME. Research results and practical guidelines*. Olten: FHNW. https://kmu-transformation.ch/digitale-nachrichten/

Pinzone, M., Albè, F., Orlandelli, D., Barletta, I., Berlin, C., Johansson, B., & Taisch, M. (2020). A framework for operative and social sustainability functionalities in Human-Centric Cyber-Physical Production Systems. *Computers & Industrial Engineering*, *139*, 105132. doi:10.1016/j.cie.2018.03.028

Portney, K. E. (2015). *Sustainability*. MIT Press.

Puron-Cid, G., & Gil-Garcia, J. R. (2022). Are smart cities too expensive in the long term? Analyzing the effects of ICT infrastructure on municipal financial sustainability. *Sustainability (Basel)*, *14*(10), 6055. doi:10.3390/su14106055

Puschmann, T. (2017). Fintech. *Business & Information Systems Engineering*, *59*(1), 69–76. doi:10.1007/s12599-017-0464-6

Qiu, Y., Shaukat, A., & Tharyan, R. (2016). Environmental and social disclosures: Link with corporate financial performance. *The British Accounting Review*, *48*(1), 102–116. doi:10.1016/j.bar.2014.10.007

Roca-Puig, V. (2019). The circular path of social sustainability: An empirical analysis. *Journal of Cleaner Production*, *212*, 916–924. doi:10.1016/j.jclepro.2018.12.078

Rogers, D. S., Duraiappah, A. K., Antons, D. C., Munoz, P., Bai, X., Fragkias, M., & Gutscher, H. (2012). A vision for human well-being: Transition to social sustainability. *Current Opinion in Environmental Sustainability*, *4*(1), 61–73. doi:10.1016/j.cosust.2012.01.013

Sala, S., Ciuffo, B., & Nijkamp, P. (2015). A systemic framework for sustainability assessment. *Ecological Economics*, *119*, 314–325. doi:10.1016/j.ecolecon.2015.09.015

Salvioni, D. M., & Almici, A. (2020). Transitioning toward a circular economy: The impact of stakeholder engagement on sustainability culture. *Sustainability (Basel)*, *12*(20), 8641. doi:10.3390/su12208641

Sarkodie, S. A., Adams, S., Owusu, P. A., Leirvik, T., & Ozturk, I. (2020). Mitigating degradation and emissions in China: The role of environmental sustainability, human capital and renewable energy. *The Science of the Total Environment*, *719*, 137530. doi:10.1016/j.scitotenv.2020.137530 PMID:32143100

Schlaepfer, R., Von Radowitz, K., Koch, M., & Merkofer, P. (2017). *Digital future readiness - How do companies prepare for the opportunities and challenges of digitalisation?* Deloitte. https://www2.deloitte.com/content/dam/Deloitte/ch/Documents/consumer-business/ch-cip-en-swiss-transformation.pdf

Schönborn, G., Berlin, C., Pinzone, M., Hanisch, C., Georgoulias, K., & Lanz, M. (2019). Why social sustainability counts: The impact of corporate social sustainability culture on financial success. *Sustainable Production and Consumption*, *17*, 1–10. doi:10.1016/j.spc.2018.08.008

Schumacher, A., Erol, S., & Sihn, W. (2016). A maturity model for assessing Industry 4.0 readiness and maturity of manufacturing enterprises. *Procedia CIRP*, *52*, 161–166. doi:10.1016/j.procir.2016.07.040

Scoones, I. (2007). Sustainability. *Development in Practice*, *17*(4-5), 589–596. doi:10.1080/09614520701469609

Singh, R. K., Murty, H. R., Gupta, S. K., & Dikshit, A. K. (2012). An overview of sustainability assessment methodologies. *Ecological Indicators*, *15*(1), 281–299. doi:10.1016/j.ecolind.2011.01.007

Šlaus, I., & Jacobs, G. (2011). Human capital and sustainability. *Sustainability (Basel)*, *3*(1), 97–154. doi:10.3390/su3010097

Soini, K., & Dessein, J. (2016). Culture-sustainability relation: Towards a conceptual framework. *Sustainability (Basel)*, *8*(2), 167. doi:10.3390/su8020167

Sutton, P. (2004). A perspective on environmental sustainability. *Paper on the Victorian Commissioner for Environmental Sustainability*, *1*, 32.

Székely, F., & Knirsch, M. (2005). Responsible leadership and corporate social responsibility: Metrics for sustainable performance. *European Management Journal*, *23*(6), 628–647. doi:10.1016/j.emj.2005.10.009

Tehulu, T. A. (2013). Determinants of financial sustainability of microfinance institutions in East Africa. *European Journal of Business and Management*, *5*(17), 152–158.

Teichert, R. (2019). Digital transformation maturity: A systematic review of literature. *Acta Universitatis Agriculturae et Silviculturae Mendelianae Brunensis*, *67*(6), 1673–1687. doi:10.11118/actaun201967061673

Valdez-de-Leon, O. (2016). A digital maturity model for telecommunications service providers. *Technology Innovation Management Review*, *6*(8), 19–32. doi:10.22215/timreview/1008

Vallance, S., Perkins, H. C., & Dixon, J. E. (2011). What is social sustainability? A clarification of concepts. *Geoforum*, *42*(3), 342–348. doi:10.1016/j.geoforum.2011.01.002

VanBoskirk, S., Gill, M., Green, D., Berman, A., Swire, J., & Birrell, R. (2017). *The digital maturity model 5.0.* Forrester Research. https://foloop.in/uploads/images/stock/The-Digital-Maturity-Model-5.0-1.pdf

Watson, R. T., Corbett, J., Boudreau, M. C., & Webster, J. (2012). An information strategy for environmental sustainability. *Communications of the ACM*, *55*(7), 28–30. doi:10.1145/2209249.2209261

Westerman, G., Bonnet, D., & McAfee, A. (2014). The nine elements of digital transformation. *MIT Sloan Management Review*, *55*(3), 1–6.

Williams, C., Schalimo, D. and Lang, K. (2019). Digital Maturity Models for Small and Medium-sized Enterprises: A Systematic Literature Review. ISPIM Innovation Conference – Celebrating Innovation: 500 Years Since daVinci, Florence, Italy on 16-19 June 2019.

Yaakub, S., Subhan, M., Abdullah, N. A. H. N., & Gapar, N. (2015, August). Environmental sustainability strategies and impacts. In *2015 International Symposium on Technology Management and Emerging Technologies (ISTMET)* (pp. 401-406). IEEE. 10.1109/ISTMET.2015.7359067

Yeh, H. (2017). The effects of successful ICT-based smart city services: From citizens' perspectives. *Government Information Quarterly*, *34*(3), 556–565. doi:10.1016/j.giq.2017.05.001

Zhang, M. (2002). *Measuring urban sustainability in China*. Thela Thesis.

Zhao, F., Fashola, O. I., Olarewaju, T. I., & Onwumere, I. (2021). Smart city research: A holistic and state-of-the-art literature review. *Cities (London, England)*, *119*, 103406. doi:10.1016/j.cities.2021.103406

Zhuhadar, L., Thrasher, E., Marklin, S., & de Pablos, P. O. (2017). The next wave of innovation—Review of smart cities intelligent operation systems. *Computers in Human Behavior*, *66*, 273–281. doi:10.1016/j.chb.2016.09.030

Zink, K. J. (2013). Social sustainability and quality of working life: a human factors perspective on sustainable HRM. In *Sustainability and Human Resource Management: Developing Sustainable Business Organizations* (pp. 35–55). Springer Berlin Heidelberg.

KEY TERMS AND DEFINITIONS

Digital Maturity Assessment: An evaluation of an organization's digital maturity across various dimensions and facilitating them to understand their starting point and build a reliable foundation for digital transformation.

Digital Maturity: The phenomenon of evaluating an organization's capacity to generate value using digital technology, assessing its current level of digital efficacy, and providing a clear roadmap for transformation.

Digital Maturity-Sustainability Relation: The connection between an organization's digital maturity and its commitment to sustainability by ensuring that digital initiatives have a positive impact on the environment, economy, and society.

Digital Transformation: The process of adopting and implementing digital technology by an organization to create new or modify existing goods, services, and operations, aiming to increase value through innovation, experience, and efficiency.

Smart City: A city that leverages digital technology to improve the quality of life for its residents, focusing on areas such as transportation, healthcare, and urban development.

Sustainability: The practice of using resources in a way that meets the needs of the current generation while ensuring that future generations can still fulfill their own requirements, encompassing environmental, social, and economic aspects.

Urban Development: The process of planning and managing the growth and development of cities, aiming to create sustainable and livable urban environments for residents.

Chapter 5
Digitalization in Business Process Management: A Comparative Analysis of the Usability of Process Modeling Tools

Katja Kous
Faculty of Electrical Engineering and Computer Science, University of Maribor, Slovenia

Gregor Polančič
https://orcid.org/0000-0002-4746-1010
Faculty of Electrical Engineering and Computer Science, University of Maribor, Slovenia

ABSTRACT

This chapter is centered on investigating the usability of process modeling tools, which are fundamental components of business process management (BPM). It is structured into two main sections. The first part offers a theoretical overview of the lifecycle of business process management, the concept of business process modeling, and various notations for process modeling. Furthermore, the chapter presents the key knowledge of BPMN and the tools for business process modeling, along with a comparative analysis of the investigated tools. The second part of the chapter is dedicated to evaluating the usability, focusing on users' perspectives, of three process modeling tools, categorizing them into web-based and desktop-based solutions, namely Camunda Web, SAP Signavio, and Camunda Desktop. The research results indicate that Camunda Web garnered the highest scores for usability, perceived usefulness, and perceived ease of use, and it was also the most preferred choice for modeling BPMN diagrams among participants.

DOI: 10.4018/979-8-3693-0798-4.ch005

INTRODUCTION

Within organizations, both governmental and non-profit, various business processes are executed. In today's digital age, as collaboration increasingly takes place online and paperless operations become more common, many business processes require digitalization and automation (Lobacz & Szanter, 2022; Truong & Nguyen-Duc, 2023). To ensure the successful transformation of these business processes into digital formats, it is essential to follow all phases of process management.

The discipline that encompasses all activities related to managing business processes, including modeling, analyzing, automating, and continuous improvement, is known as Business Process Management (hereinafter BPM). Through process modeling, organizations map out their current processes, providing a visual representation of how work flows. Process analysis helps identify bottlenecks, redundancies, and areas for optimization. Automation is implemented to streamline routine and repetitive tasks, reducing human intervention and errors. Continuous improvement ensures that processes remain aligned with evolving business needs and market dynamics. Therefore, in this context, BPM provides a structured framework with several key and significant activities.

As reported by Polančič and Jošt (2016), BPM success depends on transparent and continuously improving business processes, which mostly result from business process-modeling techniques, approaches, and tools. Therefore, to succeed in digitalization, it is crucial not only to follow all phases of BPM but also to select suitable techniques, approaches, and tools for managing business processes, including tools for modeling processes. Additionally, Zuhaira and Ahmad (2021) emphasize that significant numbers of BPM projects face challenges and fail. It has been reported that 60 to 80% of such endeavors do not succeed (Zuhaira & Ahmad, 2021). The literature has highlighted various critical success and failure factors. One of the technology-oriented factors constraining project success is the lack of suitable and effective software tools for process modeling that assess the value of new processes before their enactment (Zuhaira & Ahmad, 2021).

Selecting a business process modeling tool is a well-established practice, and numerous investigations into evaluating these tools have been conducted over the years (Campos & Oliveira, 2011; Polančič & Jošt, 2016; Schmietendorf, 2008; Zuhaira & Ahmad, 2021). As reported by Schmietendorf (2008), this decision was already intricate 15 years ago. With the advent of new technologies and various tools with diverse functionalities and characteristics, the process of selecting an appropriate tool has grown even more complex in contemporary times. Despite its complexity, this decision is crucial because it can significantly impact the success of a BPM project. In light of this, we are motivated to investigate the usability of appropriate process modeling tools that are focused on modeling using the most widespread notation called Business Process Model and Notation (hereinafter BPMN), also known as standard ISO/IEC 19510:2013, which is identical to BPMN version 2.0.1. Hence, the primary objective of the research outlined in this chapter is to conduct a usability evaluation, including usefulness and ease of use, focusing on users' perspectives, of three process modeling tools: the Camunda online version, the Camunda desktop version, and Signavio. Based on both quantitative and qualitative results, our aim is to perform a comparative analysis of the assessment of these tools.

This chapter is structured into nine sections. The subsequent section offers a comprehensive explanation of BPM and the BPM lifecycle. Following that, in the third section, the concept of business process modeling is explained, and various notations for process modeling, including the primary graphic elements, are briefly described. The fourth section delves into the primary focus of this chapter, offering a description of BPMN and the tools for business process modeling, along with a comparative analysis of the investigated tools. The fifth section covers the fundamental elements of our research, including the research objectives, the research methodology, and the conducted research. The sixth section presents the findings with a discussion. The subsequent chapter presents the implications and contributions of our research, followed by the presentation of limitations and future work. The chapter concludes with a conclusion, which includes implications, contributions, and the originality value of the research.

BUSINESS PROCESS MANAGEMENT

BPM is a holistic approach to improving and optimizing an organization's processes for greater efficiency, effectiveness, and agility. It provides a structured framework that covers all activities related to process management, including discovery, modeling, analysis, measurement, improvement, and optimization (Gartner, 2023). Often, it incorporates the use of Information Technology (Beerepoot et al., 2023). In today's dynamic and competitive business landscape, where adaptability to changing customer needs is crucial, BPM plays a pivotal role. The proliferation of new digital technologies, such as AI, IoT, and blockchain, has significantly reshaped business processes and practices (Broccardo, Zicari, Jabeen, & Bhatti, 2023). Consequently, digitization has gained even greater importance and dimensions (Ancillai, Sabatini, Gatti, & Perna, 2023).

In the literature, various authors have defined different phases of the BPM lifecycle. For example, Houy et al. (2010) propose that the BPM lifecycle comprises the following phases: Strategy development, Definition and modeling, Implementation, Execution, Monitoring and controlling, Optimization, and improvement. Similarly, Macedo de Morais et al. (2014) and Segatto et al. (2013) define the lifecycle with identical phases, namely Initial process planning and strategy, Analysis of business processes, Design and modeling of business processes, Process implementation, Process monitoring and controlling, and Process refinement and planning review. In contrast, Dumas et al. (2018) outline the BPM lifecycle as consisting of six phases, as presented in Figure 1. The lifecycle begins with process identification, followed by process discovery, process analysis, process redesign, and process implementation, and concludes with process monitoring. Each phase includes several activities that provide key information for the management of business processes and produce output information that serves as the input for the next phase. The details of each phase are presented below.

In the first phase, called process identification, a business problem is defined. Processes connected to that problem are identified, and their boundaries and connections with each other are figured out. The result of process identification is a new or improved process architecture, showing an overall picture of the processes in an organization, including their relations. This architecture helps to select which specific processes or sets thereof to manage through the remaining phases of the lifecycle. Usually, this process-identifying phase is done in parallel with performance measures identification. (Dumas et al., 2018)

The second phase, known as process discovery, involves a more detailed exploration of how the identified processes takes place. This often includes documenting and mapping the processes or using visualization techniques to understand how they currently operate. The visualization is typically done by modeling the business process. Therefore, in this phase, business process models referred to as "as-is" process models, representing the current state, are created. These models serve as input information for the next phase, named process analysis. (Dumas et al., 2018)

Figure 1. BPM lifecycle
(Dumas et al., 2018)

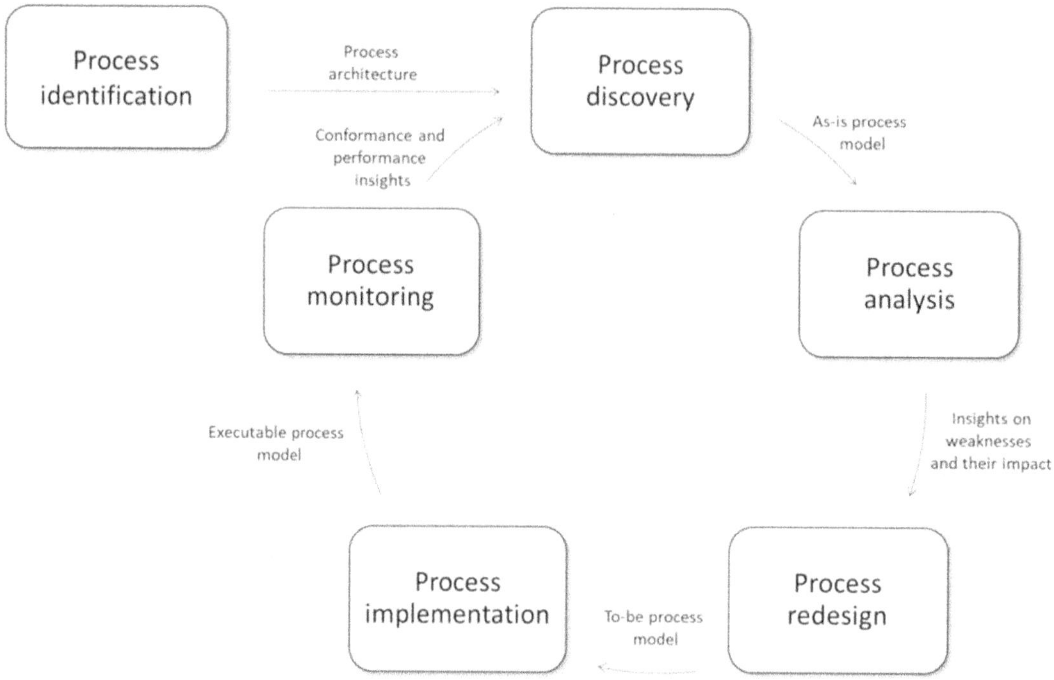

During the process analysis phase, processes undertake a comprehensive investigation using a combination of qualitative techniques, such as value-added analysis and waste analysis, and quantitative analysis approaches including flow analysis, queueing analysis, and simulation. The goal is to identify areas for improvement, bottlenecks, inefficiencies, and opportunities for optimization. This detailed analysis involves a detailed examination of the "as-is" process models to pinpoint problem areas and areas with potential for enhancement. The output of this phase is a structured issue collection that documents weaknesses and their impact on business process execution. (Dumas et al., 2018)

The fourth phase is centered around process improvement. The objective of this phase is to identify changes to the process that would address the issues identified in the previous phase. Therefore, once problem areas are identified, the processes are redesigned to enhance efficiency and effectiveness. This may involve simplifying steps, automating tasks, or reconfiguring the flow. The output of this phase is a new model that includes the identified changes, referred to as the "to-be" model. (Dumas et al., 2018)

After the redesign, the improved processes should be implemented into technical and organizational environment. In the process implementation phase, the identified changes are put into action, and therefore, the "to-be" model is implemented. This phase addresses two aspects: (1) organizational change management, which involves the set of activities required to change the way of working for all participants who are involved in the process, and (2) automation, which pertains to the development and deployment of IT systems (or enhanced versions of existing IT systems) that support the "to-be" process. (Dumas et al., 2018)

The final phase is known as monitoring, and it takes place after the process has been redesigned. This phase is essential for monitoring the newly implemented processes to ensure they deliver the desired outcomes. It involves the collection and analysis of pertinent data during the execution of the process instances. The feedback received, and the data analysis are crucial, serving as fundamental information for making any further necessary adjustments and improvements. (Dumas et al., 2018)

BUSSINES PROCESS MODELING

Business process modeling is a fundamental practice in BPM that provides a visual representation describing the structure and flow of a business process. It can be likened to creating a snapshot of real-world activities within a structured framework. As Schmietendorf (2008) observes, business process modeling serves as an image of reality, offering a clear and structured depiction of how business processes function within an organization.

Business process modeling, as a crucial component of BPM, offers numerous advantages. Firstly, it is employed for understanding processes and sharing the understanding of the process with the people who are involved with it. By visualizing and mapping processes, organizations gain a comprehensive understanding of how work is conducted from start to finish. Additionally, it allows stakeholders to identify bottlenecks, redundancies, inefficiencies, and areas for optimization within their processes. Therefore, it is crucial to identify the improvement opportunities. Moreover, process models facilitate communication. They provide a common language for discussing and improving processes, enabling better communication among teams, departments, and stakeholders. Furthermore, they play a significant role in decision-making by providing a clear overview of how different actions and tasks are interconnected. Lastly, process models serve as a blueprint for implementing changes, including automation and process redesign, once areas for improvement are identified.

To date, various approaches and notations have been developed for creating visual representations of processes. Business process modeling can manifest in multiple forms, encompassing flowcharts, and diagrams, such as Petri Nets, Flow Chart, Data Flow Diagrams (hereinafter DFD), the Unified Modeling Language (hereinafter UML), Event-driven Process Chain (hereinafter EPC), BPMN, and more. Each of these notations possesses different characteristics, and an overview of their key features is presented below.

Petri nets are defined as a graphical and mathematical modeling framework applicable to discrete event systems. They are versatile tools for representing and studying information processing systems characterized as concurrent, asynchronous, distributed, parallel, nondeterministic, and stochastic. As a graphical tool, Petri nets serve as a visual communication aid, akin to flowcharts, block diagrams, and networks. These graphical representations help convey the structure and dynamics of systems. Moreover, Petri nets employ tokens to simulate the dynamic and concurrent activities within systems. This token-based approach enables the modeling of various processes and interactions. As a mathematical formalism, Petri nets allow the establishment of state equations, algebraic equations, and other mathematical models governing the behavior of systems. This mathematical foundation makes Petri nets valuable for rigorous analysis and formal reasoning about system behavior (Pawlewski, 2010). The elements of Petri nets are presented in Figure 2.

Figure 2. Petri nets elements

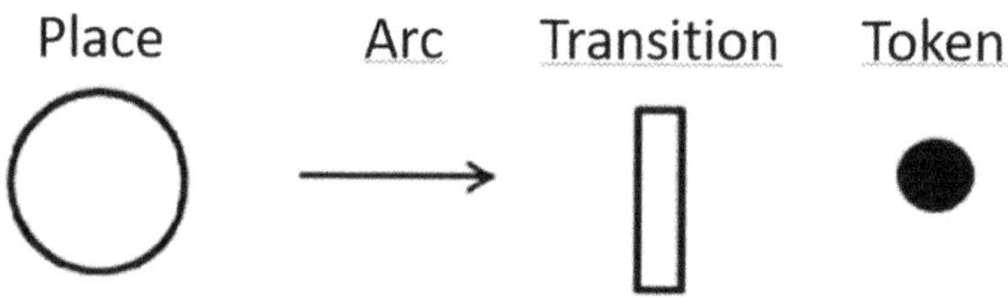

A flowchart is a visualization diagram that illustrates a process, system, or computer algorithm. Flowcharts are employed across various fields to document, study, plan, improve, and communicate complex processes through clear and easily comprehensible diagrams. Flowcharts utilize a minimal set of elements, as presented in Figure 3, allowing for the creation of models ranging from simple to complex. They are closely associated with other popular diagram types, including Data Flow Diagrams (DFDs) and Unified Modeling Language (UML) Activity Diagrams. (Lucidchart, 2023b)

Figure 3. Flowchart elements

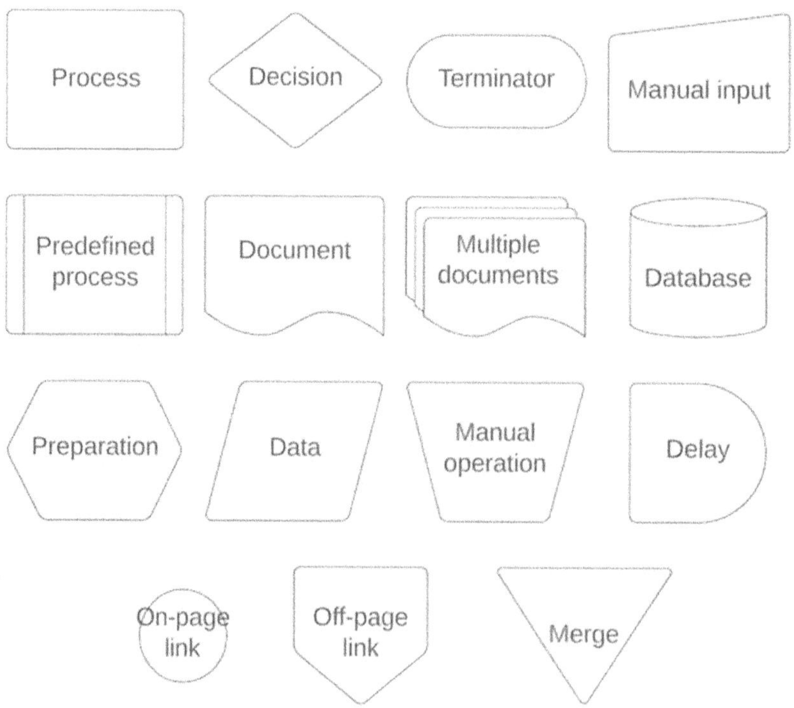

A DFD maps out the flow of information within a process or system. DFDs can be used to analyze an existing system or model a new one. While they are well-suited for visualizing data flow in software and systems, they may be less applicable for representing interactive, real-time, or database-oriented software or systems. Using a small set of elements, as presented in Table 1, it is possible to create both simple and in-depth, multi-level DFDs that progressively delve into the intricacies of how data is handled.

Table 1. DFD elements

Notation	Elements
Yourdon and Coad	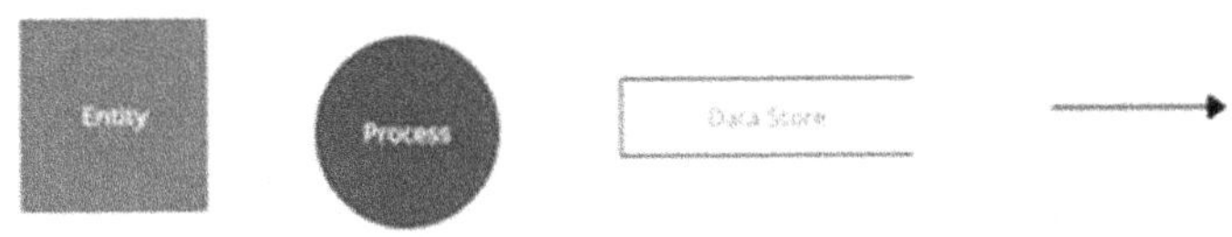
Gane and Sarson	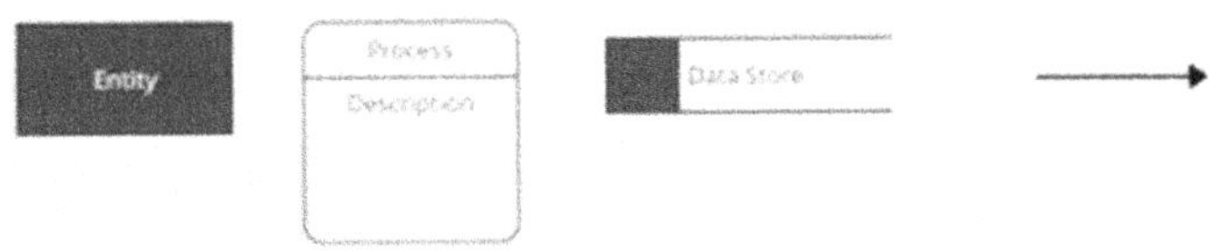

UML is primarily a standardized modeling language that comprises an integrated set of diagrams. The notation was developed to aid system and software developers in specifying, visualizing, constructing, and documenting software system artifacts. However, it also serves as a notation for business modeling and can be applied to model non-software systems. UML includes two types of diagrams (Visual Paradigm, 2023): (1) structure diagrams, like Class Diagram, Component Diagram, Deployment Diagram, Object Diagram, Package Diagram, Composite Structure Diagram, and Profile Diagram) and (2) behavior diagrams, such as the Use Case Diagram (Figure 4), Activity Diagram, State Machine Diagram, Sequence Diagram, Communication Diagram, Interaction Overview Diagram, and Timing Diagram.

Figure 4. Elements of UML use case diagram

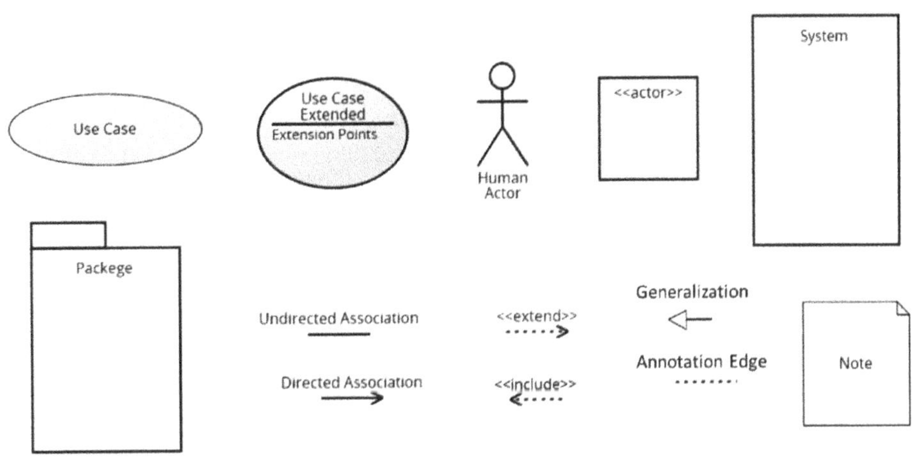

The EPC is a flowchart for business process modeling that was introduced by August-Wilhelm Scheer in the early 1990s. It serves to illustrate the workflows of business processes. EPC diagrams employ graphical symbols to represent the control-flow structure of a business process as a sequence of events and functions. This notation is not limited to modeling alone but is also used for analyzing, visualizing, and modifying business processes. (Zen Flowchart, 2023)

Figure 5. EPC elements

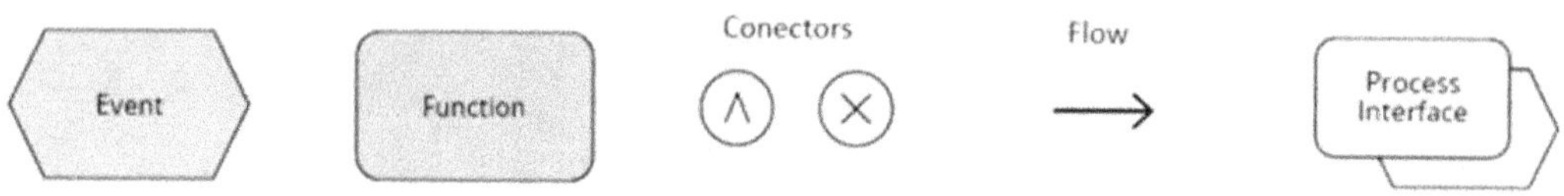

In summary, these notations offer a diverse range of approaches for business process modeling, catering to various system characteristics and modeling needs. Among these notations, BPMN stands as one of the most widely adopted in both industry and academia. Further details about BPMN are provided in the following section.

BUSINESS PROCESS MODEL AND NOTATION (BPMN)

Overview of BPMN

BPMN, also known as the ISO/IEC 19510:2013 standard, is managed by the Object Management Group (OMG) and is widely accepted as the de facto standard for business process modeling in both the industry and academia (Compagnucci, Corradini, Fornari, & Re, 2023). It offers a visual representation of business processes, making them easier to understand, analyze, and communicate. BPMN provides a graphical notation for representing business processes in models and establishes a meta-model that serves as the basis for representing business processes in machine-readable files. These models are mainly used for communication, especially for process-related purposes, while machine-readable models are primarily employed for process automation. (Polančič & Jošt, 2016).

BPMN is widely across various industries and organizations to improve process management and efficiency. It is designed to be easily understood by both business users and technical stakeholders. As a result, the BPMN diagram can be easily recognized and understood by a wide audience. The five fundamental categories of elements in BPMN are (1) Flow Objects, (2) Data, (3) Connecting Objects, (4) Swimlanes, and (5) Artifacts, as detailed in Table 2.

All sets of elements are classified into three distinct subclasses: (1) descriptive, (2) analytic, and (3) common executable. "Descriptive" is concerned with visible elements and attributes used in high-level modeling. "Analytic" includes all "descriptive" elements and approximately half of the constructs found in the complete set of elements. Both "Descriptive" and "Analytic" focus on visible elements and a minimal subset of supporting attributes/elements. In contrast, the "common executable" subclass focuses on the essential components necessary for creating executable process models (Object Management Group, 2012). More details of notation can be found in (Object Management Group, 2012).

Table 2. Basic modeling elements (Object Management Group, 2012)

Name		Meaning	Symbols
Flow Objects	Event	Something that "happens" during a Process. There are three types of various events, such as start events (initiating a process), intermediate events (triggered during a process), and end events (concluding a process).	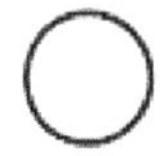
	Activity	A generic term for work that a company performs in a Process. It can be atomic or non-atomic (compound).	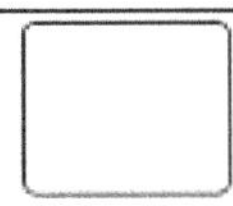
	Gateway	Represents decision points within a process, allowing for branching and merging of paths based on conditions.	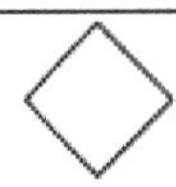
Data		Used for modeling of data objects and data associations, helping to illustrate data flows and dependencies within a process (Data Objects, Data Inputs, Data Outputs, and Data Stores).	
Connecting Objects		Used to connect elements or information (Sequence Flows, Message Flows, Associations, and Data Associations).	
Swimlanes		Used to show how processes are related across different organizational units or participants (like Pools and Swimlanes).	
Artifacts		Used to provide additional information about the Process (like Group and Text Annotation).	

Therefore, BPMN is a powerful tool for process modeling, analysis, and optimization, and it plays a crucial role in BPM initiatives. It is widely supported by modeling tools, as outlined in the following subsection.

Process Modeling Tools for BPMN

Business process modeling tools offer a wide range of functionalities and capabilities, making them essential for various aspects of process management. These tools are capable of custom modeling, steady-state and dynamic simulation, optimization, and parameter estimation based on data. As reported in Zuhaira and Ahmad (2021), a business process modeling system "is a process management system or tool that assimilates capabilities of software systems for workflow management, modeling, redesigning and reengineering, process analysis, business intelligence, monitoring and measuring, improvement, process enactment, and enterprise application integration."

To date, hundreds of tools have been developed for business process management (Zuhaira & Ahmad, 2021). Several researchers have supported the use of these tools for various reasons (Lim, Village, Salustri, & Neumann, 2014; Rigby, 2013; Zuhaira & Ahmad, 2021). These tools are classified into different categories, such as graphics tools, organizational modeling tools, business process modeling tools, process simulation tools, statistical tools, business process monitoring tools, workflow management systems, Business Process Management Systems, Business Process Reengineering tools, unified modeling language (UML) tools, business process modeling notation (BPMN) software, etc. (P. Harmon, 2015; Reijers, Vanderfeesten, & Aalst, 2016; Zuhaira & Ahmad, 2021).

Focusing on process modeling tools for BPMN, Polančič, and Jošt (2016) classified those tools along two dimensions. The first dimension divides BPMN tools into those that enable the implementation of the BPMN meta-model and those that do not. The second dimension categorizes BPMN tools into web-based and desktop tools. In our research, our focus lies on the latter dimension, encompassing web-based BPMN tools like the Camunda web version and SAP Signavio, as well as desktop-based BPMN tools like the Camunda desktop version. In light of this, these two categories are presented below.

The choice between web-based and desktop-based BPMN tools largely depends on specific needs and preferences. Each type of tool brings its own strengths and weaknesses. Some of the primary but key points of comparison of tools are presented in the following. Web-based tools offer flexibility in terms of accessibility. Users can access these tools from anywhere with an internet connection, enabling remote work and easy collaboration. They allow for real-time collaboration, with multiple users editing and sharing work simultaneously. In contrast, desktop tools require local installation on a user's machine. They often necessitate additional solutions for collaborative work, which can be less convenient for remote teams. However, they are well-suited for offline work, making them a preferred choice in areas with limited or unreliable internet connectivity. Desktop tools provide enhanced security as data remains on the local machine, reducing the risk of data breaches or unauthorized access. In contrast, web-based tools rely on secure online platforms, which may be susceptible to online threats.

Focusing on our investigated tools, all of them have their own strengths and weaknesses. Web-based BPMN tools, such as Camunda and SAP Signavio, offer distinct advantages. Both tools do not require installation, as they operate within a web browser. This eliminates the need for any specific software installation on users' devices, making them accessible from anywhere with an internet connection. Both tools promote collaborative work as multiple users can simultaneously access and edit models. This inclusion of all team members throughout the entire BPM lifecycle can have a positive impact on productivity and efficiency, ultimately enhancing the likelihood of a successful outcome. SAP Signavio, for example, is known for its comprehensive feature set and user-friendly interface. It provides various functionalities for process modeling, analysis, and optimization, serving as an all-in-one solution for BPM needs. Its web-based nature simplifies collaboration and data sharing within teams and organizations. Camunda, on the other hand, is a powerful web-based BPMN tool known for its flexibility and integration capabilities. It offers workflow management and process simulations, enabling the modeling and execution of complex business processes. Its accessibility via a web browser makes it the preferred choice for teams distributed across different locations.

On the other hand, the Camunda desktop version provides a different set of advantages. It requires installation on the user's local machine, which offers greater control and security over the modeling environment. Users can work offline without depending on a constant internet connection, which can be advantageous in certain scenarios. Although the Camunda desktop version may have limitations regarding collaboration and sharing models among team members, it offers comparable functionalities in process modeling, execution, and automation. Additionally, it provides the opportunity for in-depth modeling and analysis, making it suitable also for complex process structures.

The detailed comparative analysis of investigated tools is presented in Table 3.

USABILITY EVALUATION OF PROCESS MODELING TOOLS

Research Objective

The primary objective of the research outlined in this chapter is to conduct a usability evaluation, including usefulness and ease of use, focusing on users' perspectives, of three process modeling tools: the Camunda online version, the Camunda desktop version, and Signavio. Based on both qualitative and quantitative results, our aim is to perform a comparative analysis of the assessment of these tools.

Investigated Tools For Business Process Modeling

As mentioned earlier, the participants evaluated three different tools for modeling business processes: the Camunda online version, the Camunda desktop version, and Signavio. Two of them are classified as web-based tools, while one is a desktop tool. The comparisons of the main characteristics and functionalities are presented in Table 3.

Research Methodology

The research in this chapter was based on empirical investigation, where structured questionnaires were used as the primary research instruments. The survey was divided into three parts:

- The first part included demographic questions.
- The second part focused on questions related to participants' knowledge of existing notations for modeling and their familiarity with modeling tools.
- The final part concentrated on gathering information regarding the duration of use of the evaluated tools and on measuring three variables: usability, usefulness, and ease of use.

Variable »Usability« was assessed using a standardized questionnaire known as the System Usability Scale (hereinafter SUS) (Sauro, 2011). SUS is used to measure the usability perception of computer interfaces. Variables »Usefulness« and »Ease of use« were measured using the Technology Acceptance Model framework (hereinafter TAM) (Davis, 1989). Perceived Usefulness (hereinafter PU) is defined as »the degree to which a person believes that using a particular system would enhance his/her job performance« (Davis, 1989), while Perceived Ease of Use (hereinafter PEU) presents »the degree to which an individual believes that using a particular technology would be free from effort« (Davis, 1989).

The survey consisted of both closed and open-ended questions. The variables were assessed using a 5-point Likert scale, where a rating of 1 indicated »Strongly Disagree,« and a rating of 5 indicated »Strongly Agree«. Open-ended questions were primarily used to allow participants to explain their answers and provide additional opinions about the tools.

Table 3. Comparisons of investigated BPMN tools

Attribute	Camunda desktop	Camunda Web	SAP Signavio
General characteristic			
Type	Desktop	Web	Web
Product's website	https://camunda.com//	https://camunda.com	https://www.signavio.com/
Supported platforms	Windows, Mac, Linux	-	-
License used	Free	Free	Academic license
Model creation functionalities[a]			
BPMN elements support	Complete set of elements	Complete set of elements	Complete set of elements
Grouping of BPMN elements	Yes	Yes	Yes
BPMN syntax validation	Yes	Yes	Yes
Dictionary support	No	No	Yes
Model creation functionalities[a]			
Generation of reports	No	No	Yes
Birds-eye view	Yes	Yes	Yes
Automatic layout	Yes	Yes	Yes
Layout direction	Yes	Yes	Yes
Zoom-in/out	Yes	Yes	Yes
Model storage and interchange functionalities[a]			
Repository	No	No	Yes
Revision history	No	Yes	Yes

[a] The attributes are summarized by (Polančič & Jošt, 2016)

Executed Survey and Analysis

The survey was prepared, administered, and executed using the online tool »1ka« (https://www.1ka.si/). Prior to performing the survey, an ethical approval was obtained. The online survey was conducted independently three times, once for each modeling tool, after the participants had used the investigated process modeling tool for one to two weeks. During this time, students received two process descriptions and were required to create models based on these descriptions. Therefore, they created at least two models during the lab work or at their homes. They were not supervised during the creation of models. If they had substantial questions, we provided an answer. However, if the question was related to the tool's usage, we did not provide them with answers.

The data was collected using the online surveying tool 1ka, extracted into Excel, and analyzed using Excel. We conducted both quantitative and qualitative analyses. Demographic data, data on participants' knowledge of existing notations for modeling, and data on the measured variables were analyzed using quantitative methods. Participants' comments, on the other hand, were analyzed using the coding approach.

RESULTS AND DISCUSSIONS

Participants

The target participants for this research comprised individuals who possessed prior experience with modeling (e.g., UML) but had not previously used BPMN for modeling. A total of 46 participants took part in the research. Detailed information about included participants is presented in Table 4.

Table 4. Characteristics of participants

Characteristics	N	%
Gender		
Male	38	83%
Female	6	13%
Other	2	4%
Age group (Years)		
18-25	44	96%
26-35	2	4%
Finished education level		
IV. secondary vocational education (3 years)	7	16%
V. high school, secondary vocational-technical education, secondary technical or other professional education	38	82%
VI/1st post-secondary program (until 1994), post-secondary professional program	1	2%
Knowledge of diagram technique		
Yes	44	96%
No	2	4%
Known technique diagrams (multiple answers)		
Unified Modeling Language (UML)	44	96%
Flow Chart	40	87%
Data Flow Diagrams	28	61%
Event-driven Process Chain	5	11%
Petri Nets	5	11%
Other	1	2%

The typical participant was a male student aged 18-25 years old who had already completed high school, secondary vocational-technical education, secondary technical education, or other professional education. Additionally, participants had prior knowledge of at least one modeling notation, such as UML, Flow Chart and Data Flow Diagrams Petri nets, or EPC.

Quantitative Analysis

The final assessment of the variable "Usability" with the SUS evaluation method is presented as a score out of 100, and it does not represent a percentage. Different authors have used various interpretations. For example, Sauro (2011) reports that the average SUS score is 68. Consequently, a SUS score above 68 is considered above average, and anything below 68 is considered below average (Sauro, 2011). Bangor et al. (2009) interpret the SUS results with assessments from A to F, where A corresponds to scores between 90 and 100, B corresponds to scores between 80 and 89, C corresponds to scores between 70 and 79, D corresponds to scores between 60 and 69, and F means scores below 60.

As shown in Table 5, the average SUS evaluation of the Camunda Web version was approximately 69, which, according to Sauro's (2011) interpretation, slightly surpasses the threshold for an average SUS score. In contrast, the average assessments for the other two tools were below the average SUS score. The Camunda Desktop scored 58.18, and Signavio received a score of 59.24. According to Bangor et al. (2009), Camunda Web is rated with assessment D, while both Camunda Desktop and Signavio are rated with assessment F.

Table 5. Usability evaluation

Tool	Average	Median	Mode	Standard Deviation
Camunda Web	68.86	72.50	72.50	15.00
Camunda Desktop	58.18	50.00	50.00	13.43
Signavio	59.24	55.00	50.00	12.03

The next measured variable was PU. As shown in Table 6, participants perceive Camunda Web as the most useful tool with an average rating of 3.6, followed by the tool Signavio with an average rating of 3.5, and the tool Camunda Desktop with an average rating of 3.4. Similar results were reported for variable ease of use. Although the overall score was slightly higher, the ranking of the best-rated tool remained unchanged. Therefore, Camunda Web was rated as the easiest to use with an average of 3.9, followed by Camunda Desktop and Signavio, both with an average rating of 3.6.

Table 6. Evaluation of usefulness and ease of use

Tools	Average	Standard Deviation
PU		
Camunda Web	3.60	0.06
Camunda Desktop	3.40	0.08
Signavio	3.50	0.09
PEU		
Camunda Web	3.90	0.05
Camunda Desktop	3.60	0.05
Signavio	3.60	0.14

The participants were also asked to indicate which tool they chose as their primary tool for creating BPMN models. Their results are presented in Figure 6.

Figure 6. The primary tool of choice for modeling BPMN diagrams

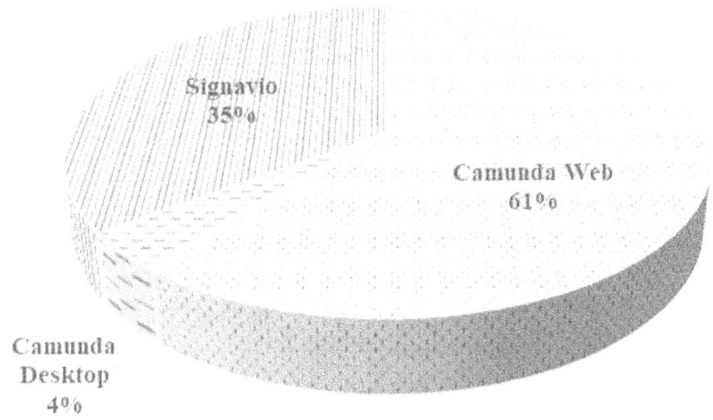

Qualitative Analysis

At the end of each questionnaire, participants were given the opportunity to provide their feedback about the tool. The majority of participants did not have any additional comments on any of the tools. However, a few participants offered additional comments, which are presented in Table 7. These comments reflect individual user preferences, experiences, and challenges faced when they were using these tools.

Table 7. Participants' comments

Tools	Participants' Comments
Camunda Web	
	»In the beginning, you may spend time searching for certain elements of the tool, like the collapsed pool, but after a few days, you become accustomed to it.«
	»A very useful tool.«
	»Web application is better.«
Camunda Desktop	
	»I dislike the desktop version primarily because it is written in Java, and you need to download the JDK version first, which is available on Java's website, but it can only be downloaded if you log into their system.«
Signavio	
	»Otherwise, it's a very interesting tool, but it is not sufficiently well explained and intuitive right from the start. It requires a bit more knowledge compared to Camunda.«

Additionally, a slightly higher number of comments were made to explain the reasons for choosing their primary tool, and these are presented in Table 8. The results indicate that Camunda Web and

Signavio are marked as easier/simpler to use (N=18). Participants have an opinion that Signavio has a friendlier user interface (N=4) and offers a greater range of functionalities (N=5) compared to the other two tools. Camunda Desktop, which received the lowest ratings, consequently received the fewest comments in comparison to the other two tools. One comment was based on personal preference, and the second one stated that it was simpler to use.

Table 8. Reasons for choosing the primary tool

Comments\tools	Camunda Web	Camunda Desktop	Signavio
Easier to use.	13	-	5
Simpler to use.	5	1	2
Items are easily found.	2	-	1
Friendlier user interface.	3	-	4
Greater range of functionalities.	-	-	5
Easy file sharing for collaborative work.	1	-	-
More accessibility and simplicity.	1	-	-
A matter of personal preference.	-	1	-

Results Summary

In summary, the differences between the average values for the evaluation of usefulness and ease of use across all three tools are minimal and they align with the usability evaluation. Camunda Web was rated as the top tool in terms of usability, perceived usefulness (PU), and perceived ease of use (PEU), with an average SUS score of 68.86, a PU score of 3.60, and an average PEU score of 3.90. These results indicated a slightly higher level of usefulness and ease of use. The lower standard deviation suggested a relatively consistent opinion among the participants. Additionally, 61% of the participants chose the Camunda Web as their primary tool for modeling BPMN diagrams.

Camunda Desktop received the lowest scores in all three variables, with average scores of 58.18 (usability), 3.40 (PU), and 3.60 (PEU). It had a higher standard deviation in the usability category, suggesting a higher variation in participants' perceptions of its usability. Conversely, it had a lower standard deviation in PU and PEU, indicating a more consistent response from participants regarding perceived usefulness and ease of use.

Signavio, while still competitive, fell in between the other two tools in terms of usability (SUS 59,24 scores). It obtained an average PU score of 3.50 and an average PEU score of 3.60. However, it had a higher standard deviation in the PEU category, indicating that participants had more diverse opinions about its ease of use.

The analysis of the comments confirmed the quantitative results. The results indicate that the Camunda Web tool is the highest-rated tool in terms of usability, usefulness, and ease of use. It also received the most positive comments, particularly regarding its ease and simplicity of use, further validating the measured variables. In contrast, the Camunda Desktop tool was rated the lowest in all three variables, and even when chosen as the primary tool, it consistently ranked at the bottom. Consequently, only one participant chose it as more straightforward to use the tool.

IMPLICATIONS AND CONTRIBUTION

This chapter has both practical and theoretical implications for various audiences, including academia, education, and BPM professionals, such as business process owners, business process analysts, process improvement specialists, etc. The implication and contribution are presented below.

Academic and Research Spheres

In the academic and research spheres, this chapter contributes to the theoretical understanding of BPM and its lifecycle, including the significant activities related to process discovery, improvement, and digitalization. It also offers theoretical and practical insights into the usability evaluation process, not only in the specific domain of BPM and process modeling tools but also in a general context (e.g., SUS, TAM). This research has the potential to serve as a foundational framework for further exploration in this field and could find applications beyond BPM in various domains. Therefore, other researchers can build upon this approach/evaluation method for their investigations.

Education Sphere

Within the education sphere, the final usability evaluation outcomes could provide insights into selecting most-user friendly tool for business process modeling. Those selected tools could contribute to the learning process of business process modeling. Additionally, this chapter could offer an educational resource for theoretical and practical knowledge related to BPM and the usability realm.

BPM Professionals

For BPM professionals, this research offers insights into the characteristics of the evaluated tools and their final usability assessment. This could aid professionals in making decisions about tool selection and adoption. Organizations undergoing digital transformation or process improvement initiatives can benefit from this research, as it provides structured guidance within the BPM lifecycle and assists in selecting the most suitable tool for their process discovery and improvement needs.

LIMITATION AND FUTURE WORK

Like any research, this study has certain limitations that warrant consideration. Firstly, using the process modeling tools was not conducted within an experimental method, and thus, it was not executed in a controlled environment. Secondly, the order in which the tools were used was not randomized, which might introduce a potential bias in the learning component. Additionally, it is important to stress that the participants in this study were not a representative sample. They were intentionally selected in a targeted manner. The target participants for this research were individuals who had prior experience with modeling, such as UML but had not previously used BPMN for modeling. This specific participant selection may limit the generalizability of the findings to a broader population. These limitations should be considered when interpreting the results and may provide directions for future research to address these constraints and further enhance the understanding of usability in the context of BPMN and process modeling tools.

Our future work will delve into a comprehensive exploration of the significance of BPM in connection with emerging technologies, with a specific focus on advancements such as AI, IoT, and blockchain. This entails a thorough examination of various facets of BPM, including global trends, approaches to digitalization in diverse cultural and regulatory contexts, and considerations for data security and regulatory compliance, particularly within digital frameworks. Furthermore, our upcoming work will concentrate on evaluating the usability of process modeling tools, emphasizing those that seamlessly integrate AI and advanced analytics into their functionalities. We believe that the integration of AI not only simplifies process modeling but also enhances the value of these tools in supporting BPM initiatives. This augmentation improves their usability from end-users' perspectives, allowing them to benefit from AI-driven features that provide intelligent insights, recommendations, and support throughout the modeling process.

CONCLUSION

This chapter provides insights into the realm of BPM, concentrating on the usability evaluation of three process modeling tools from the user's perspective. While selecting a business process modeling tool is a well-established practice, the modern world introduces complexity with the existence of various tools boasting diverse functionalities and characteristics. The emergence of new technologies presents both advantages and challenges, making the choice of a suitable tool a complicated and crucial decision that significantly impacts the success of a BPM project.

Through quantitative analysis of three key variables, namely usability, perceived usefulness, and perceived ease of use, for three different tools (Camunda Web, Camunda Desktop, and SAP Signavio), the research discovered that Camunda Web garnered the highest scores of usability, perceived usefulness, and perceived ease of use. Additionally, it emerged as the preferred choice among participants for modeling BPMN diagrams. In contrast, the Camunda Desktop tool was rated the lowest. The subsequent qualitative analysis further corroborated the quantitative findings, reinforcing the preference for the Camudna web over the Camudna desktop version.

The survey findings emphasize a growing trend towards adopting online tools in BPM, credited to their superior usability and user-friendly features. Considering the additional and improved characteristics of tools leveraging advanced technologies like AI and IoT, we anticipate a further surge in their popularity. Consequently, leveraging the benefits of these technologies in the realm of BPM becomes a logical step, promising to streamline activities within the BPM domain.

ACKNOWLEDGMENT

The authors acknowledge financial support from the Slovenian Research Agency (research core funding No. P2-0057).

REFERENCES

Ancillai, C., Sabatini, A., Gatti, M., & Perna, A. (2023). Digital technology and business model innovation: A systematic literature review and future research agenda. *Technological Forecasting and Social Change, 188* (September 2022), 122307. doi:10.1016/j.techfore.2022.122307

Bangor, A., Kortum, P., & Miller, J. (2009). Determining What Individual SUS Scores Mean: Adding an Adjective Rating Scale. *Journal of Usability Studies*, *4*(3), 114–123.

Beerepoot, I., Di Ciccio, C., Reijers, H. A., Rinderle-Ma, S., Bandara, W., Burattin, A., … Zerbato, F. (2023). The biggest business process management problems to solve before we die. *Computers in Industry, 146* (October 2022). doi:10.1016/j.compind.2022.103837

Broccardo, L., Zicari, A., Jabeen, F., & Bhatti, Z. A. (2023). How digitalization supports a sustainable business model: A literature review. *Technological Forecasting and Social Change, 187* (October 2022). doi:10.1016/j.techfore.2022.122146

Campos, A. L. N., & Oliveira, T. C. (2011). Modeling work processes and software development: Notation and tool. *ICEIS 2011 - Proceedings of the 13th International Conference on Enterprise Information Systems, 3 ISAS*(January), (pp. 337–343). ACM. 10.5220/0003581403370343

Compagnucci, I., Corradini, F., Fornari, F., & Re, B. (2023). A Study on the Usage of the BPMN Notation for Designing Process Collaboration, Choreography, and Conversation Models. *Business & Information Systems Engineering*, (March). doi:10.1007/s12599-023-00818-7

Davis, F. D. (1989). Perceived Usefulness, Perceived Ease of Use, and User Acceptance of Information Technology. *Management Information Systems Quarterly*, *13*(3), 319. doi:10.2307/249008

Dumas, M., Rosa, M., La, Mendling, J., & Hajo, A. Reijers. (2018). Fundamental Business Process Management. *Lecture Notes in Business Information Processing*, *168*.

Gartner. (2023). *Business Process Management (BPM)*. Gartner. https://www.gartner.com/en/information-technology/glossary/business-process-management-bpm

Harmon, P. (2015). The State of Business Process Management. *BP Trends*. https://www.bptrends.com/bpt/wp-content/uploads/2015-bpt-survey-report.pdf

Houy, C., Fettke, P., & Loos, P. (2010). Empirical research in business process management – analysis of an emerging field of research. *Business Process Management Journal*, *16*(4), 619–661. doi:10.1108/14637151011065946

Lim, A. J., Village, J., Salustri, F. A., & Neumann, W. P. (2014). Process mapping as a tool for participative integration of human factors into work system design. *European Journal of Industrial Engineering*, *8*(2), 273–290. doi:10.1504/EJIE.2014.060477

Lobacz, K., & Szanter, R. (2022). Measuring innovation process digitalisation in SMEs - a methodological approach. *Procedia Computer Science*, *207*, 3520–3529. doi:10.1016/j.procs.2022.09.411

Lucidchart. (2023a). *What is a data flow diagram?* Lucidchart. https://www.lucidchart.com/pages/data-flow-diagram

Lucidchart. (2023b). *What is a Flowchart*. Lucidchart. https://www.lucidchart.com/pages/what-is-a-flowchart-tutorial

Macedo de Morais, R., Kazan, S., de Pádua, S. I. D., & Costa, A. L. (2014). An analysis of BPM lifecycles: From a literature review to a framework proposal. *Business Process Management Journal*, *20*(3), 412–432. doi:10.1108/BPMJ-03-2013-0035

Object Management Group. (2012). *Business Process Model and Notation. Lecture Notes in Business Information Processing* (*Vol. 125 LNBIP*). doi:10.1007/978-3-642-33155-8

Pawlewski, P. (2010). *Petri Nets: Applications.*

Polančič, G., & Jošt, G. (2016). The impact of the representatives of three types of process modeling tools on modeler's perceptions and performance. *Journal of Software (Malden, MA)*, *28*(12), 27–56. doi:10.1002/smr.1764

Reijers, H. A., Vanderfeesten, I., & Aalst, W. (2016). The effectiveness of workflow management systems: A longitudinal study. *International Journal of Information Management*, *36*(1), 126–141. doi:10.1016/j.ijinfomgt.2015.08.003

Rigby, D. K. (2013). Management Tools 2013: An executive guide. *Bain & Company*, 1–68.

Sauro, J. (2011). Measuring Usability with the System Usability Scale (SUS). *MeasuringU*. https://www.measuringu.com/sus.php

Schmietendorf, A. (2008). Assessment of business process modeling tools under consideration of business process management activities. Lecture Notes in Computer Science (Including Subseries Lecture Notes in Artificial Intelligence and Lecture Notes in Bioinformatics), 5338 LNCS, 141–154. doi:10.1007/978-3-540-89403-2_13

Segatto, M., Pádua, S., & Martinelli, D. (2013). Business process management: A systemic approach? *Business Process Management Journal*, *19*(4), 698–714. doi:10.1108/BPMJ-Jun-2012-0064

Truong, B. Q., & Nguyen-Duc, A. (2023). A Quantitative Review of the Research on Business Process Management in Digital Transformation: A Bibliometric Approach. *Software*, (2), 377–399. https://doi.org/https://www.mdpi.com/2674-113X/2/3/18

Visual Paradigm. (2023). *What is Unified Modeling Language (UML)?* Visual Paradigm. https://www.visual-paradigm.com/guide/uml-unified-modeling-language/what-is-uml/

Zen Flowchart. (2023). *EPC Diagram: A Complete Guide*. Zen Flowchart. https://www.zenflowchart.com/guides/epc-diagram

Zuhaira, B., & Ahmad, N. (2021). Business process modeling, implementation, analysis, and management: The case of business process management tools. *Business Process Management Journal*, *27*(1), 145–183. doi:10.1108/BPMJ-06-2018-0168

Chapter 6
Performance Evaluation of Digital Platform Business Models:
A Study on Emerging Markets

Indrajanaka Mahakalanda
https://orcid.org/0000-0002-1480-2042
University of Moratuwa, Sri Lanka

Ishari Siriwardena
Sri Lanka Telecom PLC, Sri Lanka

ABSTRACT

The motivation of this study stems from the need to evaluate the platform business model design criteria to maximize benefits to all stakeholders. The authors develop an evaluation framework for platform business models incorporating sustainability as one of the dimensions of ontology. This design criteria evaluation framework is based on the analytical hierarchy process. The authors consider five main criteria and 12 sub criteria. A case study was performed by taking responses from nine experts attached to different digital business platforms. Product innovation receives a weight of 31.8%. This follows customer relationship and financials with weights of 26.4% and 23.8% respectively. The lowest weight is assigned to sustainability. The effect would be somewhat consistent with the existing literature, only over a shorter time scale within which the above results may be acceptable. While only preliminary, this ranking suggests that developments along these lines may be important in creating a pre-evaluated criterion that is acceptable to informed decision making process of a firm.

DOI: 10.4018/979-8-3693-0798-4.ch006

INTRODUCTION

Digital technologies organized as platforms are often regarded as a promising way of transforming organizations and markets in the era of digital economy (Porter & Heppelmann, 2015). With businesses entering Industry 4.0, business models compatible with digitalization can be both conceptually and practically appealing, to efficiently identify and respond to the diverse needs of agents in value chains. Unlike traditional linear business models, digital multi-side platforms are able to create greater value to its participants as they can operate with minimum coordination costs among the market participants (Allweins et al., 2021).

The objective of this chapter is to develop a framework to evaluate the relative importance of a number of design criteria for digitally enabled multi-side business models. We extend Osterwalder and Pigneur (2002) and Latora et al. (2018) to incorporate sustainability as one of the dimensions. Business model ontology elements such as customer segment, value proposition, capabilities, information strategy, feel and serve, trust and loyalty, resources, activity configuration, partner network, revenue model, profitability and cost structure are mapped against the dimensions. Our objective is accomplished through a proposed MCDM framework. This determines weights for the dimensions (criteria) and the ontology (sub-criteria) of several commercially available business model platforms. The effects are assessed by considering the sustainability aspects of digital business models.

The rest of the chapter is organized in the following way: Section 2 reviews the literature on digital business models, Section 3 methodology, Section 4 data analysis and results, Section 5 contains a discussion, Section 6 highlights the originality value and contributions, and Section 7 concludes this chapter.

DIGITAL BUSINESS MODELS

A digital business model engages in the development of new forms of business models to improve coordination of some aspects of the traditional ones beyond what has been achieved, to date. As defined by Osterwalder et al. (2005), a business model conceptually encapsulates a set of elements having many-to-many interactions at a firm level, enabling them to express complex business logic. While generating substantial profits and sustainable revenue streams, a successful business model seeks to create a value to its customer segments and other network partners. Digitalization has decreased reliance of business models on physical resources such as the brick and mortar stores front and physical channels used for marketing and promotions (Erevelles et al., 2016).

To better understand the digitalization drivers, researchers focused their attention toward examining the architecture, ecosystem and business model attributes. This has made them to developing conceptual models, blue prints or frameworks for further analysis. As a result, today, we see several different innovative business model architectures such as multi-sided platform business models, freemium business models, subscription-based business models and vertically integrated supply chain business models that are adopting digital infrastructure (Warner & Wäger, 2019).

On the other hand, the business model concept is well documented in strategic management literature (Morris et al., 2005). Budler et al. (2021) provides a useful and succinct bibliometric review of business model development research and emphasizes the importance of new frontiers such as Industry 4.0, sustainability, and networks for better inter-connectedness of business models and their overall performance. Ho (2020) categorizes business model literature into business model value and ontology, sustainability, and business model development. Cuc (2019) performs a similar bibliometric analysis to recognise key themes of business models. They are business model innovation and sustainability, digital technologies, Industry 4.0, social entrepreneurship, and theory development.

Sohl et al. (2020) discuss the interplay between operating experience and the business model. This has enabled firms to develop capabilities for individual business model design (Cortimiglia et al., 2016). Caputo et al. (2021) identify technological innovation, strategic management and digital transformation as the three main thematic clusters of business model literature. Timmers (1998) appears to be the pioneering article that incorporates architecture, value proposition, business actors and roles, revenue sources into a business model framework. Timmers article was extended from product architecture, value proposition and revenue sources to R&D / technology management as a mediator for economic value creation by the works of Chesbrough and Rosenbloom (2002) and Hedman and Kalling (2003). Business Model Canvas (BMC) outlined by Osterwalder and Pigneur (2010) is considered the most comprehensive framework as it explicitly attempted to analyze the e-business models. BMC not only is a visual generic framework to describe existing business models but supports either redeveloping existing businesses or designing and new ones (Carter & Carter, 2020). Allweins et al. (2021) adopt the BMC to develop a Platform Canvas that can be used to illustrate the essential elements of a multi-sided platform business, their inter-play and the network dynamics (Sorri et al., 2019).

The existing literature identifies value architecture, value network, value finance, and value proposition as main dimensions of a business model (Al-Debei & Avison, 2010). Osterwalder et al. (2005) defines a business model using 9 building blocks (business model ontology): value proposition, target customer, distribution channel, relationship, value configuration, core competency, partner network, cost structure and revenue model. They have categorized the above under 4 pillars: product, customer interface, infrastructure management and financial aspects. Recently, Urbinati et al. (2017) identified the customer value proposition & interface and the value network as the two major dimensions of a digital multi-sided platform business that supports circular economy. On the other hand, Osterwalder and Pigneur (2002) introduced an e-Business model ontology comprising 4 dimensions: product innovation, customer relationship, infrastructure management and financials. Further, the literature also explains the tensions created because of conflicting elements in the business models (Mini & Widjaja, 2019).

The literature on performance evaluation of platform business models is still emerging. For example, Eisape (2020) deploys a balanced scorecard-based approach to compare the success of business models. The inspiration of Eisape's study pertains to the problem of missing mechanisms for assessing relative importance of digital multi-side platform model design criteria in its performance and selection. Süß et al. (2021), provide an extensive literature review on assessment of business models. They focus on the issue of sustainability aspects of a business model evaluation. They considered evaluation approaches such as single indicator, indicator framework, simulation-based evaluation and Multi-Criteria Decision-Making (MCDM) to determine the benefits and gaps in each approach.

In works of Süß et al. several future research directions for designing and evaluating business models are proposed (e.g., circular business models, multi-layered business models). For example, Godina et al. (2020) use an indicator framework (example: balanced scorecard) to assess the social, environmental and economic impacts on business models. There has been less attention paid in the literature to the issue of simulation-based business model evaluation. For example, Melkonyan et al. (2017) have developed a system dynamics model including a causal loop diagram (CLD) and a stock and flow diagram (SFD) to understand the feedback loops of an energy utility business model. Nosratabadi, et al. (2020) present a Delphi – Analytical Hierarchy Process (Delphi AHP) based MCDM approach to evaluate the sustainability of banking business models.

To summarize our discussion so far, we have looked at how different types of business model architectures and dimensions have benefited the advancement of digital business ecosystems. We identified that performance evaluation of business models provides quantitative insight into the e-Business ontology (criteria and sub-criteria). In this chapter, we seek to bridge two gaps in the above literature. Firstly, the literature has not given sufficient attention to the structure of digital business canvas model elements (criteria and sub-criteria) and how they can impact different types of businesses. Secondly, we argue that when a business reaches different stages in its lifecycle (e.g., initial, growth, maturity), quantitative measures of the relative importance of digital business model elements can support stakeholder responses which in turn can build sustainable digital business models. This chapter considers business model elements (or criteria) such as value proposition, financials, business processes, core competency, customer interface, resources, partner network, target customers and technology based on the e-Business Model ontology defined by Osterwalder and Pigneur, (2002). We seek to construct a multi-dimensional evaluation framework for the e-Business elements and ontology using a quantitative research approach.

METHODOLOGY

Multi Criteria Decision Making

Choosing the most appropriate digital business model for any product or service involves evaluating a set of criteria and prioritizing them based on the stakeholder preference. This can be a complex and multi-dimensional problem. Multiple criteria decision-making (MCDM) is a widely used framework for evaluating and selecting criteria. Bhola et al. (2023) argue that MCDM can capture the diverse perspectives and preferences of stakeholders. Thus, MCDM can be thought of as a tool that enables a participatory and inclusive decision-making process.

MCDM is a sophisticated decision-making tool that incorporates both quantitative and qualitative elements (Aruldoss at al., 2013; Kumar et al., 2017; Taherdoost & Madanchian, 2023). MCDM is also an area of operations research that focuses on developing computational and mathematical tools to assist decision-makers in subjectively evaluating performance criteria.

The literature shows an approach to solving an MCDM problem. It involves choosing the most preferred alternative from a set of alternatives. The MCDM gives a trade-off solution where the decision maker is able to select a solution-set from the set of non-dominated ones (Aruldoss et al., 2013). Following Taherdoost and Madanchian (2023), an MCDM problem can be formulated as shown below:

Suppose A denotes a distinct and finite set of alternatives: $A = \{A_i| \, i=1,2,3,\ldots,n\}$. C is a set of certain criteria that can be used to evaluate alternatives, A: $C = \{C_j| \, j=1,2,3,\ldots,m\}$. W represents a set of weights that can be assigned to each criterion based on their level of importance: $W = \{\omega j_{|} \, j=1,2,3,\ldots,m\}$.

This is the main input to the MCDM (M) matrix:

$$M = \begin{pmatrix} x_{11} & \cdots & x_{1n} \\ \vdots & \ddots & \vdots \\ x_{m1} & \cdots & x_{mn} \end{pmatrix}_{m,n} \quad (1)$$

Where x_{ij} is the value of a_i that corresponds to c_j.

The optimization literature mainly refers to the following MDCM methods: Analytical Hierarchy Process (AHP) (Saaty, 1977), Techniques for Order of Preference by Similarity to Ideal Solution (TOPSIS) (Hwang et al., 1981), Fuzzy AHP, Elimination and Choice Expressing Reality (ELECTRE) (Benayoun et al., 1966), and Grey theory (Aruldoss et al., 2013). Majumder and Majumder (2015) identify compensatory (example: AHP) and out ranking (example: ELECTRE) as the two major ways of determining the weights of alternatives. Ciurea and Filip (2015) have used MCDM techniques to evaluate ICT platforms for creative digital works. Van Looy et al. (2013) developed a MCDM based decision tool for business process maturity model selection purposes.

Out of all MCDM implementation methods, the AHP is widely used. According to Goodwin and Wright (2004), the AHP provides a formal structure to a MCDM problem. Further, simplicity of pairwise comparisons of judgments and simple consistency assessment are other advantages. In other words, the AHP evaluates the consistency between the judgments (Salomon et al., 2019). This chapter deploys Analytic Hierarchy Process (AHP), a widely used multi-criteria decision-making model, to evaluate platform business models.

Analytical Hierarchy Process

Saaty (1976) introduced the Analytical Hierarchy Process (AHP). This algorithm works on pairwise comparison among criteria, sub-criteria and alternatives. The AHP produces a decision based on the ranking of criteria and alternative constructed via weights. A pairwise comparison reflects the relative importance between elements, according to a criterion.

The AHP is a structured technique used to deal with complex decision-making processes. Rather than recommending a "right" decision, the AHP assists decision-makers in determining the method that best meets their goals. The AHP method's strength is its capacity to arrange complex, multi-person, multi-attribute, multi-period problems hierarchically. As a result, it has been explored in a wide range of decision contexts, including business planning, resource allocation, priority setting, and alternative selection. Vaidya and Kumar (2006) performed a comprehensive review of AHP applications in different disciplines.

The basic components/building blocks for the platform business model canvas, are derived from the literature. Outlined below are the essential evaluation e-business model dimensions (main criteria) and ontology sub-criteria that can be employed to assess the efficacy of a platform business model. Table 1 shows main criteria (e-Business Model dimensions) and sub-criteria (e-Business Model ontology) derived from the platform business model canvas that will be later structured into the AHP hierarchy (see Figure 1).

Table 1. e-Business Model dimensions and ontology

Main Criteria (e-Business Model Dimensions), C_i	Sub-criteria (e-Business Model Ontology) C_{ij}	Sub-criteria Description and Source
Product Innovation $(C_1) \rightarrow \omega 1$	Innovation & Technology $(C_{11}) \rightarrow \omega 1_1$	Assess the platform's ability to adapt to technological advancements and innovate to meet changing user needs (Bouwman, 2005).
	Competitive Positioning $(C_{12}) \rightarrow \omega 1_2$	The competitive position of a platform business refers to its relative standing within the market in relation to its competitors. It encompasses various factors including Market share and Differentiated offerings (Iñiguez et al., 2007).
Customer Relationship $(C_2) \rightarrow \omega 2$	User Engagement $(C_{21}) \rightarrow \omega 2_1$	User engagement can be assessed using many metrics, such as number of active users, the frequency of user interactions, the duration of time spent on the platform, and the volume of user-generated content etc (McCarthy, 2008; Currie, 2004).
	Platform Quality $(C_{22}) \rightarrow \omega 2_2$	Assessing Platform Quality through User Feedback and Satisfaction Scores.
	Growth Metrics $(C_{23}) \rightarrow \omega 2_3$	Growth metrics refer to the quantitative measures used to assess and evaluate the progress and expansion of the platform.
	Regulatory and Legal Compliance $(C_{24}) \rightarrow \omega 2_4$	Ensure the platform complies with relevant regulations and legal requirements in the regions it operates. Non-compliance can lead to legal issues and reputational damage (Methlie & Pedersen, 2007).
Infrastructure Management $(C_3) \rightarrow \omega 3$	Market-place Dynamics $(C_{31}) \rightarrow \omega 3_1$	Maintaining an Equilibrium of Supply and Demand: Ensuring a harmonious equilibrium between the availability of goods and services (suppliers, providers) and the desire for them (buyers, consumers) on the platform (Pousttchi et al., 2007).
	Ecosystem Health $(C_{32}) \rightarrow \omega 3_2$	Ecosystem health refers to the overall condition and functioning of an ecosystem, including its components and processes (Rochet & Tirole, 2003)
Financials $(C_4) \rightarrow \omega 4$	Financial Performance $(C_{41}) \rightarrow \omega 4_1$	Financial performance measures the Revenue growth and profitability of the platform (Bouwman et al., 2005)
Sustainability and Social Impact $(C_5) \rightarrow \omega 5$	Environment $(C_{51}) \rightarrow \omega 5_1$	Evaluates the platform's environmental and social impact, as sustainability and corporate social responsibility are increasingly important to users and stakeholders (Nosratabadi et al., 2020).
	Social $(C_{52}) \rightarrow \omega 5_2$	
	Governance $(C_{53}) \rightarrow \omega 5_3$	

Figure 1 shows the 3 - Level hierarchical structure of main criteria, sub-criteria and alternatives. ωi and ωij denote relative importance weights among main criteria (Ci) and sub-criteria (Cij). i and j represents the number of main and sub criteria. is computed using the pair-wise comparison responses given by the industry experts.

Figure 1. AHP Hierarchical Structure for e-Business model performance using the relative importance of main and sub-criteria

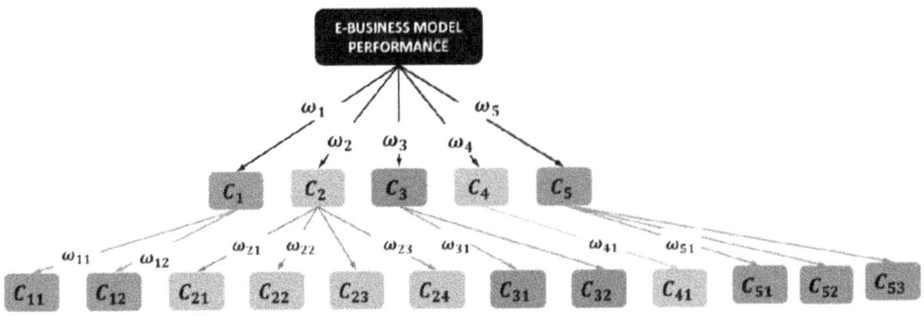

Pair-Wise Comparison

It is sufficient to record a relative verbal appreciation on the comparison of each criteria in pair-wise manner. A relative importance reflects a judgment made by the decision maker (response). For example, $C_i \succ C_j$ denotes decision maker's preference to criteria, C_i over the criteria, C_j. Here the pair-wise comparison value between criteria *i* and criteria *j* is c_{ij}. A pair-wise comparison matrix can be constructed to record all responses of the decision maker as shown in Equation (02).

$$C = \begin{bmatrix} 1 & c_{12} & & c_{1n} \\ c_{21} & 1 & c_{ij} & .. \\ & c_{ji} = \dfrac{1}{c_{ij}} & 1 & .. \\ c_{n1} & & & 1 \end{bmatrix}_{n,n} \tag{2}$$

The AHP adopts a linear '1' to '9' judgment scale to record the pair-wise responses of decision makers. Therefore, a pair-wise comparison value, c_{ij} can be expressed as: $c_{ij} = \alpha.x \forall \alpha > 0$; $x = \{1,2,3,4,\ldots,9\}$

Normalized pair-wise comparison element c'_{ij} can be determined by dividing column elements by respective column, *j* sum:

$$c'_{ij} = \frac{c_{ij}}{\sum_{i=1}^{n} c_{ij}} \forall i, j \tag{3}$$

Mean of row, *i* computes the ωi weight of criteria ci:

$$\omega_i = \frac{\sum_{j=1}^{n} c_{ij}}{n} \tag{4}$$

Saaty (1995) has used a consistency indexed eigen value approach to check the consistency of the results.

DATA ANALYSIS AND RESULTS

Assessing the performance of a platform business model can present a complex and varied task, as it necessitates the evaluation of diverse dimensions pertaining to the platform's operations, growth, and contribution to building its ecosystem.

This chapter aims at assessing and prioritizing the e-business model dimensions (criteria) and ontology elements (sub-criteria). Industry experts working at leading platform businesses operating in Sri Lanka provide their professional opinion on the above criteria and sub-criteria.

Table 2 illustrates the platform businesses considered in this study and the type of business operations that are being carried out. Out of the sample selected for the study some of the businesses consists of a brick and mortar store(s) while others purely operate as digital native businesses.

Table 2. Platform business models in Sri Lanka

Platform Business	Nature of Business
BM 1	Women's clothing
BM 2	Electronics, Telecommunications Customer Premise Equipment and Smart Home related IOT devices
BM 3	Educational course contents, materials & conduct online classes
BM 4	Travel Platform that acts as a one stop shop for Hotel Bookings, Excursion Bookings, Ticket Bookings
BM 5	Multi-Category, Multi-store marketplace
BM 6	Multi-category E-commerce Site
BM 7	Electronics and Home Appliances
BM 8	Consumer Electronics, Home Appliances, Furniture
BM 9	Grocery Items, Fruits and Vegetables, Home Appliances,

Apply the AHP Model for the Main Criteria

Each expert provides their judgment on the relative importance of one criterion against the other. This study uses a linear Likert scale from judgment score '1' to judgement score '9' following. A score of '1' refers to an equal importance of one criterion over the other. Similarly, a score of 9 refers to an extreme importance. Both even values (example: 2, 4, 6, 8) and reciprocal values (example: 1/3, 1/5, 1/7, 1/9) are accepted (see Table 3).

Table 3. Example of pairwise-comparison importance responses

Criteria – 1	Pair-wise Comparison Preferred Values	Criteria - 2
Product Innovation (C_1)	9 8 7 6 5 4 3 2 1 2 3 4 5 6 7 8 9	Customer Relationship (C_2)
Product Innovation (C_1)	9 8 7 6 5 4 3 2 1 2 3 4 5 6 7 8 9	Infrastructure Management (C_3)

For example, the pair-wise comparison score of 5 for Product Innovation (C_1) versus Customer Relationship (C_2) implies that Product Innovation (C_1) has 5 times relative importance over the Customer Relationship (C_2). Here, the main criteria are assumed to be feasible based on the availability of responses.

Table 4 shows the pair-wise comparison responses given by the experts for the main criteria. The values given are either arithmetic mean values or geometric mean values depending on the response data.

Table 4. Pair-wise comparison of relative importance

Main Criteria	Product Innovation (C_1)	Customer Relationship (C_2)	Infrastructure Management (C_3)	Financials (C_4)	Sustainability & Social Impact (C_5)
Product Innovation (C_1)	1.0	5.50	2.94	0.61	3.31
Customer Relationship (C_2)	0.18	1.00	6.15	1.40	5.00
Infrastructure Management (C_3)	0.34	0.16	1.00	0.86	4.90
Financials (C_4)	1.63	0.71	1.20	1.0	5.50
Sustainability & Social Impact (C_5)	0.30	0.20	0.20	0.18	1.0

Following Saaty (1977), the normalized pair-wise comparison of relative importance matrix can be developed (see Table 5).

Table 5. Normalized pair-wise comparison of relative importance

Main Criteria	C_1	C_2	C_3	C_4	C_5	Criteria Weights
C_1	0.29	0.73	0.3	0.15	0.2	$\omega 1_=31.8\%$
C_2	0.05	0.13	0.5	0.35	0.3	$\omega 2_=26.4\%$
C_3	0.1	0.02	0.1	0.21	0.2	$\omega 3_=13.4\%$
C_4	0.47	0.09	0.1	0.25	0.3	$\omega 4_=23.8\%$
C_5	0.09	0.03	0.0	0.04	0.1	$\omega 5_=4.5\%$

The row average gives the criteria weight. In this case, the experts argue that higher weight is given to financial criteria, $\omega 1_=29.4\%$ in the overall performance measure of digital business platform business models. Lowest weight, $\omega 5 =_4.5\%$ is given to the sustainability and social impact criteria out of five main criteria considered.

The consistency ratio of the above AHP analysis is 0.2. A consistency ratio ideally must be sufficiently lower than the given threshold value 0.10. This means the best solution is achieved within a set of potential alternatives.

Apply the AHP Model for the Sub-Criteria

This section illustrates application of AHP for each set of sub-criteria under each main criterion (refer Table 1). Table 6 summarizes the normalized pair-wise comparison of relative importance and criteria weights for innovation & technology (C_{11}) and competitive positioning (C_{12}) sub-criteria.

Table 6. Normalized pair-wise comparison of relative importance of C_{11} and C_{12}

Sub-criteria	C_{11}	C_{12}	Criteria Weights
C_{11}	0.6	0.6	$\omega 1_{1=}$62%
C_{12}	0.4	0.4	$\omega 1_{2=}$38%

AHP algorithm assigns 62% and 38% weights for the sub-criteria innovation & technology (C_{11}) and competitive positioning (C_{12}). It records a very small consistency ratio which is less than 0.1.

Table 7 provides normalized pair-wise comparison of relative importance of the following sub-criteria: user engagement (C_{21}), platform quality (C_{22}), growth metrics (C_{23}) and regulatory and legal compliance (C_{24}).

Table 7. Normalized pair-wise comparison of relative importance of C_{21}, C_{22}, C_{23}, and C_{24}

Sub-criteria	C_{21}	C_{22}	C_{23}	C_{24}	Criteria Weights
C_{21}	0.28	0.48	0.18	0.26	$\omega 2_{1=}$27.9%
C_{22}	0.11	0.18	0.25	0.24	$\omega 2_{2=}$18.6%
C_{23}	0.49	0.24	0.33	0.32	$\omega 2_{3=}$32.7%
C_{24}	0.22	0.24	0.21	0.21	$\omega 2_{4=}$20.9%

AHP finds 32.7%, 27.9%, 20.9% and 18.6% weights for growth metrics, user engagement, regulatory and legal compliance, and platform quality, respectively. The consistency ration, CR=0.095, is accepted.

Table 8 shows the sub criteria weights for market-pace dynamic (C_{31}) and ecosystem health (C_{32}) with an underlying consistency ratio close to zero.

Table 8. Normalized pair-wise comparison of relative importance of C_{31} and C_{32}

Sub-criteria	C_{31}	C_{32}	Criteria Weights
C_{31}	0.4	0.4	$\omega 3_{1=}$43%
C_{32}	0.6	0.6	$\omega 3_{2=}$57%

Finally, the AHP computes the weights for the last set of sub-criteria: environment (C_{51}), social (C_{52}) and governance (C_{53}) (see Table 9). The consistency ratio is 0.03 and it is within the norms.

Table 9. Normalized pair-wise comparison of relative importance of C_{51}, C_{52}, and C_{53}

	C_{51}	C_{52}	C_{53}	**Criteria Weights**
C_{51}	0.27	0.34	0.23	$\omega 5_{1=}$28.1%
C_{52}	0.25	0.31	0.36	$\omega 5_{2=}$30.8%
C_{53}	0.48	0.35	0.41	$\omega 5_{3=}$41.1%

The AHP constructs the following hierarchical structure that shows the priorities of the course of action at different levels. Higher level objective is determined by the priorities (weights) of the immediate lower level.

Figure 2. AHP hierarchical structure with main criteria and sub-criteria weights

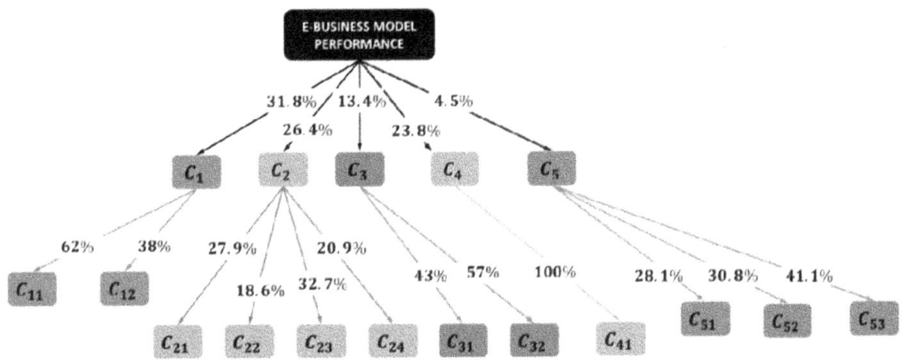

Figure 3 shows the local weights of platform business model alternatives under each main criterion. We exclude the analysis of local weights under sub-criteria for the sake of simplicity. It is both practically and conceptually appealing to conduct the alternative weight analysis for the main criterion.

Figure 3. Local weights of platform business model alternatives

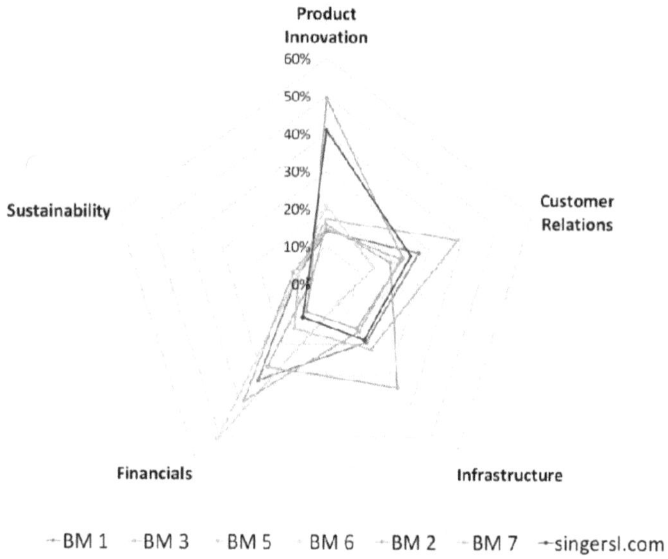

Based on the spider web diagram plotted on the responses received from the platform experts, the relative significance of each main criteria perceived by the experts have varied. Sub-Criteria related to Customer Relations have been weighed with a similar score by many experts. Significance of Product Innovation and Financials are perceived with higher varied significance by the experts based on the type of platform business they operate. Sustainability criteria also have been perceived at a lower significance with an equal weight from the experts considered in this study.

DISCUSSION

The primary aim of this chapter is to construct a comprehensive framework for evaluating the performance criteria associated with digitally enabled multi-side platform business models. Based on the MCDM methodology adopted to assess the performance of 9 leading platform business operations in Sri Lanka, this chapter aims to identifying the significance and impact of the evaluation criteria listed above and its contribution to the proposed framework.

When assessing the study results, higher significance is weighed on Financial Performance, Product Innovation and Customer Relationships, out of the 5 main criteria assessed.

Implications of the Main Criteria

Product Innovation

The success of platform business models is heavily reliant on the pivotal role played by product innovation. Platform business models facilitate the connection and interaction between diverse user groups, hence fostering the creation of mutual value. Product innovation plays a pivotal role in bolstering the success of platform business models. The user experience can be considerably improved through innovations in the platform's user interface, functionalities, and general design. Consequently, this phenomenon generates a greater influx of users and sustains their active involvement. The continual introduction of novel features and functionalities ensures the platform remains dynamic and pertinent. Additionally, this feature enables the platform to effectively address a broader spectrum of customer requirements, hence attracting a heterogeneous user demographics. The introduction of novel product features and innovations has the potential to create fresh avenues for generating revenue. Possible options for monetization in this context encompass the incorporation of premium features, implementation of subscription models, or establishment of collaborative alliances with third-party services.

In the context of product development and innovation, the utilization of modular platform architectures has facilitated the attainment of economies of scale for enterprises. This is accomplished by the utilization of standardized platform components, which enable the design and development of new products and services. The adoption of this approach promotes the creation of a diverse range of products, often referred to as a "family" of products. Within the realm of advanced technology, companies like Alphabet, Apple, Facebook, and Intel have effectively utilized platforms to enable external application and software developers, known as complementors, to engage in innovation and include their own products or services onto a standardized platform interface (Gawer, 2014).

The concept of competitive advantage suggests that innovation plays a crucial role in gaining a favorable position within the market. Platforms that continuously deliver novel and distinctive features are more inclined to differentiate themselves from competitors and effectively engage and keep consumers.

Successful platform designers think about competition when designing their business model; they recognize that platform business models do not operate in a vacuum and consider how their model interacts with those of rivals, using product innovations and technological tools such as data analytic tools. Platform leaders use both business model innovation and imitation to create complex business models; they generate a tightly coupled system in which various components bond with one another in complementary and consistent ways, and scale the model rapidly (Zhao et al., 2020).

The expansion of an ecosystem can be facilitated by the implementation of innovative strategies, which have the potential to attract third-party developers and enterprises. The utilization of open APIs and developer tools fosters the facilitation of external contributions, hence broadening the spectrum of services accessible on the platform.

The utilization of Industry 4.0 technologies such as Artificial Intelligence, AR/VR based solutions, advanced data analytics and machine learning methods can improve customer experience, yield important insights into user behavior, preferences, and trends. This information can be utilized to customize the platform's features and services to more effectively align with user expectations.

The long-term sustainability of the platform is enhanced by innovations that effectively tackle regulatory concerns and address data privacy issues. The implementation of creative solutions in response to evolving rules fosters the development of trust among both users and partners.

The enhancement of a platform's agility and flexibility through innovative measures also allows for its adaptation to both market fluctuations and developments in technology. It is imperative to remain proactive to maintain a competitive advantage and prevent becoming outdated.

In essence, the success of platform business models is heavily reliant on product innovation, as it serves as a crucial catalyst in attracting customers, generating value, and maintaining competitiveness within dynamic marketplaces.

Customer Relationships

The significance of customer interactions is rated the third most important criteria for successful platform business strategies. Platforms function as mediators that facilitate connections between various user groups, like buyers and sellers, service providers and consumers, or content creators and audiences (Uludag et al., 2016).

There are multiple justifications for the significance of establishing and sustaining robust client relationships in the context of platform business models. The concepts of trust and credibility are significant in various academic disciplines. The establishment and maintenance of trust play a crucial role in platform business models. For users to engage in transactions with confidence, it is imperative that they place trust in the platform's ability to effectively enable fair and secure transactions, safeguard their data, and deliver a dependable and valued service. The establishment of robust client relationships plays a pivotal role in fostering trust and enhancing credibility.

User retention refers to the ability of a company or organization to retain its users or customers over a certain period of time. Platforms depend on the presence of a substantial number of users engaging in interactions with one another. Developing robust connections with users enhances their loyalty, hence diminishing the probability of customer attrition. The establishment of a dedicated user base is crucial for ensuring the long-term prosperity of a platform.

The concept of user engagement refers to the level of involvement and interaction exhibited by individuals with a certain product, service, or platform. The active involvement of users is crucial for maintaining their interest and engagement with the site. Platforms that cultivate a sense of community and provide tailored experiences are more inclined to sustain user engagement and activity on the platform.

Customer interactions serve as a key means of obtaining feedback. Frequent engagements with consumers might reveal areas of dissatisfaction, individual inclinations, and recommendations for enhancement. The feedback loop plays a vital role in the process of refining the platform, including new features, and rapidly addressing any difficulties that may arise (Smedlund, 2012).

Network effects refer to the phenomenon where the value or utility of a product or service increases as more people use it. The efficacy of numerous platforms is contingent upon network effects, whereby the inherent worth of the platform escalates in tandem with the augmentation of its user base. Positive customer interactions play a significant role in fostering positive word-of-mouth, thereby recruiting new users and strengthening network effects (Rohn, et al., 2021). Platforms frequently experience success when they possess a dynamic ecosystem consisting of third-party developers and partners. Cultivating partnerships with these external contributors is crucial for broadening the scope of services and solutions available on the platform.

The establishment of robust client relationships plays a pivotal role in enabling the implementation of personalized experiences. Platforms can leverage data derived from client interactions in order to tailor the user experience, offer pertinent content recommendations, and deliver tailored services, hence augmenting overall satisfaction.

The concept of brand advocacy refers to the practice of individuals actively promoting and endorsing a certain brand. It involves voluntarily advocating in favour of a brand. Users who are content and actively involved are more inclined to become brand advocates, thereby endorsing the platform to a wider audience. The establishment of robust client relationships has the potential to produce favorable reviews, feedback, recommendations, word-of-mouth promotions, which can significantly contribute to the acquisition of new users.

In summary, the establishment and maintenance of client relationships plays a fundamental role in driving the success of platform business models. By prioritizing the establishment of trust, cultivation of engagement, and utilization of consumer information, platforms can establish a mutually beneficial and enduring ecosystem for both users and the platform itself.

Financial Performance

Platform business models depend on financial performance for numerous reasons. Financial performance is a critical indicator of a platform's profitability and sustainability (Parker et al., 2016). A sustainable platform must earn more income than it spends. For operating costs, technology and infrastructure investments, and investor returns, this is critical. Growth and expansion of platform enterprises drive investor confidence. A platform with good financial performance attracts and retains investors. This can lead to more money for development, marketing, and expansion. Consumers and businesses/ platform service providers trust platforms based on their stability and financial health (Rochet & Tirole, 2003). Financial stability makes a platform more trustworthy, increasing user adoption and retention. Financial success allows a platform to invest in innovation and development (Zhu et al., 2016). This includes improving user experience, adding features, and keeping up with technology. A platform needs money for research and development to evolve and compete. Platform firms need effective marketing and expansion to attract new users and partners. Financial resources enable marketing efforts, partnerships, and regional growth, expanding the platform's audience and user base. The platform can invest in new technologies and ecosystem growth provided they maintain effective income models and execute strategies for earning money.

Sustainability and Social Impact

Olah et al. (2022) cites sustainability is widely recognized as a crucial concern in contemporary discourse in the prevailing socio-economic and environmental issues of the era. There is a growing consumer need for enterprises to adopt eco-friendly practices to promote sustainable e-commerce. The realm of electronic commerce presents a significant and formidable challenge associated with frequent shipping and high return rates. The utilization of non-recyclable packaging materials contributes to a detrimental impact on the environment. The research indicates that e-commerce is poised for substantial and quick expansion, while also gaining widespread acceptance. Nevertheless, the primary concern lies in determining the means to maintain the ongoing expansion of platform businesses.

Based on a research study conducted in Kenyan E-commerce market, the findings suggest that allocating resources towards the implementation of sustainable practices yields favorable outcomes for the environment. Based on the survey data, it was inferred that a significant majority of customers, specifically two-thirds, consider the adoption of sustainability practices by online merchants to be of considerable importance. A mere 25% of customers have chosen to reject enterprises that fail to adhere to sustainable practices. Hence, the examination of sustainable e-commerce holds significant importance. The results suggest that the majority of European nations have implemented policies pertaining to the sustainability of e-commerce, whereas only a limited number of African countries, especially Kenya, have done so (Olah et al., 2022).

When considering the present research findings based on Sri Lanka's e-commerce market the sustainability and environmental impacts were deemed to be less significant. This could be mainly due to the immaturity of the market and Sri Lanka being an emerging market.

Presently, in nations characterized by well-established marketplaces, electronic commerce is subject to appropriate regulatory frameworks. Hence, it can be observed that the digital economy is flourishing in various countries and areas, particularly in Europe and China, when contrasted to Africa (Miethlich et al., 2020). Nevertheless, the e-commerce market in Sri Lanka continues to present challenges mostly stemming from a dearth of comprehensive policies. Hence, it is imperative to establish and execute rules that align with the principles of business and e-commerce sustainability. In Sri Lankan context, with the widespread availability and adoption of internet connectivity across the country, the advantages of electronic commerce (e-commerce) have been apparent, primarily in terms of enhanced ease and the availability of a diverse range of items at competitive rates and more and more brick and mortar stores extending their products to online channels. This phenomenon has been facilitated by intense rivalry among e-commerce platforms, the presence of eager shoppers and sellers, and the exponential growth in digital adoption and transformation during the covid-19 pandemic.

Sub-Criteria Assessment

Innovation and Technology

The success of platform business models is intricately linked to the pivotal role of technologies and innovations, as highlighted in several academic articles. Research by Hagiu and Wright (2019) underscores the criticality of platform design and the technological infrastructure underpinning these models, emphasizing that innovative features and functionalities significantly contribute to user engagement and platform growth. Additionally, Eisenmann et al. (2006) argue that successful platforms harness the power of technology to facilitate interactions among users and create network effects, a key driver of their competitive advantage. Moreover, Akter et al. (2022) illustrates in their study that technological innovations, such as data analytics and artificial intelligence, empower platforms to extract valuable insights from user interactions, enabling personalized services and enhancing overall user experience. These academic perspectives collectively emphasize that continuous technological innovation is not merely advantageous but fundamental to the success, sustainability, and evolution of platform business models in today's dynamic and digitally driven business landscape.

Growth Metrics

Platform business models have gained significant attention in academic study because of their importance and impact. Evans and Schmalensee (2016) argue that the attainment of critical mass and the ability to maintain user growth are crucial factors for the success of a platform. This is because network effects enhance the value proposition of the platform as the user base expands. Parker et al. (2016) emphasizes the clear relationship between the extent of user engagement and the effectiveness of two-sided platforms. According to Eisenmann et al. (2006), metrics such as user acquisition rates, retention rates, and engagement levels play a crucial role in assessing the life of a platform. Zhu et al. (2016) emphasizes the significance of user expansion in cultivating a dynamic ecosystem and enticing supplementary services, thereby strengthening the overall worth of the platform. Within the domain of platform enterprises, there exists a prevailing scholarly consensus that supports the idea that growth measures play a crucial role as benchmarks. These metrics are indicative of a platform's capacity to generate and maintain a flourishing network effect, which is a basic factor in determining its success within a competitive environment.

Ecosystem Health

Academic research suggests that platform business success depends on their ecosystem. Zott and Amit (2010) emphasize ecosystem health in platform-based business models. They claim that platform firm success depends on the health and vitality of their ecosystem as well as their internal skills. Hagiu and Wright (2015) also stress the importance of external complementors and the ecosystem in platform company success, arguing that a vibrant ecosystem boosts value and attracts more users. Rochet and Tirole (2003) also emphasize the necessity of a healthy ecosystem in maintaining network effects, which underpin many platform enterprises' success.

Governance

As a part of sustainability and Environmental impact analysis, establishing a well-articulated governance structure is vital for the success of platform business models. Governance structures are crucial to platform design, coordination, and incentive alignment, according to Hagiu and Wright (2019). Governance systems must ensure compliance with regulatory requirements, adhering to standards and compliances, trust & privacy, and effective collaboration among varied platform ecosystem players (Hagiu & Wright, 2015). Osiyevskyy and Dewald (2015) further propose that effective governance frameworks reduce conflicts and encourage user and complementor cooperation, sustaining platform ecosystems. Governance systems shape participant behavior by setting rules, conventions, and incentives, affecting the platform business model's health and success.

ORIGINALITY, VALUE, AND CONTRIBUTION

This chapter contributes to the existing body of knowledge by determining the relative importance of dimensions (main criteria) and ontology elements (sub-criteria) of platform business models. To the best of our knowledge, literature on prioritizing digital business canvas dimensions and ontology is limited. Our main contribution in this chapter is to introduce widely accepted MCDM methodologies in operations research literature (for example, AHP in this study) to perform the above. We have shown how to determine relative weights of alternative commercial platform business models corresponding to the main and sub- criteria using the AHP.

In addition, sustainability and social impact are proposed as new dimensions to e-Business Model Canvas ontology (Osterwalder & Pigneur, 2002). This dimension helps to measure factors such as Environment (E), Social (S) and Governance (G). This proposed 5th dimension is an important construct to achieve sustainable operation of digital business platform models.

Incorporating sustainability and social effect into the e-Business Model Canvas Ontology is essential for numerous reasons. Being a Responsible business entity is one predominant contributor. By integrating sustainability and social impact into the canvas, an e-business entity demonstrates its recognition of its obligation to the environment, society, and future generations. Consumers are becoming more aware of the influence their purchases have. Companies that include sustainability and social impact as part of their operations might have a competitive advantage by attracting consumers who prioritize ethical considerations.

Given the continuous growth of digital commerce, it is imperative to pay attention to consumers who possess significant purchasing power and exert substantial effects on brand views.

Sustainability and ethical considerations in platform business models contribute significantly towards risk mitigation. Companies that neglect sustainability are susceptible to encountering regulatory obstacles, disruptions in their supply chain, or harm to their brand. By incorporating strategies to tackle these concerns into their company model, businesses can effectively reduce these risks.

The implementation of sustainability principles frequently results in the ability to endure and recover over an extended timeframe. Companies that prioritize sustainability are more likely to engage in innovation, efficiently utilize resources, and cultivate robust partnerships with stakeholders.

By including sustainability and social effect into the e-Business Model Canvas Ontology, researchers and practitioners enhance the understanding of how organizations can succeed while acting responsibly and ethically in the global ecosystem.

CONCLUSION

The primary aim of this research is to construct a comprehensive framework for evaluating the performance criteria associated with digitally enabled multi-side platform business models. Based on the AHP adopted to assess the performance of leading platform business operations in Sri Lanka, this study identifies the significance and impact of the evaluation criteria listed i and its contribution to the proposed framework.

Our numerical illustration of the platform business model evaluation criteria model draws from the BMC (Osterwalder & Pigneur, 2010) and the BM- DST (Latora et al., 2018). Assessing the evaluation criteria of a platform business model's effectiveness might have substantial implications for business organizations that operate multi-sided platform business models. Gaining insight into the performance of a platform and identifying areas for improvement enables a firm to make informed decisions, effectively respond to evolving market dynamics, and ultimately attain its strategic objectives. The examination of these criteria yields several significant business insights. Overall, evaluating and applying a platform business model's success criterion would help firms to ascertain the previous performance and perform planning for the future. It helps firms make strategic decisions, optimize operations, and adapt to a fast-changing business environment. Our framework helps decision makers to take informed decisions by pre-evaluating all possible criteria and sub-criteria (ontologies) of platform business model, prior to design and implementation.

The study conducted in Sri Lanka encompassed various types of platform businesses. However, the study has not taken into consideration, the relative importance of main criteria and sub-criteria in relation to the specific type of platform business operations. For instance, it did not differentiate between brick-and-mortar businesses with an online presence and digital native online stores, or between physical products and software products.

There is potential for enhancing this study by expanding its scope to evaluate the importance of both primary and secondary criteria across various platform categories. The major limitation of the AHP based decision making process are system errors and judgment errors. System error is caused during the pair-wise comparison using a scale. The latter occurs due to wrong human judgment. Future research can consider improved MCDM methods. In addition, we see research opportunities in discussing design aspects of digital business canvas models using MCDM and design science methodologies.

This study was only conducted for platform business operators. This can be extended to obtain the viewpoint of the e-commerce buyers, sellers and delivery partners and assess whether the importance of main criteria and sub-criteria remain the same across all eco-system partners.

REFERENCES

Akter, S., Michael, K., Uddin, M. R., McCarthy, G., & Rahman, M. (2022). Transforming business using digital innovations: The application of AI, blockchain, cloud and data analytics. *Annals of Operations Research, 308*(1-2), 1–33. doi:10.1007/s10479-020-03620-w PMID:35935743

Al-Debei, M. M., & Avison, D. (2010). Developing a unified framework of the business model concept. *European Journal of Information Systems, 19*(3), 359–376. doi:10.1057/ejis.2010.21

Allweins, M. M., Proesch, M., & Ladd, T. (2021). The platform canvas—Conceptualization of a design framework for multi-sided platform businesses. *Entrepreneurship Education and Pedagogy, 4*(3), 455–477. doi:10.1177/2515127420959051

Aruldoss, M., Lakshmi, T. M., & Venkatesan, V. P. (2013). A survey on multi criteria decision making methods and its applications. *The African Journal of Information Systems, 1*(1), 31–43. doi:10.12691/ajis-1-1-5

Benayoun, R., Roy, B., & Sussman, N. (1966). Manual de reference du programme electre. *Note de synthese et Formation, 25(*79).

Bhola, P., Chronis, A. G., Kotsampopoulos, P., & Hatziargyriou, N. (2023). Business Model Selection for Community Energy Storage: A Multi Criteria Decision Making Approach. *Energies, 16*(18), 6753. doi:10.3390/en16186753

Bouwman, H., Faber, E., & Van der Spek, J. (2005). *Connecting future scenarios to business models of insurance intermediaries*. AIS. https://aisel.aisnet.org/bled2005/16

Budler, M., Župič, I., & Trkman, P. (2021). The development of business model research: A bibliometric review. *Journal of Business Research, 135*, 480-495.

Caputo, A., Pizzi, S., Pellegrini, M. M., & Dabić, M. (2021). Digitalization and business models: Where are we going? A science map of the field. *Journal of Business Research, 123*, 489–501. doi:10.1016/j.jbusres.2020.09.053

Carter, M., & Carter, C. (2020). The creative business model canvas. *Social Enterprise Journal, 16*(2), 141–158. doi:10.1108/SEJ-03-2019-0018

Cenamor, J., Sjödin, D. R., & Parida, V. (2017). Adopting a platform approach in servitization: Leveraging the value of digitalization. *International Journal of Production Economics, 192*, 54–65. doi:10.1016/j.ijpe.2016.12.033

Chesbrough, H., & Rosenbloom, R. S. (2002). The role of the business model in capturing value from innovation: Evidence from Xerox Corporation's technology spin-off companies. *Industrial and Corporate Change, 11*(3), 529–555. doi:10.1093/icc/11.3.529

Ciurea, C., & Filip, F. G. (2015). Multi-Criteria Analysis in Choosing IT&C Platforms for Creative Digital Works. *Uncommon Culture*, 20-27.

Cortimiglia, M. N., Ghezzi, A., & Frank, A. G. (2016). Business model innovation and strategy making nexus: Evidence from a cross-industry mixed-methods study. *R & D Management*, *46*(3), 414–432. doi:10.1111/radm.12113

Currie, W. L. (2004). Value creation from the application service provider e-business model: The experience of four firms. *Journal of Enterprise Information Management*, *17*(2), 117–130. doi:10.1108/17410390410518763

EisapeD. (2020). Comparing platform business models: A balanced scorecard approach based on the platform business model canvas. *Nordic Journal of Media Management, 1*(3), 401-432. doi:10.5278/njmm.2597-0445.5842

Eisenmann, T., Parker, G., & Van Alstyne, M. W. (2006). Strategies for two-sided markets. *Harvard Business Review*, *84*(10), 92. https://www.binhphuongnguyen.com/wp-content/uploads/2021/07/HBR-Strategy-for-2-side-market-Egg-and-Chicken-Dilemma-Startup.pdf

Erevelles, S., Fukawa, N., & Swayne, L. (2016). Big Data consumer analytics and the transformation of marketing. *Journal of Business Research*, *69*(2), 897–904. doi:10.1016/j.jbusres.2015.07.001

Evans, D. S., & Schmalensee, R. (2016). *Matchmakers: The new economics of multisided platforms*. Harvard Business Review Press.

Gawer, A. (2014). 'Bridging differing perspectives on technological platforms: Toward an integrative framework'. *Research Policy*, *43*(7), 1239–1249. doi:10.1016/j.respol.2014.03.006

Godina, R., Ribeiro, I., Matos, F. T., Ferreira, B., Carvalho, H., & Peças, P. (2020). Impact assessment of additive manufacturing on sustainable business models in industry 4.0 context. *Sustainability*, *12*(17), 7066. doi:10.3390/su12177066

Goodwin, P., & Wright, G. (2014). *Decision analysis for management judgment*. John Wiley & Sons.

Hagiu, A., & Wright, J. (2015). Marketplace or reseller? *Management Science*, *61*(1), 184–203. doi:10.1287/mnsc.2014.2042

Hagiu, A., & Wright, J. (2019). The status of workers and platforms in the sharing economy. *Journal of Economics & Management Strategy*, *28*(1), 97–108. doi:10.1111/jems.12299

Ho, M. H. C. (2022). Evolutionary network of business model studies and applications in emerging economies. *The Singapore Economic Review*, *67*(03), 1005–1028. doi:10.1142/S0217590820550012

Hwang, C. L., Yoon, K., Hwang, C. L., & Yoon, K. (1981). Methods for multiple attribute decision making. Multiple attribute decision making: methods and applications a state-of-the-art survey, 58-191. doi:10.1007/978-3-642-48318-9_3

Iñiguez de Onzoño, S., & Carmona, S. (2007). The changing business model of B-schools. *Journal of Management Development*, *26*(1), 22–32. doi:10.1108/02621710710720059

Kalling, T. (2003). The business model concept: Theoretical underpinnings and empirical illustrations. *European Journal of Information Systems*, *12*(1), 49–59. doi:10.1057/palgrave.ejis.3000446

Kumar, A., Sah, B., Singh, A. R., Deng, Y., He, X., Kumar, P., & Bansal, R. C. (2017). A review of multi criteria decision making (MCDM) towards sustainable renewable energy development. *Renewable & Sustainable Energy Reviews*, *69*, 596–609. doi:10.1016/j.rser.2016.11.191

Latora, A. G., Compagno, L., & Trapani, N. (2018). A decision support tool for business model analysis. International. *Journal of the Analytic Hierarchy Process*, *10*(2). doi:10.13033/ijahp.v10i2.516

Majumder, M., & Majumder, M. (2015*). Multi criteria decision making. Impact of urbanization on water shortage in face of climatic aberrations*, 35-47. doi:10.1007/978-981-4560-73-3_2

McCarthy, B. (2008). Case study of an artists' retreat in Ireland: An exploration of its business model. *Social Enterprise Journal*, *4*(2), 136–148. doi:10.1108/17508610810902020

Melkonyan, A., & Gottschalk, D., & VP, V. K. (. (2017). Sustainability assessments and their implementation possibilities within the business models of companies. *Sustainable Production and Consumption*, *12*, 1–15. doi:10.1016/j.spc.2017.04.001

Methlie, L. B., & Pedersen, P. E. (2007). Business model choices for value creation of mobile services. *info*, *9*(5), 70-85. doi:10.1108/14636690710816462

Miethlich, B., Belotserkovich, D., Abasova, S., Zatsarinnaya, E., & Veselitsky, O. (2020). Digital economy and its influence on competitiveness of countries and regions. *Revista espacios, 41*(12). http://ww.revistaespacios.com/a20v41n12/20411220.html

Mini, T., & Widjaja, T. (2019). *Tensions in Digital Platform Business Models: A Literature Review*. ICIS.

Nosratabadi, S., Pinter, G., Mosavi, A., & Semperger, S. (2020). Sustainable banking; evaluation of the European business models. *Sustainability (Basel)*, *12*(6), 2314. doi:10.3390/su12062314

Oláh, J., Popp, J., Khan, M. A., & Kitukutha, N. (2023). Sustainable E-Commerce and Environmental Impact on Sustainability. *Economics & Sociology (Ternopil)*, *16*(1), 85–105. doi:10.14254/2071-789X.2023/16-1/6

Osiyevskyy, O., & Dewald, J. (2015). Explorative versus exploitative business model change: The cognitive antecedents of firm-level responses to disruptive innovation. *Strategic Entrepreneurship Journal*, *9*(1), 58–78. doi:10.1002/sej.1192

Osterwalder, A., & Pigneur, Y. (2002). *An eBusiness model ontology for modeling eBusiness*. AIS. https://aisel.aisnet.org/bled2002/2

Osterwalder, A., Pigneur, Y., & Tucci, C. L. (2005). Clarifying business models: Origins, present, and future of the concept. *Communications of the Association for Information Systems*, *16*(1), 1. doi:10.17705/1CAIS.01601

Parker, G. G., Van Alstyne, M. W., & Choudary, S. P. (2016). *Platform Revolution: How Networked Markets Are Transforming the Economy—And How to Make Them Work for You*. W. W. Norton & Company.https://www.injaplus.ir/wp-content/uploads/2023/05/Platform_Revolution_Previewinjaplus.ir_.pdf

Porter, M. E., & Heppelmann, J. E. (2015). How smart, connected products are transforming companies. *Harvard Business Review, 93(*10), 96-114. http://www.knowledgesol.com/uploads/2/4/3/9/24393270/hbr-how-smart-connected-products-are-transforming-companies.pdf

Pousttchi, K., Schiessler, M., & Wiedemann, D. G. (2007, July). Analyzing the elements of the business model for mobile payment service provision. In *International Conference on the Management of Mobile Business (ICMB 2007)* (pp. 44-44). IEEE. DOI: 10.1109/ICMB.2007.16

Rochet, J. C., & Tirole, J. (2003). Platform competition in two-sided markets. *Journal of the European Economic Association, 1*(4), 990–1029. doi:10.1162/154247603322493212

Rohn, D., Bican, P. M., Brem, A., Kraus, S., & Clauss, T. (2021). Digital platform-based business models–An exploration of critical success factors. *Journal of Engineering and Technology Management, 60*, 101625. doi:10.1016/j.jengtecman.2021.101625

Saaty, T. L. (1995). Transport planning with multiple criteria: The analytic hierarchy process applications and progress review. *Journal of Advanced Transportation, 29*(1), 81–126. doi:10.1002/atr.5670290109

Salomon, M. F. B., Mello, C. H. P., & Salgado, E. G. (2019). Prioritization of product-service business model elements at aerospace industry using analytical hierarchy process. *Acta Scientiarum. Technology, 41*(1), e37934. doi:10.4025/actascitechnol.v41i1.37934

Smedlund, A. (2012). Value cocreation in service platform business models. *Service Science, 4*(1), 79–88. doi:10.1287/serv.1110.0001

Sorri, K., Seppänen, M., Still, K., & Valkokari, K. (2019). Business model innovation with platform canvas. *Journal of Business Models, 7*(2), 1–13. https://cris.vtt.fi/ws/portalfiles/portal/26015079/JOBM_2019_Sorri_et_al_business_model_innovation_with_platform_canvas.pdf

Süß, A., Höse, K., & Götze, U. (2021). Sustainability-oriented business model evaluation—a literature review. *Sustainability, 13*(19), 10908. https://doi.org/ 131910908 doi:10.3390/su

Taherdoost, H., & Madanchian, M. (2023). Multi-criteria decision making (MCDM) methods and concepts. *Encyclopedia, 3*(1), 77–87. doi:10.3390/encyclopedia3010006

Tarhan, A., Turetken, O., & Reijers, H. A. (2016). Business process maturity models: A systematic literature review. *Information and Software Technology, 75*, 122–134. doi:10.1016/j.infsof.2016.01.010

Timmers, P. (1998). Business models for electronic markets. *Electronic Markets, 8*(2), 3–8. doi:10.1080/10196789800000016

Uludag, O., Hefele, S., & Matthes, F. (2016). Platform and ecosystem governance. *Digital Mobility Platforms and State of the Art Report*, 1-24.

Urbinati, A., Chiaroni, D., & Chiesa, V. (2017). Towards a New Taxonomy of Circular Economy Business Models. *Journal of Cleaner Production, 168*, 487–498. doi:10.1016/j.jclepro.2017.09.047

Van Looy, A., De Backer, M., Poels, G., & Snoeck, M. (2013). Choosing the right business process maturity model. *Information & Management, 50*(7), 466–488. doi:10.1016/j.im.2013.06.002

Vijayvargiya, A., & Dey, A. K. (2010). An analytical approach for selection of a logistics provider. *Management Decision*, *48*(3), 403–418. doi:10.1108/00251741011037774

Warner, K. S., & Wäger, M. (2019). Building dynamic capabilities for digital transformation: An ongoing process of strategic renewal. *Long Range Planning*, *52*(3), 326–349. doi:10.1016/j.lrp.2018.12.001

Zavadskas, E. K., Turskis, Z., & Kildienė, S. (2014). State of art surveys of overviews on MCDM/MADM methods. *Technological and Economic Development of Economy*, *20*(1), 165–179. doi:10.3846/20294913.2014.892037

Zhao, Y., Von Delft, S., Morgan-Thomas, A., & Buck, T. (2020). The evolution of platform business models: Exploring competitive battles in the world of platforms. *Long Range Planning*, *53*(4), 101892. doi:10.1016/j.lrp.2019.101892

Zhu, F., Li, K. J., & Liu, H. (2016). Incentive alignment and resource allocation in innovation platforms: Evidence from the IT service market. *Management Science*, *62*(4), 1040–1059.

Zott, C., & Amit, R. (2007). Business model design and the performance of entrepreneurial firms. *Organization Science*, *18*(2), 181–199. doi:10.1287/orsc.1060.0232

Chapter 7
How Do Digital Transformation and Environmental Sustainability Innovations Intertwine?
Environmental Sustainability Innovations

Korhan Arun
https://orcid.org/0000-0001-7494-9591
Tekirdag Namik Kemal University, Turkey

Saniye Yildirim Özmutlu
Tekirdag Namik Kemal University, Turkey

ABSTRACT

By integrating digital technologies and sustainable practices, organizations can enhance their environmental performance, contribute to environmental sustainability, and create innovative solutions to address environmental challenges. Thus, the main aim of this chapter is to shed light on the effects of digital transformation on environmental sustainability innovations. The data were collected from the 1st, 2nd, and 3rd Party Logistics (PL) companies registered with the International Transporters Association (UND) in Turkey. Data were collected from mid-level managers of these companies by administering a questionnaire. Relationships have been analyzed with the help of partial least squared-based structural equation modeling, correlations, and path analysis. The investigation results have found that logistics firms' high level of digital transformation is the strongest predictor of adopting sustainability innovations. This study provides a valuable contribution to the emerging fields of supply chain sustainability and the digitalization of environmental sustainability innovations.

DOI: 10.4018/979-8-3693-0798-4.ch007

INTRODUCTION

The relationship between environmental sustainability innovations in corporate organizations and digital transformation has garnered increasing attention in recent years. Digital transformation has improved logistics operations responsiveness, efficiency, and transparency by integrating cutting-edge technologies and data-driven solutions (Gritsenko et al., 2022). Additionally, it has been determined that digital technologies in sustainable logistics are a critical facilitator for developing environmentally friendly and sustainable logistics systems that comply with sustainability imperatives (Sun et al., 2022). However, broader sustainability objectives and outcomes of the convergence of digital transformation and environmental sustainability innovations in the logistics sector are still uncertain (Feroz et al., 2021). It is this challenge that forms the motivation for our chapter.

Sustainability innovations have the potential to impact environmental sustainability significantly (Truong, 2022). They can support long-term environmental goals, advocate for beneficial improvements in business procedures, and promote the use of sustainable solutions. However, the effective application of sustainability innovations requires a supportive corporate climate, a collaborative work environment, and an emphasis on instrumental and symbolic attributes.

"Digital transformation" describes how digital technology is used and integrated into corporate settings and strategies to promote innovation, increase output, and change various organizational procedures, practices, and business models (Nadeem et al., 2018). Digital transformation entails injecting technology to improve organizational capabilities and create value in the virtual world and web, such as cloud computing, artificial intelligence, big data analytics, and the Internet of Things (IoT) (Wujarso, 2023). Thus, digital transformation has a big impact on business models, processes, interactions, and how organizations handle the environment. To keep up with this, organizations must engage their workforce and encourage a culture of creativity. It also poses obstacles, though, which must be removed for implementation to be successful.

The literature emphasizes the importance of digital transformation and environmental options in driving environmental sustainability and performance (Feroz et al., 2021; Kamal et al., 2017; Melnyk et al., 2002). Further research is needed to explore the relationship between digital transformation and environmental sustainability in the context of organizational level and other environmental options.

Environmental sustainability and digital transformation advances significantly impact the logistics industry and provide many benefits. A key factor driving change in the logistics sector is using digital technologies to increase and improve environmentally sustainable practices. Logistics or supply chain operations can be made more efficient and sustainable through the use of Industry 4.0 or newer technologies, cloud computing, artificial intelligence and digitization—a process known as digital transformation (Feroz et al., 2021; Sun et al., 2022; Zondervan et al., 2022). Moreover, entrepreneurship and adopting digital business models have been linked to achieving the United Nations Sustainable Development Goals, emphasizing the potential of digitalization to further sustainability objectives (Bican & Brem, 2020). Businesses in a variety of industries, including logistics, have realized the potential of digital technologies as a tool for improving social, economic, and environmental sustainability (Bednarčíková & Repiská, 2021). Moreover, the concept of Logistics 4.0, underpinned by digital transformation, has been identified as a critical enabler for establishing future-proof and sustainable logistics systems, aligning with sustainability imperatives (Lin & Ho, 2009).

There has indeed been much innovation in the Turkish logistics industry, especially in sustainability and technology adoption. The logistics sector in Turkey has seen a significant transformation thanks to the incorporation of sustainable practices and technical improvements (Wang et al., 2022). Multiple decoupling points in supply chains have emerged as a result of the use of environmental sustainability-focused technologies in logistics operations, demonstrating the revolutionary influence of sustainability initiatives in the Turkish logistics sector (Denktaş Şakar et al., 2018; Kabadurmuş, 2019; Korucuk et al., 2023). Decoupling points are well-located locations in the supply chain where material flow is split into several streams, allowing for distinctive strategies appropriate for certain customer demands and market circumstances. By positioning many decoupling points in various locations, the supply chain can be segmented into customer-driven and forecast-driven sectors according to the customer's demands (Olhager, 2010; Shahin et al., 2016). This separation increases the flexibility and responsiveness of the supply chain overall by making it simpler to use lean approaches in forecast-driven segments and agile methods in customer-driven sectors (Faur & Bungau, 2019; Mason-Jones & Towill, 1999).

In conclusion, integrating digital technologies and sustainable practices characterizes the relationship between environmental sustainability innovations and digitalization in the logistics sector. Sustainable supply chain management and the potential of digital transformation play important roles in driving environmental sustainability outcomes. By embracing digitalization and integrating environmental sustainability innovations, organizations can enhance their environmental performance, contribute to environmental sustainability, and create innovative solutions to address environmental challenges. Furthermore, logistics businesses have been urged to proactively contribute to sustainability transformation within the framework of alternative sustainable supply chains, emphasizing the role of logistics in fostering a green economy (Gruchmann et al., 2018).

This chapter has four original components. Firstly, researching the effects of digital transformation on environmental sustainability innovations is an essential and new research area. Secondly, the digital transformation and sustainability innovation scales are operationalized as second-order constructs. That approach allowed us to investigate the variables from a holistic perspective. Thirdly, sustainability has become important in the logistics sector; our chapter is the first to explore the relationship between these two variables. Fourthly, even if more research is required regarding the Turkish logistics sector, environmental sustainability innovations and digital transformation variables are first mentioned in the Turkish logistics sector (Yildiz & Tabak, 2019).

LITERATURE REVIEW

Importance of Environmental Sustainability in the Logistics Sector

Logistics and supply chains are closely related concepts but not synonymous. Logistics refers to managing the flow of goods, information, and resources between the point of origin and the point of consumption. In contrast, supply chain management encompasses a broader perspective that includes coordinating and integrating various activities and stakeholders in delivering products or services to customers (Lambert et al., 1998). Logistics and supply chains are closely related, and effective logistics management is essential for successfully implementing supply chain management practices. Thus, the supply chain encompasses logistics activities. However, in this chapter, both concepts are used interchangeably.

Globalization directly affects the logistics industry's rising emphasis on environmental sustainability. The logistics industry is vital to world trade and business, but it also significantly impacts the environment through its activities. These impacts include trash production, resource depletion, noise pollution, and carbon emissions (Jayarathna et al., 2023; Seroka-Stolka et al., 2015). Consequently, environmental sustainability is of paramount importance in the logistics sector. To ensure environmental sustainability, sustainable supply chain management practices and the adoption of green logistics principles are crucial (Martínez-Jurado & Moyano Fuentes, 2014).

Carter and Rogers (2008) introduce the concept of sustainability to the field of supply chain management and demonstrate the relationships among environmental, social, and economic performance within a supply chain management context. The notion of sustainability is treated more theoretically in their framework of sustainable supply chain management, which advances the theory of supply chain management.

A study by Pagell and Wu (2009) examined ten exemplar firms to build a model of the elements necessary to create a sustainable supply chain. The study highlights the necessity of looking at the supply chain as a whole and specifically taking its operations' social and environmental effects into account. This strategy emphasizes how crucial it is to incorporate environmental sustainability practices up the supply chain to meet sustainability objectives.

When analyzing the significance of environmental sustainability in the logistics sector, another area of focus is green logistics, particularly in the textile industry. While green logistics is a specific set of practices within the logistics domain and supply chain operations, environmental sustainability extends beyond logistics operations to encompass a broader perspective on the responsible use of resources and the preservation of the natural environment. Green logistics contributes to environmental sustainability by reducing the environmental impact of logistics operations, promoting the use of green energy resources, and implementing environmentally friendly practices (Ceniga & Sukalova, 2020; Evangelista et al., 2018; Horani, 2023; Nur et al., 2018). A recent study explored the advantages, challenges, and best practices of green logistics for the chemical sector. It underscores the need for environmentally friendly techniques for handling, storing, and transporting chemical products to lessen their detrimental impacts (Vivek et al., 2023). To achieve environmental sustainability, the chemical industry must use green logistics strategies, like optimizing shipping routes, reducing emissions, and implementing waste management programs.

Digital Transformation in Logistics Organizations

Numerous facets and contexts of business enterprises are significantly impacted by digital transformation. Moreover, digital transformation impacts new business models, business procedures, and how businesses collaborate and compete between organizations (Härting et al., 2020). Organizations can optimize their operations beyond their rivals by using digital technologies, improving customer experiences, and developing more successful business models (Wujarso, 2023). Furthermore, thanks to digital transformation, organizations can increase operational efficiency, make more informed decisions, and allocate resources more wisely. Additionally, digital transformation helps businesses strategically reinvent themselves by enabling them to adjust to shifting customer expectations, market situations, and legal forces (Wang et al., 2022).

Digitization within the framework of outstanding, sustainable development depends on the logistics industry. It enables logistics firms to employ environmentally friendly practices, reduce their environmental footprint, and make the most use of their resources while minimizing waste. Examples of digital technologies that can be used to evaluate environmental performance, examine carbon emissions, and promote sustainable logistics and transportation methods are IoT sensors, data analytics, automation, and artificial intelligence (Luo & Wang, 2023). Consequently, it has been noted that digital transformation plays a significant role in improving the performance of logistics service providers (LSPs) on environmental issues, with digitalization acting as a method of achieving improved service delivery, differentiation, and competitive advantages (Taufani & Widjaja, 2022). Additionally, digitization makes it easier for logistics companies to comply with regulations and accomplish sustainability goals by integrating green practices across the supply chain (Luo & Wang, 2023).

Digital transformation is required to improve supply chain management practices. Logistics organizations can make better decisions by using digital and data analytics, optimizing workflows, and boosting visibility. Digitizing procedures enable logistics firms to streamline operations, reduce costs, and boost efficiency (Chen & Paulraj, 2004). Digitalization also facilitates collaboration and information sharing among supply chain partners, improving coordination and responsiveness.

Examining how the shift to digital media impacts operational effectiveness is another crucial area of research. Digital technologies can significantly boost output, streamline operations, and enhance workflows. Organizations adopting digital transformation can increase productivity, reduce costs, and simplify operations (Wujarso, 2023).

The digital transformation has numerous and substantial implications on the organizations, especially those operating in logistics. Digital breakthroughs and technologies have transformed logistics operations, improving customer satisfaction, visibility, and efficiency by reducing carbon footprint. The literature covered in this chapter provides information on digital transformation and environmental practices in logistics, such as supply chain management, the impact of technological assimilation, and the function of digital technologies in the logistics industry.

Additionally, the digital revolution has facilitated the creation of innovative logistical services and models. Integrating digital technologies such as artificial intelligence and machine learning has enabled the automation of some logistical activities, such as last-mile delivery, warehouse management, and route optimization. Delivery has become more accurate and timely, and as a result, transportation costs have gone down, and customer satisfaction has gone up (Zhu et al., 2006).

Moreover, the logistics industry may adopt sustainable practices thanks to the digital revolution (Song et al., 2022). Digital technology has simplified the process of optimizing transportation routes, leading to a reduction in fuel consumption and greenhouse gas emissions. Digital platforms and technology have enabled the sharing economy and collaborative logistics models while also decreasing waste and increasing resource efficiency (Sanders et al., 2019; Zhu et al., 2006). For example, Minh et al. (Nguyen et al., 2023)found that green supply chain management techniques favor environmental performance when paired with digital transformation and a green digital learning approach. Furthermore, in the era of Industry 4.0, the digital transformation of supply chains is essential to the long-term sustainability of businesses (Bag et al., 2018; Pyun & Rha, 2021).

Digital change is not without its challenges. Organizations may need assistance managing organizational change, integrating digital technology into current systems and procedures, and preparing for technological advancements (Kutnjak, 2021). The intricacy of the transformation process may result in several difficulties and issues that must be resolved (Kutnjak, 2021). Concerns regarding security, data privacy, and the moral use of digital technology might also exist. Organizations must handle privacy, data security, and ethical technology use. Furthermore, for the workforce to adjust to the rapidly evolving technology world, they may need to retrain and upskill (Zhu et al., 2006).

Digital transformation or digitalization is of paramount importance for logistics firms. It optimizes supply chain management practices, facilitates green and high-quality development, and enhances green performance. By embracing digital technologies and leveraging data-driven insights, logistics firms can improve efficiency, reduce environmental impact, and achieve sustainable and competitive advantages in the industry.

Digital Transformation and Sustainability Innovations in the Turkish Logistics Sector

Since transportation, warehousing, and inventory management activities account for a growing percentage of Turkey's GDP, logistics is becoming increasingly important (Balkan & Akyuz, 2023; Gökalp, 2014). As a result, the Turkish logistics industry has been significantly changing due to technical improvements and digital transformation.

Turkey's logistics sector has concentrated on sustainable practices and green supply chain management. Scholarly investigations have delved into the effects of environmentally conscious logistics on global trade, presenting data from developed and developing nations and underscoring the worldwide significance of sustainable logistics methodologies (Bulgurcu & Nakiboglu, 2018). Research has investigated the relationships between financial performance, environmental reputation, and sustainable logistics practices (Bacak & Aydin, 2018). The findings indicate that sustainable logistics practices substantially impact the Turkish logistics sector's financial performance and environmental reputation.

HYPOTHESIS DEVELOPMENT

Environmental Sustainability and Innovation Relationship

The relationship between creativity and environmental sustainability is a significant area of research. The sources listed below provide information on several aspects of this relationship, including how creativity works in corporate environments, the relationship between sustainability and creativity, and the impact of environmental commitment on green creativity.

Silveira et al. (2022) emphasized the necessity of putting creativity as a resource at the core of sustainability by highlighting the intimate connection between sustainability and creativity. They contend that innovation is a key component of sustainable growth.

Awan et al. (2019) examine how creativity supports sustainable development, particularly how creativity fosters green innovation. They contend that supplier engagement acts as a boundary condition for the positive impact of creativity on green innovation, highlighting the importance of partnerships and collaboration in fostering creative and sustainable solutions.

Song et al. (2023) studied the relationship between corporate environmental ethics, environmental commitment, and radical green creativity. They contend that environmental commitment is a conduit between business environmental ethics and radical green creativity, arguing that a strong dedication to environmental principles can foster innovative thinking and advancements in sustainability.

Digital Transformation Impacts on Environmental Sustainability Innovations

Big data and digitalization are significant sources of information that highlight the implementation of sustainability in the logistics sector (Ashby et al., 2012; Kamble et al., 2023). Digital transformation and the intensity of digitalization affect the relationship between supply chain effectiveness and environmental sustainability (Chauhan et al., 2022).

The short-term output of digital transformation focuses on measurable increases in new digital services (Joyce & Paquin, 2016). However, long-term effects and results center on raising citizen happiness and effectiveness (Mergel et al., 2019). However, rather than focusing on long-term sustainability objectives, the literature has typically examined the economic advantages of supply networks. On the other hand, these objectives are the foundation of sustainable supply chain causation (Tseng et al., 2021).

The effects of digital transformation on environmental sustainability are multifaceted and can have both positive and negative impacts.

The positive impacts include:

1. Resource Efficiency: Organizations may minimize waste and optimize resource utilization with the help of digital transformation. For instance, waste, water, and energy management systems may be monitored and improved using IoT sensors and data analytics (Feroz et al., 2021). Significant reductions in resource use and environmental effects may result from this.
2. Sustainable Supply Chains: Digital technologies can improve the traceability and transparency of the supply chain, allowing businesses to recognize and resolve sustainability-related problems through the chain. For example, supply chain reconfiguration and new practices based on blockchain technology might encourage ethical sourcing and lower environmental hazards (Feroz et al., 2021; Holmström et al., 2017).
3. Remote Work and Telecommuting: The COVID-19 pandemic has accelerated the adoption of remote work and telecommuting, both of which have positive environmental effects. By decreasing the need for commuting, digital transformation can minimize air pollution and greenhouse gas emissions (Feroz et al., 2021).
4. Environmental Monitoring and Conservation: Real-time environmental condition monitoring and conservation activities can be facilitated by digital technologies. For example, deforestation, biodiversity loss, and the consequences of climate change can be tracked using data analytics and remote sensing technology, enabling quick reactions and informed decision-making (Feroz et al., 2021).

However, there are some negative effects of digital transformation on environmental sustainability innovations (Bednarčíková & Repiská, 2021). These negative effects include:

1. E-waste and Energy Consumption reduction: Electronic garbage (e-waste) production and energy consumption may rise with the widespread use of digital devices and technology. Production, use, and disposal of electronic devices can have a substantial negative influence on the environment, resulting in pollution, resource depletion, and greenhouse gas emissions in the total carbon footprint of the logistics operations and organizations (Kunkel & Matthess, 2020).
2. Digital Divide: Inequalities in social and environmental outcomes may worsen due to unequal access to digital technology and the internet. The digital gap may limit the benefits of digital transformation for environmental sustainability since underprivileged populations may not have access to the infrastructure and resources that are needed (Bednarčíková & Repiská, 2021).
3. Data Privacy and Security: Security and privacy issues are brought up by digital transformation's massive data collection and processing. Given that data breaches may impact the environment,

organizations must make sure that the necessary safeguards are in place to protect sensitive and personal information (e.g., through unauthorized access to energy consumption data) (Feroz et al., 2021).

Overall, the effects of digital transformation on environmental sustainability are complex and context-dependent. While digital technologies offer opportunities for improving resource efficiency, supply chain sustainability, and environmental monitoring, they also pose challenges regarding e-waste, energy consumption, and digital inequalities. To maximize the positive impacts and mitigate the negative effects, organizations need to adopt a holistic and responsible approach to digital transformation, considering environmental sustainability as a key objective and integrating it into their strategies, operations, and decision-making processes.

Effects of Digital Transformation on Environmental Sustainability Innovations

The major aim of Turkish environmental politics mentioned in the Environmental Law is "taking precautions before the pollution as a modern approach, instead of treatment after pollution" (Coşkun & Turker, 2011). At the organizational level, firms must adopt new technologies to innovate and comply with these laws by devising strategies that embrace environmental sustainability and drive better operational performance (Vial, 2019). As "digital" forms the deep technological factors, digital transformations are the basis of innovations. Integrating digital technologies and sustainability innovations can lead to several positive effects on environmental sustainability. These effects include improved resource efficiency, enhanced environmental monitoring and reporting, adopting circular economy practices, and promoting sustainable supply chains in digital environments (Bican & Brem, 2020).

Logistics companies maintain their competitive position by routinely assessing environmental issues and technology. By employing these intangible assets, businesses can steer clear of expensive and disruptive instances of government intervention in the form of mandatory compliance. They are also favorably inclined to be innovation-driven from outside the company and successfully utilize the creative potential found within it (Achillas, 2019). On the other hand, Camodeca and Almici (2021) highlighted the conflicting consequences of digital transformation and noted that the literature is ambiguous about the beneficial relationship between digitalization and sustainability. Concerns over potential sustainability issues related to digitization were also expressed by recent research, especially concerning social and environmental well-being, due to the automation of information processing and service delivery (Camodeca & Almici, 2021; Linkov et al., 2018).

While the research cited above highlights how digital transformation might improve environmental sustainability, other studies also cited express apprehensions about possible drawbacks and contentious outcomes. Nevertheless, sustainable entrepreneurship, sustainability innovation, and the potential of digital transformation all play important roles in driving environmental sustainability outcomes. By embracing digital transformation and integrating sustainability principles, organizations can enhance their environmental performance, contribute to environmental sustainability, and create innovative solutions to address environmental challenges.

In light of the literature, we hypothesize that digital transformations positively affect environmental sustainability innovations.

H1: Digital transformations increase environmental sustainability innovations in organizations.

METHODOLOGY

Environmental sustainability innovation measures (ESI) are adapted from Tiwari and Thakur's (2021) work for the hospitality sector. The scale of environmental sustainability innovations consists of four dimensions and twenty-four questions. The original environmental sustainability innovation measure combined eight subscales: "*sustainability management, food waste and purchase management, environmental communication and pollution, resource and energy conservation, transportation energy conservation, water recycling, wastewater management, and guestroom sustainability*." We excluded guestroom sustainability and adapted some questions for the logistics sector.

The digital transformation scale developed by Kontić and Vidicki (2018) consists of ten dimensions and thirty-two questions. The scale of digital transformation consists of a digital mindset, digitized applications, data-driven decisions, empowered capabilities, and data access - collaboration tools. We adapted some of the questions on this scale for the logistics industry. In this context, a research model was created considering ESI and digital transformation structures. The created research model is shown in Fig. 1.

Figure 1. Path analysis with structural equation model

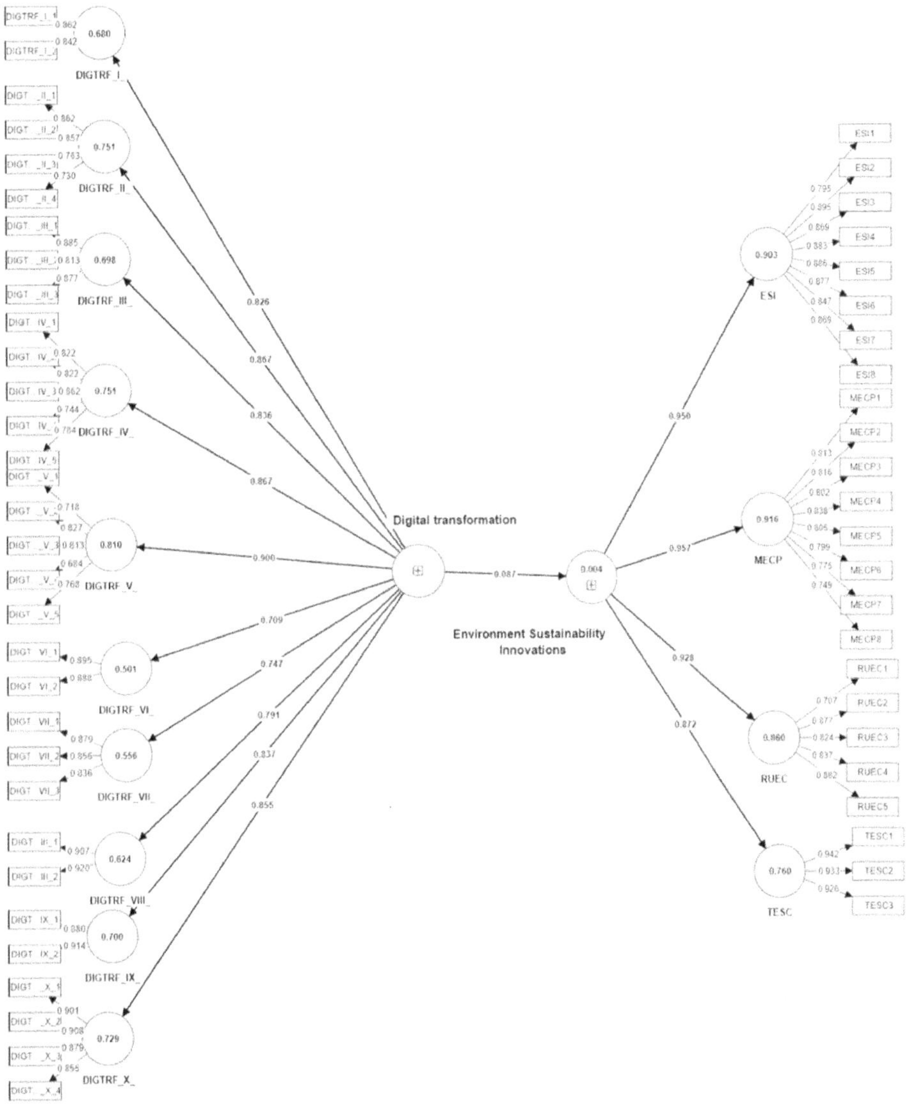

Sample

The research population consists of 1st, 2nd, and 3rd party logistics companies registered with the International Transporters Association (UND) in Turkey and continue their activities in the Thrace Region. The research population also forms the study sample. Are 310 companies registered with this association and continuing their activities in the Thrace region (https://www.und.org.tr/users). Managers were reached through communication channels (phone or e-mail) on these companies' websites. A total of 297 companies' mid-level managers were contacted, and a questionnaire form was sent. A participation rate of 63% was achieved, with 189 managers who filled out the questionnaire completely and provided feedback. The research questionnaire included 4 questions, seeking information about companies and managers and answers to Likert-type problems.

The term "first-party logistics" (1PL) describes businesses that manage logistical processes, such as distribution, warehousing, and transportation. They oversee the flow of commodities from the point of origin to the point of consumption and have direct control over their supply chain operations. Transportation providers are usually second-party logistics (2PL) companies, which include shipping lines, airplanes, and freight carriers. The shipper or sender hires them to move items from one place to another. By serving as a middleman between the shipper and the recipient, 2PL companies enable the actual transportation of goods. Businesses can outsource their logistical needs to third-party logistics (3PL) companies. Transportation, warehousing, inventory control, order fulfillment, and other value-added services are among the many services they provide. 3PL companies manage and coordinate the logistics operations for their clients by operating as a middleman between the shipper and other service providers.

The nature of the interaction between various logistics companies can change based on the particular agreements and contracts. For some transit requirements, first-party logistics companies may work with second-party logistics companies. On the other hand, businesses can hire outside logistics providers to manage all or just some of their logistical needs. Partnerships and cooperation between these logistics companies can result in lower costs, higher supply chain efficiency, and better service quality (Moore, 1998). Overall, the relationship between first, second, and third-party logistics firms is characterized by collaboration, specialization, and sharing of resources and expertise. These relationships contribute to the efficient and effective management of logistics operations within the supply chain. Thus, these three-party logistics companies were chosen for the research.

Logistics companies develop sustainable services that provide a high level of digital transformation that responds quickly to market changes. Thus, logistics companies within the service sector make important contributions to the Turkish economy. In addition to providing economic benefits by increasing their efficiency thanks to their digital transformation systems, these companies also provide significant environmental benefits by reducing their energy consumption and emissions. Turkey's 1st, 2nd, and 3rd PL companies have a high technological level that accelerates commercial activity. By establishing digital solid systems, these companies can gain efficiency, productivity, and environmentally sustainable advantages in their business processes. One of the main reasons for choosing these companies is that they can proactively see problems and take measures before problems arise, with digital operations and instant customer solutions. In this way, they try to create environmentally sustainable innovations. These companies can quickly perceive the needs of their customers, organize their supply chain through different channels, and develop solutions against sudden changes or demand increases. They can configure a flexible logistics network system thanks to their digital systems. If digital systems are used, logistics companies can turn their supply chain into a competitive advantage, and with this advantage, they can develop new digital business models (De Andres Gonzalez et al., 2021). With the use of digital technologies in their business processes, logistics companies can gain benefits such as optimization of resource use, low cost, increased productivity of employees, increased business efficiency, optimization of supply chains, increased customer satisfaction, and increased customer loyalty (Rachinger et al., 2019). As a result, digital transformation is studied in 1st, 2nd, and 3rd PL firms.

Descriptive Statistics and Other Analysis

The descriptive information of the companies and company managers within the scope of the research was examined. In addition, descriptive statistics, correlation between variables, reliability analysis, and data quality assessment were made (see Table 1).

Examining the gender of 189 mid-level managers, it was determined that 73% of them were male. When the ages of all managers were examined, it was seen that they were between 30 and 39 (54%). When the ages of the companies were examined, it was seen that they were between the ages of 11 and 20 (41%). In addition, when the operating structures of the companies were examined, it was determined that the majority (61%) were international companies.

Table 1 (a). Descriptive statistics, correlation between variables, and data quality assessment

7	8	9	10	11	12	13	14	15	16
0.620	0.691	0.868	0.802	0.932	0.078	0.085	0.091	0.084	0.072
0.633	0.682	0.908	0.768	0.972	0.092	0.087	0.094	0.081	0.045
0.657	0.623	0.878	0.776	0.947	0.105	0.106	0.110	0.113	0.062
0.782	0.730	0.851	0.963	0.968	0.124	0.132	0.127	0.153	0.098
0.734	0.716	0.976	0.906	1.060	0.100	0.104	0.093	0.094	0.124
0.912	0.810	0.822	0.719	0.897	0.164	0.144	0.121	0.157	0.090
0.857	0.905	0.794	0.600	0.839	0.101	0.098	0.084	0.099	0.093
0.708	**0.892**	0.896	0.578	0.845	0.151	0.110	0.096	0.078	0.056
0.653	0.698	**0.764**	0.851	1.012	0.117	0.099	0.090	0.086	0.069
0.526	0.477	0.740	**0.886**	0.903	0.127	0.138	0.131	0.159	0.114
0.747	0.709	0.900	0.855	**0.702**	0.125	0.120	0.114	0.121	0.087
0.080	0.125	0.085	0.116	0.107	**0.865**	0.987	0.945	0.873	0.812
0.057	0.077	0.042	0.123	0.087	0.952	**0.792**	1.014	1.000	0.912
0.019	0.044	0.022	0.107	0.072	0.884	0.958	**0.800**	0.960	0.820
0.058	0.040	0.009	0.140	0.080	0.801	0.926	0.863	**0.828**	0.942
0.052	0.046	0.006	0.099	0.042	0.764	0.869	0.758	0.859	**0.934**

Correlation The square root of AVE Heterotrait–monotrait ratio
M: Mean, SD: Standard Deviation, CA: Cronbach's Alpha, CR: Composite Reliability, AVE: Average Variance Extracted

Table 1 (b). Descriptive statistics, correlation between variables, and data quality assessment

6	7	8	9	10	11	12	13	14	15	16
0.668	0.620	0.691	0.868	0.802	0.932	0.078	0.085	0.091	0.084	0.072
0.715	0.633	0.682	0.908	0.768	0.972	0.092	0.087	0.094	0.081	0.045
0.784	0.657	0.623	0.878	0.776	0.947	0.105	0.106	0.110	0.113	0.062
0.816	0.782	0.730	0.851	0.963	0.968	0.124	0.132	0.127	0.153	0.098
0.881	0.734	0.716	0.976	0.906	1.060	0.100	0.104	0.093	0.094	0.124
0.914	0.912	0.810	0.822	0.719	0.897	0.164	0.144	0.121	0.157	0.090
0.744	**0.857**	0.905	0.794	0.600	0.839	0.101	0.098	0.084	0.099	0.093
0.624	0.708	**0.892**	0.896	0.578	0.845	0.151	0.110	0.096	0.078	0.056
0.669	0.653	0.698	**0.764**	0.851	1.012	0.117	0.099	0.090	0.086	0.069
0.617	0.526	0.477	0.740	**0.886**	0.903	0.127	0.138	0.131	0.159	0.114
0.791	0.747	0.709	0.900	0.855	**0.702**	0.125	0.120	0.114	0.121	0.087
0.145	0.080	0.125	0.085	0.116	0.107	**0.865**	0.987	0.945	0.873	0.812
0.127	0.057	0.077	0.042	0.123	0.087	0.952	**0.792**	1.014	1.000	0.912
0.103	0.019	0.044	0.022	0.107	0.072	0.884	0.958	**0.800**	0.960	0.820
0.131	0.058	0.040	0.009	0.140	0.080	0.801	0.926	0.863	**0.828**	0.942
0.074	0.052	0.046	0.006	0.099	0.042	0.764	0.869	0.758	0.859	**0.934**

Correlation The square root of AVE Heterotrait–monotrait ratio
M: Mean, SD: Standard Deviation, CA: Cronbach's Alpha, CR: Composite Reliability, AVE: Average Variance Extracted

Applying Structural equation modeling (SEM) in the analysis of the logistics sector offers advantages in capturing complex relationships, assessing mediating effects, and integrating observed and latent variables, thereby providing a robust framework for understanding and improving logistics performance. Furthermore, SEM allows for integrating observed and latent variables, providing a comprehensive understanding of the logistics landscape.

Structural Equation Modeling (SEM) offers several advantages in analyzing the logistics sector. Firstly, SEM allows for examining complex relationships between multiple variables, making it suitable for studying the intricate interplay between various factors influencing logistics performance (Yeo & Deng, 2020). This is particularly relevant in the context of logistics, where numerous interconnected elements such as trade facilitation, digitalization processes, infrastructure, and green logistics applications can impact overall performance (Ismayil & Karagulle, 2023; Munim & Schramm, 2018; Yeo et al., 2020). SEM's ability to incorporate latent constructs and measurement error makes it well-suited for capturing the underlying constructs in logistics, such as infrastructure, trade mediation, and green logistics management (Yeo et al., 2020; Yongrok & Ning, 2011).

SEM enables the assessment of mediating effects, which is crucial in understanding the indirect pathways through which factors influence logistics performance. For instance, SEM has been used to demonstrate the mediating role of logistics performance in the relationship between trade facilitation and international trade (Yeo & Deng, 2020). Similarly, SEM has been employed to model the mediating role of seaborne trade in the impacts of port infrastructure and logistics performance on economic growth (Munim & Schramm, 2018). This capability is valuable in uncovering the mechanisms by which various aspects of logistics contribute to overall performance.

This study investigated the relationship between digital transformation and environmental sustainability innovation using structural equation modeling. The digital transformation and sustainability innovation scales were operationalized to investigate this relationship as second-order constructs. The relationships between variables related to this study are given in Table 2.

Table 2. Relationships between the variables

Relationships between the Variables	Path coefficients	T statistics (|O/ STDEV|)V|)	P values
Digital transformation -> DIGTRF_III_	0.836	28.073	0.000
Digital transformation -> DIGTRF_II_	0.867	30.602	0.000
Digital transformation -> DIGTRF_IV_	0.867	28.967	0.000
Digital transformation -> DIGTRF_IX_	0.837	27.400	0.000
Digital transformation -> DIGTRF_I_	0.826	24.569	0.000
Digital transformation -> DIGTRF_VIII_	0.791	18.413	0.000
Digital transformation -> DIGTRF_VII_	0.747	14.906	0.000
Digital transformation -> DIGTRF_VI_	0.709	12.416	0.000
Digital transformation -> DIGTRF_V_	0.900	37.630	0.000
Digital transformation -> DIGTRF_X_	0.855	29.672	0.000
Digital transformation -> Env. Sus. _Innovations	0.087	-	0.000
ESI -> Environment Sustainability _Innovations	0.379	22.734	0.000
MECP -> Environment Sustainability _Innovations	0.326	25.717	0.000
RUEC -> Environment Sustainability _Innovations	0.211	25.205	0.000
TESC -> Environment Sustainability _Innovations	0.151	18.134	0.000

Note: The dimensions of digital transformation are shown as DIGTRF_ I - DIGTRF_X in the research model and in Table 2, which shows the relationships between variables. In addition, the scale items of each dimension are shown, for example, DIGIT_I_1.

RESULTS AND DISCUSSION

Structural equation model path analysis shows that digital transformation positively impacts environmental sustainability innovations. The coefficient is 0.087, meaning that every one-point increase in digital transformation will increase environmental sustainability innovations by almost 0.1%. In other words, if we can transform the organizations digitally 100%, environmental innovations will also increase by almost 10%.

Many studies support this result at the organizational level (Kache & Seuring, 2017; Ordieres-Meré et al., 2020; Schallmo et al., 2017; Westerman et al., 2011). However, firms' degree of digitization capability may vary within and across industries depending on two main reasons (Ritter & Pedersen, 2020). First, the type of technologies varies across industries (Vial, 2019). Second, the value of the outputs added by digital transformation is also relative to the industry structure (Fosso Wamba et al., 2015). As a result, longitudinal results may be different for logistics firms than other firms in other sectors.

One of the interesting results of this chapter depends on the operationalization of the variables. Dependent and independent variables are operationalized as a second-order construct. In other words, instead of analyzing the effects of the variables depending on the effects of subdimensions separately, we operationalized the subdimensions as first-order and variables as second-order constructs. As an independent variable, digital transformation has ten subdimensions. Table 2 shows that each subdimension has almost the same effect on the digital transformation variables. Logistics firms should consider each dimension separately, and firms can integrate the dimension sequentially.

On the other hand, the Environmental sustainability innovation (ESI) variable (dependent) has four dimensions: environmental sustainability management, managing environmental communication and pollution, Resource use and energy conservation, and Transportation energy conservation. According to Table 2, sustainability management (0.379) and environmental communication and pollution (0.326) are the most important dimensions of ESI. Moreover, the Resource use and energy conservation dimension affect ESI by a score of 0.211, and the Transportation energy conservation dimension impacts ESI by 0.151. So, logistics firms should focus on sustainability management, environmental communication, and pollution management more cautiously than the other dimensions of ESI. One interesting result is that the Transportation energy conservation dimension of ESI has a minimal impact on the four subdimensions of ESI. This result is interesting because it naturally comes to mind that logistics firms depend more on transportation energy conservation than the other dimensions; however, results show the opposite. So, for logistics firms to be innovative in transportation energy conservation, it takes considerable work to establish and make an impact.

As can be seen from the results, logistics firms in Turkey choose the management function to improve creatively, which needs less investment than operational functions like transportation or resource use and energy conservation. This result may contradict recent research highlighting the challenges the logistics industry faces regarding high-factor input, high-energy consumption, and high-pollution emissions (Wang et al., 2022). So, naturally, firms can improve these functions through innovations; however, Grawe (2009) highlights that the economic culture has been seen as an opportunity for logistics innovation. Dwivedi et al. (2021) and Daugherty et al. (2011) highlighted the importance of innovation capability in logistics and supply chain firms. So, Turkish logistics firms still need to develop innovation capability to the desired level. These firms more easily improved customer value-oriented innovation by managing environmental communication and recognizing the importance of customer value-oriented logistics innovation in enhancing overall performance (Flint et al., 2005; Wagner, 2013).

CONCLUSION

The effects of digital transformation on the logistics sector are significant and wide-ranging. Digital technologies and innovations have revolutionized logistics operations, improving efficiency, visibility, and customer experience.

Many authors emphasized the necessity of putting creativity as a resource at the core of sustainability by highlighting the intimate connection between sustainability and creativity. They contend that innovation is crucial to sustainable growth (Awan et al., 2019; Silveira et al., 2022; W. Song et al., 2023).

As a result, this chapter has three original components. First, researching the effects of digital transformation on environmental sustainability innovations is an essential and new research area. Second, the digital transformation and sustainability innovation scales are operationalized as second-order constructs.

That approach allowed us to investigate the variables from a holistic perspective. Third, sustainability has become essential in the logistics sector; the relationship between these two variables is first explored according to our knowledge.

As can be understood from the results of this section, it has been determined that logistics companies in Turkey can improve many of their functions through innovations. However, developing digital transformation and environmental sustainability innovations in logistics and supply chain companies is important in ensuring the continuity of innovation capabilities. For this reason, these companies need to develop their innovation capabilities while performing their functions.

CONTRIBUTION

This chapter has three significant contributions to the literature. First, The effects of digital transformation on environmental sustainability are multifaceted and can have both positive and negative impacts. Prior studies demonstrated that digital transformation can positively and negatively affect environmental sustainability innovations. While digital technologies offer opportunities for improving environmental performance and driving sustainability initiatives, some challenges and uncertainties must be addressed. Factors such as innovation capabilities, organizational culture, board characteristics, and the specific context of implementation can influence the relationship between digital transformation and environmental sustainability. Thus, more research is needed to explore the relationship between digital transformation and environmental sustainability innovations.

Second, to our knowledge, the logistics sector is first investigated to explore the relationship between digital transformation and environmental sustainability innovations. For several reasons, environmental sustainability innovations are crucial in supply chain management. These innovations have the potential to drive positive environmental outcomes, improve operational efficiency, enhance brand reputation, and meet the growing demand for sustainable products and practices (Carter & Rogers, 2008).

Lastly, prior research has explored different facets of sustainability innovation and digital transformation only on the sub-dimensional level. However, in this chapter, we operationalized the variables as second-order constructs that allowed us to see the relationship from a wholistic perspective.

REFERENCES

Achillas, C. (2019). *Green supply chain management*. Routledge, Taylor & Francis Group.

Ashby, A., Leat, M., & Hudson-Smith, M. (2012). Making connections: A review of supply chain management and sustainability literature. *Supply Chain Management, 17*(5), 497–516. doi:10.1108/13598541211258573

Awan, U., Sroufe, R., & Kraslawski, A. (2019). Creativity Enables Sustainable Development: Supplier Engagement as a Boundary Condition for the Positive Effect on Green Innovation. *Journal of Cleaner Production, 226*, 172–185. doi:10.1016/j.jclepro.2019.03.308

Bacak, S., & Aydin, Y. (2018). Üretim İşletmelerindeki Lojistik Faaliyetlerin Finansal Performansa Etkisinin İşletme Yetkilileri Algısı: Sivas İlinde Bir Araştırma. *Kahramanmaraş Sütçü İmam Üniversitesi Sosyal Bilimler Dergisi, 15*(1), 1.

Bag, S., Telukdarie, A., Pretorius, J. H. C., & Gupta, S. (2018). Industry 4.0 and supply chain sustainability: Framework and future research directions. *Benchmarking: An International Journal*, BIJ-03-2018-0056. doi:10.1108/BIJ-03-2018-0056

Balkan, D., & Akyuz, G. A. (2023). Logistics Sector Turnover: Forecasting for Turkey, EU27 and EA19 under Effects of COVID-19. *Logistics*, *7*(2), 23. doi:10.3390/logistics7020023

Bednarčíková, D., & Repiská, R. (2021). Digital Transformation in the Context of the European Union and the Use of Digital Technologies as a Tool for Business Sustainability. *SHS Web of Conferences*. 10.1051/shsconf/202111501001

Bican, P. M., & Brem, A. (2020). Digital Business Model, Digital Transformation, Digital Entrepreneurship: Is There A Sustainable "Digital"? *Sustainability (Basel)*, *12*(5239), 5239. doi:10.3390/su12135239

Bulgurcu, B., & Nakiboglu, G. (2018). An extent analysis of 3PL provider selection criteria: A case on Turkey cement sector. *Cogent Business & Management*, *5*(1), 1469183. doi:10.1080/23311975.2018.1469183

Camodeca, R., & Almici, A. (2021). Digital Transformation and Convergence toward the 2030 Agenda's Sustainability Development Goals: Evidence from Italian Listed Firms. *Sustainability (Basel)*, *13*(21), 11831. doi:10.3390/su132111831

Carter, C. R., & Rogers, D. S. (2008). A framework of sustainable supply chain management: Moving toward new theory. *International Journal of Physical Distribution & Logistics Management*, *38*(5), 360–387. doi:10.1108/09600030810882816

Ceniga, P., & Sukalova, V. (2020). Sustainable Business Development in the Context of Logistics in the Globalization Process. *SHS Web of Conferences*, *74*, 04003. 10.1051/shsconf/20207404003

Chauhan, S., Singh, R., Gehlot, A., Akram, S. V., Twala, B., & Priyadarshi, N. (2022). Digitalization of Supply Chain Management with Industry 4.0 Enabling Technologies: A Sustainable Perspective. *Processes (Basel, Switzerland)*, *11*(1), 96. doi:10.3390/pr11010096

Coşkun, A. A., & Turker, O. (2011). Analysis of environmental impact assessment (EIA) system in Turkey. *Environmental Monitoring and Assessment*, *175*(1–4), 213–226. doi:10.1007/s10661-010-1507-3 PMID:20521100

Daugherty, P. J., Chen, H., & Ferrin, B. G. (2011). Organizational Structure and Logistics Service Innovation. *International Journal of Logistics Management*, *22*(1), 26–51. doi:10.1108/09574091111127543

De Andres Gonzalez, O., Koivisto, H., Mustonen, J. M., & Keinänen-Toivola, M. M. (2021). Digitalization in Just-In-Time Approach as a Sustainable Solution for Maritime Logistics in the Baltic Sea Region. *Sustainability (Basel)*, *13*(3), 1173. doi:10.3390/su13031173

Denktaş Şakar, G., Yıldırım, E., & Mansuroğlu, E. (2018). Value Creation in Project Cargo Logistics: A Delphi Study. *Journal of ETA Maritime Science*, *6*(3), 255–274. doi:10.5505/jems.2018.48343

Dwivedi, P., Chaturvedi, V., & Vashist, J. K. (2021). Innovation for Organizational Sustainability: The Role of HR Practices and Theories. *The International Journal of Organizational Analysis*. Advance online publication. doi:10.1108/IJOA-07-2021-2859

Evangelista, P., Santoro, L., & Thomas, A. (2018). Environmental Sustainability in Third-Party Logistics Service Providers: A Systematic Literature Review from 2000–2016. *Sustainability (Basel), 10*(5), 1627. doi:10.3390/su10051627

Faur, M., & Bungau, C. (2019). Outsourcing Towards Greater Agility Through Investigating Decoupling Points in Leagile Supply Chains. *MATEC Web of Conferences, 290*, 07006. 10.1051/matecconf/201929007006

Feroz, A. K., Zo, H., & Chiravuri, A. (2021). Digital Transformation and Environmental Sustainability: A Review and Research Agenda. *Sustainability (Basel), 13*(3), 1530. doi:10.3390/su13031530

Flint, D. J., Larsson, E., Gammelgaard, B., & Mentzer, J. T. (2005). Logistics Innovation: A Customer Value-Oriented Social Process. *Journal of Business Logistics, 26*(1), 113–147. doi:10.1002/j.2158-1592.2005.tb00196.x

Fosso Wamba, S., Akter, S., Edwards, A., Chopin, G., & Gnanzou, D. (2015). How 'big data' can make big impact: Findings from a systematic review and a longitudinal case study. *International Journal of Production Economics, 165*, 234–246. doi:10.1016/j.ijpe.2014.12.031

Grawe, S. J. (2009). Logistics Innovation: A Literature-based Conceptual Framework. *International Journal of Logistics Management, 20*(3), 360–377. Advance online publication. doi:10.1108/09574090911002823

Gritsenko, S., Karpun, Oi., & Kolisnichenko, A. (2022). Digitalization of logistics company business process in conditions of industry 4.0. *Electronic Scientific Journal Intellectualization of Logistics and Supply Chain Management, 11*, 46–56. doi:10.46783/smart-scm/2022-11-4

Gruchmann, T., Melkonyan, A., & Krumme, K. (2018). Logistics Business Transformation for Sustainability: Assessing the Role of the Lead Sustainability Service Provider (6PL). *Logistics, 2*(4), 25. doi:10.3390/logistics2040025

Härting, R.-C., Reichstein, C., Sandkuhl, K., Hoppe, N., & Yesilay, H. (2020). *Potential Benefits of Enterprise Architecture Management in the Digital Transformation Process*. Complex Systems Informatics and Modeling Quarterly., doi:10.7250/csimq.2020-24.04

Holmström, J., Liotta, G., & Chaudhuri, A. (2017). Sustainability outcomes through direct digital manufacturing-based operational practices: A design theory approach. *Journal of Cleaner Production, 167*, 951–961. doi:10.1016/j.jclepro.2017.03.092

Horani, L. F. (2023). Sustainable design concepts and their definitions: An inductive content-analysis-based literature review. *Technological Sustainability, 2*(3), 225–243. doi:10.1108/TECHS-10-2022-0041

Ismayil, N., & Karagulle, O. A. (2023). *The Effect of Digitalization Process and Green Logistics Applications on Logistics Performance: Measuring Azerbaijan Logistics Companies* [Preprint]. SOCIAL SCIENCES. doi:10.20944/preprints202301.0189.v1

Jayarathna, C. P., Agdas, D., & Dawes, L. (2023). Exploring sustainable logistics practices toward a circular economy: A value creation perspective. *Business Strategy and the Environment, 32*(1), 704–720. doi:10.1002/bse.3170

Joyce, A., & Paquin, R. L. (2016). The triple layered business model canvas: A tool to design more sustainable business models. *Journal of Cleaner Production, 135*, 1474–1486. doi:10.1016/j.jclepro.2016.06.067

Kache, F., & Seuring, S. (2017). Challenges and opportunities of digital information at the intersection of Big Data Analytics and supply chain management. *International Journal of Operations & Production Management, 37*(1), 10–36. doi:10.1108/IJOPM-02-2015-0078

Kamal, N., Imran, M., & Tripati, N. K. (2017). Greening the Urban Environment Using Geospatial Techniques, A Case Study of Bangkok, Thailand. *Procedia Environmental Sciences, 37*, 141–152. doi:10.1016/j.proenv.2017.03.030

Kamble, S. S., Mor, R. S., & Belhadi, A. (2023). Big Data Analytics for Supply Chain Transformation: A Systematic Literature Review Using SCOR Framework. In S. S. Kamble, R. S. Mor, & A. Belhadi (Eds.), *Digital Transformation and Industry 4.0 for Sustainable Supply Chain Performance* (pp. 1–50). Springer International Publishing., doi:10.1007/978-3-031-19711-6_1

Karaman Kabadurmuş, F. N. (2019). The Relationship Between Logistics Performance and Innovation: An Empirical Study of Turkish Firms. *Alphanumeric Journal, 7*(2), 157–172. doi:10.17093/alphanumeric.614170

Korucuk, S., Aytekin, A., Ecer, F., Pamucar, D. S. S., & Karamaşa, Ç. (2023). Assessment of ideal smart network strategies for logistics companies using an integrated picture fuzzy LBWA–CoCoSo framework. *Management Decision, 61*(5), 1434–1462. doi:10.1108/MD-12-2021-1621

Kunkel, S., & Matthess, M. (2020). Digital transformation and environmental sustainability in industry: Putting expectations in Asian and African policies into perspective. *Environmental Science & Policy, 112*, 318–329. doi:10.1016/j.envsci.2020.06.022

Kutnjak, A. (2021). Covid-19 Accelerates Digital Transformation in Industries: Challenges, Issues, Barriers and Problems in Transformation. *Ieee Access*. doi:10.1109/ACCESS.2021.3084801

Lambert, D. M., Cooper, M., & Pagh, J. D. (1998). Supply Chain Management: Implementation Issues and Research Opportunities. *International Journal of Logistics Management, 9*(2), 1–20. doi:10.1108/09574099810805807

Lin, C., & Ho, Y. (2009). RFID technology adoption and supply chain performance: An empirical study in China's logistics industry. *Supply Chain Management, 14*(5), 369–378. doi:10.1108/13598540910980288

Linkov, I., Trump, B., Poinsatte-Jones, K., & Florin, M.-V. (2018). Governance Strategies for a Sustainable Digital World. *Sustainability (Basel), 10*(2), 440. doi:10.3390/su10020440

Martínez-Jurado, P. J., & Moyano-Fuentes, J. (2014). Lean Management, Supply Chain Management and Sustainability: A Literature Review. *Journal of Cleaner Production, 85*, 134–150. doi:10.1016/j.jclepro.2013.09.042

Mason-Jones, R., & Towill, D. R. (1999). Using the Information Decoupling Point to Improve Supply Chain Performance. *International Journal of Logistics Management, 10*(2), 13–26. doi:10.1108/09574099910805969

Melnyk, S. A., Sroufe, R., & Calantone, R. J. (2002). Assessing the Impact of Environmental Management Systems on Corporate and Environmental Performance. *Journal of Operations Management*. doi:10.1016/S0272-6963(02)00109-2

Mergel, I., Edelmann, N., & Haug, N. (2019). Defining digital transformation: Results from expert interviews. *Government Information Quarterly*, *36*(4), 101385. doi:10.1016/j.giq.2019.06.002

Moore, K. R. (1998). Trust and Relationship Commitment in Logistics Alliances: A Buyer Perspective. *International Journal of Purchasing and Materials Management*, *34*(4), 24–37. doi:10.1111/j.1745-493X.1998.tb00039.x

Munim, Z. H., & Schramm, H.-J. (2018). The impacts of port infrastructure and logistics performance on economic growth: The mediating role of seaborne trade. *Journal of Shipping and Trade*, *3*(1), 1. doi:10.1186/s41072-018-0027-0

Nadeem, A., Abedin, B., Cerpa, N., & Chew, E. (2018). Editorial: Digital Transformation &Amp;amp; Digital Business Strategy in Electronic Commerce—The Role of Organizational Capabilities. *Journal of Theoretical and Applied Electronic Commerce Research*, *13*(2), I–VIII. Advance online publication. doi:10.4067/S0718-18762018000200101

Nguyen, N. M., Hoai, T. T., Vo, H. V., & Nguyen, N. P. (2023). Digital approach toward environmental sustainability in supply chains: Evidence from Vietnamese firms. *Sustainable Development (Bradford)*, *31*(5), 3303–3317. doi:10.1002/sd.2586

Nur, Y. A., & Wahyuni, Rr. E., Saidah, D., & Octaviani, R. D. (2018). *INFORMATION TECHNOLOGY, GREEN INITIATIVES AND ORGANIZATIONAL PERFORMANCE: CONTINGENCY MODELS.* Global Research on Sustainable Transport (GROST 2017), Jakarta, Indonesia. 10.2991/grost-17.2018.26

Olhager, J. (2010). The role of the customer order decoupling point in production and supply chain management. *Computers in Industry*, *61*(9), 863–868. doi:10.1016/j.compind.2010.07.011

Ordieres-Meré, J., Prieto Remón, T., & Rubio, J. (2020). Digitalization: An Opportunity for Contributing to Sustainability From Knowledge Creation. *Sustainability (Basel)*, *12*(4), 1460. doi:10.3390/su12041460

Pagell, M., & Wu, Z. (2009). Building a More Complete Theory of Sustainable Supply Chain Management Using Case Studies of 10 Exemplars. *The Journal of Supply Chain Management*, *45*(2), 37–56. Advance online publication. doi:10.1111/j.1745-493X.2009.03162.x

Pyun, J., & Rha, J. S. (2021). Review of Research on Digital Supply Chain Management Using Network Text Analysis. *Sustainability (Basel)*, *13*(17), 9929. doi:10.3390/su13179929

Rachinger, M., Rauter, R., Müller, C., Vorraber, W., & Schirgi, E. (2019). Digitalization and its influence on business model innovation. *Journal of Manufacturing Technology Management*, *30*(8), 1143–1160. doi:10.1108/JMTM-01-2018-0020

Ritter, T., & Pedersen, C. L. (2020). Digitization capability and the digitalization of business models in business-to-business firms: Past, present, and future. *Industrial Marketing Management*, *86*, 180–190. doi:10.1016/j.indmarman.2019.11.019

Sanders, N. R., Boone, T., Ganeshan, R., & Wood, J. D. (2019). Sustainable Supply Chains in the Age of AI and Digitization: Research Challenges and Opportunities. *Journal of Business Logistics*, *40*(3), 229–240. doi:10.1111/jbl.12224

Schallmo, D., Williams, C. A., & Boardman, L. (2017). DIGITAL TRANSFORMATION OF BUSINESS MODELS — BEST PRACTICE, ENABLERS, AND ROADMAP. *International Journal of Innovation Management*, *21*(08), 1740014. doi:10.1142/S136391961740014X

Seroka-Stolka, O., Tomski, P., & Pabian, A. (2015). Environmental strategies in the management of transport & logistics sector companies. *2015 4th International Conference on Advanced Logistics and Transport (ICALT)*, (pp. 122–127). IEEE. 10.1109/ICAdLT.2015.7136607

Shahin, A., Gunasekaran, A., Khalili, A., & Shirouyehzad, H. (2016). A new approach for estimating leagile decoupling point using data envelopment analysis. *Assembly Automation*, *36*(3), 233–245. doi:10.1108/AA-07-2015-063

Silveira, C., Luo, J., Reis, L., & Mamede, H. S. (2022). CRESustain: Approach to Include Sustainability and Creativity in Requirements Engineering. *Journal of Engineering Research and Sciences*. doi:10.55708/js0108004

Song, M., Zheng, C., & Wang, J. (2022). The role of digital economy in China's sustainable development in a post-pandemic environment. *Journal of Enterprise Information Management*, *35*(1), 58–77. doi:10.1108/JEIM-03-2021-0153

Song, W., Ma, Y., Fan, X., & Peng, X. (2023). Corporate Environmental Ethics and Employee's Green Creativity? The Perspective of Environmental Commitment. *Corporate Social Responsibility and Environmental Management*, *30*(4), 1856–1868. doi:10.1002/csr.2459

Sun, X., Yu, H., Solvang, W. D., Wang, Y., & Wang, K. (2022). The application of Industry 4.0 technologies in sustainable logistics: A systematic literature review (2012–2020) to explore future research opportunities. *Environmental Science and Pollution Research International*, *29*(7), 9560–9591. doi:10.1007/s11356-021-17693-y PMID:34893953

Taufani, M., & Widjaja, A. W. (2022). Digital transformation for enhancing LSP (Logistic Service Provider) performance. *Proceeding of the International Conference on Family Business and Entrepreneurship, 2*(1). 10.33021/icfbe.v2i1.3518

Tiwari, V., & Thakur, S. (2021). Environment sustainability through sustainability innovations. *Environment, Development and Sustainability*, *23*(5), 6941–6965. doi:10.1007/s10668-020-00899-4

Truong, T. C. (2022). The Impact of Digital Transformation on Environmental Sustainability. *Advances in Multimedia*, *2022*, 1–12. doi:10.1155/2022/6324325

Tseng, M.-L., Bui, T.-D., Lim, M. K., & Lewi, S. (2021). A Cause and Effect Model for Digital Sustainable Supply Chain Competitiveness under Uncertainties: Enhancing Digital Platform. *Sustainability (Basel)*, *13*(18), 10150. doi:10.3390/su131810150

Vial, G. (2019). Understanding digital transformation: A review and a research agenda. *The Journal of Strategic Information Systems*, *28*(2), 118–144. doi:10.1016/j.jsis.2019.01.003

Vivek, H., Gajjar, K. M., & Daruwala, S. B. (2023). A RESEARCH PAPER STUDY ON IMPLICATION OF GREEN LOGISTICS IN CHEMICAL INDUSTRIES. *International Research Journal of Modernization in Engineering Technology and Science*, *5*(3). doi:10.56726/IRJMETS33989

Wagner, S. M. (2013). Partners for Business-to-Business Service Innovation. *IEEE Transactions on Engineering Management*, *60*(1), 113–123. doi:10.1109/TEM.2012.2198066

Wang, D., Tarasov, A., & Zhang, H. (2022). Environmental Regulation, Innovation Capability, and Green Total Factor Productivity of the Logistics Industry. *Kybernetes*. Advance online publication. doi:10.1108/K-04-2022-0591

Westerman, G., Calméjane, C., Bonnet, D., Ferraris, P., McAfee, A., & ... (2011). Digital Transformation: A roadmap for billion-dollar organizations. *MIT Center for Digital Business and Capgemini Consulting*, *1*, 1–68.

Wujarso, R. (2023). Effect of Digital Transformation on Company Operational Efficiency. *Central European Management Journal*, *31*(2), 2. doi:10.57030/23364890.cemj.31.2.16

Yeo, A. D., & Deng, A. (2020). Logistics performance as a mediator of the relationship between trade facilitation and international trade: A mediation analysis. *Suid-Afrikaanse Tydskrif vir Ekonomiese en Bestuurswetenskappe*, *23*(1). doi:10.4102/sajems.v23i1.3453

Yeo, A. D., Deng, A., & Nadiedjoa, T. Y. (2020). The Effect of Infrastructure and Logistics Performance on Economic Performance: The Mediation Role of International Trade. *Foreign Trade Review*, *55*(4), 450–465. doi:10.1177/0015732520947676

Yildiz, K., & Tabak, Ç. (2019). LPI Based Comparison of Turkey And Mexican Logistics Sector. *Politeknik Dergisi*, *22*(4), 4. doi:10.2339/politeknik.479410

Yongrok, C., & Ning, Z. (2011). Does proactive green logistics management improve business performance? A case of Chinese logistics enterprises. *African Journal of Business Management*, *5*(17), 7564–7574. doi:10.5897/AJBM11.613

Zhu, K., Kraemer, K. L., & Xu, S. (2006). The Process of Innovation Assimilation by Firms in Different Countries: A Technology Diffusion Perspective on E-Business. *Management Science*, *52*(10), 1557–1576. doi:10.1287/mnsc.1050.0487

Zondervan, N. A., Tolentino-Zondervan, F., & Moeke, D. (2022). Logistics Trends and Innovations in Response to COVID-19 Pandemic: An Analysis Using Text Mining. *Processes (Basel, Switzerland)*, *10*(12), 2667. doi:10.3390/pr10122667

Chapter 8
Corporate Social Responsibility (CSR) and Sustainable Development (SD) in the Digital Age

Siriyama Kanthi Herath
Clark Atlanta University, USA

Laksitha Maheshi Herath
New York University, USA

ABSTRACT

The primary objective of this chapter is to offer readers a thorough grasp of the intricate relationships that exist between organizational policies, digital tools, and the impacts that technology has on people and the natural world. Today's businesses profit from having easy access to a plethora of online resources and tools that promote improved communication, openness, gathering and interpreting information, and the spurring of innovation. These capabilities have allowed for the integration of CSR and SD principles into major company planning, promoting long-term sustainability and beneficial social results. The chapter examines how CSR and SD practices have grown as a result of digital technology, highlighting both the challenges and the new potential. Businesses that use the digital era for CSR and SD could open the door to a more prosperous and ecologically conscious future for humanity.

INTRODUCTION: CORPORATE SOCIAL RESPONSIBILITY AND SUSTAINABLE DEVELOPMENT IN THE DIGITAL AGE

One of the numerous economic issues that the digital revolution has greatly affected is how companies carry out their social and environmental obligations. Using freely available digital technology is becoming the standard in an array of industries, including finance, management, business, and education (Zahid et al., 2021; Singh & Hong, 2023). In the digital age, this chapter explores the complex relationship

DOI: 10.4018/979-8-3693-0798-4.ch008

between sustainable development (SD) and corporate social responsibility (CSR). It examines how CSR and SD practices have grown as a result of digital technology, highlighting both the challenges and the new potential. Rapid social change brought about by digital technology is both benefiting humanity in ways never before possible and creating significant new issues (UN, 2019; Nambisan et al., 2017).

In the digital age, there has been a significant shift in how businesses connect with their stakeholders and deal with environmental and social issues. Nowadays, companies benefit from easy access to a wide range of electronic devices and platforms that encourage more transparency, cooperation, data gathering and analysis, and the acceleration of innovation. These capabilities have allowed for the integration of CSR and SD principles into major company planning, promoting long-term sustainability and beneficial social results. More options are available than ever, thanks to digital technology, but there are also frequent instances of misuse and unforeseen consequences (UN, 2019). Policymakers should embrace technological innovation and consider how digitization contributes to ecological preservation in the framework of corporate social responsibility to accomplish the goals of sustainable development (Kwilinski, et al., 2023).

The next section will discuss several creative ways businesses can use digital technologies to improve their social responsibility programs and promote sustainable business practices. It will look at the advantages and drawbacks of using cutting edge technology. With the advent of the digital era, there are numerous ways to tackle pressing social and environmental problems, including greater accountability and transparency, data-driven planning, and innovative problem-solving.

Because of growing technologies, people and businesses can now work globally, share ideas, and interact. The significance of global cooperation and knowledge exchange in the realm of technology will be covered in this chapter. It highlights how crucial moral technological conduct is to ensure a sustainable future and reduce harmful impacts on the environment. Given the flexibility of digital technology, social and ethical problems need to be considered (Amoako & Dartey-Baah (2020).

Organizations can use technology in the digital age to address challenges associated with sustainable development (SD) and corporate social responsibility (CSR). By appreciating the benefits of combining cutting-edge technology with sustainable practices, organizations may help create a fairer and more sustainable world. Businesses that combine creative thinking with environmentally friendly practices can harness technology as a powerful tool for revolutionary change.

A comprehensive review of the ways in which digital technology promotes innovation is required to evaluate the characteristics of sustainability and the role of CSR in the digital age. It includes assessing the ways in which companies use technology to increase operational transparency and utilize data to make informed decisions. Research is also being done on details that define the benefits and cons of living in this era of unmatched technological advancement. The principal aim is to acquire an in-depth knowledge of the complex interrelationships among digital tools, organizational rules, and the effects of technology on humanity and the environment. This will help us navigate the complex, contemporary world of CSR and SD.

REVOLUTIONARY SHIFTS: PROMOTING SOCIAL RESPONSIBILITY AND ENVIRONMENTAL DEVELOPMENT IN THE DIGITAL AGE

Contemporary rapidly changing digital age, the ideas of social responsibility for businesses (CSR) and sustainable development (SD) have undergone substantial transformation. This has given rise to creative methods of upholding social and environmental responsibility, as well as fresh opportunities for socially responsible business. The notion of "corporate social responsibility", has historically placed a heavy emphasis on monetary goals and charitable contributions intended to improve society's problems. But these ideas have changed in the age of the internet, and companies now need an even broader and more advanced IT plan. The incorporation of digital technology not only facilitates the realization of novel concepts, but also expedites the shift towards sustainable business practices, signifying a paradigm shift in the perspective and execution of corporate social responsibility and development initiatives within contemporary company settings. Corporate social responsibility (CSR) is defined by Hillman and Keim (2001) as a broad concept that includes social issue management and stakeholder management. The European Commission (EC, n.d.) defines sustainable development as achieving current requirements without sacrificing the capacity of upcoming generations to achieve their own. Its basis is supported by three pillars: social, environmental, and economic. The three policy areas must work together and support one another to achieve sustainable development. Gond et al. (2022) report that during the past three decades, there has been an unprecedented surge in interest in corporate social responsibility (CSR) and the promotion of sustainable development (SD) among political and management circles on a local, national, and international level.

Companies that embrace the idea of "corporate social responsibility," voluntarily consider how their business activities affect the community and the environment. Companies that act in this way promise to do more for the environment and society than just increase their bottom line (Carroll, 1999). As part of Sustainable Development (SD), an endeavor to safeguard the welfare of present and future generations, resource management and environmental protection have gained much attention. During the past 20 years, there has reportedly been apparent growth in the adoption of business sustainability and social responsibility concepts, according to Ashrafi et al. (2020). But since the beginning of the digital era, these concepts have experienced a significant metamorphosis that has increased their importance and relevance significantly. The breadth of social and environmental factors has increased with the incorporation of digital technology, so organizations now need to adopt innovative, tech-driven initiatives that align with sustainability and social responsibility.

Traditionally, company social responsibility (CSR) initiatives have operated on the periphery of corporate strategies, sometimes being entrusted with supplementary roles. However, a paradigm shift brought about by the advancement of digital technology has made corporate social responsibility (CSR) the top priority for businesses. Companies are beginning to understand that upholding moral principles and taking on social responsibilities are not just morally right, but also strategically crucial to long-term success and adaptability in the face of a rapidly evolving commercial landscape. This idea has been strengthened by the dynamic interplay between technological progress and societal expectations.

Further evidence of the favorable relationship between corporate social responsibility (CSR), business operations, and sustainable development was offered by John Elkington's triple bottom line concept proposal in the late 1990s (Ashrafi et al., 2020). This novel approach prioritizes social responsibility over other goals, including economic growth, equitable distribution of wealth, and social justice (Elkington, 1998). Businesses are more likely to participate in corporate social responsibility (CSR) programs and build dependable connections with a variety of significant stakeholders, include regulators, employees, consumers, vendors, shareholders, financiers, and communities, according to Clarkson (1995).

The development of digital technology has substantially enhanced businesses' capacity to establish enduring relationships with their most important stakeholders. Companies can successfully incorporate stakeholders and promote openness, collaboration, and trust through the creation of interactive platforms and communication channels. The transition to digitalization affects how businesses engage with their customer base and gives them new chances to uphold social norms and enhance the communities where they do business. As organizations manage the convergence of technology, accountability, and stakeholder involvement, corporate social responsibility, or CSR, is turning into a strategic requirement. One way that companies can encourage ethical and sustainable business practices is by integrating CSR into their core operations.

Many scholars agree that it is important to make clear the benefits of combining environmental considerations with business decisions. Among the various theories they use are resource-based theories, institutional theories, stakeholder theories, and other enterprise theories. It is widely acknowledged that Hart (1995) was a trailblazer in advancing the incorporation of environmental initiatives into resource-based philosophy. As per Hart, certain environmental practices have the potential to serve as valuable assets or competencies that bolster a company's competitive edge. Expanding upon this groundbreaking research, Hart (1997) examined how sustainable development-related actions might give businesses an advantage over rivals.

The basis for developing programs and policies related to corporate social responsibility (CSR) and sustainability has also been strengthened by stakeholder theory. It emphasizes how important it is to create value for all parties engaged, as well as for internal and external stakeholders, main and secondary (Freeman, 1984). According to Freeman, this inclusive approach highlights how important it is to consider the interests of multiple groups, when developing morally and ecologically sound business practices, and acknowledges the complicated relationships that companies have with different stakeholders. When these theories are combined, it becomes clear how closely environmental sustainability, the involvement of stakeholders, technical advancement, and the growth of moral business practices are related. It also provides a thorough understanding of the strategic implications of including ecological considerations in business decisions.

With the advent of a new era of openness and accountability, digital technology has played a critical role in accelerating progress toward sustainable development (SD) and Corporate Social Responsibility (CSR). Nowadays, businesses can interact with stakeholders effectively, using a variety of digital platforms, tell them about their CSR initiatives, and give them real-time updates on their status. Transparency fosters trust and reaffirms the organization's dedication to ethical and environmentally sustainable company activities. Businesses that display transparency are more likely to win over consumers, investors, and communities because they show a sincere commitment to moral business practices.

In addition, businesses may now gather, examine, and use huge amounts of data to help with CSR and SD projects, thanks to the digital age. By utilizing sophisticated systems for organizing data and analytics tools, companies may assess and investigate their impact on the environment, make educated decisions, and keep a close eye on sustainability goals. Organizations can improve their social and environmental performance, through the identification of areas that need attention and the application of this data-driven methodology to make evidence-based decisions. Businesses can more successfully accomplish their CSR and SD goals, when they make the most of digital technology's analytical capabilities. It also equips them with the knowledge and adaptability to take proactive measures in response to emerging difficulties. Digital technology and sustainability are working together to show how revolutionary technological innovation can be in promoting a more ethical and sustainable organizational environment.

Innovative approaches to sustainability issues have a significant influence in the digital age. Digital technologies that have gained traction include the use of blockchain, artificial intelligence (AI), and the Internet of Things (IoT), which have the potential to significantly improve supply chain transparency, waste reduction, energy efficiency, and resource management. Businesses may swiftly integrate sustainable practices into their operations, which benefits both the environment and society at large, by strategically leveraging these technological advances.

The rapidly evolving digital landscape requires us to expand and modify our understandings of sustainable development and corporate social responsibility on a constant basis. As technology advances, such ideas will grow and have benefits as well as drawbacks (Nambisan et al., 2017). By embracing the potential of digital technology, businesses may address social and environmental issues, bring forth positive change, and even contribute to the building of a future that is both environmentally sustainable and more inclusive.

UTILIZING DIGITAL TECHNOLOGY TO ITS FULLEST FOR CSR AND SD

The wide range of digital tools and technology available to modern businesses can facilitate the advancement of their CSR and SD activities. Digital technology integration has the capacity to increase the efficacy, efficiency, and impact of CSR and SD activities.

Digital technology facilitates greater transparency and communication, which benefits corporate social responsibility and sustainable development (Bekele, 2023). Businesses may effectively inform a wide audience about their corporate responsibility initiatives by using websites, social media, and digital reporting processes. By enabling direct participation from stakeholders, digital platforms foster a sense of ownership and participatory discussion. Businesses can access a vast amount of data for gathering, analyzing, and application in CSR and SD projects by utilizing digital technologies. Organizations can actively monitor important sustainability criteria like energy use, carbon emissions, rubbish creation, and social effect evaluations using advanced data management systems and analytical tools. This data-driven strategy helps businesses make well-informed tactical and strategic decisions, in addition to boosting trend analysis and progress tracking.

Innovative solutions to environmental issues can be found with digital technology. The Internet of Things (IoT) makes waste reduction, energy control, and resource efficiency possible by tying together connected systems and devices. Through outcome prediction, trend identification, and process optimization, artificial intelligence (AI) and algorithmic machine learning enhance social and environmental performance. Furthermore, the transparency of the supply chain offered by blockchain technology promotes moral enterprise and responsible sourcing.

Technology has a complex impact on the intersection of corporate social responsibility and sustainable development. The relationship between CSR and SD is greatly influenced by technology. The impact of sustainable innovation in the environment is positively impacted by the social and financial aspects of company social responsibility (CSR), according to Pan et al. (2020). This highlights the potential synergies between CSR and technology in advancing sustainable development. Furthermore, in the context of natural disasters like the COVID-19 issue, Awawdeh et al. (2021) emphasized how technology may improve environmental performance, through green innovation and corporate social responsibility (CSR).

Projects involving CSR and SD require collaboration and knowledge sharing, and digital technology makes these connections feasible everywhere. Through online platforms and virtual communities, companies, associations, and people may collaborate on innovative ideas and share best practices. When everyone contributes resources, knowledge, and experiences, sustainable projects may go more quickly and have a greater societal impact.

Digital technology has many benefits, but it's crucial to be aware of any hazards or challenges and take the necessary precautions. The digital gap, privacy, technology's impact on the environment, and waste from technology are just a few of the concerns that need to be addressed ethically and with extreme caution.

Technology has been more and more integrated into initiatives pertaining to social responsibility and sustainable development. Businesses may interact with consumers, stimulate creativity, increase transparency, and develop teamwork by utilizing digital tools. Zheng et al. (2023) highlight the critical relationship between corporate social responsibility, performance, and digitalization, as well as the importance of utilizing modern technologies to advance ethical and sustainable business practices. The chapter highlights how crucial it is to consider ownership structure, when creating and implementing digital transformation programs designed to improve the company's CSR outcomes. If organizations are to create a more equitable and sustainable future, they must recognize the role that digital technology plays as a catalyst for moral corporate practices.

FOSTERING TRANSPARENCY AND ACCOUNTABILITY WITH TECHNOLOGY

In the domains of corporate social responsibility and sustainable development, transparency and accountability have critical components. In the digital age, technology has developed into a powerful tool for promoting these fundamental concepts. Businesses may improve stakeholder transparency and responsibility in their CSR operations by strategically utilizing technology. Businesses that adhere to the guidelines of corporate digital accountability, promise to manage their digital assets and technologies in an honest and open manner. This commitment means addressing ethical, legal, and societal issues surrounding the use of these resources (European Commission, 2020).

Businesses may successfully communicate CSR goals, values, and accomplishments to a range of stakeholders by utilizing digital platforms and technologies (Atanasov et al., 2023). Websites, social networking accounts, and specialized CSR portals are just a few of the easily accessible methods by which businesses can highlight their sustainability goals, methods, and successes. It renders the actions and outcomes clear to all parties involved.

Digital solutions for real-time reporting allow for quick and constant communication, making certain that stakeholders are aware of ongoing CSR projects. Companies that share information, performance indicators, and accomplishments on a regular basis can foster a candid and accountable culture. Two strategies to encourage a cooperative and participatory method of handling corporate social responsibility are to continually motivate consumers, investors, employees, and community members to participate and to provide feedback.

Using digital platforms and technologies, businesses may successfully inform a range of audiences about their CSR initiatives, values, and successes (Atanasov et al., 2023). Businesses can exhibit their environmental objectives, plans, and accomplishments to stakeholders by employing websites, social media accounts, and specialized CSR portals that provide accessible information and update sources. This helps stakeholders understand the purpose and impact of the projects.

Furthermore, the incorporation of real-time reporting via cutting-edge digital technology ensures that stakeholders are informed about the most recent CSR initiatives and enables prompt and continuous communication. Businesses can promote transparency and accountability by regularly disseminating information, benchmarks, and KPIs. Collaboratively promoting corporate social responsibility can be accomplished through actively soliciting feedback and encouraging active engagement from consumers, investors, employees, and community members. This multidimensional approach to involvement, not only improves stakeholder relationships, but also raises the general effect and efficacy of CSR initiatives.

There are many ways that technology can be utilized to encourage transparency and accountability, but there are also disadvantages that need to be considered. Sensitive information can be properly managed and protected if data safety and confidentiality measures are prioritized.

To sum up, digital technology is essential for enhancing CSR and SD transparency and accountability efforts. The act of digitizing a corporate process underscores the crucial connection between accountability and transparency inside the organization and necessitates robust information governance (Bekele, 2023). Businesses can use data analytics, digital platforms, real-time reporting, external verification, and data platforms to show their steadfast commitment to ethical standards, enhance transparency, and actively involve stakeholders. Using technology to increase accountability and transparency not only builds confidence and trust, but also puts companies in a position to serve people and the environment in the digital era (Bekele, 2023).

HARNESSING DATA FOR ENHANCED CSR AND SD INITIATIVES

In the digital era, data is more crucial than ever for focusing business activities related to sustainable development (SD) and corporate social responsibility (CSR). Data-driven operations allow businesses to evaluate and enhance their influence on society and the environment. These tactics encourage moral and ecologically conscious behavior throughout supply chains by utilizing immediate form data and statistical methods.

To better understand their sustainability successes, businesses can collect, analyze, and use data with sophisticated data management systems and analytics technologies. Key environmental indicators, such as water use, greenhouse gas emissions, trash output, and power usage, may be precisely gauged and tracked. Additionally, social impact indicators, including worker well-being, ethical supply chain practices, and community involvement, can be measured and evaluated. Al Mashalah et al. (2022) assert that technology-driven apps can ensure active stakeholder participation in supply chain management and encourage the implementation of environmentally friendly initiatives.

By identifying issue areas and establishing SMART goals (specific, measurable, doable, relevant, and time-bound), businesses can enhance their CSR and SD initiatives. Resources are allocated where they will have the greatest effect, thanks to the targeted strategies and action plans that can be created with the help of data-driven insights. Businesses can improve efficiency and prioritize actions that align with their core values and environmental aims by using this technique.

Data-driven approaches facilitate the process of tracking changes and assessing the long-term social impact of CSR and SD activities. CSR and SD initiatives provide longer-lasting effects, when they establish benchmark measurements, monitor performance metrics, and evaluate achievements in relation to predefined goals. Every one of these duties promotes ongoing assessment and development.

Data-driven solutions provide accurate reports on long-term performance, which enhances transparency and accountability. They also enable companies to provide stakeholders with up-to-date information via interactive dashboards and digital platforms. The increased amount of openness fosters confidence and allows interested parties to assess the company's conformity to moral business practices.

Data-driven initiatives have many benefits, but it's also necessary to be mindful of their disadvantages, which include problems with data privacy, quality, and interpretation. It is imperative that organizations adhere to data privacy regulations, guarantee the accuracy and dependability of acquired data, and safeguard confidential information. Carefully analyzing the facts, backed by in-depth research and contextual understanding, is essential to avoid reaching distorted or inaccurate judgments.

Improving the effectiveness and impact of CSR and SD projects in the digital age, requires harnessing the power of data. It can be used by businesses to monitor their progress, establish difficult objectives, make informed decisions, promote transparency, and foster innovation. The use of data will become increasingly important as technological developments advance, supporting the required social and environmental reforms, and contributing to the building of a sustainable future.

TECHNOLOGICAL PARADIGMS: ACHIEVING ENVIRONMENTAL SOLUTIONS IN THE MODERN ERA

Data-driven insights, contemporary technology, and dynamic ecosystems are coming together to create a confluence that is redefining consumer experiences, reshaping industries, and propelling advancement at a pace never witnessed. Modern technology, data-driven insights, and changing ecosystems combine to shatter preconceived notions and unleash a disruptive tsunami, that transforms industries and consumer experiences. Inventiveness in the digital age is exploding like a revolutionary tsunami. The emergence of digital technologies has revolutionized social and economic pursuits, resulting in novel ideas, products, and possibilities for business (Atanasov et al., 2023).

Innovation can occur in a variety of ways in an organizational context. It may entail, for instance, a reinvention of products and technologies or organizational improvements (Dorin, 2018). Even though innovations may take many different forms and interactions (Figure 1), they are usually categorized based on the impact they have on a business or organization. Below are brief overviews and comparisons of various innovation categories:

a) **Product Innovation:** Product innovation is the process of creating new or improved goods or services (Atanasov et al., 2023). One example of creativity is the introduction of a state-of-the-art smartphone with state-of-the-art features and a state-of-the-art camera; another is the development of an effective laundry detergent. These pictures illustrate how adding new features or technology to objects can make them more visually appealing and functional. Numerous empirical studies indicate that innovation and corporate social responsibility interactions result in the launch of new products. Guerrero-Villegas et al. (2018) and Battaglia et al. (2014) are two of these investigations. Research demonstrating how CSR can improve financial success through innovation lends credence to this association (Al-Shuaibi, 2016; Bahta et al., 2020; Guerrero-Villegas et al., 2018).

b) **Process Innovation:** Improving the processes and techniques used in the production or delivery of goods and services is the main objective of process innovation. Enhancing operational efficiency can be achieved through innovative methods. Companies might accomplish this, for example, by utilizing modern technologies to create a supply chain management system that is more efficient. Utilizing methods based on data in a supply chain management system to optimize manufacturing output and inventory levels is one instance of this cutting-edge technology in action.

c) **Organizational Innovation:** To increase output or adjust to the market, a company may choose to make substantial changes to its organizational structure, business plan, or corporate culture. This could entail creating a flat organizational framework, implementing flexible work hours, or applying innovative management techniques. The implementation of an organizational information sharing system that promotes improved collaboration among staff and ongoing training could serve as another illustration.

d) **Marketing Innovation:** Marketing innovation is the process of developing unique marketing concepts, campaigns, or promotional strategies to advertise products or services. This could entail coming up with a whole new marketing approach, adjusting prices, or coming up with inventive and innovative methods to use social media. Marketing innovation is the use of creative and innovative advertising techniques, such as the use of virtual reality to promote items.

e) **Business Model Innovation:** The process of creating new organizational structures with the goal of providing value is known as business model innovation. A few examples are launching a premium company plan, providing subscription services, and establishing an online store in place of an offline one. An illustration of this would be the transition from a traditional retail business to one that runs on subscription, like Amazon Prime.

f) **Service Innovation:** Defining it as the process of developing or enhancing services to better satisfy the demands of customers or the market. A few examples include developing a user-friendly website, offering an entirely new variety of customer care services, or increasing client happiness through creative service delivery. AI chatbots are utilized to give customers tailored, on-the-spot assistance and recommendations.

g) **Technological Innovation:** The development or application of new technologies to enhance products, processes, or overall corporate operations. We call this innovation in technology. Consider implementing cutting-edge technology into a product, employing sophisticated manufacturing techniques, or integrating artificial intelligence into corporate processes. The development of blockchain-based technologies will increase security and expedite financial transactions.

These innovations don't have to be mutually exclusive; in fact, prosperous businesses frequently use several creative strategies simultaneously to stay one step ahead of the competition and adapt to changing client needs.

Figure 1. Types of innovations

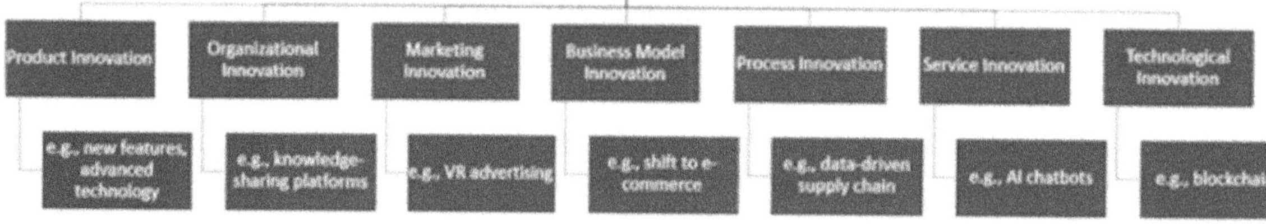

Companies aim to stay innovative to sustain a competitive advantage in the fast-paced, ever-changing business climate of today (Guerrero-Villegas et al., 2018). According to Guerrero-Villegas et al. (2018), innovation increases product quality, diversity, and turnover while also boosting market shares, operational effectiveness, cost reduction, and reputation. Because they reduce market rivalry, innovative products give businesses an even greater competitive edge (González-Fernández and González-Velasco, 2018). Businesses now have an exceptional chance to use creative solutions to solve environmental issues and advance sustainable development. Businesses may strengthen their commitment to CSR, promote SD, and carry out creative solutions to current environmental challenges by leveraging digital technologies.

One significant area where digital technology is helpful, is resource management. Real-time resource utilization optimization and monitoring are made possible by the Internet of Things (IoT), through seamless interaction between systems and devices. Intelligent sensors and data analytics play an integral part in improving supply chain, waste, energy, and water management. As a result, there are notable cost savings, higher output, and less adverse environmental impacts.

Because renewable energy technologies are becoming more widely available and affordable, it is imperative that we find solutions for environmental problems. Examples of these technologies are solar panels, wind turbines, and other sustainable sources. Businesses can reduce their reliance on fossil fuels, cut back on greenhouse gas emissions, and aid in the creation of an energy infrastructure that is more sustainable by using these technologies. Digital technology makes it possible to implement circular economy ideas and innovative waste management techniques at the same time. By using artificial intelligence (AI) and data analytics, businesses may automate waste collection, recycling, and disposal processes to boost efficiency and reduce emissions. Digital platforms facilitate resource sharing initiatives.

Companies that use digital technologies can improve the transparency of their supply chains (Al Mashalah, 2022). For example, blockchain technology can be utilized to provide an unquestionable record of transactions and sourcing processes, which could be helpful in solving sustainability-related issues. The developments in online communication technologies, cloud-based collaboration, and video conferencing have also made remote work solutions more sustainable for the environment and reduced the carbon footprint associated with business travel in the digital age.

In the digital age, businesses have a rare opportunity to come up with innovative solutions for environmental problems. However, these technological advancements also create new problems, such as rising energy output and electrical waste. When developing, using, and getting rid of digital gadgets, businesses need to abide by ethical and environmental standards. In addition, the digital era presents innovative ways to promote CSR and SD. Digital technology is used by responsible and ethical businesses to reduce carbon emissions, adopt the circular economy, manage resources more effectively, and ensure supply chain transparency. It is interesting to note that businesses are inadvertently addressing social issues that have traditionally been the purview of governments and taking on an increasing number of governmental responsibilities (Barnett et al., 2020).

INTERNATIONAL COOPERATION AND INFORMATION EXCHANGE IN CSR AND SD

The continuing growth of corporate social responsibility (CSR) and sustainable development (SD) activities in the digital age depends on international collaboration and information sharing. The cross-border exchange of ideas and best practices is facilitated by the global interconnection of neighborhoods, corporations, and individuals. Businesses can learn about local problems and cultural quirks, through international collaboration, which stimulates ingenuity and the creation of more effective CSR and SD strategies.

International information sharing has expanded, thanks in part to cooperative platforms and digital networks. Through social media and online forums, like-minded people and organizations can swap experiences and creative, environmentally friendly, practices to establish a worldwide learning community. Modern technologies like webinars and video calls have also significantly changed worldwide CSR and SD cooperation by enabling real-time communication, removing the need for travel, lowering carbon footprints, and increasing resource usage.

One of the most significant settings for cross-border cooperation and knowledge sharing in CSR and SD, is collaboration between corporations, nonprofit organizations, educational institutions, and government departments. Using a variety of networks, resources, and expertise, cross-sector collaboration creates synergy that increases the success of sustainability programs. Organizations can exchange best practices, consolidate resources, and cooperate to achieve the Sustainable Development Goals (SDGs) of the UN through such collaborations. It is commonly acknowledged in academia and politics that the Sustainable Development Goals (SDGs) apply to both developed and developing countries (Eichler & Schwarz, 2019).

For CSR and SD projects, it is imperative to identify and address any potential barriers to international collaboration as well as data sharing. Language barriers, cultural differences, and differences in the legal system are a few issues that could make collaboration and communication difficult. Diversity, transparency, and trust must be prioritized when attempting to overcome such challenges and foster a truly global cooperative environment.

In the digital age, CSR and SD must grow via worldwide collaboration and knowledge exchange. Businesses can find it easier to handle complex sustainability concerns by collaborating, learning worldwide, and networking. However, when negotiating the Sustainable Development Goals (SDGs), digitalization poses hurdles for multinational corporations, because different digital technologies have diverse implications (Ciulli & Kolk, 2023). Together, we can build a future that is equitable and sustainable through collaborative alliances, technology, and open communication.

NAVIGATING THE PROS AND CONS OF TECHNOLOGY IN CSR AND SD

Technology has a big impact on sustainable development (SD) and social responsibility in business (CSR) in the digital age. While technology can significantly enhance environmental efforts, there are also disadvantages that need to be carefully considered. Digital platforms, data analytics, and automation may help organizations monitor performance, streamline operations, and better manage their resources. Productivity growth improves environmental awareness and waste reduction, which supports the real-time tracking of sustainability goals for enhanced accountability and transparency.

Technology plays an important role in facilitating stakeholder participation in corporate social responsibility (CSR) and sustainable development (SD). Social media, online forums, and digital platforms give people a place to voice concerns, share ideas, and get involved in sustainability initiatives—all of which help promote inclusion and a sense of ownership. However, addressing problems like the "digital gap," which prevents access and participation, involves targeted initiatives, the development of infrastructure, and digital literacy initiatives to be able to guarantee balanced gains across society.

Two dimensions of technology's environmental impact are electronic trash and data center energy use. Organizations must employ sustainable practices, such as managing energy costs and handling e-waste in an ethical manner. Data privacy and security problems in the context of CSR and SD technology call for stringent protections and moral data management to protect consumer rights and comply with legal responsibilities.

Therefore, technology has the potential to greatly enhance CSR and SD operations, but it's important to weigh the advantages and disadvantages of it. Organizations can use technology to affect positive change and contribute to a more sustainable and inclusive future by properly using it, reducing access barriers, decreasing its negative effects on the environment, and preserving privacy.

ADVANCING SUSTAINABILITY: RESPONSIBLE TECHNOLOGY PRACTICES FOR A BETTER FUTURE

In the digital age, it is more crucial than ever to promote sustainable development (SD) and corporate social responsibility (CSR). As technology advances and becomes more and more ingrained in our daily lives, organizations need to adopt ethical habits and lessen the possibility of unfavorable repercussions. Technology lifecycle management is one of the fundamental elements of ethical technology practices (Zheng et al., 2023). To do this, legislation that fosters recycling, extends the life of technology, and minimizes electronic waste is required. By providing items that can be repaired and are sturdy, upgradable, and repairable, businesses may encourage responsible consumption. Businesses can reduce the negative environmental effects of technology manufacturing and removal, save energy, and minimize resource exploitation by using the concepts of the circular economy.

One of the most significant elements of moral technical action is energy efficiency. The primary driver of greenhouse gas emissions and global warming is the growing energy needs of digital infrastructure, cloud computing, and data centers. Businesses that utilize energy-efficient technologies ought to exercise extraordinary vigilance, including low-power application servers, energy management systems, and the integration of renewable energy sources. By reducing energy use and prioritizing renewable energy sources, businesses can substantially lower their carbon footprint, while contributing to a more sustainable energy transition.

Furthermore, initiatives centered around ethical technology prioritize the security of data and privacy above everything else. Companies need to emphasize how important it is to safeguard consumers' right to privacy, because the amount of personal data being utilized and collected is increasing. Strong data protection bills, safe, informed consent processes, and the adoption of open data standards are all essential. Preventing the misuse of personal data and advocating ethical data usage, are additional facets of ethical IT practices (Zahid et al., 2021). Businesses operating under the Corporate Social Responsibility (CSR) framework are obligated to demonstrate moral behavior in addition to using appropriate data processing and collection techniques. This means preventing the misuse or intrusion of private information, protecting people's privacy, and being open and honest about the purposes behind data processing (Quach et al., 2022).

Data security and privacy are also given prominence in initiatives centered around ethical technology. Businesses must stress the significance of respecting customers. Right to privacy as an increasing quantity of personal data is being used and collected. Adoption of open data standards, secure informed consent procedures, and robust data protection regulations are all crucial. Further components of ethical IT practices include preventing the misuse of personal data and promoting ethical data usage.

Expanding the use of ethical technologies requires encouraging collaboration and associations. Collaboration across industry, government, academia, and civil society will be necessary to create the institutions, rules, and guidelines that will encourage ethical and environmentally friendly technological practices. These collaborations might guarantee that ethical technology is employed in all global CSR and SD projects and foster innovation by communicating best practices, conducting research, and cooperating to develop solutions.

Lastly, Zheng et al. (2023) claim that the application of ethical technical principles is necessary for the creation of a sustainable digital age. Organizations that prioritize collaboration, lifecycle management, energy efficiency, data security, digital inclusion, and CSR and SD goals can leverage technology to drive change. While reducing potential negative consequences, responsible technical practices promote innovation and advancement toward a more equitable and environmentally conscious society.

FOSTERING DIGITAL RESILIENCE FOR SUSTAINABLE BUSINESS PRACTICES

To advance responsible company behavior in the digital age, this section looks at the idea of digital resilience (Figure 2) and how it might help sustainably run businesses in the face of digitization.

Figure 2. Building digital resilience for sustainable business practices

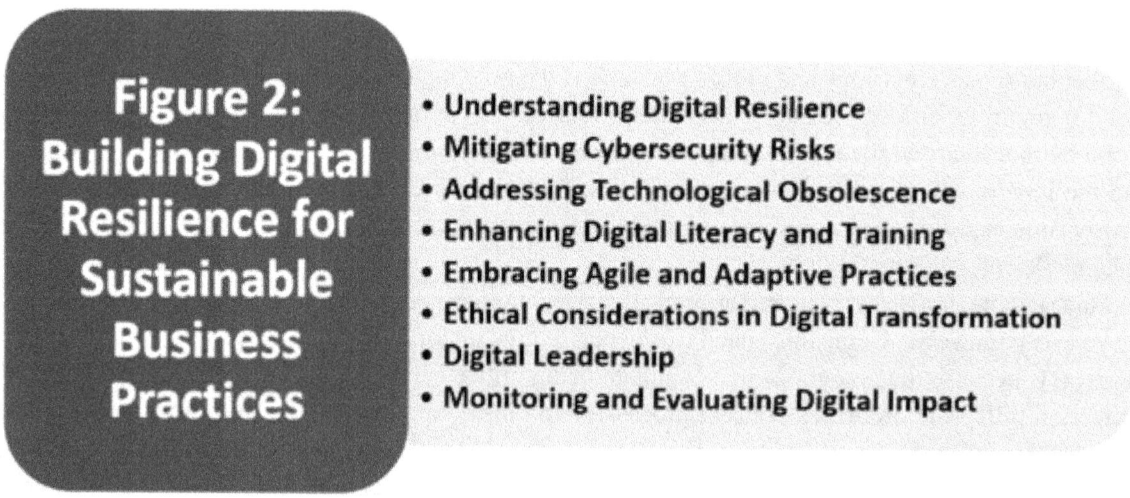

Understanding Digital Resilience: An organization needs strong defenses against threats to be digitally resilient, or able to bounce back from digital setbacks. This resilience emphasizes how crucial it is to match digital activities with morally and environmentally sound conduct. It shares a tight relationship with CSR and SD. Businesses can manage digital disruptions and promote better societal and environmental well-being by implementing reliable digital operations (Zahid et al., 2021). Proactive steps are needed to build digital resilience, like adopting agile methods, increasing digital literacy, and giving ethical considerations priority, while using digital resources. This is all part of a deliberate strategy to grow and prosper in the digital era.

Mitigating Cybersecurity Risks: It is essential to be aware of cybersecurity risks, given how much the modern business climate depends on electronic devices for data-driven decision-making and consumer interaction. The probability of a cyberattack is positively correlated with an organization's degree of digitization. While stopping cyberattacks is important from a technological point of view, protecting personal data has ethical implications as well. In this instance, maintaining your moral standards and stakeholders' trust should come before tightening organizational controls to reduce operational risks. This section highlights the two goals of preventing cyberattacks: defending against operational disruptions and maintaining moral standards to maintain stakeholders' long-term trust. In an era where digital security is essential to moral corporate conduct. As society and business grow more digitally integrated, cybersecurity is playing a bigger role in corporate responsibility. Companies need to invest in cybersecurity protocols that safeguard customer information and prevent unlawful gain or breaches of personal data (Serabian, 2015).

Addressing Technological Obsolescence: It is essential to be aware of cybersecurity dangers given how much the current corporate environment depends on electronic devices for data-driven decision-making and consumer interaction. An organization's level of digitalization and the likelihood of a cyberattack are positively correlated. This section aims to highlight how important is to identify and control specific cybersecurity risks. Not only is preventing cyberattacks technically necessary, but it also has moral ramifications, because it involves safeguarding personal information. Maintaining organization's moral principles and stakeholders' trust should come before improving organizational controls to reduce operational risks. This section outlines the two main goals of cyberattack prevention: keeping operations free from outside interference and maintaining moral standards to keep stakeholders' long-term trust. Trust is the foundation of any successful business partnership.

Enhancing Digital Literacy and Training: In the fast-paced world of contemporary business, organizations need to start staff training programs that promote digital literacy right now. This expense is necessary to ensure that employees have the skills and knowledge (Abina et al. 2022) necessary to utilize the range of digital tools available for CSR and SD projects. Considering the crucial role that human capital plays in the successful integration of digital technology, this section attempts to highlight the importance of employee upskilling. Companies can facilitate their employees' adoption of innovative sustainability practices by encouraging digital literacy and electronic device competency. Employees are viewed as a vital component of CSR and SD programs, helping them to accomplish their moral and long-term objectives. This increases the programs' overall efficacy and influence in the digital age. Setting sustainability and digital literacy as top priorities simultaneously, improves operational effectiveness.

Embracing Agile and Adaptive Practices: The idea of digital resilience forces companies to adopt adaptable and agile processes in the age of rapid digital change, so they can react quickly to new possibilities and problems. This section looks at the connection between digital resilience, sustainable development, and corporate social responsibility. Businesses may ensure success in the face of constant change and survive the rapid changes of the digital era by adopting a flexible and adaptable strategy for their CSR and SD activities. This study's objective is to clarify the ways in which concepts related to digital resilience can be integrated into CSR and SD frameworks to enhance the overall flexibility and sustainability of a business. This will help the business overcome the challenges brought on by the digital economy, while also benefiting society and the environment.

Ethical Considerations in Digital Transformation: In the process of leveraging digital technologies to improve their CSR and SD operations, companies must maintain a strong moral commitment. This section's primary goal is to uphold moral principles in the context of technical growth. The moral of the narrative will be underlined, along with the need to make morally sound judgments and utilize technology tools responsibly. Giving ethical issues top importance during the decision-making process, helps organizations enable the seamless integration of digital technology, with socially and ecologically acceptable operations (Zahid et al., 2021). This section seeks to clarify the critical role that moral behaviors play in the digital age and to show that the pursuit of advances in technology need not compromise the moral basis of CSR and SD initiatives, but rather serves as a catalyst for encouraging positive environmental and societal impact.

Digital Leadership: To become digitally resilient, one must possess solid management skills and the technological fortitude to handle the intricate and rapidly changing technology environment. This section's analysis of the crucial role that leadership plays in promoting digital resilience makes it very apparent that businesses need competent leaders to help them navigate the challenges of the digital age. The unique traits and competencies that digital executives require to oversee long-term viability, CSR and SD initiatives will be covered in this presentation. Finding the dynamic leadership qualities required to build a digitally resilient culture, that can adapt to shifting circumstances and promote positive, lasting change in the SD and CSR domains in the digital age, is the goal of the study. Improving organizational agility and having a strategic understanding of quickly changing technologies are two instances of these insights.

Monitoring and Evaluating Digital Impact: Strong monitoring and assessment techniques must be created in the complicated digital age to assess the accomplishment of SD and CSR programs. Organizations can use data analytics and KPIs (key performance indicators) to make in-depth evaluations of how technological advancement is affecting sustainability goals, as this section explains in detail. Companies can get beneficial data about the accomplishment of their CSR and SD initiatives in the digital sphere by utilizing pertinent KPIs and contemporary analytics technologies. The story will highlight the need for an approach based on information in this fast-paced period of technological growth and provide advice on how businesses can track their progress and make educated choices to optimize their strategy. This will ensure that the overall goals of sustainability are significantly enhanced by digital technologies (Bokhari & Myeong 2022).

Businesses face several opportunities as well as difficulties when integrating electronic devices into CSR and SD activities. By implementing digital resilience, businesses may effectively manage the obstacles of the internet age and promote environmentally and socially responsible operations. A future that is environmentally friendly for everybody relies on finding a careful balance between utilizing digital technology's advantages and reducing any potential risks.

HARNESSING THE DIGITAL ERA FOR CSR AND SD

The advent of the digital age ushered in a new era of opportunities and promises for sustainable development (SD) and corporate social responsibility (CSR). Nowadays, companies may use technology to enhance their sustainability initiatives, include stakeholders, and effect good change on an international level. By the end of this chapter, it should be evident that in the digital age, CSR and SD rely on technology to achieve sustainable objectives to improve the future for all people.

The emergence of the digital age and present collaboration technologies, have radically altered how businesses address SD and CSR. Businesses may now collect and analyze data to learn more about their resource usage, expectations from stakeholders, and impact on the environment, thanks to technology. This data-driven solution delivers targeted plan implementation and educated decision-making to effectively address sustainability concerns.

Technology has additionally changed stakeholder involvement, encouraging businesses to promote involvement and communication in their CSR and SD activities (Wood et al., 2021). Digital platforms, social media, and online forums have developed into devices for getting input from stakeholders, showcasing their viewpoints, and collaborating to co-create solutions. These interactive applications help CSR and SD projects become more credible and effective by encouraging accountability, transparency, and teamwork.

To enhance sustainable business growth and value, Lee (2021) carried out a thorough investigation to look at how technology innovation affects corporate social responsibility (CSR). The study emphasized how closely technology, sustainable development, and corporate social responsibility are linked. Simultaneously, Chung et al. (2019) investigated the relationship between sustainable development objectives and technology-driven eco-innovation. This study examined how travelers' views of certain destinations are influenced by technological developments, providing insights into how technology-focused corporate social responsibility initiatives could support sustainable development.

Access to knowledge sharing as well as ability building in CSR and SD is also becoming easier with the development of the internet. Through online platforms, people and businesses can access global resources, best practices, and news. This knowledge-sharing across boundaries of culture spurs creativity, quickens learning, and prepares people to collaborate for sustainable development. In a world that is changing rapidly, the digital age makes sure that current knowledge and insights are freely accessible, enabling businesses to adapt and take on new sustainability concerns.

While there are quite many benefits to adopting technology, it's equally crucial to handle the risks and problems that come with it. Addressing privacy, cybersecurity, and uneven access to technological concerns is essential to realizing a responsible and inclusive digital revolution. If businesses want to benefit from technology's advantages without becoming victims of its disadvantages, they must place the utmost importance on maintaining moral principles, preserving personal information, closing the digital divide, and developing digital literacy.

In conclusion, CSR and SD have a special chance to grow and make a big difference in the digital age. Businesses may include stakeholders, improve sustainability, and lead to major change by effectively utilizing technology. A complete strategy integrating information exchange, stakeholder involvement, ethical technology practices, and data-driven decision-making, will be necessary for success in the digital era. Corporations that subscribe to these principles will be able to use technology to build an equitable, fair, and sustainable future that's good for both current and future generations.

CONCLUSION AND SUGGESTIONS

By leveraging the disruptive landscape created by the intersection of creative thinking, digitization, and environmentally friendly development (SD), businesses may enhance their CSR programs to contribute to a future that is healthier (Dionisio et al., 2023). This chapter emphasized the crucial role technological advancement plays in addressing global concerns, by examining the substantial impact that technological advances have had on the growth of CSR and SD initiatives, throughout the corporate sector. As we conclude this chapter, we will revisit the most significant findings and offer recommendations for utilizing the age of digital technology to advance sustainability in business and society.

Digital Transformation: Empowering CSR and SD

The digital age has created new prospects for social responsibility and sustainable development. Modern technologies, such as machine learning (AI), the Internet of Things (IoT), big data analysis, and digital currencies enable organizations to collect, process, and analyze enormous amounts of data (Piccarozzi et al., 2022). These tools assist companies in making more informed decisions and achieving higher success with their sustainable projects, by obtaining data on environmental, social, and governance (ESG) challenges. Digital platforms facilitate more openness and stakeholder involvement, which in turn helps investors and consumers hold businesses accountable for their corporate social responsibility (CSR) pledges.

Harmonizing Sustainability with Digital Innovation: Businesses can now develop ecologically sound, sustainable goods and services, that satisfy customer demands and save the environment, all thanks to digital innovation. Businesses can create products that help society and the environment in addition to achieving economic success, by integrating sustainable development (SD) ideas into their innovation processes (Dionisio et al., 2023). In addition, the latest innovations have the power to totally transform an industry and pave the way for a more sustainable and green future. Examples of these technologies are smart cities, circular economy principles, and renewable energy sources.

Addressing Digital Divides for Inclusive Sustainable Development: Digital divides, which have the potential to widen already-existing socioeconomic sections, are among the difficulties and growth potential brought about by the digital age (Dionisio, 2021). If businesses want to fully benefit from digital technologies for CSR and SD, they must prioritize accessibility and diversity. Closing the technology gap guarantees that those in need have fair access to digital opportunities and resources. To promote more fair and sustainable growth, businesses can use technology to address community issues like access to healthcare, financial, and educational resources. Digital technologies provide a plethora of innovative and inventive prospects. Organizations that prioritize CSR play a crucial role in closing the digital gap by working to ensure equitable access to and utilization of digital technologies across all socioeconomic sectors (Basu, 2017).

Fostering Collaborative Partnerships for Collective Impact: In the digital age, partnerships and collaboration are essential to achieve sustainable development goals. Partnership between businesses, governments, non-governmental groups, and academic institutions is necessary to advance systemic change and create a shared sustainability vision. Digital platforms can deeply impact society as a whole and enable stakeholders to take part in the resolution of tricky issues and the achievement of agreed-upon goals.

Ensuring Responsible and Ethical Use of Digital Technology: As they move into the digital age, businesses need to be aware of the dangers and legal ramifications connected to digital technology. To preserve trust among consumers and protect people's rights, businesses need to give information privacy, cybersecurity, and ethical AI use top priority. Integrity and accountability will serve as a strong basis for CSR and SD projects, that use digital technology in accordance with ethical frameworks and industry norms.

Guidelines for Sustainability in the Digital Era

We support a digital-first approach that prioritizes data-driven decision-making, diversity, and teamwork. Think about the significance of transparent AI applications, ethical technology use, and data protection. To foster public trust, we prioritize decision-making transparency, incorporating ideas from de Fine & de Fine (2020). We also emphasize how important it is to provide money for digital literacy initiatives, that will enable interested parties to promote environmentally responsible behavior.

Develop a Digital-First Sustainability Strategy: Businesses should integrate digital technology into their sustainability strategies to enhance data-driven decision-making, stakeholder engagement, and impact measurement.

Foster Collaboration and Partnerships: To pool assets and knowledge for sustainable development projects, form cooperative alliances with an array of stakeholders, including governments, communities, and non-governmental organizations.

Promoting Inclusivity and Accessibility: When employing AI and data analysis apps, prioritize data security, privacy, and transparency, while following ethical and responsible guidelines.

Integrate Ethics and Responsibility: When utilizing technology, follow responsible and ethical practices. Give data security, privacy, and accessibility top priority in applications employing artificial intelligence (AI) and data analysis. As evidenced by the work of de Fine and de Fine (2020), the argument implies that openness is vital not only in the design of AI agents, but also throughout the process of making decisions. This approach aims to increase trust in the public domain, rather than focusing solely on the procedural side.

Promote Digital Literacy and Training: Digital literacy education and tools are offered to support communities, partners, and staff in harnessing digital resources for sustainable practices.

Organizations now have the best opportunity in history to advance their CSR and SD projects, due to the digital era. Businesses may have a significant and long-lasting effect on the lives of people and the environment, by embracing digital innovation, encouraging inclusivity, and emphasizing ethical standards. Businesses that use the digital era for CSR and SD could open the door to a more prosperous and ecologically conscious future for humanity. New kinds of digital collaboration are vitally needed to make sure that the advancement of digital technology is founded on a commitment to human rights and offers genuine opportunity for all people and nations (UN, 2019).

REFERENCES

Abina, A., Batkovič, T., Cestnik, B., Kikaj, A., Kovačič Lukman, R., Kurbus, M., & Zidanšek, A. (2022). Decision Support Concept for Improvement of Sustainability-Related Competences. *Sustainability (Basel)*, *14*(14), 8539. doi:10.3390/su14148539

Adi, A., Crowther, D., & Grigore, G. (2015). Introduction to Corporate Social Responsibility in the Digital Age. In Corporate Social Responsibility in the Digital Age (pp. ix-xvi). Emerald Group Publishing Limited. doi:10.1108/S2043-052320150000007028

Al Mashalah, H., Hassini, E., Gunasekaran, A., & Bhatt, D. (2022). The impact of digital transformation on supply chains through e-commerce: Literature review and a conceptual framework. *Transportation Research Part E, Logistics and Transportation Review*, *165*, 102837. doi:10.1016/j.tre.2022.102837

Al-Shuaibi, K. M. (2016). A structural equation model of CSR and performance: Mediation by innovation and productivity. *Journal of Management and Sustainability*, *6*(2), 139–153. doi:10.5539/jms.v6n2p139

Amoako, G. K., & Dartey-Baah, K. (2020). *Corporate social responsibility: strategy for boosting brand perception and competitive advantage. CSR and Socially Responsible Investing Strategies in Transitioning and Emerging Economies*. IGI Global. doi:10.4018/978-1-7998-2193-9.ch004

Ashrafi, M., Magnan, G. M., Adams, M., & Walker, T. R. (2020). Understanding the Conceptual Evolutionary Path and Theoretical Underpinnings of Corporate Social Responsibility and Corporate Sustainability. *Sustainability (Basel)*, *12*(3), 760. doi:10.3390/su12030760

Atanasov, A., Chipriyanova, G., & Krasteva-Hristova, R. (2023). Integration of Digital Technologies in Corporate Social Responsibility (CSR) Activities: A Systematic Literature Review and Bibliometric Analysis. *Journal of Risk and Financial Management*, *16*(8), 373. doi:10.3390/jrfm16080373

Awawdeh, A. E., Ananzeh, M., El-khateeb, A. I., & Aljumah, A. (2022). Role of green financing and corporate social responsibility (CSR) in technological innovation and corporate environmental performance: A COVID-19 perspective. *China Finance Review International*, *12*(2), 297–316. doi:10.1108/CFRI-03-2021-0048

Bahta, D., Yun, J., Islam, M. R., & Ashfaq, M. (2021). Corporate social responsibility, innovation capability, and firm performance: Evidence from SME. *Social Responsibility Journal*, *17*(6), 840–860. doi:10.1108/SRJ-12-2019-0401

Barnett, M. L., Henriques, I., & Husted, B. W. (2020). Beyond Good Intentions: Designing CSR Initiatives for Greater Social Impact. *Journal of Management*, *46*(6), 937–964. doi:10.1177/0149206319900539

BasuS. (2017). Beyond Agenda: Digital Divide and Corporate Social Responsibility. ResearchGate. DOI: doi:10.13140/RG.2.2.32149.63206

Battaglia, M., Testa, F., Bianchi, L., Iraldo, F., & Frey, M. (2014). Corporate Social Responsibility and Competitiveness within SMEs of the Fashion Industry: Evidence from Italy and France. *Sustainability (Basel)*, *6*(2), 872–893. doi:10.3390/su6020872

Bekele, S. (2023). *The Role of Transparency and Accountability in Digital Transformation*. ISACA https://www.isaca.org/resources/news-and-trends/industry-news/2023/the-role-of-transparency-and-accountability-in-digital-transformation

Bohnsack, R., Bidmon, C. M., & Pinkse, J. (2022). Sustainability in the digital age: Intended and unintended consequences of digital technologies for sustainable development. *Business Strategy and the Environment*, *31*(2), 599–602. https://doi-org.proxy.library.nyu.edu/10.1002/bse.2938. doi:10.1002/bse.2938

Bokhari, S. A. A., & Myeong, S. (2022). Use of Artificial Intelligence in Smart Cities for Smart Decision-Making: A Social Innovation Perspective. *Sustainability (Basel)*, *14*(2), 620. doi:10.3390/su14020620

Carmo, C., Correia, I., Leite, J., & Carvalho, A. (2023). Towards the Voluntary Adoption of Integrated Reporting: Drivers, Barriers, and Practices. *Administrative Sciences*, *13*(6), 148. https://doi-org.proxy.library.nyu.edu/10.3390/admsci13060148. doi:10.3390/admsci13060148

Carroll, A. B. (1991). The pyramid of corporate social responsibility: Toward the moral management of organizational stakeholders. *Business Horizons*, *34*(4), 39–48. doi:10.1016/0007-6813(91)90005-G

Carroll, A. B. (1999). Corporate Social Responsibility: Evolution of a Definitional Construct. *Business & Society*, *38*(3), 268–295. doi:10.1177/000765039903800303

Charamba, K. (2022). Beyond the Corporate Responsibility to Respect Human Rights in the Dawn of a Metaverse. *International & Comparative Law Review*, *30*(1), 110–149.

Chung, N., Tyan, I., & Lee, S. J. (2019). Eco-Innovative Museums and Visitors' Perceptions of Corporate Social Responsibility. *Sustainability (Basel)*, *11*(20), 5744. doi:10.3390/su11205744

Ciulli, F., & Kolk, A. (2023). International Business, Digital Technologies, and Sustainable Development: Connecting the Dots. *Journal of World Business*, *58*(4), 101445. doi:10.1016/j.jwb.2023.101445

Clarkson, M. E. (1995). A stakeholder framework for analyzing and evaluating corporate social performance. *Academy of Management Review*, *20*(1), 92–117. doi:10.2307/258888

Cook, K. A., Romi, A. M., Sánchez, D., & Sánchez, J. M. (2019). The influence of corporate social responsibility on investment efficiency and innovation. *Journal of Business Finance & Accounting*, *46*(3-4), 494–537. doi:10.1111/jbfa.12360

de Fine Licht, K., & de Fine Licht, J. (2020). Artificial intelligence, transparency, and public decision-making. *AI & Society*, *35*(4), 917–926. doi:10.1007/s00146-020-00960-w

Dionisio, M. (2021). Corporate social innovation in practice : People with disabilities project in Brazil. *International Journal of Business and Globalisation*, *1*(1), 1–18. https://www.researchgate.net/publication/348131612_Corporate_Social_Innovation_CSI_in_practice_People_with_disabilities_project_in_Brazil. doi:10.1504/IJBG.2021.10034457

Dionisio, M., de Souza Junior, S. J., Paula, F., & Pellanda, P. C. (2023). The role of digital social innovations to address SDGs: A systematic review. *Environment, Development and Sustainability*, *34*, 100442. doi:10.1007/s10668-023-03038-x PMID:36855437

Dorin, M. (2018). Product and process innovation: A new perspective on organizational development. *International Journal of Advanced Engineering and Management Research*, *3*(6), 132–138.

Ebinger, F., & Omondi, B. (2020). Leveraging digital approaches for transparency in sustainable supply chains: A conceptual paper. *Sustainability (Basel)*, *12*(15), 6129. https://doi-org.proxy.library.nyu.edu/10.3390/su12156129. doi:10.3390/su12156129

Eichler, G. M., & Schwarz, E. J. (2019). What Sustainable Development Goals Do Social Innovations Address? A Systematic Review and Content Analysis of Social Innovation Literature. *Sustainability (Basel)*, *11*(2), 522. doi:10.3390/su11020522

Elkington, J. (1998). *Cannibals with Forks: The Triple Bottom Line of Sustainability*. New Society Publishers.

European Commission. (2019). *Corporate Social Responsibility, Responsible Business Conduct, and Business and Human Rights: Overview of Progress, Commission Staff Working Document No. 143*. EC. https://ec.europa.eu/docsroom/documents/34963

European Commission. (2020). Directorate General for Communications Networks, Content and Technology. In *Shaping Europe's Digital Future*. Publications Office of the European Union.

European Commission. (n.d.). *Sustainable Development*. EC. https://ec.europa.eu/environment/eussd/

Fallah, S. N., Mohabbati-Kalejahi, N., Alavi, S., & Zahed, M. A. (2022). Sustainable Development Goals (SDGs) as a Framework for Corporate Social Responsibility (CSR). *Sustainability (Basel)*, *14*(3), 1222. doi:10.3390/su14031222

Freeman, E. R. (1984). *Strategic Management: A Stakeholder Approach*. Harpercollins College Div: Pitman.

Gond, J., Augustine, G., Shin, H., Tirapani, A., & Mosonyi, S. (2022). *How corporate social responsibility and sustainable development functions impact the workplace: A review of the literature*. (ILO Working Paper 71). Geneva, ILO. https://www.ilo.org/wcmsp5/groups/public/---dgreports/---inst/documents/publication/wcms_850856.pdf

González-Fernández, M., & González-Velasco, C. (2018). Innovation and Corporate Performance in the Spanish Regions. *Journal of Policy Modeling*, *40*(5), 998–1021. doi:10.1016/j.jpolmod.2018.05.005

Guerrero-Villegas, J., Sierra-García, L., & Palacios-Florencio, B. (2018). The role of sustainable development and innovation on firm performance. *Corporate Social Responsibility and Environmental Management*, *25*(6), 1350–1362. doi:10.1002/csr.1644

Hart, S. L. (1995). A natural-resource-based view of the firm. *Academy of Management Review*, *20*(4), 986–1014. doi:10.2307/258963

Hart, S. L. (1997). Beyond greening: Strategies for a sustainable world. *Harvard Business Review*, *75*, 66–77.

Hillman, A. J., & Keim, G. D. (2001). Shareholder Value, Stakeholder Management, and Social Issues: What's the Bottom Line? *Strategic Management Journal*, *22*(2), 125–139. doi:10.1002/1097-0266(200101)22:2<125::AID-SMJ150>3.0.CO;2-H

Hu, Y., & Liu, Q. (2023). Local Digital Economy and Corporate Social Responsibility. *Sustainability (Basel)*, *15*(11), 8487. https://doi-org.proxy.library.nyu.edu/10.3390/su15118487. doi:10.3390/su15118487

Irshad, A. U. R., Safdar, N., Younas, Z. I., & Manzoor, W. (2023). Impact of Corporate Governance on Firms' Environmental Performance: Case Study of Environmental Sustainability-Based Business Scenarios. *Sustainability (Basel)*, *15*(10), 7775. doi:10.3390/su15107775

Kwilinski, A., Lyulyov, O., & Pimonenko, T. (2023). Environmental Sustainability within Attaining Sustainable Development Goals: The Role of Digitalization and the Transport Sector. *Sustainability (Basel)*, *15*(14), 11282. doi:10.3390/su151411282

Lee, H., & Lee, K. (2021). The Effects of Technology Innovation Activity on CSR: Emphasizing the Nonlinear and Heterogeneous Effects. *Sustainability (Basel), 13*(19), 10893. doi:10.3390/su131910893

Li, R., Xin, Y., Sotnyk, I., Kubatko, O., Almashaqbeh, I., Fedyna, S., & Prokopenko, O. (2022). Energy poverty and energy efficiency in emerging economies. *International Journal of Environment and Pollution, 69*(1/2), 1–21. doi:10.1504/IJEP.2021.125188

Nambisan, S., Lyytinen, K., Majchrzak, A., & Song, M. (2017). Digital innovation management: Reinventing innovation management research in a digital world. *Management Information Systems Quarterly, 41*(1), 223–238. doi:10.25300/MISQ/2017/41:1.03

Nidumolu, R., Prahalad, C. K., & Rangaswami, M. R. (2013). Why Sustainability is now the key driver of innovation. *IEEE Engineering Management Review, 41*(2), 30–38. doi:10.1109/EMR.2013.6601104

Ode, E., & Avavoo, R. (2020). The mediating role of knowledge application in the relationship between knowledge management practices and firm innovations. *Journal of Innovation & Knowledge, 5*(3), 210–218. doi:10.1016/j.jik.2019.08.002

Ortiz-Martínez, E., Marín-Hernández, S., & Santos-Jaén, J.-M. (2023). Sustainability, corporate social responsibility, non-financial reporting and company performance: Relationships and mediating effects in Spanish small and medium sized enterprises. *Sustainable Production and Consumption, 35*, 349–364. doi:10.1016/j.spc.2022.11.015

Pan, X., Sinha, P., & Chen, X. (2020). Corporate social responsibility and eco-innovation: The triple bottom line perspective. *Corporate Social Responsibility and Environmental Management, 28*(1), 214–228. doi:10.1002/csr.2043

Paris, B., Michas, D., Balafoutis, A. T., Nibbi, L., Skvaril, J., Li, H., Pimentel, D., da Silva, C., Athanasopoulou, E., Petropoulos, D., & Apostolopoulos, N. (2023). A Review of the Current Practices of Bioeconomy Education and Training in the EU. *Sustainability (Basel), 15*(2), 954. doi:10.3390/su15020954

Pfajfar, G., Shoham, A., Małecka, A., & Zalaznik, M. (2022). Value of Corporate Social Responsibility for Multiple Stakeholders and Social Impact – Relationship Marketing Perspective. *Journal of Business Research, 143*, 46–61. doi:10.1016/j.jbusres.2022.01.051

Piccarozzi, M., Silvestri, C., Aquilani, B., & Silvestri, L. (2022). Is this a new story of the 'Two Giants'? A systematic literature review of the relationship between industry 4.0, sustainability and its pillars. *Technological Forecasting and Social Change, 177*, 121511. doi:10.1016/j.techfore.2022.121511

Piecyk, M. I., & Björklund, M. (2015). Logistics service providers and corporate social responsibility: Sustainability reporting in the logistics industry. *International Journal of Physical Distribution & Logistics Management, 45*(5), 459–485. doi:10.1108/IJPDLM-08-2013-0228

Quach, S., Thaichon, P., Martin, K. D., Weaven, S., & Palmatier, R. W. (2022). Digital technologies: Tensions in privacy and data. *Journal of the Academy of Marketing Science, 50*(6), 1299–1323. doi:10.1007/s11747-022-00845-y PMID:35281634

Serabian, D. (2015). Consumer Protection and Cybersecurity: The Consumer Education Gap (pp. 1–16). Digital Scholarship. https://digitalscholarship.unlv.edu/brookings_pubs/33 (accessed on November 26, 2023).

Singh, N., & Hong, P. (2023). CSR, Risk Management Practices, and Performance Outcomes: An Empirical Investigation of Firms in Different Industries. *Journal of Risk and Financial Management, 16*(69), 69. doi:10.3390/jrfm16020069

UN (United Nations). (2019). *The Age of Digital Interdependence*. UN. https://www.un.org/en/pdfs/DigitalCooperation-report-for%20web.pdf

Vogler, D., & Eisenegger, M. (2021). CSR Communication, Corporate Reputation, and the Role of the News Media as an Agenda-Setter in the Digital Age. *Business & Society, 60*(8), 1957–1986. https://doi-org.proxy.library.nyu.edu/10.1177/0007650320928969. doi:10.1177/0007650320928969

Wang, K., & Guo, F. (2022). Towards Sustainable Development through the Perspective of Construction 4.0: Systematic Literature Review and Bibliometric Analysis. *Buildings, 12*(10). https://doi-org.proxy.library.nyu.edu/10.3390/buildings12101708

Wood, D. J., Mitchell, R. K., Agle, B. R., & Bryan, L. M. (2021). Stakeholder Identification and Salience after 20 Years: Progress, Problems, and Prospects. *Business & Society, 60*(1), 196–245. doi:10.1177/0007650318816522

World Commission on Environment and Development. (1987). *Our Common Future*. Oxford University Press.

Yu, D., & Zhao, P. (2022). Global Value Chain Governance of the Apparel Design Industry under the Background of Global Sustainable Economic Development. *Journal of Environmental and Public Health, 2022*, 1–11. doi:10.1155/2022/5178301 PMID:36507463

Zahid, M., Naeem, H., Aftab, I., & Mughal, S. A. (2021). From corporate social responsibility activities to financial performance: Role of innovation and competitive advantage. *Asia Pacific Journal of Innovation and Entrepreneurship, 15*(1), 2–13. doi:10.1108/APJIE-04-2020-0046

Zheng, L. J., Zhang, J. Z., Au, A. K. M., Wang, H., & Yang, Y. (2023). Leveraging technology-driven applications to promote sustainability in the shipping industry: The impact of digitalization on corporate social responsibility. *Transportation Research Part E, Logistics and Transportation Review, 176*, 103201. doi:10.1016/j.tre.2023.103201

Chapter 9

The Differences in Perceptions of Continuous Intention to Use Mobile Banking Apps: Evidence From Kuwait and Serbia

Vladimir Simovic
Australian University, Kuwait & Institute of Economic Sciences, Serbia

Faidon Theofanidis
Australian University, Kuwait

Marija Antonijevic
Institute of Economic Sciences, Serbia

Massouma Rahat
Australian University, Kuwait

Yamen Nissi
https://orcid.org/0000-0001-9080-8289
Australian University, Kuwait

ABSTRACT

The literature on continuous mobile banking use lacks research on cross-cultural variations and comparisons between countries at different levels of economic and technological development. These differences can lead to varying perceptions and attitudes among residents. This study aimed to identify significant differences between Kuwaiti and Serbian university students in their use of mobile banking applications and their perceptions of factors influencing such usage. The data on eight constructs that have been hypothesized in previous literature to impact continuous mobile banking app use were collected: perceived usefulness, perceived ease of use, confirmation, perceived trust, compatibility, privacy, environmental awareness, and satisfaction. The Mann-Whitney U-test was employed to test for differences in perceptions between the two groups. The findings suggest that differences in perceptions between the two countries are influenced by cultural backgrounds, development levels, user habits, mobile banking app characteristics, and socio-economic factors.

DOI: 10.4018/979-8-3693-0798-4.ch009

INTRODUCTION

Digital transformation is one of the biggest challenges in all industries, including banking (Schuchmann and Seufert 2015). The changes in people's habits and the way they access financial services are a result of the increasing use of the Internet and mobile devices. As a result, people are more interested in banking services that are available anywhere, anytime and are easy to understand and use. Economies from all around the world, especially developing countries, face challenges with financial inclusion (M. S. Antonijević et al. 2022). Digital banking, i.e. the creation and delivery of products/services through digital channels using state-of-the-art technology to identify individuals' needs, automate services and interact with customers across all channels, seems to be an obvious solution for enhancing financial inclusion and constantly changing customer habits and preferences. Mobile banking is a form of digital banking where the customer is connected to a bank via a mobile device such as a smartphone or tablet (Laukkanen 2017). Mobile banking is known to be a digital financial service offered by banks to enable customers to do their banking without having to be physically present in the bank or having ATMs available.

Over the past decade, the academic community has become increasingly interested in studying factors and measuring their impact on the continuous intention to use mobile banking services. Albashrawi and Motiwalla (2019) define continuance intention as intent to continue using mobile banking services after the initial adoption phase.As banks seek to provide the best digital solution to their customers, it is important to understand the factors that influence the continuous use of digital banking services. The continuous use of mobile banking apps has been extensively studied by many authors (Tsai et al. 2014; Hanafizadeh et al., 2014; Yuan et al. 2014; Vedadi and Warkentin 2016; Lema, 2017; Kumar et al. 2018; Albashrawi and Motiwalla 2019; Avornyo et al. 2019; Waheed et al. 2019; Merhi et al. 2019; Lukić et al. 2019; Kuncoro et al. 2020; Jerene and Sharma 2020; Asnakew 2020; Poromatikul et al. 2019; Antonijević et al. 2021; Rabaa'i and AlMaati 2021; Abu-Taieh et al. 2022; Shetu et al. 2022; Yin and Lin 2022; Alghareeb 2022; Inan et al. 2023). The most obvious gap in the current literature on the continuous use of mobile banking concerns the study of cross-cultural variations and comparisons between countries with different levels of economic and technological development, as residents may have different perceptions and attitudes. These cross-cultural differences and country comparisons have been recognised by many authors and recommended for future research (Yuan et al. 2014; Kumar et al. 2018; Avornyo et al. 2019; Asnakew 2020; Shetu et al. 2022; Yin and Lin 2022; Inan et al. 2023). In one of the rare comparative studies of this type, Malaquias and Hwang (2019) examined differences in mobile banking use between Brazilian and US citizens. As far as the authors are aware, there are no comparative studies on the continuous use of mobile banking apps between Kuwait and Serbia.

The second area that requires additional research is to examine the influence of other variables to gain a better understanding of the predictors of continuance intention (Yuan et al. 2014; Jerene and Sharma 2020; Asnakew 2020; Inan et al. 2023). The addition of new variables will provide a comprehensive insight into the main drivers of future behaviour.

To address these challenges, the primary objective of this chapter is to identify statistically significant differences between Kuwaiti and Serbian students in their use of mobile banking applications and in their perceptions of critical factors that might influence such use. A second focus is to explain these differences in perceptions based on the different socio-economic environments in Kuwait and Serbia.

This chapter aims to contribute to the literature by providing evidence of differences in the perceptions of students in the two countries, which are characterised by different cultural backgrounds, levels of development (high income vs. upper-middle income) and other socio-economic characteristics. In addition, the authors examine perceptions of environmental awareness, as this variable has not been the subject of previous studies.

THEORETICAL BACKGROUND

Previous Work on Continuous Use of Mobile Banking Apps

The emergence of mobile banking has completely changed the financial industry by enabling users to access banking services from their smartphones, whenever and wherever they want. The rising demand for mobile banking, especially due to the emergence of COVID-19, has led to a growing interest in the scientific community to examine variables that influence an individual's decision to use this digital service in the future. Numerous studies (Tsai et al. 2014; Hanafizadeh et al., 2014; Yuan et al. 2014; Vedadi and Warkentin 2016; Lema, 2017; Kumar et al. 2018; Albashrawi and Motiwalla 2019; Avornyo et al. 2019; Waheed et al. 2019; Merhi et al. 2019; Lukić et al. 2019; Kuncoro et al. 2020; Jerene and Sharma 2020; Asnakew 2020; Poromatikul et al, 2020; Antonijević et al. 2021; Rabaa'i and AlMaati 2021; Abu-Taieh et al. 2022; Shetu et al. 2022; Yin and Lin 2022; Alghareeb 2022; Inan et al. 2023) have investigated the factors that drive the continuous use of mobile banking, such as perceived usefulness, perceived ease of use, privacy, confirmation, compatibility, perceived trust, and satisfaction.

Research conducted by Yuan et al. (2014) found that perceived usefulness and satisfaction were significant predictors of continuance intention, while perceived ease of use was not statistically significant. The results regarding perceived usefulness were in line with Yin and Lin's (2022) findings. Kumar et al. (2018) highlighted the important role of satisfaction in the continuance intention to use mobile banking. Moreover, Lema (2017) identified the crucial role of perceived usefulness, perceived ease of use, and perceived trust. Albashrawi and Motiwalla (2019) found that satisfaction was a statistically significant predictor of the continued intention to use mobile banking. This finding is confirmed by Vedadi and Warkentin (2016), whereby the authors discovered a significant influence of perceived usefulness. Perceived usefulness and satisfaction were the key drivers of continuous intention, while perceived ease of use did not represent a good predictor of future behavior in a study by Avornyo et al. (2019). The same findings arose in Abu-Taieh et al. (2022) and Hanafizadeh et al., (2014). Inan et al. (2023) found perceived usefulness as a significant variable, while Kuncoro et al. (2020) claimed that privacy and satisfaction also had a significant influence.Waheed et al. (2019) revealed that perceived usefulness influenced continuous intention, while compatibility influenced perceived ease of use and perceived usefulness. Jerene and Sharma (2020) highlighted the importance of perceived usefulness, but found no significance of perceived ease of use. Additionally, Asnakew (2020) identified the relevance of perceived trust. The behavior of users was influenced by compatibility, perceived ease of use, and perceived usefulness in Shetu et al. (2022). The significance of compatibility and satisfaction was confirmed, but perceived ease of use to some extent did not represent a crucial driver in Tsai et al. (2014). Results of the study conducted by Poromatikul et al. (2019) showed that the key antecedents of future behavior were perceived trust and satisfaction, while confirmation was not a significant predictor. Merhi et al. (2019) conducted a cross-cultural analysis and found that privacy concerns and perceived trust played a significant role in continuous intention.

Two studies examining continuous intention have been conducted in the Republic of Serbia. Lukić et al. (2019) found that perceived usefulness and perceived ease of use were good predictors of students' intention to exclusively use mobile banking in the future, while Antonijević et al. (2021) indicated that perceived usefulness was a statistically significant factor, but perceived ease of use was not a good predictor of an individual's intention. In Kuwait, two studies have examined users' behavior regarding continuous intention. Alghareeb (2022) found a low mean score for security issues, particularly individual fears about personal data abuse (2.28), while users were satisfied with the application with an average score of 4.41. Additionally, Rabaa'i and AlMaati (2021) identified a significant influence of perceived trust and satisfaction on continuous intention, while satisfaction was directly influenced by confirmation, privacy, and perceived trust.

The Driving Factors of Continuous Use of Mobile Banking Apps

The literature reveals that the continuous intention to use mobile banking apps is determined by different factors. Different models are usually combined and extended with additional variables resulting in the significant predictive power of continuance intention. The most commonly used is the expectation-confirmation model (ECM) (Hidayat-ur-Rehman et al. 2021), which comprises four variables: Perceived usefulness (PU), Confirmation (CONF), Satisfaction (SATISF), and Continuance intention (CI). Additionally, the TAM model, which consists of Perceived usefulness (PU) and Perceived ease of use (PEOU), is often combined with ECM to better understand the decision-making process regarding the continuous intention to use mobile banking apps (Al-Laheebi 2022).

The mentioned models have been extended by incorporating Perceived trust (PT), Compatibility (COMPAT), and Privacy (PRIV) (Raza et al. 2017; Kumar et al. 2018; Poromatikul et al. 2019; Merhi et al. 2019; Waheed et al. 2019; Kuncoro et al. 2020; Petrović et al. 2021; Rabaa'i and AlMaati 2021; Van et al. 2021; Nguyen et al. 2021; Kabakuş and Küçükoğlu 2022; Shetu et al. 2022). In addition, we used Environmental awareness (ENV), which has not been considered in previous studies on the continuous use of mobile banking apps. Table 1 shows the literature sources and the items for all constructs used in our study.

Perceived Usefulness

Perceived usefulness indicates the extent to which a person believes that using mobile banking services is useful to them (Jeong and Yoon 2013). A mobile banking app is perceived as useful if users believe that there is a positive relationship between usage and performance on the one hand and effectiveness and satisfaction on the other (Priya et al. 2018). Perceived usefulness has been shown to be a strong predictor of continuous use of mobile banking apps and its positive impact has been confirmed by many authors (Gu et al. 2009; Hanafizadeh et al., 2014; Avornyo et al. 2019; Foroughi et al. 2019; Hidayat-ur-Rehman et al. (2021). In our study, we used the items proposed by Albashrawi and Motiwalla (2019) that measure the overall perception of usefulness of mobile banking, performance, speed and productivity in conducting financial transactions using mobile banking.

Perceived Ease of Use

Perceived ease of use refers to the extent to which people believe it is easy to log in and use mobile banking (Le et al. 2020). The TAM model, which is the basis for understanding user behaviour when using a particular system, states that people who perceive the system to be easy to use are more likely to want to use it (Altin Gumussoy et al. 2018). The possession of the appropriate level of digital competences is important for accessing and using digital services (Domazet et al. 2023; Ivanovic et al. 2021; Simovic et al. 2023; Simović and Domazet 2021; Simovic et al. 2022). Many studies (Gu et al. 2009; Hanafizadeh et al., 2014; Priya et al. 2018; Le et al. 2020; Tiwari et al. 2021; Prastiawan et al. 2021; Shetu et al. 2022) confirm the positive impact of perceived ease of use on intention to use mobile banking apps continuously. In our study, we adopted the approach proposed by Yuan et al. (2014) to measure the perceived ease of use of mobile banking apps using perceived mental effort, learning curve and ease of performing banking transactions with the m-banking app.

Satisfaction

Satisfaction implies the fulfillment of expectations, and if the performance of the product or service is better than expected, the level of satisfaction is higher (Marinković et al. 2020). The positive impact of satisfaction on the continuous use of mobile banking apps is confirmed in several studies (Avornyo et al. 2019; Foroughi et al. 2019; Hidayat-ur-Rehman et al. 2021; Inan et al. 2023). In our study, satisfaction was assessed using performance of mobile banking services, positive experience of using the mobile banking app, reflection on the decision to use the mobile banking app, and the feeling when using the mobile banking app compared to the traditional branch visit, following Tsai et al. (2014).

Privacy

Privacy refers to "the individual's ability to control when, how and to what extent his or her personal information is communicated to others" (Hong et al. 2006). Privacy concerns tend to be higher with monetary transactions via mobile devices (Chong 2013). Several studies have confirmed the positive impact of privacy on continuous intention to use mobile banking (Arcand et al. 2017; Kuncoro et al. 2020; Rabaa'i and AlMaati 2021). We used items from Albashrawi and Motiwalla (2019) to assess university students' perceptions of privacy related to mobile banking app use. The following items were used: the likelihood of the bank using the data obtained from customers for other purposes or selling the data and the likelihood of a data breach.

Compatibility

The suitability of using the mobile banking app to the person's lifestyle and needs constitutes compatibility (Hanafizadeh et al., 2014). As reported by Shetu et al. (2022), compatibility has a positive impact on continuous intention to use mobile banking apps. In our study, the construct Compatibility assessed university students' perceptions of the compatibility of mobile banking apps with their lifestyle, personal finance management and work style (Giovanis et al. 2019).

Trust

Trust in mobile banking is related to a sufficient level of ability, benevolence and integrity of the system (Gefen et al. 2003), as well as the willingness of individuals to accept the risk (Hidayat-ur-Rehman et al. 2021). It has been confirmed that trust has a positive impact on the intention to adopt and continue using mobile banking apps (Gu et al. 2009; Hanafizadeh et al., 2014; Le et al. 2020; Marinković et al.

2020; Saparudin et al. 2020). Two types of trust (Köksal 2015) are associated with the adoption and continuous use of mobile banking applications: institutional trust and trust in the technology or channel. Our research focused on the second type of trust associated with the technology or channel, and we explored users' perceptions based on perceptions of trust and trustworthiness of mobile banking and the security and reliability of mobile banking transactions (Sharma 2019).

Confirmation

Confirmation in using mobile banking apps is associated with higher performance and exceeding expectations (Hidayat-ur-Rehman et al. 2021). Confirmation of the initial expectations of mobile banking services contributes to subsequent users' satisfaction, whereas the reverse causes dissatisfaction and discontinuance intention (Foroughi et al. 2019). In our study, the users' perceptions of Confirmation were assessed on the basis of the experience in using mobile banking apps, the features mobile banking apps provide and confirmation of the expectations (Kumar et al. 2018).

Environmental Awareness

Digital services play an important role in addressing environmental issues by promoting reduced usage of paper, energy, fuel, and other resources. One possible way to enhance sustainable banking is by encouraging individuals to use digital banking services instead of traditional ones (Burhanudin et al. 2019). Previous research on continuous intention to use mobile banking did not consider individuals' awareness of the environment. In this regard, the authors adapted items from Taneja and Ali (2021), who examined the factors influencing customers' intentions towards environmentally sustainable banking. The adapted items are related to the environmentally friendly aspects of mobile banking and its important role in reducing pollution, protecting the environment, and providing environmental benefits compared to traditional banking. In this study the environmental awareness was assessed using students' perceptions regarding the use of mobile banking apps as an environmentally friendly alternative, reduction of pollution, environment protection, and environmental benefits compared to other forms of banking (Taneja and Ali 2021).

METHODS

The questionnaire was first prepared in English and then translated into Arabic and Serbian. The students in Kuwait answered the bilingual questionnaire (English and Arabic) and the data from the students in Serbia were collected using the Serbian version of the questionnaire. The questionnaire consisted of the following parts:

- Part 1 contained 5 questions to collect the respondent's demographic data (i.e. gender, age, nationality, university and major).
- Part 2 captured the respondent's behavioural profile of mobile banking use (i.e. bank account ownership, average years of bank affiliation, average years of mobile banking use, number of times mobile banking is used per week, most frequently used mobile banking features).

- Part 3 measured 9 constructs identified in the literature review as critical factors influencing mobile banking application use, as well as the construct of continuous intention to use mobile applications.

The 9 constructs measured are specifically the following: 1. Perceived usefulness (PU), 2. Perceived ease of use (PEOU), 3. Satisfaction (SATISF), 4. Privacy (PRIV), 5. Compatibility (COMPAT), 6. Perceived trust (PT), 7. Confirmation (CONF), 8. Environmental awareness (ENV), 9. Continuous intention to use (CI). The operationalisation of these constructs was based on scales/items from previous studies (see Table 1) and was scaled on a five-point Likert scale with which respondents expressed their degree of agreement (1 - strongly disagree, 5 - strongly agree). The questionnaire was pre-tested with two focus groups from each of the two countries and the scales were tested for internal consistency reliability (Cronbach's $\alpha > 0.7$, Table 1) for all measurement scales used (DeVellis 2003). The items measuring the constructs of Satisfaction and Environmental awareness were modified accordingly to fit the research context (insertion of "mobile banking" in the items). Table 1 shows the constructs, Cronbach's alpha per construct, the items used per construct and the source from which the items were taken.

Table 1. Research constructs and items employed in the study

Constructs / Cronbach' alpha	Items	Source
Perceived usefulness (PU) Cronbach' alpha: 0.766	1. Overall, I find mobile banking to be useful. 2. Using mobile banking improves my performance in conducting financial transactions. 3. Using mobile banking enables me to process financial transactions quickly. 4. Using mobile banking enhances my productivity with financial transactions.	Albashrawi, M., & Motiwalla, L. (2019)
Perceived ease of use (PEOU) Cronbach' alpha: 0.718	1. Learning to operate m-banking is easy for me. 2. It is easy to use m-banking to accomplish banking transactions. 3. Interaction with m-banking does not require a lot of mental effort.	Yuan, S., Liu, Y., Yao, R., & Liu, J. (2016)
Satisfaction (SATISF) Cronbach' alpha: 0.801	1. I am satisfied with the performance of mobile banking services. 2. I am pleased with the experience of using mobile banking services. 3. My decision to use mobile banking services was a wise one. 4. My feeling with using mobile banking services was better than traditional "brick and mortar" bank branch.	Adapted from Tsai, H. T., Chien, J. L., & Tsai, M. T. (2014)
Privacy (PRIV) Cronbach' alpha: 0.935	1. I am concerned that when I give personal information to mobile banking for some reason, the bank would use the information for other reasons. 2. I am concerned that my information could be breached when using mobile banking 3. I am concerned that my information could be shared or sold when using mobile banking.	Albashrawi, M., & Motiwalla, L. (2019)
Compatibility (COMPAT) Cronbach' alpha: 0.840	1. Mobile banking is compatible with my lifestyle. 2. Using mobile banking fits well with the way I like to manage my finances. 3. Using mobile banking fits into my working style.	Giovanis, A., Athanasopoulou, P., Assimakopoulos, C., & Sarmaniotis, C. (2019)
Perceived trust (PT) Cronbach' alpha: 0.936	1. I trust in mobile banking. 2. Mobile banking is trustworthy. 3. Mobile banking transactions are safe. 4. Mobile banking transactions are reliable.	Sharma, S. K. (2019)
Confirmation (CONFIR) Cronbach' alpha: 0.835	1. My experience with mobile banking was better than what I expected. 2. The various features of mobile banking apps were better than what I expected. 3. Overall, most of my expectations towards mobile banking apps were confirmed.	Kumar, R. R., Israel, D., & Malik, G. (2018)
Environmental awareness (ENV) Cronbach' alpha: 0.897	1. Using mobile banking is environment-friendly. 2. By using mobile banking, I help reduce pollution due to less usage of paper and energy. 3. By using mobile banking, I help protect the environment. 4. Using mobile banking has more environmental benefits as compared to traditional banking services.	Adapted from Taneja, S., & Ali, L. (2021)
Continuous intention (CI) Cronbach' alpha: 0.856	1. I intend to continue using mobile banking in the future. 2. I will always try to use mobile banking in my daily life. 3. I plan to continue to use mobile banking frequently.	Farzin, M., Sadeghi, M., Kharkeshi, F. Y., Ruholahpur, H., & Fattahi, M. (2021)

Two surveys were conducted, one in Serbia and one in Kuwait. Both surveys were conducted in November 2022 using an online data collection method (convenience sampling). Only university students of all disciplines and years of study at public and private universities in Kuwait and Serbia were eligible to participate in the survey, regardless of their gender and nationality. During data cleaning and filtering, only responses from Kuwaitis and Serbs were selected for a final sample (other nationalities were excluded). A total of 329 participants responded to the questionnaire, and after excluding non-users of mobile banking, non-Kuwaitis and non-Serbs, the final sample consisted of 212 students in Serbia and 83 students in Kuwait.

The study was conducted following the guidelines of the Declaration of Helsinki and received ethical approval from the Scientific Research Center of the Australian University in Kuwait before it was conducted. The study was anonymous and participating students were informed that they were giving consent to participate in a study by clicking the 'Continue' button on the questionnaire.

Table 2 compares the demographic and behavioural characteristics of participants in Kuwait and Serbia.

Table 2. Comparison of demographics and behavioral characteristics of the survey participants (Serbia and Kuwait)

Demographics & Behavioral	Serbia	Kuwait
Gender		
Female	67%	55.4%
Male	33%	44.6%
Age (average)	22.27 years, SD=3.33	23.00 years, SD=3.37
Major		
Business	59%	90.4%
Engineering	9.4%	8.4%
Other	31.6%	1.2%
Average years of affiliation with the bank	3.91 years, SD=2.92	6.69 years, SD=4.22
Average years using mobile banking	3.95 years, SD=1.22	4.14 years, SD=1.25
Number of times using mobile banking per week		
Less than once a week	28.8%	6.0%
About once a week	23.1%	9.6%
2–3 times a week	25.0%	19.3%
4–5 times a week	13.2%	19.3%
About once a day	6.6%	16.9%
Several times each day	3.3%	28.9%
Functions used more often		
Checking account balance(s)	52.8%	21.7%
Transferring money between accounts	4.2%	37.3%
Paying a bill	20.8%	18.1%
Sending money to another individual	11.3%	9.6%
Paying for products or services using Apple Pay or Google Pay	5.7%	9.6%
Locating the closest ATM or branch	0.5%	1.2%
Cardless ATM withdrawal	2.4%	0%
Viewing statements	1.9%	2.4%
Exchange to other currency	0.5%	0%

RESULTS

Since the data were not normally distributed, the differences in students' perceptions between Kuwait and Serbia were examined using the non-parametric Mann-Whitney U test. The Mann-Whitney U test was designed to test differences between two independent groups using a continuous (in our case) or ordinal measure. "It converts the scores on the continuous variable into ranks across the two groups. It then tests whether the ranks for the two groups differ significantly" (Pallant 2020). Checking the shape of the distributions (using histograms) of all 9 constructs per group (Serbia/Kuwait) showed that all pairs of distributions had a similar pattern, so the medians (rather than the mean ranks) should be used to summarise the differences in students' perceptions between the two countries. Furthermore, according to Daly and Cohen (1978), the effect size (symbolised by r) for the Mann-Whitney U-test can be calculated by dividing the z-value by the square root of N, where N is the total number of cases (of the Serbian and Kuwaiti samples). Based on Daly and Cohen's (1978) criteria, r = 0.1 indicates a small effect, r = 0.3 a medium effect and r = 0.5 a large effect. Table 3 summarises the results of the tests conducted to determine the differences in perceptions between the Serbian and Kuwaiti student samples.

Table 3. Summary of results (Mann-Whitney U Test)

Constructs	Median Score	Standard Deviation	Mann-Whitney U-test
Perceived usefulness (Kuwait)	4.75	0.67	*U=6783 z = -3.407*
Perceived usefulness (Serbia)	5.00	0.51	***p = 0.00*** *r= 0.198*
Perceived ease of use (Kuwait)	4.67	0.75	*U=6724 z = -3.435*
Perceived ease of use (Serbia)	5.00	0.57	***p = 0.00***, *r =0.199*
Satisfaction (Kuwait)	4.75	0.68	*U=6765 z = -3.304*
Satisfaction (Serbia)	5.00	0.54	***p = 0.00*** *r=0.192*
Privacy (Kuwait)	3.00	1.18	*U=5927 z = -4.429*
Privacy (Serbia)	2.00	1.29	***p = 0.00*** *r =0.258*
Compatibility (Kuwait)	4.33	0.79	*U=7136 z = -2.130*
Compatibility (Serbia)	5.00	0.71	***p = 0.007***, *r = 0.124*
Perceived trust (Kuwait)	4.00	0.85	*U=6864 z = -3.050*
Perceived trust (Serbia)	4.75	0.74	***p = 0.002***, *r =0.177*
Confirmation (Kuwait)	4.33	0.68	*U=8404 z = -0.615*
Confirmation (Serbia)	4.33	0.78	*p = 0.539 r=0.036*
Environmental awareness (Kuwait)	4.50	0.93	*U=7429 z = -2.245*
Environmental awareness (Serbia)	5.00	0.82	***p = 0.025***, *r =0.131*
Continuous intention to use (Kuwait)	4.67	0.70	*U=6559 z = -3.931*
Continuous intention to use (Serbia)	5.00	0.57	***p = 0.00*** *r =0.229*
Note: Statistically significant differences (i.e. p < 0.05) appear in bold.			

The Mann-Whitney U Test revealed statistically significant differences in the perception of the following constructs:

- Usefulness: for Kuwaitis (Md = 4.75, n =83) and Serbs (Md = 5, n = 212), U = 6783, z = -3.407, p = .00, with a small effect size (r = .198).
- Ease of use: for Kuwaitis (Md = 4.67, n =83) and Serbs (Md = 5, n = 212), U = 6724, z = -3.435, p = .00, with a small effect size (r = .199).
- Satisfaction: for Kuwaitis (Md = 4.75, n =83) and Serbs (Md = 5, n = 212), U = 6765, z = -3.050, p = .00, with a small effect size (r = .192).
- Privacy: for Kuwaitis (Md = 3, n =83) and Serbs (Md = 2, n = 212), U = 5927, z = -4.429, p = .00, with a medium effect size (r = .258).
- Compatibility: for Kuwaitis (Md = 4.33, n =83) and Serbs (Md = 5, n = 212), U = 7136, z = -2.130, p = .007, with a small effect size (r = .124).
- Trust: for Kuwaitis (Md = 4, n =83) and Serbs (Md = 4.75, n = 212), U = 6864, z = -3.050, p = .002, with a small effect size (r = .177).
- Environmental awareness: for Kuwaitis (Md = 4.5, n =83) and Serbs (Md = 5, n = 212), U = 7429, z = -2.245, p = .025, with a small effect size (r = .131).
- Continuous intention to use mobile banking applications: for Kuwaitis (Md = 4.67, n = 83) and Serbs (Md = 5, n = 212), U = 6559, z = -3.931, p = .00, with a medium effect size (r = .229).

The Mann-Whitney U Test revealed no statistically significant differences in perceptions of the Confirmation construct:

- Confirmation: for Kuwaitis (Md = 4.33, n =83) and Serbs (Md = 4.33, n = 212), U = 8404, z = -0.615, p = .539, r = .036.

DISCUSSION

This research primarily addressed the differences in perceptions of continuous mobile banking app use between university students in Kuwait and Serbia and their relationship with the different socio-economic environments in the two countries. The results show that there are statistically significant differences between the two countries on seven out of eight determinants of continuous intention to use mobile banking apps.

For the construct "Perceived usefulness", students in Serbia perceive usefulness at a higher level than students in Kuwait. Given that PU has a positive impact on CI (Li and Fang 2019; Avornyo et al. 2019; Foroughi et al. 2019: Hidayat-ur-Rehman et al. 2021), it can be assumed that university students in Serbia intend to continue using mobile banking apps to a higher extent than their counterparts in Kuwait. Our results in Table 3 confirm this assumption. Students in Serbia perceive intention to continue using mobile banking apps at a higher level than students in Kuwait. One possible explanation for the higher perception of students in Serbia on PU and consequently CI is that PU is associated with various characteristics of mobile banking apps such as design aesthetics (Chaouali et al. 2019) and interactivity (Gupta et al. 2021), suggesting that students in Serbia perceive the characteristics of mobile banking apps in this country at a higher level. It is very important to note that according to the data in Table 2, students in Serbia most frequently use mobile banking apps to check account balances (52.8%), while students in Kuwait most frequently use mobile banking apps to transfer money between accounts (37.3%). The design aesthetics and the interactivity of the specified features could be the explanation for the differences in the perception of PU.

For the construct "Perceived ease of use", our results show that university students in Serbia perceive this determinant of continuous mobile banking app use at a higher level than university students in Kuwait. In other words, students in Serbia find mobile banking apps easier to use than their peers in Kuwait. One way to explain this result is to relate it to information and digital literacy. This is in line with the evidence suggesting that information and digital literacy have a direct impact on PEOU of technology (Nikou et al. 2022). The value of the Digital Skills Gap Index - DSGI ("Digital skills gap index" 2021), which ranks countries according to the level of digital skills of their citizens, is in line with our findings. The DSGI ranks Serbia 64th and Kuwait 67th in the world, which is consistent with the fact that students in Serbia perceive ease of use of mobile banking apps at a higher level than students in Kuwait. Another interesting perspective of our finding relates to the positive impact of PEOU on PU, as shown in many studies (Yuan et al. 2014; Avornyo et al. 2019; Waheed et al. 2019; Asnakew 2020). Our findings are consistent with this argumentation and show that higher student perceptions of PEOU in Serbia co-exist with higher perceptions of PU.

The results for the construct "Satisfaction" show that university students in Serbia perceive a higher level of satisfaction with mobile banking apps than students in Kuwait. Satisfaction is positively related to the benefits that mobile banking offers (Hoffmann et al. 2017), suggesting that students in Serbia perceive mobile banking apps to be more beneficial in this country than in Kuwait. Design and enjoyment are also factors that influence customer satisfaction with mobile banking apps (Rejman-Petrovic et al. 2022) and their close association with design aesthetics and interactivity leads to a very similar conclusion as in the case of perceived usefulness - students in Serbia perceive the features of mobile banking apps in this country at higher level. Also, higher perceptions of the SATISF of the students in Serbia co-exist with their higher perceptions of the PU and PEOU which is in line with the evidence suggesting that PU (Albashrawi and Motiwalla 2019; Foroughi et al. 2019; Inan et al. 2023) and PEOU (Priya et al. 2018; Albashrawi and Motiwalla 2019; Yin and Lin 2022) have a positive impact on SATISF of mobile banking users.

For all three constructs elaborated so far (perceived usefulness, perceived ease of use and satisfaction), students in Serbia and Kuwait showed differences in their perceptions and students in Serbia had higher levels of agreement with the statements under these determinants of continuation intention. "Privacy" was the only construct where students in Serbia disagreed to a higher degree with the statements under this construct and showed higher levels of trust in privacy issues related to continuous use of the mobile banking app compared to students in Kuwait. One way to explain the difference in privacy perceptions between students in Serbia and Kuwait is the regulatory environment. In Serbia (as a candidate country for accession to the European Union), the regulatory environment is aligned with EU legislation in many areas, including data privacy. For example, Serbian data privacy laws are in line with the GDPR act (General Data Protection Regulation), which regulates the way organisations and government agencies collect and manage personal customer data. Kuwait does not have such an initiative and to date this country does not have a personal data protection law ("Law in Kuwait - DLA Piper global data protection laws of the world" n.d.) In addition, World Bank data on the Global Indicator of Regulatory Governance (which ranges from 0 for worst performance to 5 for best performance) for Serbia is 4.5 ("Economy data" n.d.), while in Kuwait it is 1 ("Economy data" n.d.).

The results for the construct "Compatibility" suggest that students in Serbia perceive that mobile banking apps fit their lifestyle and work style better and help them manage their personal finances better than students in Kuwait. There is strong evidence of a positive relationship between parental wealth and children's (students') personal financial management (Novitasari et al. 2021), suggesting that children (students) in a country with a higher GDP per capita (in Kuwait GDP per capita is 24,300 USD compared to Serbia where GDP per capita is 9,230 USD ("GDP per capita (current US$)" n.d.) World Bank ("GDP per capita (current US$)" n.d.) have a greater need for, and higher expectations of, more sophisticated personal financial management tools (mobile banking apps). Following this line of reasoning, the difference in students' perceptions of this construct can be attributed to similar reasons as PU and PEOU - students in Kuwait expect more from their mobile banking apps in terms of features. Another interesting fact (Table 2) that may shed light on this finding is that students in Kuwait use the mobile banking apps more frequently (28.9% of students in Kuwait use the mobile banking app several times a day compared to 3.3% of students in Serbia), suggesting that their expectations are higher. Higher expectations, when properly met, lead to higher PU and vice versa (Yuan et al. 2014). A number of studies confirm the positive impact of COMPAT on PU (Raza et al. 2017; Altin Gumussoy et al. 2018; Waheed et al. 2019).

"Trust" in app-based transactions and the mobile banking system is closely related to privacy concerns when using mobile banking, and our results show the same tendency. Students in Serbia perceive trust in mobile banking apps at a higher level than students in Kuwait. In addition to the arguments used to explain the differences in privacy perceptions, the differences in trust perceptions could also be related to the differences in country rankings between Kuwait (65) and Serbia (39) according to the Global Cybersecurity Index - GCI ("ITU publications" n.d.). The apparent difference in the commitment of Serbian authorities to cybersecurity compared to Kuwait could be one reason for the differences in students' perceptions of confidence in using mobile banking apps. In other words, the general sense of higher cybersecurity among citizens in Serbia is likely to have an impact on students' perceptions of cyber trust associated with use of mobile banking apps. Another way to explain the differences in trust and privacy perceptions of mobile banking use between students in Kuwait and Serbia is that, as shown in Table 2, students in Serbia use mobile banking apps mainly for simple transactions such as checking account balances (52.8%), which is associated with a lower risk of security breach and lower privacy concerns, compared to more complex transactions such as money transfers between accounts, which students in Kuwait use most often (37.3%). Due to lower perceptions of privacy and trust, students in Kuwait might also perceive Usefulness (PU) and Ease of Use (PEOU) at a lower level, which is in line with findings suggesting a positive impact of PRIV on PU and PEOU (Petrović et al. 2021; Van et al. 2021; Kabakuş and Küçükoğlu 2022).

Only in the case of the construct "Confirmation," was no statistically significant difference identified between the perceptions of university students in Kuwait and Serbia. This result suggests that university students in Kuwait and Serbia have similar levels of perception regarding their expectations towards mobile banking apps in the two countries. When compared with other constructs, the median values for CONF are lower for both countries, indicating that university students in Kuwait and Serbia perceive that their expectations towards mobile banking apps are not fully met. One way to interpret this finding is to associate it with the experience of using mobile banking apps, which can lead to greater familiarity with the technology (Alba and Hutchinson 1987). The experience and familiarity with the technology result in higher expectations as one of the main aspects of the construct CONF (Kumar et al. 2018). The data in Table 2 show that both students in Kuwait and Serbia have been using mobile banking apps for approximately four years on average, placing them in the category of more experienced users who are more familiar with this technology and, in turn, have higher expectations towards mobile banking apps. This could explain the lower perceptions of university students in Kuwait and Serbia in terms of CONF.

Apart from the fact that our study adds value by comparing university students' perceptions of continuous mobile banking use at a cross-national level (between Kuwait and Serbia), the inclusion of the construct "Environmental awareness" in the analysis also represents an original contribution to the topic under discussion. The results show that students in Serbia perceive a higher level of environmental awareness compared to students in Kuwait. One way to interpret these results is to relate them to the Environment Performance Index (EPI) for the two countries. The EPI score for Serbia is 43.90, ranking 79th in the world, while the EPI index for Kuwait is 42.40, with a corresponding rank of 87 (Wolf et al. 2022). The score of the EPI index shows a difference in terms of environmental protection in the two countries, indicating a difference in environmental awareness, which is also reflected in the perception of environmental awareness in relation to the use of the mobile banking app in our research.

Considering that satisfaction (Humbani and Wiese 2019), perceived usefulness (Daragmeh et al. 2021) and other constructs used in our study are the predictors of continuous mobile banking app use, the higher perceptions of university students from Serbia on 7 (out of 7) constructs (which were found to be statistically significant) suggest that their perceptions of intention to use mobile banking apps continuously should also be higher compared to university students in Kuwait. Our results confirm this assumption. University students in Serbia have a higher intention to continue using mobile banking apps compared to their peers in Kuwait.

CONCLUSION

Mobile banking has radically changed the financial sector by enabling consumers to access banking services anytime, anywhere via their smartphones. With so many features that are easy to use, mobile banking became very popular. The academic community is increasingly interested in studying factors that influence an individual's decision to use this digital service. The aim of this chapter was to investigate the differences in perceptions between Serbian and Kuwaiti university students regarding their continuous intention to use mobile banking.

The scientific contribution of this chapter is evident in the fact that it provides a comparison of perceptions between two countries with different socio-economic environments. This is one of the few studies that compares mobile banking users' perceptions with their intention to continue using mobile banking apps. The results of this chapter suggest that the differences in perceived usefulness, satisfaction and compatibility between users in different countries can be attributed to the characteristics of mobile banking apps. Differences in perceptions of perceived ease of use could be related to different levels of digital literacy, and differences in perceptions of privacy and trust in the use of mobile banking apps between countries could be due to the different characteristics of the regulatory environment and the different attitudes and approaches of country authorities towards cybersecurity. The chapter also found that higher perceptions of the predictors of continuous use of mobile banking in a country (usefulness, ease of use, privacy, trust, compatibility, environmental awareness and satisfaction) are in line with higher perceptions of intention to use mobile banking continuously.

In addition, the inclusion of a new construct - environmental awareness - designed specifically for this study, improves the understanding of individual behaviour. The results of this chapter suggest that differences in perceptions of environmental awareness as a driver of continuous mobile banking use may be associated with levels of the Environment Performance Index (EPI).

The results of this research have multiple managerial and strategic implications. From managerial perspective, understanding the differences in perceptions between users in two countries may result in localized marketing strategies, improved user experience and customer satisfaction and retention strategies which are adapted to cultural preferences and technological habits of the users in two countries. From strategic point, understanding socio-economic factors associated with continuous use of mobile banking apps can lead to better tailored market penetration strategies, better strategic partnerships and alliances with local businesses, and better policy and regulation alignment. Also, insights gained from cross-cultural differences in perceptions of mobile banking app continuous use can inspire innovation in mobile banking services.tailored to diverse user preferences.

Despite the significance of this research in enhancing the scientific literature in this area, this chapter has some limitations. Firstly, it didn't examine the differences in perceptions regarding other variables such as bank reputation, innovativeness of the app's features, and habit. Future studies should consider adding new variables to better understand user behavior. Secondly, the study didn't investigate the interplay between variables and measure their influence on continuous intention. Further research should focus on developing a model to examine the relationships between variables. Thirdly, the chapter only compared user's perceptions in high-income and upper-middle-income countries. Future studies should include other countries categorized as low-income and lower-middle-income to compare the results. Lastly, the influence of socio-demographic factors on students' perceptions was not considered in this chapter. Regarding this, further research should investigate the impact of age, gender, education levels and other socio-demographic characteristics on users' behavior.

ACKNOWLEDGMENTS

This paper is supported by Australian University, Kuwait under internal seed grant No.IRC-2021/2022-SRC-PR16, and by the Ministry of Science, Technological Development and Innovation of the Republic of Serbia under contract number 451-03-47/2023-01/200005.

REFERENCES

Abu-Taieh, E. M., AlHadid, I., Abu-Tayeh, S., Masa'deh, R., Alkhawaldeh, R. S., Khwaldeh, S., & Al-rowwad, A. (2022). Continued Intention to Use of M-Banking in Jordan by Integrating UTAUT, TPB, TAM and Service Quality with ML. *Journal of Open Innovation*, *8*(3), 120. doi:10.3390/joitmc8030120

Al-Laheebi, G. A. J. (2022). Continuous Intention to Use Mobile Banking Apps: Empirical Study in Iraq. *THEORY METHODOLOGY PRACTICE-REVIEW OF BUSINESS AND MANAGEMENT, 18*(1), 61–74. http://real.mtak.hu/144917/1/5_k.pdf

Alba, J. W., & Hutchinson, J. W. (1987). Dimensions of Consumer Expertise. *The Journal of Consumer Research*, *13*(4), 411–454. doi:10.1086/209080

Albashrawi, M., & Motiwalla, L. (2019). Privacy and Personalization in Continued Usage Intention of Mobile Banking: An Integrative Perspective. *Information Systems Frontiers*, *21*(5), 1031–1043. doi:10.1007/s10796-017-9814-7

Alghareeb, S. (2022). Mobile banking adoption among undergraduate students in Kuwait university. *OAlib*, *09*(06), 1–13. doi:10.4236/oalib.1106458

Altin Gumussoy, C., Kaya, A., & Ozlu, E. (2018). Determinants of Mobile Banking Use: An Extended TAM with Perceived Risk, Mobility Access, Compatibility, Perceived Self-efficacy and Subjective Norms. In *Industrial Engineering in the Industry 4.0 Era* (pp. 225–238). Springer International Publishing. doi:10.1007/978-3-319-71225-3_20

Antonijević, M., Ivanović, Đ., & Simović, V. (2021). Adoption of Mobile Banking in the Republic of Serbia. In *Finance, Innovation and Technology: new models and structures* (p. 197). Institute of Economics - Ss. Cyril & Methodius University. http://ebooks.ien.bg.ac.rs/1594/

Antonijević, M. S., Ljumović, I., & Ivanović, Đ. (2022). Is there a Gender Gap in Financial Inclusion across Countries? *JWEE*, (1-2), 79–96. doi:10.28934/jwee22.12.pp79-96

Arcand, M., PromTep, S., Brun, I., & Rajaobelina, L. (2017). Mobile banking service quality and customer relationships. *International Journal of Bank Marketing*, *35*(7), 1068–1089. doi:10.1108/IJBM-10-2015-0150

Asnakew, Z. S. (2020). Customers' continuance intention to use mobile banking: Development and testing of an integrated model. *The Review of Socionetwork Strategies*, *14*(1), 123–146. doi:10.1007/s12626-020-00060-7

Avornyo, P., Fang, J., Odai, R. O., Vondee, J. B., & Nartey, M. N. (2019). Factors affecting continuous usage intention of mobile banking in Tema and Kumasi. *International Journal of Business and Social Science*, *10*(3). doi:10.30845/ijbss.v10n3p11

Burhanudin, B., Ronny, R., & Sihotang, E. T. (2019). Connecting Intention to Use Online Banking, Commitment to Environmental Sustainability, and Happiness: The Role of Nature Relatedness. *Procedia Computer Science*, *161*, 341–349. doi:10.1016/j.procs.2019.11.132

Chaouali, W., Imene, B. Y., Lunardo, R., & Triki, A. (2019). Reconsidering the "what is beautiful is good" effect: When and how design aesthetics affect intentions towards mobile banking applications. *International Journal of Bank Marketing*, *37*(7), 1525–1546. doi:10.1108/IJBM-12-2018-0337

Chong, A. Y.-L. (2013). A two-staged SEM-neural network approach for understanding and predicting the determinants of m-commerce adoption. *Expert Systems with Applications*, *40*(4), 1240–1247. doi:10.1016/j.eswa.2012.08.067

Daly, J. C., & Cohen, J. (1978). Statistical power analysis for the behavioral sciences. Journal of the American Statistical Association, 73(363), 680. doi:10.2307/2286629

Daragmeh, A., Lentner, C., & Sági, J. (2021). FinTech payments in the era of COVID-19: Factors influencing behavioral intentions of "Generation X" in Hungary to use mobile payment. *Journal of Behavioral and Experimental Finance*, *32*, 100574. doi:10.1016/j.jbef.2021.100574 PMID:34540592

DeVellis, R. F. (2003). *Scale Development: Theory and Applications*. SAGE. https://play.google.com/store/books/details?id=BYGxL6xLokUC

Digital skills gap index. (2021, June 1). Wiley. https://dsgi.wiley.com/.

Domazet, I. S., Marjanović, D., Ahmetagić, D., & Stantić, J. (2023). Innovation and ICT: Key Factors of Successful Business. In Innovation, Strategy, and Transformation Frameworks for the Modern Enterprise (pp. 327-345). IGI Global. doi:10.4018/979-8-3693-0458-7.ch014

Dragana, R. P., Nedeljković, I., & Marinković, V. (2022). The role of the hedonistic and utilitarian quality dimensions in enhancing user satisfaction in mobile banking. *International Journal of Bank Marketing*, *40*(7), 1610–1631. doi:10.1108/IJBM-03-2022-0112

Economy data. (n.d.). World Bank. https://rulemaking.worldbank.org/en/data/explorecountries/serbia

Farzin, M., Sadeghi, M., Yahyayi Kharkeshi, F., Ruholahpur, H., & Fattahi, M. (2021). Extending UTAUT2 in M-banking adoption and actual use behavior: Does WOM communication matter? *Asian Journal of Economics and Banking*, *5*(2), 136–157. doi:10.1108/AJEB-10-2020-0085

Foroughi, B., Iranmanesh, M., & Sean, H. S. (2019). Understanding the determinants of mobile banking continuance usage intention. *Journal of Enterprise Information Management*, *32*(6), 1015–1033. doi:10.1108/JEIM-10-2018-0237

GDP per capita (current US$). (n.d.). World Bank Open Data. https://data.worldbank.org/indicator/NY.GDP.PCAP.CD?name_desc=true.

Gefen, D., Karahanna, E., & Straub, D. W. (2003). Trust and TAM in Online Shopping: An Integrated Model. *Management Information Systems Quarterly*, *27*(1), 51–90. doi:10.2307/30036519

Giovanis, A., Athanasopoulou, P., Assimakopoulos, C., & Sarmaniotis, C. (2019). Adoption of mobile banking services: A comparative analysis of four competing theoretical models. *International Journal of Bank Marketing*, *37*(5), 1165–1189. doi:10.1108/IJBM-08-2018-0200

Gu, J.-C., Lee, S.-C., & Suh, Y.-H. (2009). Determinants of behavioral intention to mobile banking. *Expert Systems with Applications*, *36*(9), 11605–11616. doi:10.1016/j.eswa.2009.03.024

Gupta, P., Prashar, S., Vijay, T. S., & Parsad, C. (2021). Examining the influence of antecedents of continuous intention to use an informational app: The role of perceived usefulness and perceived ease of use. *International Journal of Business Information Systems*, *36*(2), 270–287. doi:10.1504/IJBIS.2021.112829

Hanafizadeh, P., Behboudi, M., Koshksaray, A. A., & Tabar, M. J. S. (2014). Mobile-banking adoption by Iranian bank clients. *Telematics and Informatics*, *31*(1), 62–78. doi:10.1016/j.tele.2012.11.001

Hidayat-ur-Rehman, I., Ahmad, A., Khan, M. N., & Mokhtar, S. A. (2021). Investigating Mobile Banking Continuance Intention: A Mixed-Methods Approach. *Mobile Information Systems*, *2021*, 1–17. doi:10.1155/2021/9994990

Hoffmann, S. C., Junior, L. W., & De Oliveira, S. F. (2017). Apps for mobile banking and customer satisfaction: A cross-cultural study. *International Journal of Bank Marketing*, *35*(7), 1133–1153. doi:10.1108/IJBM-09-2015-0146

Hong, S., Thong, J. Y. L., & Tam, K. Y. (2006). Understanding continued information technology usage behavior: A comparison of three models in the context of mobile internet. *Decision Support Systems, 42*(3), 1819–1834. doi:10.1016/j.dss.2006.03.009

Humbani, M., & Wiese, M. (2019). An integrated framework for the adoption and continuance intention to use mobile payment apps. *International Journal of Bank Marketing, 37*(2), 646–664. doi:10.1108/IJBM-03-2018-0072

Inan, D. I., Hidayanto, A. N., Juita, R., Soemawilaga, F. F., Melinda, F., Puspacinantya, P., & Amalia, Y. (2023). Service quality and self-determination theory towards continuance usage intention of mobile banking. *Journal of science and technology policy management, 14*(2), 303–328. doi:10.1108/JSTPM-01-2021-0005

Ivanovic, D., Simovic, V., Domazet, I., & Antonijevic, M. (2021). Average Matching Levels for Two DigComp Competence Areas of the Female Entrepreneurs in Serbia. *JWEE*, (3-4), 42–60. doi:10.28934/jwee21.34.pp42-60

Jeong, B. K., & Yoon, T. E. (2013). An Empirical Investigation on Consumer Acceptance of Mobile Banking Services. *Business and Management Research, 2*(1), 31–40. https://ideas.repec.org/a/jfr/bmr111/v2y2013i1p31-40.html

Jerene, W., & Sharma, D. (2020). The adoption of financial technology in Ethiopia: A study of bank customers perspective. *Journal of Banking and Financial Technology, 4*(1), 53–63. doi:10.1007/s42786-020-00015-0

Kabakuş, A. K., & Küçükoğlu, H. (2022). THE EFFECT OF TRUST ON MOBILE BANKING USAGE: THE MEDIATING ROLES OF PERCEIVED USEFULNESS AND PERCEIVED EASE OF USE. *Ekonomski vjesnik/Econviews - Review of Contemporary Business. Entrepreneurship and Economic Issues, 35*(2), 231–246. doi:10.51680/ev.35.2.1

Köksal, Y. A. D. P. (2015). An Investigation of the Important Factors Influence Web Trust in Online Shopping, *6*(1), 28–40. https://search.proquest.com/openview/39b4398d3c177cf881a6467140794ba7/1?pq-origsite=gscholar&cbl=2032031

Kumar, R. R., Israel, D., & Malik, G. (2018). Explaining customer's continuance intention to use mobile banking apps with an integrative perspective of ECT and Self-determination theory. *Editorial Introduction, 10*(2), 79–112. doi:10.17705/1pais.10204

Laukkanen, T. (2017). Mobile banking. *International Journal of Bank Marketing, 35*(7), 1042–1043. doi:10.1108/IJBM-10-2017-0218

DLA. (n.d.). Law in Kuwait - *DLA Piper global data protection laws of the world.* DLA. https://www.dlapiperdataprotection.com/index.html?t=law&c=KW

Le, H. B. H., Ngo, C. T., Trinh, T. T. H., & Nguyen, T. T. P. (2020). Factor affecting customers' decision to use mobile banking service: A case of Thanh Hoa province, Vietnam. *Journal of Asian Finance Economics and Business, 7*(2), 205–212. doi:10.13106/jafeb.2020.vol7.no2.205

Lema, A. (2017). Factors influencing the adoption of mobile financial services in the unbanked population. Inkanyiso. *Journal of the Humanities and Social Sciences*, *9*(1), 37–51.

Li, C.-Y., & Fang, Y.-H. (2019). Predicting continuance intention toward mobile branded apps through satisfaction and attachment. *Telematics and Informatics*, *43*, 101248. doi:10.1016/j.tele.2019.101248

Lukić, V., Čolić, L., & Prica, I. (2019). Perspectives and adoption of mobile banking in Serbia: The case of young adults. *Ekonomika preduzeca, 67*(5-6), 334–344. doi:10.5937/EKOPRE1906334L

Malaquias, R. F., & Hwang, Y. (2019). Mobile banking use: A comparative study with Brazilian and U.S. participants. *International Journal of Information Management*, *44*, 132–140. doi:10.1016/j.ijinfomgt.2018.10.004

Marinković, V., Đorđević, A., & Kalinić, Z. (2020). The moderating effects of gender on customer satisfaction and continuance intention in mobile commerce: A UTAUT-based perspective. *Technology Analysis and Strategic Management*, *32*(3), 306–318. doi:10.1080/09537325.2019.1655537

Merhi, M., Hone, K., & Tarhini, A. (2019). A cross-cultural study of the intention to use mobile banking between Lebanese and British consumers: Extending UTAUT2 with security, privacy and trust. *Technology in Society*, *59*, 101151. doi:10.1016/j.techsoc.2019.101151

Nguyen, T. T. P., Van Nguyen, A., & Han, S.-L. (2021). The Role of Trust Factors Toward Technological Innovation in Explaining the Effects of CSR Concerns on Mobile Banking Adoption: A Comparative Study Between Vietnam and South Korea. *Academy of Asian Business Review, 7*(1). https://repository.hanyang.ac.kr/handle/20.500.11754/176357

Nikou, S., Mark, D. R., & Matin, M. K. (2022). Workplace literacy skills—How information and digital literacy affect adoption of digital technology. *The Journal of Documentation*, *78*(7), 371–391. doi:10.1108/JD-12-2021-0241

Novitasari, D., Juliana, J., Asbari, M., & Purwanto, A. (2021). The Effect of Financial Literacy, Parents' Social Economic and Student Lifestyle on Students Personal Financial Management. *Economic Education Analysis Journal, 10*(3), 522–531. https://journal.unnes.ac.id/sju/index.php/eeaj/article/view/50721

Pallant, J. (2020). *SPSS Survival Manual: A Step by Step Guide to Data Analysis using IBM SPSS.* McGraw-Hill Education (UK). https://play.google.com/store/books/details?id=CxUsEAAAQBAJ

Petrović, M., Rajin, D., Milenković, D., & Marić, D. (2021). The influence of eWOM on the use of mobile banking. *Ekonomika preduzeca, 69*(3-4), 95–104. doi:10.5937/EKOPRE2102095P

Poromatikul, C., Peter, D. M., Leelapanyalert, K., & Zaby, S. (2019). Drivers of continuance intention with mobile banking apps. *International Journal of Bank Marketing*, *38*(1), 242–262. doi:10.1108/IJBM-08-2018-0224

Prastiawan, D. I., Aisjah, S., & Rofiaty, R. (2021). The Effect of Perceived Usefulness, Perceived Ease of Use, and Social Influence on the Use of Mobile Banking through the Mediation of Attitude Toward Use. [Asia Pacific Management and Business Application]. *APMBA*, *9*(3), 243–260. doi:10.21776/ub.apmba.2021.009.03.4

Priya, R., Vikas, G. A., & Shaikh, A. (2018). Mobile banking adoption in an emerging economy: An empirical analysis of young Indian consumers. *Benchmarking*, *25*(2), 743–762. doi:10.1108/BIJ-01-2016-0009

Rabaa'i, A. A., & AlMaati, S. (2021). Exploring the determinants of users' continuance intention to use mobile banking services in Kuwait: Extending the expectation-confirmation model. *Asia Pacific Journal of Information Systems, 31*(2), 141–184. https://www.researchgate.net/profile/Ahmad-Rabaai-2/publication/353175206_Exploring_the_Determinants_of_Users'_Continuance_Intention_to_Use_Mobile_Banking_Services_in_Kuwait_Extending_the_Expectation-Confirmation_Model/links/60ebf0eab8c0d5588cee77cf/Exploring-the-Determinants-of-Users-Continuance-Intention-to-Use-Mobile-Banking-Services-in-Kuwait-Extending-the-Expectation-Confirmation-Model.pdf

Raza, S. A., Umer, A., & Shah, N. (2017). New determinants of ease of use and perceived usefulness for mobile banking adoption. *International Journal of Electronic Customer Relationship Management*, *11*(1), 44–65. doi:10.1504/IJECRM.2017.086751

Rejman-Petrovic, D., Nedeljković, I., & Marinković, V. (2022). The role of the hedonistic and utilitarian quality dimensions in enhancing user satisfaction in mobile banking. *International Journal of Bank Marketing*, *40*(7), 1610–1631. doi:10.1108/IJBM-03-2022-0112

Saparudin, M., Rahayu, A., Hurriyati, R., & Sultan, M. A. (2020). Exploring the role of trust in mobile-banking use by Indonesian customer using unified theory of acceptance and usage technology. *International journal of financial research, 11*(2), 51. doi:10.5430/ijfr.v11n2p51

Schuchmann, D., & Seufert, S. (2015). Corporate learning in times of digital transformation: A conceptual framework and service portfolio for the learning function in banking organisations. [iJAC]. *International Journal of Advanced Corporate Learning*, *8*(1), 31. doi:10.3991/ijac.v8i1.4440

Sharma, S. K. (2019). Integrating cognitive antecedents into TAM to explain mobile banking behavioral intention: A SEM-neural network modeling. *Information Systems Frontiers*, *21*(4), 815–827. doi:10.1007/s10796-017-9775-x

Shetu, S. N., Islam, M. M., & Promi, S. I. (2022). An Empirical Investigation of the Continued Usage Intention of Digital Wallets: The Moderating Role of Perceived Technological Innovativeness. *Future Business Journal*, *8*(1), 1–17. doi:10.1186/s43093-022-00158-0

Simovic, V., Domazet, I., Bhagat, R., Sarhan, H., & Ivanovic, D. (2022). Identification of Opportunities as the Component of Digital Entrepreneurial Competences of University Students: A pilot study in Kuwait and Serbia. In *Proceedings of the 6th International Conference on E-Commerce, E-Business and E-Government* (pp. 85–90). New York, NY, USA: Association for Computing Machinery. 10.1145/3537693.3537724

Simovic, V., Domazet, I., Bugarcic, M., Safi, M., Sarhan, H., Bhagat, R., & Bradic Martinovic, A. (2023). The association of socio-demographic characteristics of university students and the levels of their digital entrepreneurial competences. *Heliyon*, *9*(10), e20897. doi:10.1016/j.heliyon.2023.e20897 PMID:37867828

Simović, V. M., & Domazet, I. S. (2021). An Overview of the Frameworks for Measuring the Digital Competencies of College Students: A European Perspective. In *Stagnancy Issues and Change Initiatives for Global Education in the Digital Age* (pp. 259–282). IGI Global. doi:10.4018/978-1-7998-4993-3.ch012

Taneja, S., & Ali, L. (2021). Determinants of customers' intentions towards environmentally sustainable banking: Testing the structural model. *Journal of Retailing and Consumer Services*, *59*(102418), 102418. doi:10.1016/j.jretconser.2020.102418

Tiwari, P., Tiwari, S. K., & Gupta, A. (2021). Examining the impact of customers' awareness, risk and trust in M-banking adoption. *FIIB business review, 10*(4), 413–423. doi:10.1177/23197145211019924

Tsai, H.-T., Chien, J.-L., & Tsai, M.-T. (2014). The influences of system usability and user satisfaction on continued Internet banking services usage intention: Empirical evidence from Taiwan. *Electronic Commerce Research*, *14*(2), 137–169. doi:10.1007/s10660-014-9136-5

Van, H. N., Pham, L., Williamson, S., Chan, C.-Y., Thang, T. D., & Nam, V. X. (2021). Explaining intention to use mobile banking: Integrating perceived risk and trust into the technology acceptance model. *International Journal of Applied Decision Sciences*, *14*(1), 55–80. doi:10.1504/IJADS.2021.112933

Vedadi, A., & Warkentin, M. (2016). Continuance Intention on Using Mobile Banking Applications: A Replication Study of Information Systems Continuance Model. *AIS Transactions on Replication Research*, *2*(1), 7. doi:10.17705/1atrr.00014

Waheed, S. A., Ding, D., & Siyal, S. (2019). M-banking barriers in Pakistan: A customer perspective of adoption and continuity intention. *Data Technologies and Applications*, *53*(1), 58–84. doi:10.1108/DTA-04-2018-0022

Wolf, M. J., Emerson, J. W., Esty, D. C., de Sherbinin, A., & Wendling, Z. A. (2022). *2022 Environmental Performance Index (EPI) results*. BVEARNB. https://bvearmb.do/handle/123456789/2828.

Yin, L.-X., & Lin, H.-C. (2022). Predictors of customers' continuance intention of mobile banking from the perspective of the interactivity theory. *Ekonomska Istrazivanja*, *35*(1), 6820–6849. doi:10.1080/1331677X.2022.2053782

Yuan, S., Liu, Y., Yao, R., & Liu, J. (2014). An investigation of users' continuance intention towards mobile banking in China. *Information Development*. doi:10.1177/0266666914522140

Chapter 10
Forms of Bias in Online Reviews and Their Implications for Management of Customer Knowledge:
A Literature Review

Apostolos Skotis
https://orcid.org/0000-0002-7393-5793
University of Piraeus, Greece

Christos Livas
https://orcid.org/0000-0002-9166-8799
University of Patras, Greece

ABSTRACT

This study conducts a systematic literature review to identify forms of user behavioral bias, affecting the generation of content, evaluation patterns, and the impact of online reviews. Furthermore, it indicates the resulting implications for organizations' management of customer knowledge. The authors collected studies dating from 2009 to 2023 in Scopus, where a high dimensionality of bias definitions is observed. As a result of this review, a series of thematic distinctions is proposed, distinguishing sentiment and evaluation asymmetries, motivational factors, as well as on-platform effects that can amplify, adjust, or create biased behaviors. The authors draw analogies with cognitive bias literature regarding cognitive limitations, preconceptions and motives, and contextual adaptations that lead to biased behaviors. Suggested methods and analyses aiming at bias understanding and mitigation are also presented in detail. The authors provide a comprehensive framework of bias-centered management in online review platforms, incorporating customer knowledge flows and practices to monitor and address bias effects.

DOI: 10.4018/979-8-3693-0798-4.ch010

INTRODUCTION

Online Review Platforms and Customer Knowledge

Online review communities are a valuable source for the understanding of customer behavior, expectations and satisfaction. Evaluations posted by reviewers are viewed as quality and performance indicators of businesses, as well as an information source affecting potential customers of products or services (Chatterjee, 2019). Several studies have indicated the effect of online review evaluations on product sales (Lee et al., 2018; Millwood, 2015). In recent years, studies urge for the utilization of online review communities as platforms of customer knowledge, a topic which has attracted significant attention in many industries (Pan et al., 2020). The scope of Customer Knowledge Management (CKM) has been outlined in a variety of ways throughout literature, but was defined by (Gibbert et al., 2002) as being about "gaining, sharing, and expanding the knowledge residing in customers, to both customer and corporate benefit". CKM comprises knowledge collected about customers, knowledge received from customers and knowledge created for customers (Ourzik, 2022; Gebert et al., 2003). As monitoring and utilization of consumer-generated data in online reviews becomes a relevant subtopic of customer knowledge management, several challenges emerge. Grasping customer behavior patterns, developing models and technologies for collecting and analyzing customer feedback that can lead to product and service improvements, management of trends and online assessments that can greatly affect customer intentions, in a big data context (Centobelli & Ndou, 2019; Ractham et al., 2021). Recent research urges for transforming online customer reviews into customer knowledge databases, as part of the incorporation of customer e-word-of-mouth (e-WoM) in CKM strategies and the development of customer knowledge systems (Ractham et al., 2021).

Behavioral Bias

Consumer decision making behaviors according to models of behavioral economics are systematically biased (Suomala, 2020). For several decades, cognitive bias has been a subject of psychology studies, but has recently gained attention in Information Systems research (Fleischmann, 2014). Literature often refers to the term "cognitive bias" either to group a range of decision making, motivational, and heuristic judgement behaviors, or to specifically refer to the ways people process information, viewing motivational biases as a separate category (Browne & Parsons, 2012; Wilke & Mata, 2012). This is in line with the lack of standard typologies of biased behaviors in information systems (Fleischmann, 2014), which can often be misleading for researchers. However, cognitive bias literature offers paradigms that can provide insight regarding the understanding of consumer decision behavior biases in an online review context. Defining cognitive bias as errors occurring in judgement and decision making, it can reflect behaviors caused by cognitive limitations, motivations, or adaptations to contextual or environmental factors (Wilke and Mata, 2012). An important view applying in decision support systems environments and consumer decision is that choices are to a large degree endogenously determined (Aral et al, 2011), and that biased behaviors are defined by the balance between a starting point of prior belief and initial judgement and the influence of additional information on perception, as in the "anchoring and adjustment" approach (George et al., 2000; Huang et al., 2012; Suomala, 2020). Analogies of consumer experience and the online review process can be drawn from cognitive bias theory in how initial judgements are shaped, stating the importance of recency and vividness of memories, tendency to ignore new or contradictory information (anchoring and perseverance) and favoring familiar patterns (Haley & Stumpf, 1989; Bazerman & Moore, 2013; Fleishmann et al., 2014).

Bias Effects on Customer Knowledge

In consequence, the question is raised regarding how users' behavioral bias can affect online review platforms as a source of customer knowledge. Several studies have questioned the representativeness of online reviews, and their validity as collective indicators of product and services' true quality. Online reviews representativeness is one of the critical factors for an effective internet economy (Karamana, 2021). Representativeness discrepancies are usually addressed as a problem occurring due to the joint effects of behavioral biases (Askalidis, 2017) by current reviewers, potential reviewers and managers, that can be observed on multiple stages of buying and evaluation process. Bias in reviews can lead to an unrepresentative corpus of online review information and knowledge, both through text content and ratings (Zhang et al., 2018). In this direction, our study conducts a systematic literature review aiming to identify forms of user behavioral bias affecting generation of reviews, direction of evaluations, and their impact. Moreover, it attempts to group and categorize user bias terms found in literature, describe their multi-dimensional nature, and place them in a common management perspective. We try to demonstrate how evaluation reporting and formation are affected by user biased behaviors in online review communities, and how bias can have multiple repercussions for decision-making of existing and potential customers. Also, we indicate that bias can have significant implications for organizations' management of customer feedback and knowledge. Finally, we present a comprehensive framework consolidating categories of user bias and targeted areas of bias mitigation, to aid the establishment of balanced information environments for both organizations and customers.

METHODOLOGY

We conducted our search in the Scopus database, to locate and collect studies related to user behavioral bias in an online review context. More specifically, we queried the database for the occurrences of "online review" in abstracts, titles and keywords of publications, together with the occurrence of the word "bias" in either the title or the keywords fields, aiming at studies in which bias in online review platforms is of central importance. Furthermore, we added limitations regarding subject area in a filter provided by Scopus, to exclude areas not relevant to business research (e.g. "Physics and Astronomy"). The use of Scopus database was selected as one of the dominant indexes worldwide, offering customized search functionality, as well as exporting abstract and keywords information into a dataset for further processing. Our search returned 104 publications in which we examined exported abstracts carefully, to locate non-relevant articles. We specifically excluded studies where behavioral bias in review platforms was not the main object of analysis, as well as studies on online communities, outside the context of customer or consumer behavior. This resulted in a set of 95 studies, which were subsequently downloaded to be thoroughly read, evaluated, and synthesized to the direction of the study's objectives. In parallel, we used the extracted abstracts dataset from Scopus to perform a simple text mining approach. Abstract texts were text-mined by developing a custom program, to extract bigrams and trigrams containing the word "bias". The script was developed in Python, using Numpy, Pandas, NLTK and Sklearn libraries to perform importing of data, text pre-processing (tokenization, lemmatization), recognition of bigrams and trigrams and extraction in a common dataset. Subsequently, we performed an identification of terms associated with user behavior in online reviews and applied data cleansing, removing instances that were not valid references to bias types.

All relevant term instances were mapped to the corresponding publication, so studies' data were organized in a common dataset including extracted user bias terminology by study, to aid reconciliation and identification of groupings. We performed a chronological analysis of topic's evolution in literature, a qualitative analysis of main themes and an analysis of multiple perspectives related to the topic of bias in online reviews. Additionally, we performed an identification of proposed managerial practices of mitigation of bias triggers and effects. The most influential studies of the field, according to number of citations are presented in a separate table. Also, a table demonstrating forms of user bias, observed themes, and citations was created for a comprehensive overview of literature. In many cases, studies on online review bias may elaborate on certain bias types with no explicit reference as "bias", but they were included as a result of our review analysis (for example, studies on review bias may refer to "bandwagon bias" or "bandwagon effect"). Since literature is characterized by a considerable dispersion of terms and dimensions, we tried to group bias references using a broad conceptual approach. Finally, management practices, approaches and practical interventions of de-biasing were collected, and subsequently complemented and associated with customer knowledge flows, in a common framework.

RESULTS AND DISCUSSION

Overview and Research Trends

Figure 1 demonstrates the historical trend of research on bias in online review communities, as derived from Scopus database. Studies ranging from 2009 to today display a peak in 2020, however it could be argued that the number of studies annually has remained stable since 2017. Moreover, as displayed in Table 2, the extent of user bias terms and contexts reveals several areas being under-researched.

Figure 1. Number of studies by year

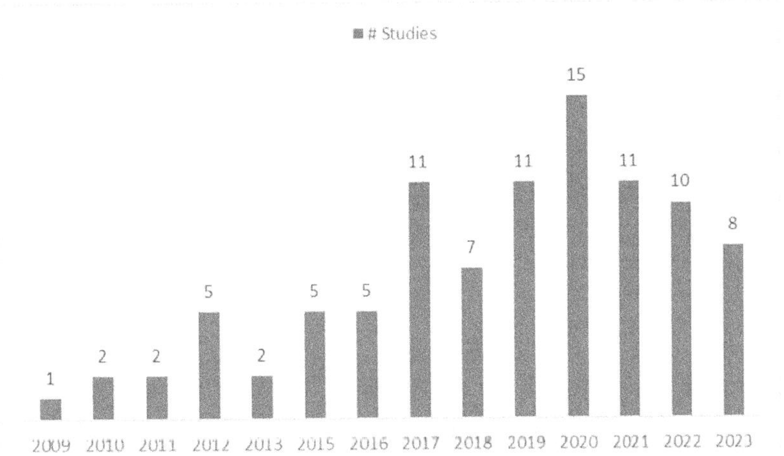

In Table 1, the most influential studies are presented, according to citations (Scopus) as of November of 2023.

Table 1. Most influential studies

Authors/Year	Source title	Title	# Citations (Scopus)
Chen & Lurie, 2013	Journal of Marketing Research	Temporal contiguity and negativity bias in the impact of online word of mouth	291
Yin et al., 2016	Information Systems Research	When do consumers value positive vs. negative reviews? An empirical investigation of confirmation bias in online word of mouth	235
Kuan et al., 2015	Journal of the Association for Information Systems	What makes a review voted? An empirical investigation of review voting in online review systems	183
Wu, 2013	Psychology and Marketing	In search of negativity bias: An empirical study of perceived helpfulness of online reviews	181
Koh et al., 2010	Electronic Commerce Research and Applications	Do online reviews reflect a product's true perceived quality? An investigation of online movie reviews across cultures	159
Hu et al., 2017	MIS Quarterly: Management Information Systems	On self-selection biases in online product reviews	147
Bridges & Vásquez, 2018	Current Issues in Tourism	If nearly all Airbnb reviews are positive, does that make them meaningless?	132
Ho et al., 2017	Information Systems Research	Disconfirmation effect on online rating behavior: A structural model	114
Naylor et al., 2011	Journal of Marketing Research	Seeing ourselves in others: Reviewer ambiguity, Egocentric anchoring, and persuasion	103
Eslami et al., 2018	Decision Support Systems	Which online reviews do consumers find most helpful? A multi-method investigation	99
Gao et al., 2017	Decision Support Systems	Follow the herd or be myself? An analysis of consistency in behavior of reviewers and helpfulness of their reviews	85
Liu & Karahanna, 2017	MIS Quarterly: Management Information Systems	The dark side of reviews: The swaying effects of online product reviews on attribute preference construction	74
Plotkina et al., 2020	Journal of Business Research	Illusions of truth—Experimental insights into human and algorithmic detections of fake online reviews	57
Wu et al., 2011	International Conference on Information Systems 2011, ICIS 2011	The influences of negativity and review quality on the helpfulness of online reviews	57
Mehraliyev et al., 2020	Tourism Management	From measurement scale to sentiment scale: Examining the effect of sensory experiences on online review rating behavior	56

Figure 2 demonstrates percentages by publication type. More than 3 in 4 studies on online review bias behaviors are journal articles.

Figure 2. Percentages by publication type

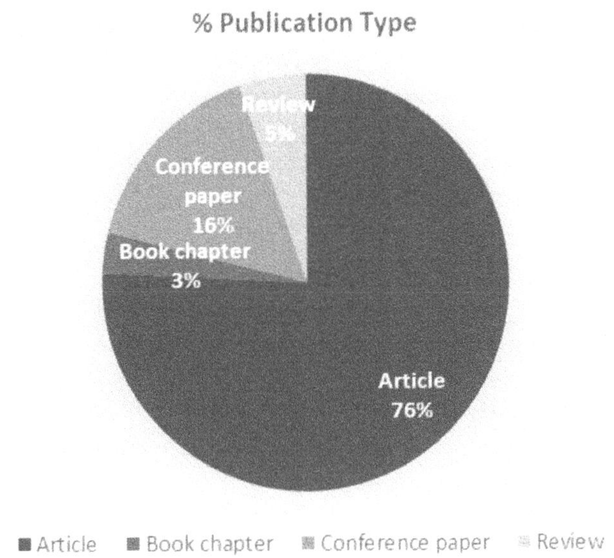

In Table 2, we thematically group bias references in three categories and five sub-categories which were identified as the main concepts of focus in literature. We define an "asymmetry aspect" group comprising negativity, positivity and extremity, which are effects intertwined with motivational biased behaviors and reflect the asymmetrical evaluation output of online review platforms. Motivational aspect groups all biases centered in motivations created by self-view, preference, and beliefs of individuals. Selection refers to behaviors related to choice, initiative, and individual preferences.

Confirmation and disconfirmation are common terms related to customer experience and expectations gaps, as well as the tendencies of users to approve their initial beliefs. We also define a group comprising bias effects related to user background and off-platform intrinsic and extrinsic motivations. Finally, we suggest a thematic group of bias effects related to on-platform experience, grouping biases caused by design, information and social features of platforms. It is also worth mentioning instances of bias terms observed in more than one category, such as "rating bias" or "review bias", used by studies in different contexts. Thematic categorizations are analyzed in detail in the following sections.

Table 2. Thematic categories, bias terms and citations

Forms of Bias and Identified Themes	
Asymmetry aspect	
negativity bias	Bing & Yang, 2020; Chen & Lurie, 2013; Eslami et al., 2018; Filieri et al., 2021; Guo et al., 2019; Hu et al., 2022a; Jabr et al., 2022; Kim et al., 2020; Kuan et al., 2015; Lei et al., 2023; Li et al., 2017; Li et al., 2020; Liu & Hu, 2021; Liu et al., 2020; Mehraliyev et al., 2020; Nicolau et al., 2022; Ozcan et al., 2023; Purnawirawan et al., 2012; Qahri-Saremi & Montazemi, 2023; Shi et al., 2020; Skotis et al., 2023; Tata et al., 2020; Vali et al., 2015; Wen et al., 2021; Wu et al., 2011; Wu, 2013; Yin et al., 2016; Zhao et al., 2022
positivity bias	Askay, 2015; Bridges & Vásquez, 2018; Lei et al., 2023; Skotis et al., 2023
extremity bias	Bhole & Hanna, 2017; Brandes et al., 2022; Choi, 2022; Karamana, 2021; Kuan et al., 2015; Liu & Hu, 2021; Nicolau et al., 2022; Zhao et al., 2022
Motivational aspect	
Selection	
selection bias	Askalidis et al., 2017; Kuan et al., 2015; Liu & Karahanna, 2017; Marinescu et al., 2021; Wu et al., 2018
self-selection bias	Bhole & Hanna, 2017; Hu et al., 2017; Shen et al., 2020; Yuan et al., 2012; Zhang et al., 2018
reporting bias	Bhole & Hanna, 2017; Chen et al., 2016; de Barra, 2017; Han & Anderson, 2020; Hu et al., 2017; Jurca et al., 2010; Karamana, 2021; Koh et al., 2010; Osman et al., 2019; Yuan et al., 2012
under-reporting bias	Bhole & Hanna, 2017; Koh et al., 2010; Wu et al., 2018; Yuan et al., 2012
response bias	Han & Anderson, 2020
dimensional bias	Ge & Li, 2015; Liu & Karahanna, 2017; Wu et al., 2018
purchasing Bias	Wu et al., 2018
acquisition bias	Hu et al., 2017
preference bias	Ge & Li, 2015
rating bias	Ge & Li, 2015; Li et al., 2016
review bias	Ge & Li, 2015
Confirmation	
confirmation bias	Bao & Chau, 2016; Choi, 2022; Hu & Zhou, 2023; Jabr et al., 2022; Lei et al., 2023; Roy et al., 2017; Sengo Furtado et al., 2022; Yin et al., 2016; Zapf et al., 2021
disconfirmation bias	Ho et al., 2017; Li et al., 2020; Quan et al., 2022; Siering, 2021
rating bias	Ho et al., 2017
Reviewer characteristics and background	
egocentric bias	Naylor et al., 2011
evaluation bias	Gao & Katrompas, 2020; Skotis et al., 2023
gender bias	Fan-Osuala, 2019; Nesdoly et al., 2020
homophily bias	Yu & Liao, 2023
intrinsic bias	Gao et al., 2017
extrinsic bias	Gao et al., 2017
popularity-difference bias	Kokkodis & Lappas, 2020
regional bias	Kobayashi et al., 2009
reviewer bias	Sikora & Chauhan, 2012; Tay, 2019
rating bias	Fang et al., 2019; Gao et al., 2017; Lim & Tucker, 2017; Wan & Nakayama, 2012; Wu et al., 2023
review bias	Fang et al., 2019; Nakayama & Wan, 2019
truth bias	Bing & Yang, 2020; Chaudhary et al., 2019; Plotkina et al., 2020; Qahri-Saremi & Montazemi, 2019

Continued on following page

Table 2. Continued

Forms of Bias and Identified Themes	
social desirability bias	Swetha & Murthy, 2019
self-serving bias	Liang et al., 2021
On-platform features aspect	
bandwagon bias	Wu et al., 2018; Wu et al., 2023
sequential bias	Du et al., 2021; Jurca et al., 2010; Piramuthu et al., 2012; Purnawirawan et al., 2012; Sikora & Chauhan, 2012; Vinson et al., 2019; Wu et al., 2018
dependence bias	Wu et al., 2018
popularity bias	Hayes et al., 2021; Heck et al., 2020; Powell et al., 2017
review bias	Shen et al., 2020
social influence bias	Askalidis et al., 2017; Cicognani et al., 2022; Hu et al., 2022a; Köcher et al., 2016; Tata et al., 2020
recommendation bias	Köcher et al., 2016
rating bias	Ackerman & Chung, 2018; Hu et al., 2022a; Hu et al., 2022b; Kordzadeh, 2019
cognitive bias	Bao et al., 2018; Bao et al., 2021; Kobayashi et al., 2009; Nicolau et al., 2022; Schneider et al., 2015; Vinson et al., 2019; Zhao et al., 2022
decision bias	Liu & Karahanna, 2017
judgment bias	Antioco & Coussement, 2018
platform bias	Kordzadeh, 2019; Shen et al., 2020
information bias	Jia et al., 2020
bias effect (review quality)	Aghakhani et al., 2023; Qahri-Saremi & Montazemi, 2019

Asymmetry Aspect

Online reviews are expected to exhibit negativity, positivity and extremity trends by their very nature. However, studies indicate that these tendencies can be a result of biased behaviors and induce snowballing effects. Asymmetry of evaluations refers to the simultaneous dominance of positivity reports by humans while negative events can have an asymmetrical, higher effect (Peetrs & Czapinski, 1990). Positive bias applies in views reporting, retrieving of memories, expectations and positive favorability in reasoning. However, response of individuals in negative information is found to be stronger (Hoorens, 2014). Online reviews` J-shaped patterns of evaluations are reflective of this evaluation asymmetry. Positivity, negativity and extremity forms of bias are present at multiple analysis dimensions in literature. The terms are used to describe bias factors affecting the formation of evaluations, as well as their impact.

Effects on Evaluation Patterns

Negativity bias is widely recognized in the context of online reviews, but relevant research has been inconsistent regarding effects and scope of the topic (Guo et al., 2019). It can refer to the asymmetrical effects of negativity on readers, potential reviewers and buyers, but can also be traced in discrepancies at multiple levels of the customer experience and review process, as a trait of individual evaluation behavior. From an intrinsic point of view, literature relates selection, reporting and disconfirmation bias to negativity presence, however it can additionally affect gaps found between text review content valence and intensity and star rating choices. In this regard, the asymmetrical effect of negative references on ratings have been verified through text mining techniques in travel destination reviews (Skotis et al., 2023). Similarly, Mehraliyev et al. (2020) have demonstrated a higher impact of negative sensory experiences (compared to positive ones) on review rating levels, also indicating an asymmetrical effect contributing to discrepancies found between text sentiment and rating choice.

Positivity bias, on the other hand, is collectively present in most reviews, since reviewers tend to mainly report positive experiences, as indicated by both positive sentiment dominance and skewed distributions of star ratings (Skotis et al., 2023). Bridges & Vásquez (2018) denote that 90% of AirBnB reviews are rated with 4 or 5 stars. Additionally, positive text content follows similar patterns. However, less positive references are often expressed in more subtle or context-dependent ways. Dominance of positive views, which is often attributed to self-selection, has another aspect from the perspective of opinion expression by reviewers. Askay (2015) demonstrates that positive bias behavior can be a result of social factors and specifically the fear of isolation affecting the willingness to post neutral or negative reviews. Brandes et al. (2022) indicate that extremity is a root cause of J-Shaped distributions of ratings due to the relative rarity of moderate reviewers.

The presence of initial positive or negative signals in review communities can also create bias towards positivity or negativity in subsequent evaluations. Purnawirawan et al. (2012) focus on the influence of majority's opinion in online review contexts, in the form of positive-negative reviews ratio. When this balance is predominantly positive or negative, it is a primary source of influence on shaping recall and impressions. Zhao et al. (2022) through the prism of Prospect Theory estimate negativity bias as the deviation of subsequent decision process induced by heuristic judgements related to valence, sentiment extremity and aspiration levels. Increased aspiration level of users deepens negativity bias on review helpfulness. Shi et al. (2020) describe a negativity bias demonstrated by consumers, regarding the underestimation of products with low sales compared with high-selling ones.

Perception of Causal Attribution

Literature suggests that positivity and negativity differ in terms of causal attribution, as perceived by reviewers. So, the distinction of positivity and negativity extends to causal attribution, affecting reviewers' trust and perception through negativity bias. Negativity is usually attributed to the product or service experience, while positivity of reviews is usually attributed to the reviewer (Vali et al., 2015). The causal attribution of reviews, as positive reviews are attributed to the reviewer, leads to negativity bias, however it was found to be mitigated by the presence of temporal contiguity information (Chen & Lurie, 2013).

Effects on Satisfaction

Effects on satisfaction, buying behavior and purchasing intentions have also been a subject of studies. Liu et al. (2020) identify negativity bias in elements of negative customer experience greatly affecting levels of customer satisfaction, as well as on consumer intentions (Wen et al., 2020). However, Tata et al. (2020) mention that positivity of reviews has a marginally greater influence on purchase intentions, although influences are also dependent on consumption context, which plays a significant differentiating role in the case of private or public consumption. The latter is particularly characterized by negativity bias impact, through the social context influence, thus implicitly stating the presence of social influence bias. Nicolau et al (2022) relate text content extremity and negativity to overall satisfaction levels.

The Role of Reviewer Background

We observe that the effects of extreme negativity or positivity can significantly differ between diverse contexts as well as reviewer segments. Qahri-Saremi & Montazemi (2023) refer to the common perception of negativity bias being mainly attributed to inexperienced users influenced by peripheral cues, such as average ratings. Nevertheless, they emphasize that experienced reviewers can also reveal behaviors of negativity bias, when the focus shifts to review text content. In fact, higher experienced users can be characterized by increased negativity bias on consumer attitude when exposed to negative review content. The higher sensitivity of experienced users to negative content and consequent decision making affected by negativity bias, raises the significance of response strategies regarding negative content. Analyzing negativity bias in terms of influence towards product attitude, Ozcan et al. (2023) point out a gender disparity in review usefulness, as negative information effects on product behavior vary by gender. Li et al. (2017) show that community social identities and expert status can mitigate negativity bias of review peer evaluations.

The Role of Review Elements

Guo et al. (2019) introduce the issue of cognitive processing of reviews by users, in relation to positivity and negativity. They find that negativity bias could be attributed to a different cognitive process, due to shorter response times of users on positive reviews helpfulness, compared to negative reviews. Certain review characteristics are also influential. Investigating effects of review characteristics and review extreme negativity on helpfulness, Liu & Hu (2011) find that comprehensiveness can have a moderating role. Also, coverage of multiple product aspects in a review affects helpfulness perception. Similarly, Wu et al. (2011) confirm that certain review quality characteristics, such as readability and length, can moderate negativity bias affecting helpfulness evaluations. In the same direction, Kuan et al. (2015) find that review voting and helpfulness are affected by length and vocabulary. Regarding length, they specifically indicate the presence of a cutoff point after which a reader's additional cognitive effort becomes undesirable. Also, reviews using more elaborated language are more helpful. Finally, posts provided by top reviewers are more likely to be considered helpful. Eslami et al. (2018) discover that favorable, positive reviews are less helpful compared to negative ones, which are considered to have more targeted descriptions. Regarding extremity, reviews offering different views are more helpful, but there appears to be a threshold over which reviews appear to be overly extreme and biased. They also suggest that reviews promoting negative or neutral argument frames and lower rating scores are viewed as more helpful by reviewers. Review quality was also found to be a moderating factor of negative bias towards review helpfulness assessments (Wu, 2013).

The Role of Product/Service Quality

Finally, the moderating role of product quality is examined by several studies. Filieri et al. (2021) indicate that findings in literature regarding the effects of extremely negative reviews on helpfulness are contrasting. Since not all negative reviews appear to be influential, they propose that quality of product or service has a moderating role on helpfulness. In the context of hotel reviews, external quality indicators, such as hotel rating and certificates of excellence, are prime examples of indicators that can moderate this effect. Bing & Yang, 2020 criticize praise cash-back strategies, as a practice that reduces the trustworthiness of both evaluation systems and reviewers. Also, they link their relative importance and effectiveness to product quality levels. Increased negativity bias over time is associated with the extension of praise cash-back strategies, but in the case of very low- or high-quality products this practice is not essential.

Motivational Aspect

As mentioned in the introduction section, several cognitive bias studies have distinguished a motivational dimension in biased behaviors in decision making. Motivational bias refers to decisions made under the influence of internal preferences or desires as well as contextually induced incentives (Browne and Parsons, 2012). Mental models of individuals are connected to motivational biases, indicative of behaviors favoring specific hypotheses and seeking of confirmation, placing excess value in current beliefs (Huang et al., 2012), or making decisions promoting self-desired emotional or interest outcomes (Bazerman and Moore, 2013).

Selection

Selection or self-selection bias are terms used to describe issues of non-randomness in samples. In online reviews, selection encompasses a range of phenomena affecting the randomness and representativeness of online review content, such as the demographical mismatch between reviewers and readers, specific consumption goals and product preferences affecting perceptions, and under-reporting related to satisfaction levels (Einar et al., 2015). Bias related to customers' choices and preferences can explain evaluation and rating distributions to a great extent. Selection bias can refer to the choice and incentives (or their absence) for consumption, reporting (writing a review), and evaluation discrepancies in different product dimensions. Yuan et al. (2012) recognize self-selection bias in online reviews, manifesting in purchasing and under-reporting bias. In the same manner, Hu et al. (2017) refer to two components of self-selection bias that both affect reporting: Acquisition bias, as consumers with a positive predisposition acquire a product and write reviews, and under-reporting bias, which is related to the intensity of positivity or negativity affecting the decision to post a product or service experience. The effect of self-selection on mean ratings can distort product quality evaluations overall.

Effects on Rating Patterns

Selection bias can explain rating patterns' evolution through time. Initial high rating effects observed are a product of this selective behavior, and businesses should develop specific marketing strategies to adjust these effects (Zhang et al., 2018). Similarly, Bhole & Hanna (2017) posit that mean star-rating effectiveness decreases due to under-reporting bias, but that this is mainly evident in products of extremely poor or high quality. Askalidis et al. (2017) examined rating trends over time in self-motivated reviews (characterized by selection bias) and observed a downward trend because of social influence bias, in agreement with several studies.

Reporting/Under-Reporting

Reporting or under-reporting bias is one of the most common forms of bias mentioned in literature, which influences the specific population of customers making the decision to evaluate a product or service. Studies outline both positive and negative motives to post a review evaluation. De Barra (2017) suggests that users with positive experiences are more inclined to report information of their experience in the form of reviews. Thus, reporting bias can seriously affect decisions of people relying on online word-of-mouth. Reporting bias has been closely associated with satisfaction levels. Chen et al (2016) in the context of movie reviews, estimate that probabilities of a highly satisfied customer posting a review are significantly higher than in cases of lower satisfaction. However, studies indicate extremity as a motive for reporting bias, regardless of evaluation direction (positive or negative). This is line with J-shaped distributions of ratings observed in online review communities across domains.

People with extreme opinions have a higher motivation to share them in online review communities, in contrast to moderately positioned customers (Marinescu et al., 2021). Han & Anderson (2020) identify the effects of extremity and negativity of experience on reporting decisions. Karamana (2021) recognizes extremity and conformity as existing factors in under-reporting communities of unsolicited reviews. However, biased phenomena can be weakened with solicited reviewers that are found to enhance representativeness of reviews and rating distributions. Different contexts of interaction with service providers can also affect intentions and decisions to report an experience. Personal bonds developed in peer-to-peer accommodations can deter customers from posting negative reviews (Osman et al., 2019). Verifying that under-reporting bias can vary in different contexts, Koh et al. (2010) compared online movie reviews networks between United States, China, and Singapore, finding that under-reporting is more prevalent among US reviewers.

Attribute Selection

Selection can also refer to reviewer bias towards specific product aspects or dimensions. The existence of a dimensional review bias that is related to consumer preference (dimensional preference bias) has been proposed by Ge & Li (2015). They quantify a dimensional bias of two levels, namely preference and rating bias. Liu & Karahanna (2017) define decision bias and put emphasis on specific review characteristics that affect attribute preferences and ultimately selection: distribution of information about attribute-level performance, degree of attribute information conflict and attribute rating-performance relationship. Li et al. (2016) observe the existence of a rating bias between individual aspect rating and overall rating. These discrepancies can affect rating prediction models.

Confirmation

Confirmation and disconfirmation effects are closely related to initial beliefs, expectations, and preconceptions. Bazerman and Moore (2013) describe aspects of anchoring and overconfidence regarding the confirmation heuristic, when decision making over-emphasizes initial judgements and their correctness.

Effects on Evaluations and Helpfulness

In the online review context, customer initial expectations exhibit a strong relation to confirmation bias (Lei et al. 2023). Literature also emphasizes positivity, negativity and extremity as aspects intertwined with confirmation or disconfirmation bias. According to Roy et al. (2017), expectations of potential consumers can provide motivation to read reviews with a positive stance, asserting the presence of confirmation bias. Consequently, as readers navigate towards positive reviews due to this confirmation tendency, positive word-of-mouth has a higher effect on sales compared to neutral contributions. Yin et al. (2016) in their study on product review helpfulness, confirm the existence of confirmation bias, as consumers; initial beliefs play a crucial role on finding a review helpful. Also, they demonstrate the combined effect of overall average ratings positivity or negativity, which can amplify the level of confirmation bias to their respective directions. Choi (2022) relates review extremity to the existence and effect of confirmation bias. Review content extremity can thus offer a confirmation of initial beliefs, affecting trust cues on review helpfulness in parallel.

Disconfirmation can be particularly observed in circumstances of gaps between expected and actual customer experience. Ho et al. (2017) indicate that disconfirmation effect leads to biases of reporting selection and rating direction and level. Siering (2021) investigates the field of restaurant health violations prediction with the use of online review content, and essentially associates disconfirmation bias with the choice of posting by users, emanating from a poor hygiene restaurant experience. This however is dependent on the restaurant's prior rating performance and reputation, which naturally affects expectations and subsequent disconfirmation effects.

The Role of Platform Features

Platform features and information can help form and deteriorate confirmation or disconfirmation bias. Zapf et al. (2021) associate rating patterns evolution with confirmation bias induced by average ratings at the initial stage. Bias from this perspective is created as subsequent users, rate similarly to the majority of previous ratings, albeit in a weakening manner, as extremity tends to diminish over time. According to Bao & Chau (2016), the cue of collective rating can also induce confirmation bias in review perception of potential customers. However, this is found to be moderated by their prior expectations, thus linking collective rating to the individuals' primary source of confirmation bias. Jabr et al. (2022) examine platforms' feature of hidden text content and its effect on user behavior, relating confirmation bias, as the perceived value of hidden content strengthens prior positive beliefs. Finally, reviewer characteristics have been found to affect confirmation bias, such as status and recommendation source (Hu & Zhou, 2023).

Reviewer Characteristics and Background

Reviewer-centered analysis of bias is often observed in literature in relation to effects attributed to reviewer background or evaluation patterns that reflect reviewer personality. However, definitions covering these aspects are not always concise (e.g. "rating bias"). Tay (2019) considers reviewer characteristics as of central importance in opinion mining efforts, and a necessary component of modeling of biased behaviors, using the term "reviewer bias".

Historical Evaluation Patterns

Several studies refer explicitly or implicitly to rating bias behaviors, focusing on rating behavioral patterns of users. Users' rating historical behavior is a strong indicator of the existence of a biased rating behavior. Lim & Tucker (2017) posit an approach for addressing the multiple different criteria defining user consumption and rating choices, as well as the identification of true product quality and unbiased behavior, through the monitoring and analysis of users' rating tendencies and patterns. Consistent rating behavior of users can often lead to influential traits or intrinsic motives that can affect rating choices, regardless of product or service true quality levels. Gao et al. (2017) indicate the consistency of users' rating behavior over time and how this potentially reflects a series of intrinsic characteristics that determine rating patterns of an individual. These intrinsic motives appear to be more impactful than extrinsic motives, such as social influence or social status. Skotis et al. (2023) identified reviewer segments demonstrating stable negative or positive rating patterns over time. In combination with text analysis of positivity and negativity, this is a form of evaluation bias that can be ascribed to alternate intrinsic or extrinsic motives of the reviewer, rather than emanating from customer experience.

Reviewer Background Factors

Some of the observed significant rating choice discrepancies have been attributed to differences of gender, age, cultural background, and other individual behavioral characteristics (Wan & Nakayama, 2012). Bias in review evaluations has been attributed to gender differences (Nesdoly et al., 2020; Fan-Osuala, 2019). Extending these findings, Yu & Liao (2023) discover the presence of homophily bias in the selection and review of partners regarding Airbnb stays. Homophily bias is based on similarity of gender, age and race. Kobayashi et al. (2009) suggest the existence of regional bias, observed in the phenomenon of more stringent than average evaluations of restaurants by reviewers who are inside their activity areas. Nakayama & Wan, (2019) compare emotion distributions between reviewers of western and Japanese cultural background and find significant differences among different product aspects.

Quan et al. (2022) find significant differences of users' ratings and sentiments between French and Chinese restaurants, suggesting that it is a result of implicit discriminatory bias in reviewers' behavior. Gao & Katrompas (2020) refer to evaluation bias describing overly skewed distributions of reviews towards the negative or positive side. In the case of online community of professor evaluations, they attribute disproportionally negative reviews to reviewers' motives due to their nature of relationship with professors. Reviewer identity information can also influence biased behaviors. When absent, hence when a reviewer's identity is ambiguous, users exhibit an egocentric bias assuming that they have similar tastes. Additionally, users are less persuaded by reviewers with dissimilar tastes (Naylor et al., 2011). Off-platform social factors related to customer experience can also be influential, as in the case of social desirability that can lead to overly positive reviews (Swetha & Murthy, 2019). In the same manner, offline social exclusion has been identified as a factor increasing the likelihood of a negative review. This is related to the presence of self-serving bias, representing the need of reviewers to boost their status and self-esteem (Liang et al., 2021). Kokkodis & Lappas (2020) define a different type of popularity bias, namely popularity-difference bias, which occurs when the destination under review has significantly different popularity compared to reviewer's origination, thus linked to cultural differences of reviewers. Finally, psychological effects created during customer experience, such as air quality in restaurants, even if not part of primary offerings, can affect quality perceptions and review ratings (Fang et al., 2019).

Reviewer Genuineness

Reviewer genuineness has also been a subject of recent research (Chaudhary et al., 2019). Fake reviews and fake review detection has been a subject of several studies as a widely recognized distorting phenomenon in online reviews and can be considered a form of bias, affecting knowledge representativeness. Plotkina et al. (2020) define deception effects of fake reviews as "truth bias". Malicious or dishonest reviews are listed by Wu et al. (2018) in a section of "random error", since they represent a subpopulation causing deviation from true consumer evaluations. Nevertheless, they consider fake reviews a type of biased reviewing behavior.

On-Platform Features Aspect

We propose a theme grouping bias forms related to social and other platform-based cues, that induce cognitive bias behaviors. Evaluations can be strongly affected by platform elements affecting decision making during the process of engaging in an online review community. That includes social trends and influences, product popularity and prior evaluations, review sequence and ranking, and other visual, structural or review characteristics that can serve as heuristic cues.

Popularity and Prior Evaluations

Popularity of products or services in the online community has been found to be crucial. Powell et al. (2017) define popularity bias as the influence of number of total reviews on rating scores. They find that under certain conditions, more reviewed products were preferred. Heck et al. (2020) verify that products with more reviews are more likely to be chosen. However, they also emphasize the role of coherence of representation regarding number of reviews and the indication of average rating, which was found to be a sought-after feature by customers. Prior ratings and evaluation content can also exert a strong influence on future evaluations. Ackerman & Chung (2018), find that both prior negative and positive ratings can affect subsequent ratings. Studies refer to the effect of displayed average ratings on individual rating choice, namely bandwagon bias. Bandwagon bias has been described as rating distortion, due to a shifted position of individuals towards observed average ratings (Wu et al., 2023). Wu et al. (2018) list bandwagon bias as a form of dependence bias (dependent on observed mean rating and trend) and as an opposite of differentiation effect, which represents contrasting behaviors to dominant evaluations.

Influence of previous reviews is also defined as social influence bias. According to Köcher et al. (2016), there is a social influence effect caused by previous reviews, although dependent on levels of satisfaction, which moderates the level of influence for products of high true quality. Social influence bias is also described as an asymmetrical effect. Cicognani et al. (2022), suggest that information of prior ratings can influence new reviews in cases where prior ratings are above average. Additionally, they limit social influence bias behaviors mainly to non-experienced reviewers, as frequent users are found to be less susceptible.

Review Sequence

Studies focus on the structural issue of review sequence, which is very influential on future evaluations. According to Vinson et al. (2019), sequential dependency of cognitive user behavior is a commonly acknowledged phenomenon, which leads to rating bias, due to the last encountered evaluations by the user forming an evaluation. However, the level of sequential effect decays over time. Jurca et al. (2010) verify sequential bias by analyzing text features and content. Longer and detailed reviews are more likely to converge in terms of rating agreement. The sequential structure of online review input data has also been found to affect recommendations of recommender systems (Piramuthu et al., 2012). Sequential structures also favor the creation of a contextual environment for each review, dependent on neighboring reviews, which can be a valuable source of information for bias detection (Du et al., 2021).

Social Status Influence

Hu et al. (2022a) interpret negative rating bias in reviews as a consequence of customers' need for status. However, they observe a counter-balancing effect of social conformity, as a form of social pressure from crowds, that can often have predominantly positive opinions, thus alleviating individual negativity bias. Additionally, Hu et al. (2022b) address online beauty and self-presentation as factors inducing rating bias in online shopping communities.

Between-Platform Bias

Rating bias has also been found in rating discrepancies between different technical platforms. Kordzadeh (2019) defines between-website bias in a study of online reviews of physicians, indicating that ratings of physicians in healthcare institutions websites are skewed towards more favorable scores compared to independent websites. Shan et al. (2020), in a similar manner identify elements of social-cultural complexity and technical platform particularities in Chinese networks that create unique layers of bias.

Other Cognitive Biases

Finally, even though cognitive bias has a broad scope across many scientific fields, many online review studies use the term to refer to design, visual and structural elements of platforms and their effect on evaluation decisions, through user heuristic judgements. Bao et al. (2018) emphasize that tag functions affect review evaluations and helpfulness perception. Schneider et al. (2015) discern prominent heuristics that lead to cognitive bias of online review behaviors, namely availability, triggered by most easily acceptable thoughts, anchoring in previous reviews, and response styles, triggered by the absence of default values in rating scales. E-WoM literature has also associated consumers' assessments of message credibility and quality with heuristic cues that can induce bias. Qahri-Saremi & Montazemi (2019) suggest two dominant factors, namely message consistency and source trustworthiness. Message consistency refers to which a message's arguments are consistent with other messages covering the same topic. Source trustworthiness affects heuristics by creating expectations for review quality. Aghakhani et al., 2023 also identify review topic consistency as a factor positively affecting review usefulness. Finally, Antioco & Coussement (2018) support that managers are characterized by judgement bias, which is found to be heavily dependent on specific language markers in review tests, resulting in misinterpretation of messages.

Bias Mitigation

This section covers bias mitigation methods, as well as bias analysis directions proposed by literature. Hu et al. (2022a) urge for a balanced management of informative elements in a community, to enable a dynamic adjustment to various biased behavior circumstances. Our review reveals that studies propose multiple practices, including approaches of direct prompting to affect reporting populations, balanced opinions, and control of informative or structural elements to adjust on-platform bias. Additionally, methods utilizing bias-related information can enhance monitoring efforts and improve quality and accuracy of extracted information.

Practices to Affect Reviewer Population and Quality

Representativeness of reviews is greatly affected by the characteristics of the population of reviewers that contribute to the community. A common approach to address issues of under-reporting is review solicitations, of customers less affected by extremity or self-selection. This was found to increase representativeness of ratings and review content, in comparison to unsolicited reviewers (Karamana, 2021). Marinescu et al. (2021) find that selection bias can be reduced by attracting customers of moderate opinion, through appropriate incentives, overcoming low initial motivations. Askalidis et al. (2017) propose that email invitations to verified customers improve representativeness, as the segment of solicited reviewers was found to be less prone to social influence bias.

Another direction of direct prompting involves prompting reviewers to avoid extremity and provide a quality contribution. Kuan et al. (2015) indicate the need of developing prompts for reviewers to provide more balanced views. Similarly, Askay (2015) suggests providing prompts to contribute balanced and sincere review descriptions, to attract postings of higher knowledge value. Wu et al. (2018) propose prompting of unbiased behavior and weighted information flow methods to highlight opposite views, for addressing bandwagon and differentiation effects.

Finally, manipulative reviews detection and filtering algorithms (which is a thriving separate stream of research) are among the methods of improving representativeness of reviews and associated biases (Wu et al., 2018). Plotkina et al. (2020) propose a micro-linguistic algorithm for automated detection to filter online review content, suggesting that advanced filtering techniques are essential for management of online content of review communities.

Platform Informative Adjustments

Studies suggest that on-platform bias behavior escalations can be mitigated by making targeted informative interventions towards users. Additional knowledge provided to reviewers can reduce effects of prior evaluations, promote balanced views, and optimize the contextual space in which reviewers make decisions. One of the most crucial bias factors is collective ratings and popularity of products. According to Bao & Chau (2016) collective rating can be an amplifying factor of prior expectations and confirmation bias. Average rating and majority opinion can crucially affect expectations' formation, confirmation effects and future rating patterns (Zaof et al., 2021). Ho et al. (2017) propose an indicator providing the standard deviation of ratings' distribution, to promote uncertainty in cases of high variation, and make it more difficult to infer product quality from average rating alone. Cicognani et al. (2022), urge for the development of adjusted online rating and evaluation systems to mitigate social influence bias due to prior ratings. Regarding popularity bias, Hayes et al. (2021) propose a mechanism of providing information such as "time on the market", to mark products old enough to explain part of their popularity. Shi et al. (2020) claim that presenting a percentage of positive reviews information can eliminate rating differences due to negativity bias induced by low-sales products. Kordzadeh (2019) indicate that institutions should systematically try to help users bypass rating biases and make informed decisions. This could be achieved by providing additional or comparative information that can mitigate biased accumulated evaluations within platforms.

Counterbalancing negativity bias due to causal attribution can be achieved through providing peripheral cues of temporal closeness to consumption (Chen & Lurie, 2013) or by developing indicators of repeated purchase of products and services (Vali et al., 2015). Additionally, attending to negative reviews and developing timely and appropriate response strategies can greatly reduce related negativity bias effects, especially in experienced users. An important factor is to satisfy the needs of cognition, attenuating negativity biased behaviors and potential escalations of reactionary decision making (Qahri-Saremi & Montazemi, 2023).

Enriching information context regarding reviews and reviewers is an important aspect. Studies propose providing information to lead reviewers to more quality and helpful contributions, by promoting identifiers on reviewer contribution record (Kuan et al., 2015) and developing social status peripheral cues (Li et al., 2017), which can mitigate negativity bias. In a similar direction, Guo et al. (2019) propose the use of indicators or recommendation mechanisms of neutral or positive reviews to enhance cognitive processing and alleviate short response times by users. Finally, to cope with cognitive bias effects caused by the extent use of glorified terms, Kobayashi et al. (2009) suggest providing additional information to support accurate understanding by users.

Platform Structural and Design Adjustments

Design and structural enhancements can also address biased behaviors aiming at crucial areas affecting heuristic judgements of users. Schneider et al. (2015) propose a series of targeted design interventions. The effect of anchoring can be toned down with the use of hidden reviews feature. The effect of availability could be addressed by providing more granular, multi-aspect forms of evaluations to reviewers. The response style effect, which refers to the tendency of users to select the very end of the star rating scale, could be mitigated by setting a default value in the center of the scale. In a similar direction, Liu & Hu (2021) emphasize covering multiple aspects in reviews, which can be enhanced by design features enabling separate assessment areas for different product aspects. Hidden text features are also highlighted by Jabr et al. (2022), as hidden text perceived value is related to prior beliefs and confirmation bias behaviors.

Studies also outline review-level features. Wu et al. (2011) propose promoting reviews with certain language characteristics found to moderate negativity bias. Kuan et al. (2015) distinguish two review quality aspects affecting evaluations, namely length and vocabulary. They suggest developing design aspects that guide or restrict review length (which was shown to induce extremity) and providing infrastructure of vocabulary help to reviewers to promote more elaborated review representations. Also, the use of tag function applications on reviews has been proposed, having a significant impact of review value perceptions (Bao et al., 2018). Finally, studies focus on the dynamic nature and contextual environment of online review communities and indicate the need of adjustable structures and customized information (e.g., for different reviewer segments) to adjust biased behaviors (Cicognani et al., 2022; Hu & Zhou, 2023).

Approaches of Bias Analysis

Bias in online review communities entails a series of challenges for monitoring and customer knowledge extraction. Jurca et al. (2010) identify text characteristics, text content and ratings as the three sources of primary information. Composite analyses of these sources can aid the identification of discussion elements and review features that lead to rating agreement, extraction of factors affecting reporting, and descriptions of prior expectations to assess true product quality. Jia et al. (2020) urge for holistic frameworks associating online review components and various forms of bias and promoting the understanding of review components' importance for mitigating bias. Additionally, analytical and modeling approaches emphasize the importance of assessing bias for multiple reviewer segments exhibiting deviations in evaluation behaviors.

Estimation of asymmetries between text sentiment content and ratings is suggested by several studies (Mehraliyev et al., 2020; Skotis et al., 2023) as well as between aspect ratings and overall ratings (Li et al., 2016), for rating prediction models is proposed. Also, monitoring of deviations of non-positive review content from dominant positive views is suggested by Bridges & Vásquez (2018). Additionally, association of review content and satisfaction levels has been a subject of research. Nicolau et al. (2022) focus on the identification and monitoring of extreme and moderate content and their asymmetric effects on satisfaction levels, while Chen et al. (2016) propose modeling generation of content incorporating posting probabilities based on levels of satisfaction, to address reporting bias.

Techniques to explore cognitive processes of reviewers based on review content are also proposed. Zhao et al. (2022) focus on extraction of review aspects of valence, emotional extremity and previous expectations to enable better management of heuristic judgements by users. Choi (2022) stress that identifying review content extremity, confirm initial consumer beliefs, can moderate confirmation bias. Du et al. (2021) propose a neural architecture approach to contextualize reviews, incorporating clues of neighbor reviews, to enhance understanding of sequential bias. Studies also emphasize the extraction of review linguistic features, as specific features of review language can alter or distort perceptions and interpretations. Antioco & Coussement (2018) identify that the use of discrepancy words and third-person pronouns can improve interpretations of negative reviews. Developing techniques to mark these features can thus be useful for managing judgement bias. Eslami et al. (2018) identify contributions of medium length and neutral or negative tone as more likely to be perceived as helpful. Moreover, Qahri-Saremi & Montazemi (2019) suggest that creating models to recognize the level of a message's consistency regarding a certain topic could be valuable for identifying deviating evaluations.

Research also indicates the need for organizations to be adaptive to different user backgrounds and preferences. Reviewer profiling and segmentation based on behavioral and background characteristics is an emerging topic. Koh et al. (2010) stress that reviewers of different networks and cultural backgrounds can have varying intensities of the same biased behavior forms. Tay (2019) calls for modeling of biased behaviors incorporating reviewer preferences to achieve more balanced summarizations and bias-aware representations. Ho et al. (2017) verify that experienced reviewers were found to be less affected by disconfirmation effects, while Sikora & Chauhan (2012) find that sequential bias is different for reviewer segments varying by number of votes, posts and helpfulness. Nakayama & Wan (2019) show that sentiment distributions can significantly differ between product aspects for reviewers of different cultural backgrounds and customer profiles. Regarding individual preferences, dimensional and product attribute factors can be valuable for selection bias research (Liu & Karahanna, 2017). Finally, incorporating reviewer historical rating behavior patterns in modeling and profiling approaches is suggested by Lim & Tucker (2017) and Skotis et al. (2023).

A Bias-Oriented CKM Framework

Figure 3 demonstrates a framework consolidating management challenges and practices for addressing the effects of biased behavior on customer knowledge representativeness. Biases create a distorted view of evaluations at both individual and collective levels, that require multi-dimensional analysis and crucial management interventions to address escalations. Adopting the view of online review communities as dynamic sources of customer data and knowledge, we believe that this virtual landscape creates multiple challenges for customer knowledge management that lack holistic approaches in literature. In this direction, several targeted management and analysis practices can be considered as customer knowledge flows that affect quality of information for businesses, platform management and customers, in a sustainable manner. Organizations can take into consideration advances of relevant literature and make use of bias-aware frameworks and practices.

Drawing concepts from cognitive bias literature, we view our review findings on biased behaviors in review platforms through two perspectives. The initial judgement, "anchoring" side, being the main source of biased views due to dominant mental models, preconceptions, motivations, and contextual influences of individuals, defining to a large degree the endogenous nature of decision making. On the other hand, the on-platform process, design environment and de-biasing practices focus on the "adjustment" side. Providing additional information or alternative information representations affects "framing" (Suomala, 2020) and changing structural elements inducing cognitive limitations and contextual adaptations by users can address multiple forms of cognitive bias.

Figure 3. A bias-aware CKM framework

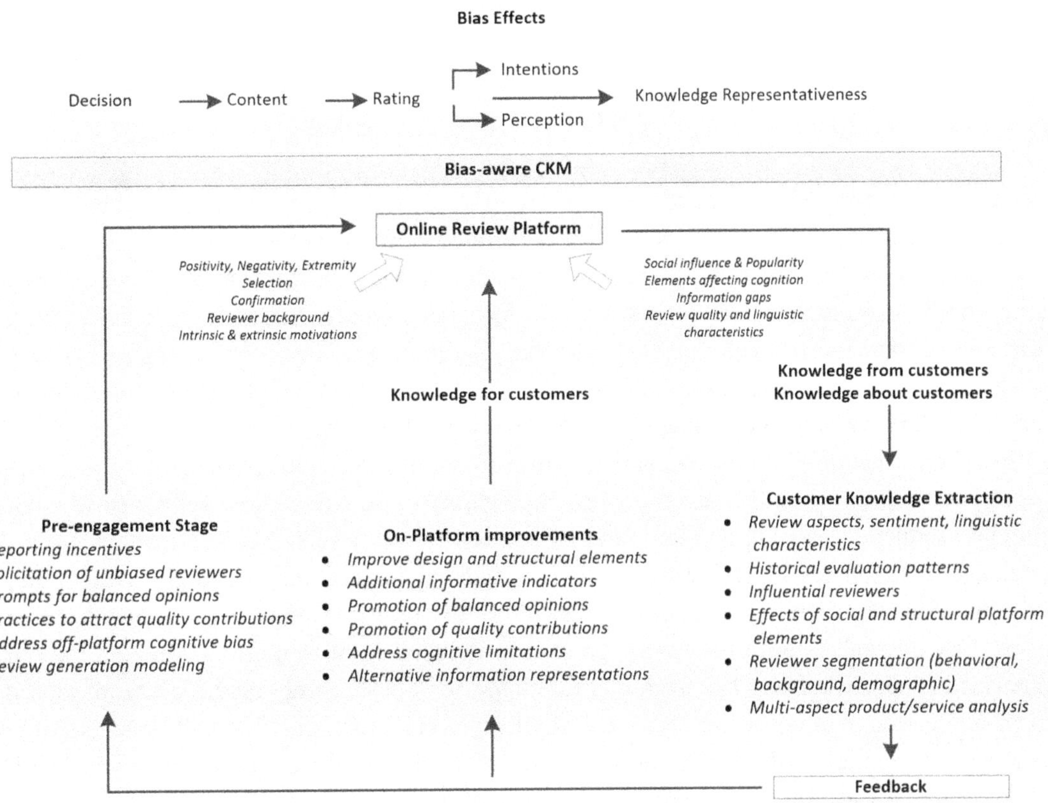

At the pre-engagement stage, management emphasizes on drawing reviewer populations with balanced and multi-aspect views that can partly address J-shaped distributions in terms of completeness, objectivity, and quality of produced knowledge. Behaviors leading to decisions to review can be part of modeling approaches incorporating bias at multiple levels. During the on-platform review process, management develops design and structural improvements, as well as additional informative cues, aiming at enriching reviewers' perceptions and forming a cognitive environment that discourages heuristic judgements inducing biased behaviors. Creating a more objective, rich in information and balanced landscape for users is manifested through flows of knowledge for customers, dynamically adjusted to bias behavior phenomena.

Customer knowledge extraction and related monitoring and analysis can be very demanding, according to literature. Review content regarding aspects, sentiment and linguistic characteristics are crucial elements of analysis, indicative of biased behaviors and impactful on review perceptions. Historical rating patterns can reveal unique customer segments at the individual level and track bias escalations at the collective level. Organizations can enhance methods for the identification of influential reviews and reviewers having specific properties and develop bias-oriented practices to utilize them. Additionally, examine how certain social and structural platform elements can create biased decisions and trends in review creation or review perceptions processes. Also, analyze asymmetries of evaluations, at multiple levels. Knowledge extraction and analysis can provide important feedback points for the improvement of processes, determine interventions, and create knowledge flows towards customers, on and off-platform, in a dynamic and sustainable manner.

CONCLUSION, LIMITATIONS, AND FUTURE RESEARCH

As behaviors of users exhibit traces of bias at multiple levels, organizations face the complex task of coping with the identification and management of associated combined effects. According to our literature review, these effects can have a multiplying nature, leading to an increasingly biased source of information affecting both businesses and customers. Certain forms of bias affect if and why a reviewer will post, the direction and historical evolution of evaluations, the impact of these on existing and potential users of products and services. Bias-aware customer knowledge management practices can aid businesses to the end of better assessing and managing online review platforms as knowledge sources. Organizations can affect the formation of online evaluations, by establishing additional information flows for customers to counter-balance cognitive and motivational bias. Also, provide a more symmetrical environment to alleviate sequential, social, and temporal influences for reviewers. Finally, develop more efficient strategies for luring potential reviewers not characterized by intense intrinsic motives affecting postings and evaluations. The thematic distinctions drawn by this study can provide novel perspectives of user behavior bias and enhance the interpretation of bias-induced combined effects. In parallel, our review summarized proposed approaches from literature regarding de-biasing practices. Our proposed framework promotes the relation of user bias effects with practices of mitigation and concepts of customer knowledge management, offering a unifying point of reference for research and practices addressing issues of online review knowledge representativeness.

Considering the importance of online review platforms for businesses and economies and observing recent trends of research, we conclude that the topic in general is under-researched, especially in relation to methods and practices of managing extracted knowledge in a bias-aware manner. Nevertheless, we distinguish a few significant research gaps demonstrating very limited research. Literature offers very few references on factors about the off-platform contextual information environment regarding products and services, or contextual limitations that can crucially pre-determine biased behaviors (Aral et al., 2011; Suomala, 2020) before users' engagement with the platform. Also, although discrepancies between review content and corresponding ratings have been mentioned in several studies (e.g., for justifying using measured sentiments instead of ratings for classification purposes) these patterns have only rarely been used for reviewer segmentation purposes. In this direction, future studies should more intensively focus on multi-dimensional segmentation of users according to emotional and historical rating patterns, affected by intrinsic and extrinsic drivers. A significant research gap was also found in bias categorizations and definitional coherence. There is a need to further address the dispersed and overlapping categorizations of cognitive bias behaviors towards a unified typology. Furthermore, future studies should further develop advanced methods of monitoring and mitigation of biases' impacts, and define crucial points for management, through alternative information representations and focused customer relationship initiatives. Regarding limitations, as mentioned in the methodology section, only the Scopus database was selected due to the additional features provided by the platform. This is an important limitation of this study, and complementary review studies on the topic could offer valuable additional insights. Finally, a review of methodologies used by the same literature stream would be a useful future research direction.

REFERENCES

Ackerman, D., & Chung, C. (2018). Is RateMyProfessors. com unbiased? A look at the impact of social modelling on student online reviews of marketing classes. *Journal of Marketing Education, 40*(3), 188–195. doi:10.1177/0273475317735654

Aghakhani, N., Oh, O., Gregg, D., & Jain, H. (2023). How review quality and source credibility interacts to affect review usefulness: An expansion of the elaboration likelihood model. *Information Systems Frontiers: A Journal of Research and Innovation, 25*(4), 1513–1531. doi:10.1007/s10796-022-10299-w

Antioco, M., & Coussement, K. (2018). Misreading of consumer dissatisfaction in online product reviews: Writing style as a cause for bias. *International Journal of Information Management, 38*(1), 301–310. doi:10.1016/j.ijinfomgt.2017.10.009

Aral, S., Ipeirotis, P., & Taylor, S. J. (2011). Content and context: Identifying the impact of qualitative information on consumer choice. *International Conference on Information Systems 2011*. SSRN. 10.2139/ssrn.1784376

Askalidis, G., Kim, S. J., & Malthouse, E. C. (2017). Understanding and overcoming biases in online review systems. *Decision Support Systems, 97*, 23–30. doi:10.1016/j.dss.2017.03.002

Askay, D. A. (2015). Silence in the crowd: The spiral of silence contributing to the positive bias of opinions in an online review system. *New Media & Society, 17*(11), 1811–1829. doi:10.1177/1461444814535190

Baeza-Yates, R. (2018). Bias on the web. *Communications of the ACM, 61*(6), 54–61. doi:10.1145/3209581

Bao, Z., & Chau, M. (2016). *The effect of collective rating on the perception of online reviews.*

Bao, Z., Li, W., Yin, P., & Chau, M. (2018). How does the review tag function benefit highly-rated popular products in online markets? In *Lecture Notes in Business Information Processing* (pp. 47–63). Lecture Notes in Business Information Processing. doi:10.1007/978-3-319-99936-4_5

Bao, Z., Li, W., Yin, P., & Chau, M. (2021). Examining the impact of review tag function on product evaluation and information perception of popular products. *Information Systems and e-Business Management, 19*(2), 517–539. doi:10.1007/s10257-021-00532-5

Bazerman, M. H., & Moore, D. A. (2013). *Judgement in Managerial Decision Making*. John Wiley & Sons, Inc.

Bhole, B., & Hanna, B. (2017). The effectiveness of online reviews in the presence of self-selection bias. *Simulation Modelling Practice and Theory, 77*, 108–123. doi:10.1016/j.simpat.2017.05.005

Bhole, B., & Hanna, B. (2017). The effectiveness of online reviews in the presence of self-selection bias. *Simulation Modelling Practice and Theory, 77*, 108–123. doi:10.1016/j.simpat.2017.05.005

Bing, X., & Yang, Z. (2020). Study of two-period pricing strategies for experiential products based onpraise cash-back'and negativity bias. *Journal of Industrial Engineering and Engineering Management, 34*(2), 21–29.

Brandes, L., Godes, D., & Mayzlin, D. (2022). Extremity Bias in Online Reviews: The Role of Attrition. *JMR, Journal of Marketing Research, 59*(4), 675–695. doi:10.1177/00222437211073579

Bridges, J., & Vásquez, C. (2018). If nearly all Airbnb reviews are positive, does that make them meaningless? *Current Issues in Tourism, 21*(18), 2065–2083. doi:10.1080/13683500.2016.1267113

Browne, G. J., & Parsons, J. (2012). More enduring questions in cognitive is research. *Journal of the Association for Information Systems, 13*(12), 1000–1011. doi:10.17705/1jais.00318

Centobelli, P., & Ndou, V. (2019). Managing customer knowledge through the use of big data analytics in tourism research. *Current Issues in Tourism, 22*(15), 1862–1882. doi:10.1080/13683500.2018.1564739

Chatterjee, S. (2019). Explaining customer ratings and recommendations by combining qualitative and quantitative user generated contents. *Decision Support Systems, 119*(February), 14–22. doi:10.1016/j.dss.2019.02.008

Chaudhary, P., Aeron, A., & Vijay, S. (2020). Quantify The Reviewer Genunity Based On Behavior Metrics And Past Trust Analysis. *International Journal of Scientific and Technology Research, 8*(8), 1116-1121.

Chen, H., Zheng, Z., & Ceran, Y. (2016). De-biasing the reporting bias in social media analytics. *Production and Operations Management, 25*(5), 849–865. doi:10.1111/poms.12509

Chen, Z., & Lurie, N. H. (2013). Temporal contiguity and negativity bias in the impact of online word of mouth. *JMR, Journal of Marketing Research, 50*(4), 463–476. doi:10.1509/jmr.12.0063

Choi, H. S. (2022). Do extraordinary claims require extraordinary evidence? Differential effect of trust cues on helpfulness by review extremity: An empirical study using big data. *European Journal of Information Systems*, 1–22. doi:10.1080/0960085X.2022.2104665

Cicognani, S., Figini, P., & Magnani, M. (2022). Social influence bias in ratings: A field experiment in the hospitality sector. *Tourism Economics*, *28*(8), 2197–2218. doi:10.1177/13548166211034645

de Barra, M. (2017). Reporting bias inflates the reputation of medical treatments: A comparison of outcomes in clinical trials and online product reviews. *Social Science & Medicine (1982)*, *177*, 248–255. doi:10.1016/j.socscimed.2017.01.033

Du, J., Rong, J., Wang, H., & Zhang, Y. (2021). Neighbor-aware review helpfulness prediction. *Decision Support Systems*, *148*, 113581. doi:10.1016/j.dss.2021.113581

Einar, B., Havro, L. J., & Moen, O. (2015). An Empirical Investigation of Self-Selection Bias and Factors Influencing Review Helpfulness. *International Journal of Business and Management*, *10*(7), 16–30. doi:10.5539/ijbm.v10n7p16

Eslami, S. P., Ghasemaghaei, M., & Hassanein, K. (2018). Which online reviews do consumers find most helpful? A multi-method investigation. *Decision Support Systems*, *113*, 32–42. doi:10.1016/j.dss.2018.06.012

Fang, J., Hu, L., Hossin, M. A., Yang, J., & Shao, Y. (2019). Polluted online reviews: The effect of air pollution on reviewer behavior. *International Journal of Electronic Commerce*, *23*(4), 557–594. doi:10.1080/10864415.2019.1655206

Filieri, R., Raguseo, E., & Vitari, C. (2021). Extremely negative ratings and online consumer review helpfulness: The moderating role of product quality signals. *Journal of Travel Research*, *60*(4), 699–717. doi:10.1177/0047287520916785

Fleischmann, M., Amirpur, M., Benlian, A., & Hess, T. (2014). Cognitive biases in information systems research: A scientometric analysis. *ECIS 2014 Proceedings - 22nd European Conference on Information Systems*.

Gao, B., Hu, N., & Bose, I. (2017). Follow the herd or be myself? An analysis of consistency in behavior of reviewers and helpfulness of their reviews. *Decision Support Systems*, *95*, 1–11. doi:10.1016/j.dss.2016.11.005

Gao, B. J., & Katrompas, A. (2020, December 10). A preliminary experimental analysis on RateMyProfessors. *2020 IEEE International Conference on Big Data (Big Data)*. IEEE. 10.1109/BigData50022.2020.9378446

Ge, Y., & Li, J. (2015). Measure and Mitigate the Dimensional Bias in Online Reviews and Ratings. In ICIS 2015.

Gebert, H., Geib, M., Kolbe, L., & Brenner, W. (2003). Knowledge-enabled customer relationship management: Integrating customer relationship management and knowledge management concepts [1]. *Journal of Knowledge Management*, *7*(5), 107–123. doi:10.1108/13673270310505421

George, J. F., Duffy, K., & Ahuja, M. (2000). Countering the anchoring and adjustment bias with decision support systems. *Decision Support Systems*, *29*(2), 195–206. doi:10.1016/S0167-9236(00)00074-9

Gibbert, M., Leibold, M., & Probst, G. (2002). Five styles of customer knowledge management, and how smart companies use them to create value. *European Management Journal, 20*(5), 459–469. doi:10.1016/S0263-2373(02)00101-9

Guo, D., Zhao, Y., Zhang, L., Wen, X., & Yin, C. (2019). Conformity feedback in an online review helpfulness evaluation task leads to less negative feedback-related negativity amplitudes and more positive P300 amplitudes. *Journal of Neuroscience, Psychology, and Economics, 12*(2), 73–87. doi:10.1037/npe0000102

Haley, U. C. V., & Stumpf, S. A. (1989). Cognitive Trails in Strategic Decision-Making: Linking Theories of Personalities and Cognitions. *Journal of Management Studies, 26*(5), 477–497. doi:10.1111/j.1467-6486.1989.tb00740.x

Han, S., & Anderson, C. K. (2020). Customer motivation and response bias in online reviews. *Cornell Hospitality Quarterly, 61*(2), 142–153. doi:10.1177/1938965520902012

Hayes, B. K., Wisken, A., & Cruz, N. (2021). Explaining the popularity bias in online consumer choice. *Journal of Experimental Psychology. General, 150*(10), 2185–2191. doi:10.1037/xge0001031 PMID:33734776

Heck, D. W., Seiling, L., & Bröder, A. (2020). The love of large numbers revisited: A coherence model of the popularity bias. *Cognition, 195*(104069), 104069. doi:10.1016/j.cognition.2019.104069 PMID:31877503

Ho, Y.-C., Wu, J., & Tan, Y. (2017). Disconfirmation effect on online rating behavior: A structural model. *Information Systems Research : ISR, 28*(3), 626–642. doi:10.1287/isre.2017.0694

Hoorens, V. (2014). Positive Bias. Encyclopedia of Quality of Life and Well-Being Research, 4938-4941. Springer. doi:10.1007/978-94-007-0753-5

Hu, N. (2017). On self-selection biases in online product reviews. MIS Quarterly: Management Information Systems, 41(2), 449–471. doi:10.25300/MISQ/2017/41.2.06

Hu, N., Pavlou, P. A., & Zhang, J. (2017). On Self-Selection Biases in Online Product Reviews. *Management Information Systems Quarterly, 41*(2), 449–471. doi:10.25300/MISQ/2017/41.2.06

Hu, X., He, L., & Liu, J. (2022). Status reinforcing: Unintended rating bias on online shopping platforms. *Journal of Retailing and Consumer Services, 67*(102995), 102995. doi:10.1016/j.jretconser.2022.102995

Hu, X., He, L., & Liu, J. (2022). The power of beauty: Be your ideal self in online reviews—an empirical study based on face detection. *Journal of Retailing and Consumer Services, 67*, 102975. doi:10.1016/j.jretconser.2022.102975

Hu, Y., & Zhou, S. (2023). Will reviewer recommendation source and cured status bias review helpfulness in online health community? *Online Information Review, 47*(4), 680–696. doi:10.1108/OIR-05-2021-0248

Huang, H. H., Hsu, J. S. C., & Ku, C. Y. (2012). Understanding the role of computer-mediated counter-argument in countering confirmation bias. *Decision Support Systems, 53*(3), 438–447. doi:10.1016/j.dss.2012.03.009

Jabr, W., Lohtia, R., Zhao, Y., & Guillory, M. D. (2022). Hidden power: Impact of the "snippet" on online consumer engagement. *Electronic Commerce Research and Applications*, *55*(101196), 101196. doi:10.1016/j.elerap.2022.101196

Jia, Q., Guo, Y., & Barnes, S. (2020). Understanding information bias: The perspective of online review component: An abstract. In Marketing Opportunities and Challenges in a Changing Global Marketplace (pp. 157–158). Springer. doi:10.1007/978-3-030-39165-2_69

Jurca, R., Garcin, F., Talwar, A., & Faltings, B. (2010). Reporting incentives and biases in online review forums. [TWEB]. *ACM Transactions on the Web*, *4*(2), 1–27. doi:10.1145/1734200.1734202

Kahneman, D., Lovallo, D., & Sibony, O. (2011). Before you make that big decision. *Harvard Business Review*, *89*(6), 50–60, 137. https://www.ncbi.nlm.nih.gov/pubmed/21714386 PMID:21714386

Karaman, H. (2021). Online review solicitations reduce extremity bias in online review distributions and increase their representativeness. *Management Science*, *67*(7), 4420–4445. doi:10.1287/mnsc.2020.3758

Karaman, H. (2021). Online Review Solicitations Reduce Extremity Bias in Online Review Distributions and Increase Their Representativeness. *Management Science*, *67*(7), 4420–4445. doi:10.1287/mnsc.2020.3758

Kim, J. M., Kim, M., & Key, S. (2020). When profile photos matter: The roles of reviewer profile photos in the online review generation and consumption processes. *Journal of Research in Interactive Marketing*, *14*(4), 391–412. doi:10.1108/JRIM-10-2019-0163

Kobayashi, T., Ohshima, H., Oyama, S., & Tanaka, K. (2009, March). Modeling and analyzing review information on the web focusing on credibility. In *Proceedings of the 2009 ACM symposium on Applied Computing* (pp. 1316-1317). ACM. 10.1145/1529282.1529577

Köcher, S., Paluch, S., & Küsgen, S. (2016). The recommendation bias: The effects of social influence on individual rating behavior. In Marketing Challenges in a Turbulent Business Environment (pp. 353–354). Springer. doi:10.1007/978-3-319-19428-8_93

Koh, N. S., Hu, N., & Clemons, E. K. (2010). Do Online Reviews Reflect a Product's True Perceived Quality? - An Investigation of Online Movie Reviews Across Cultures. *2010 43rd Hawaii International Conference on System Sciences*, (pp. 1–10). IEEE. 10.1109/HICSS.2010.154

Kokkodis, M., & Lappas, T. (2020). Your hometown matters: Popularity-difference bias in online reputation platforms. *Information Systems Research*, *31*(2), 412–430. doi:10.1287/isre.2019.0895

Kordzadeh, N. (2019). Investigating bias in the online physician reviews published on healthcare organizations' websites. *Decision Support Systems*, *118*, 70–82. doi:10.1016/j.dss.2018.12.007

Kuan, K. (2015). What makes a review voted? An empirical investigation of review voting in online review systems. Journal of the Association for Information Systems, 16(1), 48–71. doi:10.17705/1jais.00386

Lee, P., Hu, Y., & Lu, K. (2018). Assessing the helpfulness of online hotel reviews: A classification-based approach. *Telematics and Informatics*, *35*(2), 436–445. doi:10.1016/j.tele.2018.01.001

Lei, Z., Yin, D., & Zhang, H. (2023). Positive or Negative Reviews? Consumers' Selective Exposure in Seeking and Evaluating Online Reviews. *Journal of the Association for Information Systems, 24*(4), 1162–1183. doi:10.17705/1jais.00823

Li, H., Meng, F., & Pan, B. (2020). How does review disconfirmation influence customer online review behavior? A mixed-method investigation. *International Journal of Contemporary Hospitality Management, 32*(11), 3685–3703. doi:10.1108/IJCHM-03-2020-0234

Li, H., Zhang, Z., Meng, F., & Janakiraman, R. (2017). Is peer evaluation of consumer online reviews socially embedded? – An examination combining reviewer's social network and social identity. *International Journal of Hospitality Management, 67*, 143–153. doi:10.1016/j.ijhm.2017.08.003

Li, Y., Shi, C., Zhao, H., Zhuang, F., & Wu, B. (2016). Aspect mining with rating bias. In Machine Learning and Knowledge Discovery in Databases: European Conference. *Proceedings, 16*(Part II), 458–474.

Liang, S., Chu, Y., Wang, Y., Zhang, Z., Wu, Y., & Chang, Y. (2021). 'scapegoat' for offline consumption: Online review response to social exclusion. *Frontiers in Psychology, 12*, 783483. doi:10.3389/fpsyg.2021.783483 PMID:34925186

Lim, S., & Tucker, C. S. (2017). Mitigating Online Product Rating Biases Through the Discovery of Optimistic, Pessimistic, and Realistic Reviewers. *Journal of Mechanical Design, 139*(11), 111409. doi:10.1115/1.4037612

Liu, Q. B., & Karahanna, E. (2017). The dark side of reviews: The swaying effects of online product reviews on attribute preference construction. MIS Quarterly: Management. *Management Information Systems Quarterly, 41*(2), 427–448. doi:10.25300/MISQ/2017/41.2.05

Liu, Y., & Hu, H. (2021). Online review helpfulness: The moderating effects of review comprehensiveness. *International Journal of Contemporary Hospitality Management, 33*(2), 534–556. doi:10.1108/IJCHM-08-2020-0856

Liu, Y., Song, Y., Sun, J., Sun, C., Liu, C., & Chen, X. (2020). Understanding the relationship between food experiential quality and customer dining satisfaction: A perspective on negative bias. *International Journal of Hospitality Management, 87*(102381), 102381. doi:10.1016/j.ijhm.2019.102381

Marinescu, I., Chamberlain, A., Smart, M., & Klein, N. (2021). Incentives can reduce bias in online employer reviews. *Journal of Experimental Psychology. Applied, 27*(2), 393–407. doi:10.1037/xap0000342 PMID:33764122

Mehraliyev, F., Kirilenko, A. P., & Choi, Y. (2020). From measurement scale to sentiment scale: Examining the effect of sensory experiences on online review rating behavior. *Tourism Management, 79*, 104096. doi:10.1016/j.tourman.2020.104096

Millwood, A. (2015). *How star ratings influence customers' behavior.* Yotpo. https://www. yotpo.com/blog/star-ratings-influence-customers

Nakayama, M., & Wan, Y. (2019). Cross-cultural examination on content bias and helpfulness of online reviews: Sentiment balance at the aspect level for a subjective good. *Proceedings of the 52nd Hawaii International Conference on System Sciences.* HDL. http://hdl.handle.net/10125/59555

Naylor, R. W., Lamberton, C. P., & Norton, D. A. (2011). Seeing ourselves in others: Reviewer ambiguity, egocentric anchoring, and persuasion. *JMR, Journal of Marketing Research*, *48*(3), 617–631. doi:10.1509/jmkr.48.3.617

Nesdoly, N., Tulk, C., & Mantler, J. (2020). The effects of perceived professor competence, warmth and gender on students' likelihood to register for a course. *Assessment & Evaluation in Higher Education*, *45*(5), 666–679. doi:10.1080/02602938.2019.1689381

Nicolau, J. L., de Carlos Villamarín, P., Alén, E., & González, A. P. (2022). Asymmetric effects of extreme-moderate online reviews in the language-satisfaction relationship. *Tourism Management*, *91*, 104524. doi:10.1016/j.tourman.2022.104524

Osman, H., D'Acunto, D., & Johns, N. (2019). Home and away: Why do consumers shy away from reporting negative experiences in the peer-to-peer realms? *Psychology and Marketing*, *36*(12), 1162–1175. doi:10.1002/mar.21264

Ourzik, V. Y. (2022). Customer Knowledge Management: A Systematic Literature Review and Agenda for Future Research. *Proceedings of the European Conference on Knowledge Management, ECKM*, *23*(2), 1384–1394. 10.34190/eckm.23.2.780

Ozcan, T., Hair, M., & Hattat, A. M. (2022). Eric is bad, but Erica is worse: Greater negativity bias toward female brands. *Journal of Marketing Theory and Practice*, 1–16. doi:10.1080/10696679.2022.2067066

Peeters, G., & Czapinski, J. (1990). Positive-negative asymmetry in evaluations: The dis- tinction between affective and informational negativity effects. *European Review of Social Psychology*, *1*(1), 33–60. doi:10.1080/14792779108401856

Piramuthu, S., Kapoor, G., Zhou, W., & Mauw, S. (2012). Input online review data and related bias in recommender systems. *Decision Support Systems*, *53*(3), 418–424. doi:10.1016/j.dss.2012.02.006

Plotkina, D., Munzel, A., & Pallud, J. (2020). Illusions of truth—Experimental insights into human and algorithmic detections of fake online reviews. *Journal of Business Research*, *109*, 511–523. doi:10.1016/j.jbusres.2018.12.009

Powell, D., Yu, J., DeWolf, M., & Holyoak, K. J. (2017). The love of large numbers: A popularity bias in consumer choice. *Psychological Science*, *28*(10), 1432–1442. doi:10.1177/0956797617711291 PMID:28825874

Purnawirawan, N., Dens, N., & De Pelsmacker, P. (2012). Balance and sequence in online reviews: The wrap effect. *International Journal of Electronic Commerce*, *17*(2), 71–98. doi:10.2753/JEC1086-4415170203

Qahri-Saremi, H., & Montazemi, A. R. (2019). Factors affecting the adoption of an electronic word of mouth message: A meta-analysis. *Journal of Management Information Systems*, *36*(3), 969–1001. doi:10.1080/07421222.2019.1628936

Qahri-Saremi, H., & Montazemi, A. R. (2023). Negativity bias in the diagnosticity of online review content: The effects of consumers' prior experience and need for cognition. *European Journal of Information Systems*, *32*(4), 717–734. doi:10.1080/0960085X.2022.2041372

Quan, W., Li, Z., & Kim, W. (2022, December 17). *Implicit Discriminatory Bias Reflected in Yelp Reviews - A case study*. 2022 IEEE International Conference on Big Data (Big Data), Osaka, Japan. 10.1109/BigData55660.2022.10020592

Ractham, P., Abrahams, A., Gruss, R., Kim, E., Davis, Z., & Kaewkitipong, L. (2021). A Comparative Evaluation of Airline Service Quality Using Online Content Analysis: A Case Study of Korean vs. International Airlines. *Asia Pacific Journal of Information Systems, 31*(4), 491–526. doi:10.14329/apjis.2021.31.4.491

Roy, G., Datta, B., & Basu, R. (2017). Effect of eWOM valence on online retail sales. *Global Business Review, 18*(1), 198–209. doi:10.1177/0972150916666966

Schneider, C., Weinmann, M., & vom Brocke, J. (2015). Choice architecture: Using fixation patterns to analyze the effects of form design on cognitive biases. In *Lecture Notes in Information Systems and Organisation* (pp. 91–97). Information Systems and Neuroscience. doi:10.1007/978-3-319-18702-0_12

Sengo Furtado, F., Reutterer, T., & Schröder, N. (2022). The carrot and the stick in online reviews: Determinants of un-/helpfulness voting choices. *Journal of Business Economics, 92*(4), 565–590. doi:10.1007/s11573-021-01044-x

Shen, X., Pan, B., Hu, T., Chen, K., Qiao, L., & Zhu, J. (2020). Beyond self-selection: The multilayered online review biases at the intersection of users, platforms and culture. *Journal of Hospitality and Tourism Insights, 4*(1), 77–97. doi:10.1108/JHTI-02-2020-0012

Shi, Z., Zhang, C., & Wu, L. (2020). Sales or reviews, which matters more to consumer preference and online advertising? – evidence from eye-tracking and self-reporting. *International Journal of Advertising, 39*(8), 1274–1300. doi:10.1080/02650487.2020.1755181

Siering, M. (2021). Leveraging online review platforms to support public policy: Predicting restaurant health violations based on online reviews. *Decision Support Systems, 143*(113474), 113474. doi:10.1016/j.dss.2020.113474

Sikora, R. T., & Chauhan, K. (2012). Estimating sequential bias in online reviews: A Kalman filtering approach. *Knowledge-Based Systems, 27*, 314–321. doi:10.1016/j.knosys.2011.10.011

Skotis, A., Morfaki, C., & Livas, C. (2023). Identifying drivers of evaluation bias in online reviews of city destinations. *International Journal of Information Management Data Insights, 3*(2), 100184. doi:10.1016/j.jjimei.2023.100184

Suomala, J. (2020). The Consumer Contextual Decision-Making Model. *Frontiers in Psychology, 11*(September), 570430. doi:10.3389/fpsyg.2020.570430 PMID:33117237

Swetha, N., & Murthy, H. V. (2019). Indian heritage tourism—A netnographic approach. *International Journal of Innovative Technology and Exploring Engineering, 8*(7C2), 272-279.

Tata, S. V., Prashar, S., & Gupta, S. (2020). An examination of the role of review valence and review source in varying consumption contexts on purchase decision. *Journal of Retailing and Consumer Services, 52*(101734), 101734. doi:10.1016/j.jretconser.2019.01.003

Tay, W. (2019, July). Not all reviews are equal: Towards addressing reviewer biases for opinion summarization. In *Proceedings of the 57th Annual Meeting of the Association for Computational Linguistics: Student Research Workshop* (pp. 34-42). ACM. 10.18653/v1/P19-2005

Vali, H., Xu, D., & Yildirim, B. (2015). *The effects of repeating purchase cues and mixed reviews on product attribution. Thirty-Sixth International Conference on Information Systems*, Fort Worth.

Vinson, D. W., Dale, R., & Jones, M. N. (2019). Decision contamination in the wild: Sequential dependencies in online review ratings. *Behavior Research Methods, 51*(4), 1477–1484. doi:10.3758/s13428-018-1175-8 PMID:30604037

Wan, Y., & Nakayama, M. (2012). Are Amazon.com online review helpfulness ratings biased or not? In Lecture Notes in Business Information Processing (pp. 46–54). Springer. doi:10.1007/978-3-642-29873-8_5

Wen, J., Lin, Z., Liu, X., Xiao, S. H., & Li, Y. (2021). The interaction effects of online reviews, brand, and price on consumer hotel booking decision making. *Journal of Travel Research, 60*(4), 846–859. doi:10.1177/0047287520912330

Wilke, A., & Mata, R. (2012). Cognitive Bias. In Encyclopedia of Human Behavior (2nd ed., Vol. 1, pp. 531–535). Elsevier. doi:10.1016/B978-0-12-375000-6.00094-X

Wu, D., Guo, X., & Chen, G. (2017). *Mitigating the Dependence Bias in Online Ratings: A "Consider-the-Opposite"*. Strategy for Scale Prompting.

Wu, D., Guo, X., Wang, Y., & Chen, G. (2023). A Warning Approach to Mitigating Bandwagon Bias in Online Ratings: Theoretical Analysis and Experimental Investigations. *Journal of the Association for Information Systems, 24*(4), 1132–1161. doi:10.17705/1jais.00817

Wu, P. F. (2013). In search of negativity bias: An empirical study of perceived helpfulness of online reviews. *Psychology and Marketing, 30*(11), 971–984. doi:10.1002/mar.20660

Yin, D., Mitra, S., & Zhang, H. (2016). Research note—When do consumers value positive vs. negative reviews? An empirical investigation of confirmation bias in online word of mouth. *Information Systems Research, 27*(1), 131–144. doi:10.1287/isre.2015.0617

Yu, C., & Liao, W. (2023). Professionalism and homophily bias: A study of Airbnb stay choice and review positivity. *International Journal of Hospitality Management, 110*, 103433. doi:10.1016/j.ijhm.2023.103433

Yuan, W., Hong, Y., & Pavlou, P. A. (2012, December). The informational role of online product review distributions: An experimental study of biases in online product reviews. In *18th Americas Conference on Information Systems 2012, AMCIS 2012* (pp. 3780-3790). IEEE.

Zapf, B., Hütter, M., & Sassenberg, K. (2021). Are minority opinions shared less? *Zeitschrift für Psychologie, 229*(4), 251–256. doi:10.1027/2151-2604/a000471

Zhang, Y., Feng, X., Wu, Y., & Xiao, J. (2018). The dynamics of online ratings with heterogeneous preferences in online review platform. *Chaos, Solitons, and Fractals, 109*, 26–30. doi:10.1016/j.chaos.2018.02.003

Zhao, M., Shen, X., Liao, H., & Cai, M. (2022). Selecting products through text reviews: An MCDM method incorporating personalized heuristic judgments in the prospect theory. *Fuzzy Optimization and Decision Making*, *21*(1), 1–24. doi:10.1007/s10700-021-09359-8

Chapter 11
Navigating Cancer Epidemiology:
The Power of Digitalization and Visualization in Jordan, 2012-2018

Mohammad Majed Asad
https://orcid.org/0000-0003-1216-7679
Princess Sumaya University for Technology, Jordan

Abdullah Al-Refai
https://orcid.org/0000-0002-1557-3982
Princess Sumaya University for Technology, Jordan

Saqr Abushattal
Al-Hussein Bin Talal University, Jordan

Abedalrhman Alkhateeb
Lakehead University, Canada

ABSTRACT

In this chapter, the authors aimed to assess the cancer incidence and epidemiology among Jordanians from 2012 to 2018, utilizing data from the Jordan cancer registry (JCR) and Microsoft power BI for visualization. The authors collected cancer cases over this period, analyzed demographic information, and calculated incidence rates. The results revealed an overall average crude cancer incidence rate of 94.6/100,000 population, with the highest age-standardized rates observed in 2013. Breast cancer was the most prevalent among females, while bronchus and lung cancer led among males. These findings underscore the need for robust screening programs and the potential of digital tools like interactive dashboards in early detection. This study contributes valuable insights into Jordan's cancer landscape and suggests proactive healthcare strategies for the future, including predictive analytics for forecasting cancer cases.

DOI: 10.4018/979-8-3693-0798-4.ch011

OBJECTIVE

Cancer is a leading cause of morbidity and mortality worldwide. It is a group of diseases characterized by the uncontrolled growth and spread of abnormal cells in the body. Cancer can develop in any organ or tissue and can have a wide range of symptoms, depending on the type and stage of the disease (World Health Organization,2019).

According to the World Health Organization (WHO), cancer is the second leading cause of death globally and was responsible for an estimated 9.6 million deaths in 2018. The most common types of cancer worldwide are lung, breast, prostate, and colorectal cancer (World Health Organization,2019).

The causes of cancer are complex and multifactorial, with a combination of genetic, environmental, and lifestyle factors contributing to the development of the disease. Risk factors for cancer include tobacco use, alcohol consumption, poor diet, physical inactivity, UV radiation exposure, and certain chemicals and pollutants (Cancer Research UK, 2021; Harford, 2021).

Early detection and treatment of cancer can significantly improve outcomes and reduce mortality rates. Screening programs and vaccination against certain types of cancer, such as cervical and liver cancer, can also help reduce the burden of cancer (World Cancer Research Fund International, 2021).

Cancer is a leading cause of morbidity and mortality worldwide and in Jordan. According to the World Health Organization (WHO), cancer is expected to become Jordan's leading cause of death by 2020. Cancer incidence and mortality rates in Jordan have been increasing in recent years. The Jordan Cancer Registry (JCR) is the primary source of information on cancer incidence and mortality in the country. The JCR was established in 1979 and has been collecting data on cancer cases since then. The JCR data is used for cancer surveillance, research, and planning cancer control programs in Jordan.

Here, Business analytics comes into play by utilizing this vast dataset to identify trends and patterns. Predictive analytics, powered by machine learning algorithms, can forecast future trends in cancer incidence and mortality rates. By analyzing historical data, it can pinpoint areas at risk of experiencing a surge in cancer cases. Such insights are invaluable for informed decision-making and resource allocation.

Data visualization tools, such as Power BI dashboards, offer dynamic representations of the data. They enable healthcare professionals, policymakers, and researchers to quickly grasp the evolving landscape of cancer in Jordan. These visualizations can reveal trends over time, helping to identify areas where interventions are most urgently needed and allowing for targeted strategies.

The digital ecosystem also facilitates telehealth and remote consultations, making it easier for patients, especially those in remote regions, to access expert opinions and treatment recommendations without the need for extensive travel. This is particularly crucial during times like the COVID-19 pandemic.

Moreover, genomic data can be integrated into the digital ecosystem, enabling personalized treatment plans based on genetic markers and mutations associated with specific cancer types. This approach increases the chances of successful outcomes and represents a significant advancement in cancer care.

In addition to patient care, the digital ecosystem serves as a platform for cancer research and clinical trials management. It streamlines patient recruitment for trials, fosters collaboration between healthcare institutions and pharmaceutical companies, and ultimately contributes to the development of innovative treatments.

Public health interventions also benefit from business analytics. Data-driven insights inform the design and evaluation of cancer prevention and awareness campaigns. These insights allow for precise targeting of high-risk populations and the optimization of resource allocation. To ensure the success of this approach, considerations such as data security and privacy are paramount. Robust cybersecurity measures and data encryption protocols must be implemented to safeguard sensitive health information within the digital ecosystem. Continuous monitoring and a feedback loop are essential features of the system. Real-time data updates and alerts enable healthcare providers and policymakers to respond swiftly to emerging trends or outbreaks, enhancing the agility of the healthcare system.

In conclusion, the digital economy and digital ecosystems offer a transformative approach to tackling the increasing cancer cases in Jordan. By integrating data, technology, and analytics into the healthcare landscape, the country can not only monitor and understand the trends but also develop more targeted, personalized, and efficient strategies for cancer prevention, diagnosis, and treatment. This holistic approach has the potential to improve the overall healthcare infrastructure and significantly reduce the burden of cancer in Jordan.

THEORETICAL OVERVIEW

In this section, we provide a theoretical overview of the concepts and frameworks that underpin our research on cancer epidemiology in Jordan from 2012 to 2018. Theoretical foundations are essential for framing our study within the broader context of cancer research and public health strategies. We draw upon key sources of research that have shaped our understanding of cancer epidemiology and guided our approach to data analysis and interpretation.

Cancer as a Complex Health Challenge

Cancer is a multifaceted health challenge with complex etiology and epidemiology. Understanding the theoretical underpinnings of cancer as a disease is crucial for developing effective prevention and control strategies. The World Health Organization (WHO) provides a comprehensive perspective on the global burden of cancer, emphasizing its impact on morbidity and mortality (World Health Organization, 2019). Additionally, the American Cancer Society's "Cancer Facts & Figures" (American Cancer Society, 2020) offers valuable insights into cancer statistics, highlighting the prevalence of specific cancer types.

Multifactorial Nature of Cancer Development

Theoretical perspectives on cancer emphasize its multifactorial nature, where genetic, environmental, and lifestyle factors converge to influence disease development. Siegel et al. (2020) delve into cancer statistics, revealing the dynamic landscape of cancer incidence and mortality. The research by Cancer Research UK (2021) is instrumental in understanding the multifaceted risk factors associated with cancer development, including tobacco use, diet, and UV radiation exposure (Al-Mousa & Alomari, 2019; National Cancer Institute; Word Health Organization).

The Role of Early Detection and Screening

A fundamental theoretical aspect of cancer control is the significance of early detection and screening programs. The World Cancer Research Fund International (2021) highlights the importance of cancer prevention strategies, including screening initiatives. These theoretical foundations underscore the need for systematic screening programs to identify cancer at its earliest stages, improving patient outcomes and reducing mortality rates.

Data Visualization and Digitalization

In our research, we leverage the theoretical framework that emphasizes the role of data visualization and digitalization in enhancing our understanding of cancer epidemiology. Microsoft Power BI dashboards are instrumental in this regard, enabling us to transform complex data into accessible and interpretable visual representations. The integration of data visualization technology aligns with the broader theoretical perspective of harnessing digital tools for evidence-based healthcare strategies.

This theoretical overview serves as the conceptual foundation for our research on cancer epidemiology in Jordan. By grounding our study in these key theoretical concepts and sources of research, we aim to contribute to evidence-based cancer prevention and control strategies. The multifaceted approach, including early detection through screening programs and health promotion initiatives, aligns with established theoretical principles for addressing the profound impact of cancer on public health.

METHODS

Data Collection

This study encompassed a comprehensive seven-year analysis of cancer incidence within the Jordanian population, spanning from 2012 to 2018. The dataset employed for this research was meticulously acquired through official requests to the Jordan Cancer Registry (JCR) and was thoughtfully processed in CSV format utilizing the CanReg software. This dataset proved invaluable, providing a wealth of demographic data, including gender and age, as well as granular information concerning tumor characteristics such as diagnosis date, location, histology, grade, stage, and method of diagnosis. Notably, the International Classification of Diseases for Oncology 3rd Edition (ICDO-3) system was diligently employed for disease classification and mortality coding, ensuring the precision and comprehensiveness of the data underpinning our analysis. Such a robust dataset served as the cornerstone upon which our examination of cancer epidemiology in Jordan was built.

Statistical Analysis

Our research was underpinned by a rigorous statistical analysis, aimed at distilling actionable insights from the extensive dataset. Several fundamental calculations were conducted to delineate the intricate landscape of cancer epidemiology in Jordan. The Crude Incidence Rate (CIR), calculated by dividing the number of new cancer cases by the total population and subsequently multiplying by 100,000, provided a holistic perspective on cancer incidence within the entire populace. Age-Specific Incidence Rates (ASIRs) were derived by dividing the number of new cancer cases within specific age cohorts by the respective total population, once again multiplied by 100,000. This yielded nuanced insights into the differential impact of cancer across age groups. The Age-Standardized Rate (ASR) amalgamated age-specific rates, weighing them by the proportion of the population within each corresponding age group. Expressed per 100,000 individuals, ASR facilitated cross-population comparisons, considering varying age structures.

Temporal Trends and Age-Specific Analysis

In addition to these foundational calculations, the study conducted a meticulous analysis of temporal trends in cancer incidence over the seven-year period (2012-2018). This enabled the identification of notable patterns and variations, providing insight into peak years and fluctuations within the specified timeframe. Age-specific analysis provided further granularity by assessing cancer prevalence across different age strata. Age-specific incidence rates (ASIRs) were scrutinized to illuminate variations in cancer incidence linked to age.

Limitations of the Study

Acknowledging the paramount importance of transparency, it is imperative to underscore the study's limitations. Firstly, the reliance on data from the Jordan Cancer Registry (JCR) necessitates caution regarding potential limitations in data quality, completeness, and accuracy. Variations in data reporting and recording practices over the seven-year period could introduce variability. Furthermore, the study's data availability was confined to the years 2012-2018, thereby limiting the capacity to capture more recent trends or long-term changes in cancer epidemiology. The study did not explore external factors, such as shifts in healthcare infrastructure, healthcare access, or environmental influences, which might have implications for cancer incidence. Geographical specificity was also a limitation, as the study primarily offered a national perspective and may not fully capture regional or local variations. Additionally, predictive modeling to forecast future cancer incidences, while a valuable prospect, was not incorporated into this study.

Visualization Tools

Microsoft Power BI dashboards were employed for data visualization in this study. These advanced visualization tools played a crucial role in enhancing our understanding of cancer epidemiology by providing dynamic and interactive representations of cancer incidence and mortality patterns. The use of Power BI dashboards made the data more accessible and interpretable.

Figure 1. Methods for data collection, analysis, and visualization in the Jordanian cancer epidemiology study

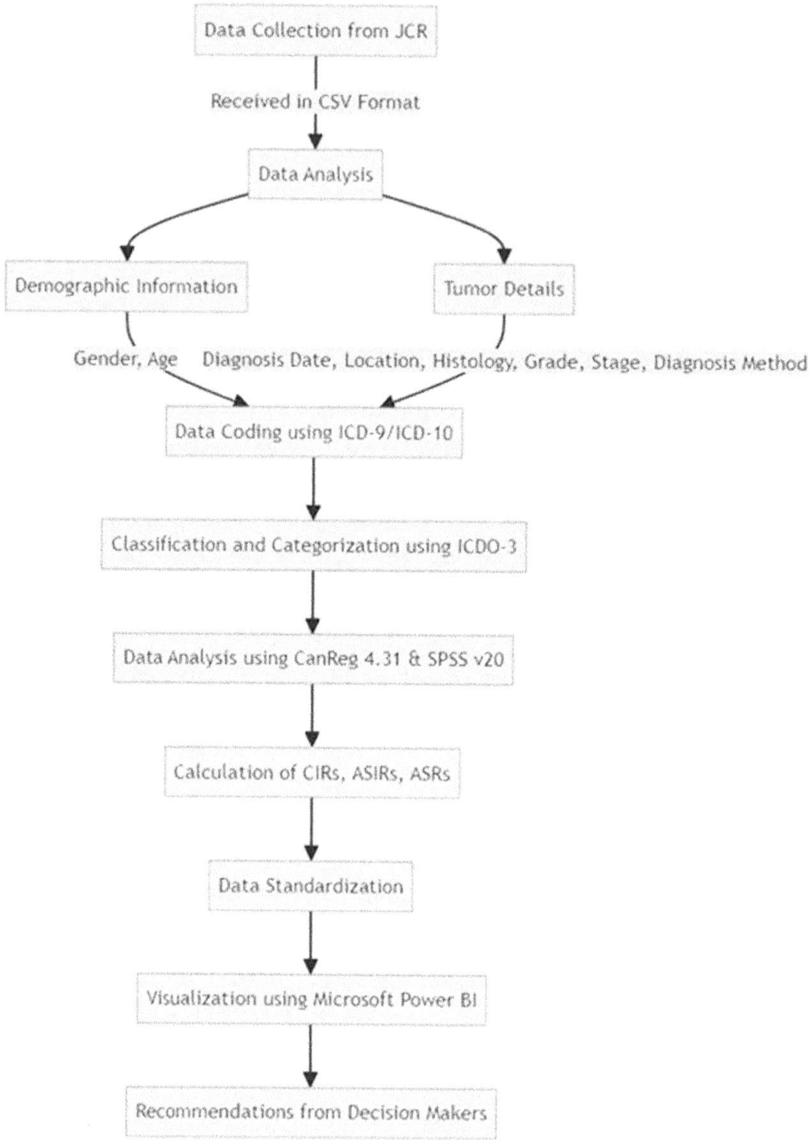

Healthcare System Capacity

The capacity of Jordan's healthcare system to effectively address the challenges posed by cancer is crucial. Understanding the healthcare system's readiness, resources, and accessibility of services sheds light on the broader context of cancer prevention, diagnosis, and treatment.

The World Health Organization (WHO) has emphasized the significance of healthcare system capacity in cancer control. In Jordan, the healthcare system comprises both public and private sectors, with varying levels of resources and infrastructure. The availability of specialized cancer centers, equipped with state-of-the-art diagnostic and treatment facilities, plays a pivotal role in early detection and management. Accessibility to these centers, particularly for remote or underserved populations, is a key determinant of timely diagnosis and treatment initiation (Bray et al., 2020; Sung et al., 2021).

Additionally, the capacity of healthcare professionals, including oncologists, radiologists, and pathologists, is critical in ensuring accurate diagnosis and treatment planning. Training and continuous medical education programs are essential for maintaining a skilled workforce capable of delivering high-quality cancer care (Abdel-Razeq, Attiga, & Mansour, 2015; American Society of Clinical Oncology, 2020; Siegel et al., 2021).

The availability of cancer screening programs, such as mammography for breast cancer and colonoscopy for colorectal cancer, is another dimension of healthcare system capacity. These programs are integral in promoting early detection and reducing cancer-related morbidity and mortality. Monitoring the participation rates in these screening initiatives can provide insights into their effectiveness and accessibility.

Furthermore, the healthcare system's capacity extends to the availability of essential cancer drugs, radiotherapy facilities, and surgical interventions. Timely access to these treatments is paramount for improving patient outcomes and survival rates.

However, it's essential to acknowledge the limitations and challenges within the healthcare system. These may include resource constraints, waiting times for specialized care, and disparities in access between urban and rural areas (Abdel-Razeq, Attiga, & Mansour, 2015; Ferlay et al., 2015). Understanding these limitations is crucial for implementing targeted interventions and policy reforms to strengthen the healthcare system's capacity in addressing cancer.

In conclusion, a comprehensive assessment of the healthcare system's capacity is integral to understanding the broader landscape of cancer epidemiology in Jordan. This assessment encompasses the availability and accessibility of cancer-related services, the readiness of healthcare professionals, and the effectiveness of screening programs. By addressing the capacity challenges and building a resilient healthcare system, Jordan can enhance its ability to prevent, diagnose, and treat cancer effectively, ultimately reducing the burden of this disease on its population (Jordan Ministry of Health Annual Reports).

RESULTS

The following section presents the results of the analysis conducted on the study data. It includes a summary of the key findings, statistical analysis, and any other relevant information related to the research objectives.

1- Cancer Incidence Rate

The overall crude cancer incidence rate observed over the seven-year period was recorded at 94.6 per 100,000 population. Notably, the highest incidence rate was documented in 2013 at 114 per 100,000 population, while the lowest incidence rate was observed in 2016, at 80.9 per 100,000 population.

Figure 2. Number of cases and incidence rates of cancer in Jordan, 2012-2018

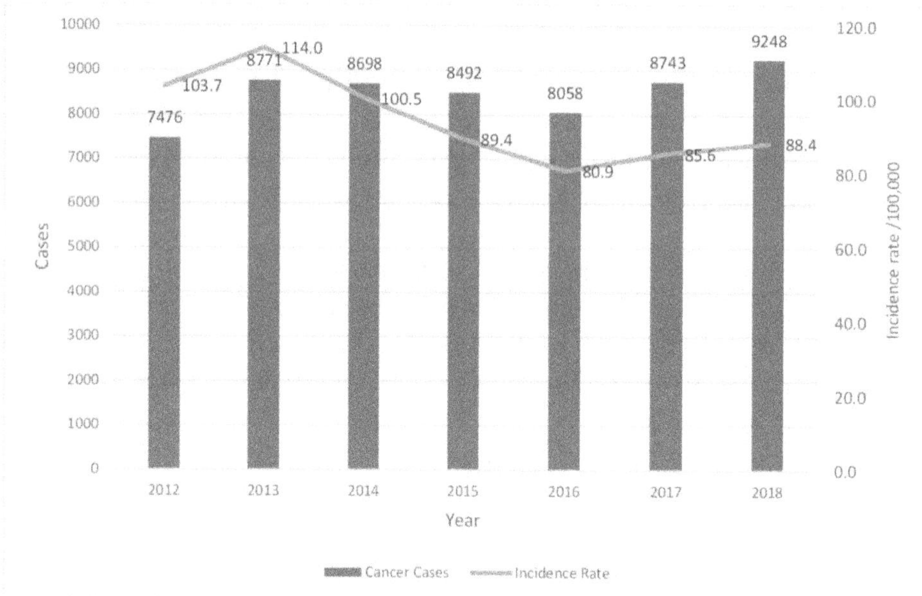

2- Cancer Rates according to age group and gender

The analysis of cancer cases revealed a significant association with age and gender. Notably, a substantial majority of cancer cases were observed in individuals aged 40 and above. Specifically, 86.8% of male cancer cases and 87.9% of female cancer cases occurred in this age group. Among males, the highest prevalence of cancer cases was found in the 75-79 age group, comprising 11.9% of total male cases. Conversely, for females, the age group 55-59 exhibited the highest number of cancer cases, representing 11.9% of the total female cases.

Table 1. Distribution of cumulative cancer cases registered in Jordan from 2012-2018, categorized by gender and age

Age group	Male	%	Female	%	Total	%
05--09	276	1.0%	193	0.6%	469	0.8%
10-14	582	2.0%	416	1.4%	998	1.7%
15-19	407	1.4%	318	1.0%	725	1.2%
20-24	467	1.6%	342	1.1%	809	1.4%
25-29	583	2.0%	523	1.7%	1106	1.9%
30-34	638	2.2%	732	2.4%	1370	2.3%
35-39	847	3.0%	1197	3.9%	2044	3.4%
40-44	1079	3.8%	1679	5.5%	2758	4.6%
45-49	1349	4.7%	2359	7.7%	3708	6.2%
50-54	1758	6.1%	3201	10.4%	4959	8.3%
55-59	2366	8.2%	3664	11.9%	6030	10.1%
60-64	2786	9.7%	3442	11.2%	6228	10.5%
65-69	3072	10.7%	3207	10.4%	6279	10.6%
70-74	3150	11.0%	3002	9.7%	6152	10.3%
75-79	3420	11.9%	2721	8.8%	6141	10.3%
80-84	2971	10.4%	1863	6.0%	4834	8.1%
85+	2936	10.2%	1940	6.3%	4876	8.2%
Grand Total	**28687**	**100.0%**	**30799**	**100.0%**	**59486**	**100.0%**

3- Age-standardized incidence rates

The Age-standardized incidence rates of cancer among males and females in Jordan from 2012-2018 were the highest for both males and females in 2013 females (117.27/100,00 pop) and males (99.95/100,00 pop.)

Figure 3. Age-standardized incidence rates of cancer among males and females in Jordan, 2012-2018.

4- Age-specific incidence rates of cancer (ASIR) in Jordan

The average ASIR was 68 /100,000 during the study period (113.9/100,000 for males and 99.3/100,000 for females). Table 2 shows the average ASIRs during the 7 -years period. Among males, the lowest average ASIR was in the age group 05-09 years (6.3/100,000) and the highest was in the age group 85+ years (4582.9/100,000). Among females, the lowest average ASIR was in the age group 05-09 years (4.6/100,000) and the highest average ASIR was in the age group 85+ years (2700.6/100,000).

Table 2. Age-specific incidence rates of cancer among males and females in Jordan, 2012-2018

	Male Cancer				female Cancer				Total Cancer			
AGE	N*	avg/n**	%	AV/ ASIR+	N*	avg/n**	%	AV/ ASIR+	N*	avg/n**	%	AV/ ASIR+
0-4	0	0	0.0%	0.0	0	0.0	0.0%	0.0	0	0.0	0.0%	0.0
05-09	276	39.4	1.0%	6.3	193	27.6	0.6%	4.6	469	33.5	0.8%	5.5
10-14	582	83.1	2.0%	16.9	416	59.4	1.4%	13.0	998	71.3	1.7%	15.0
15-19	407	58.1	1.4%	12.4	318	45.4	1.0%	10.8	725	51.8	1.2%	11.6
20-24	467	66.7	1.6%	13.4	342	48.9	1.1%	12.0	809	57.8	1.4%	12.7
25-29	583	83.3	2.0%	19.1	523	74.7	1.7%	21.1	1106	79.0	1.9%	20.0
30-34	638	91.1	2.2%	24.2	732	104.6	2.4%	32.3	1370	97.9	2.3%	27.9
35-39	847	121.0	3.0%	35.7	1197	171.0	3.9%	59.3	2044	146.0	3.4%	46.4
40-44	1079	154.1	3.8%	53.2	1679	239.9	5.5%	97.8	2758	197.0	4.6%	73.4
45-49	1349	192.7	4.7%	77.7	2359	337.0	7.7%	163.3	3708	264.9	6.2%	116.2
50-54	1758	251.1	6.1%	140.4	3201	457.3	10.4%	294.3	4959	354.2	8.3%	211.4
55-59	2366	338.0	8.2%	274.7	3664	523.4	11.9%	468.0	6030	430.7	10.1%	366.5
60-64	2786	398.0	9.7%	480.6	3442	491.7	11.2%	638.8	6228	444.9	10.5%	556.0
65-69	3072	438.9	10.7%	675.8	3207	458.1	10.4%	708.3	6279	448.5	10.6%	690.9
70-74	3150	450.0	11.0%	895.1	3002	428.9	9.7%	962.4	6152	439.4	10.3%	925.2
75-79	3420	488.6	11.9%	1584.0	2721	388.7	8.8%	1301.9	6141	438.6	10.3%	1442.4
80-84	2971	424.4	10.4%	2957.8	1863	266.1	6.0%	1826.2	4834	345.3	8.1%	2383.7
85+	2936	419.4	10.2%	4582.9	1940	277.1	6.3%	2700.6	4876	348.3	8.2%	3585.6

*N = total number of cases in the age group during the 7-years period.

** Av/N: the average number of cases in the age group during the 7-years period.

+Av/ASIR= the average ASIR in the age group during the 7-years period.

5- The cumulative top ten cancers in males and females, Jordan, 2012-2018.

The cumulative top ten cancers in males during the 7-year period were bronchus and lung (11%), bladder (8%), prostate gland (8%), colon (8%), hematopoietic and reticuloendothelial systems (7%), lymph nodes (6%), skin (6%), stomach (4%), brain (4%), and kidney (3%).

The cumulative top ten cancers in females were breast (38%), thyroid (6%), colon (6%), hematopoietic and reticuloendothelial systems (5%), lymph nodes (4%), corpus uteri (4%), skin (3%), ovary (3%), lung (3%) and stomach (3%).

Table 3. Top ten cancers registered in Jordan according to gender in the period 2012-2018

Female			Male			All			
BREAST	11720	38%	BRONCHUS AND LUNG	3157	11%	BREAST	11925	20%	
THYROID GLAND	1951	6%	BLADDER	2419	8%	COLON	4223	7%	
COLON	1930	6%	PROSTATE GLAND	2315	8%	BRONCHUS AND LUNG	3990	7%	
HEMATOPOIETIC AND RETICULOENDOTHELIAL SYSTEMS	1443	5%	COLON	2289	8%	HEMATOPOIETIC AND RETICULOENDOTHELIAL SYSTEMS	3586	6%	
LYMPH NODES	1333	4%	HEMATOPOIETIC AND RETICULOENDOTHELIAL SYSTEMS	2140	7%	LYMPH NODES	3154	5%	
CORPUS UTERI	1244	4%	LYMPH NODES	1820	6%	BLADDER	2762	5%	
SKIN	1052	3%	SKIN	1674	6%	SKIN	2727	5%	
OVARY	934	3%	STOMACH	1252	4%	THYROID GLAND	2648	4%	
BRONCHUS AND LUNG	832	3%	BRAIN	1140	4%	PROSTATE GLAND	2317	4%	
STOMACH	808	3%	KIDNEY	989	3%	STOMACH	2060	3%	
others	7552	25%	others	9492	33%	Others	20140	34%	
Total	30799	100%	Total	28687	100%	Total	59532	100%	

6- Data Analysis and Power BI Dashboards

In this study, Power BI dashboards have emerged as a transformative asset, providing dynamic and customized visualizations of cancer epidemiology in Jordan. These dashboards enhance data accessibility, transparency, and usability, enabling stakeholders to gain real-time insights into cancer incidence, mortality, and demographic associations. Geospatial mapping capabilities aid in pinpointing cancer hotspots, while trend analysis and predictive analytics facilitate long-term planning and rapid response to changing epidemiological patterns. Real-time updates, public awareness communication, and feedback mechanisms foster collaboration among healthcare professionals, researchers, and policymakers. This digital tool not only empowers data-driven decision-making but also contributes to capacity building and serves as a model for addressing complex healthcare challenges.

These findings provide valuable insights for healthcare professionals and policymakers, informing the development of targeted cancer prevention and control strategies in Jordan. Continued monitoring of cancer incidence and mortality rates is imperative to facilitate early detection and effective intervention, ultimately reducing the burden of this widespread and complex disease on the population.

DISCUSSION

Cancer represents a formidable global health challenge, exerting a significant toll on morbidity and mortality across the world. This group of diseases is characterized by the uncontrolled proliferation and dissemination of abnormal cells throughout the body, potentially affecting any organ or tissue. As reported by the World Health Organization (WHO), cancer stands as the second leading cause of death on a global scale, claiming an estimated 9.6 million lives in 2018. Predominant cancer types worldwide encompass lung, breast, prostate, and colorectal cancer. The etiology of cancer is intricate and multifaceted, stemming from a complex interplay of genetic, environmental, and lifestyle factors. The pivotal role of early detection, timely intervention, screening initiatives, and vaccination programs cannot be overstated, as they collectively contribute to enhanced patient outcomes and a reduction in cancer-related mortality rates (Bray et al., 2020; Ferlay et al., 2020; Jordan Ministry of Health Annual Reports).

Of particular concern is the burgeoning incidence and mortality rates of cancer in Jordan, where it is anticipated to surpass other causes of mortality and become the foremost cause of death by the year 2020. Within the Jordanian context, the most prevalent cancer types include lung, breast, colon, and prostate cancer for males, and breast, thyroid, and colon cancer for females. This alarming trend underscores the imperative for the formulation and implementation of effective strategies for cancer prevention and control within the Jordanian healthcare landscape (Jemal et al., 2011; Hussain, Haddad, & Fayyadh, 2018).

The findings of this study elucidate the pivotal role of digital dashboards, specifically Microsoft Power BI, in the domain of cancer epidemiology in Jordan. The utility of these tools transcends mere data representation; they are instrumental in the decision-making processes of healthcare professionals and policymakers, with significant implications for patient outcomes and public health strategies.

Enhanced Decision-Making Capabilities

The integration of digital dashboards in the analysis of cancer trends has profoundly augmented the decision-making capabilities of healthcare professionals. By facilitating a comprehensive visualization of data, these tools enable a deeper understanding of epidemiological patterns. This, in turn, supports the development of targeted interventions and informed policy decisions, tailored to address the specific needs and challenges identified through the data.

Implications for Patient Outcomes

The study underscores the potential of digital dashboards to positively influence patient outcomes. The facilitation of early detection and intervention strategies, as informed by data visualizations, can lead to a decrease in cancer-related morbidity and mortality. Furthermore, the ability to dissect and analyze data across various demographics and cancer types enables healthcare providers to adopt more personalized and effective treatment approaches.

Policy Formulation and Healthcare Strategy Development

The insights gleaned from Power BI dashboards are invaluable in shaping healthcare policies and strategies. By providing a clear and accessible depiction of cancer incidence and trends, these tools assist policymakers in identifying areas that require immediate attention and resource allocation. This capability is crucial for the optimal distribution of healthcare resources and the implementation of effective public health interventions.

Future Work and Predictive Analysis

Looking ahead, the application of advanced predictive modeling, as an extension of the current dashboard capabilities, opens new avenues for proactive healthcare strategies. Predictive analytics can potentially forecast future cancer incidences, thus enabling healthcare systems to prepare and respond more effectively to emerging public health challenges.

Broader Healthcare Implications

Beyond the scope of cancer epidemiology, the utilization of digital dashboards has broader implications in healthcare. They promote a more efficient management of healthcare resources and foster the development of educational and awareness programs tailored to specific cancer trends and demographic needs.

this study highlights the transformative impact of digital dashboards in the realm of cancer epidemiology and healthcare at large. Their application in Jordan serves as a testament to their potential in enhancing healthcare delivery, shaping public health policies, and ultimately improving patient outcomes. This approach exemplifies a paradigm shift towards a more data-driven and visually oriented methodology in healthcare research and decision-making.

CONCLUSION

In the present research, a meticulous examination of a seven-year trend in cancer incidence within the Jordanian population was undertaken, thereby providing an expansive temporal perspective for assessing the dynamics of cancer epidemiology. To ensure the utmost reliability and precision of our findings, we harnessed the comprehensive dataset available from the Jordan Cancer Registry (JCR), which had demonstrated a substantial improvement in data quality commencing in 2012. The outcomes of our rigorous analysis, encompassing cancer incidence trends and the identification of prevalent cancers, have yielded invaluable insights into the landscape of cancer in Jordan.

Our findings engender several compelling recommendations, which have profound implications for public health and healthcare strategies in Jordan. Foremost among these recommendations is the imperative need to prioritize the establishment of systematic cancer screening programs. Targeting the most prevalent forms of cancer in Jordan, for which validated screening modalities exist, is essential. By detecting malignancies at their incipient stages through the judicious utilization of screening tests, we have the potential to substantially mitigate the overall morbidity and mortality associated with cancer. Such a proactive approach is especially pertinent for those cancer types that exhibit a heightened prevalence within the Jordanian populace.

This research has meticulously analyzed the cancer incidence trends in Jordan over a seven-year period, employing data from the Jordan Cancer Registry (JCR). Our findings illuminate the dynamic landscape of cancer epidemiology in Jordan, offering crucial insights into the prevalence and patterns of various cancer types. The study underscores the escalating incidence of cancer, particularly the types most prevalent in the Jordanian populace, thereby highlighting the urgent need for comprehensive cancer control strategies.

Significantly, the employment of Microsoft Power BI dashboards in this research has revolutionized our approach to data analysis and visualization. These tools have not only enhanced our understanding of the complex epidemiological data but have also elevated its interpretability, facilitating a more nuanced analysis of trends and patterns. The interactive and real-time capabilities of these dashboards have proven indispensable in synthesizing and presenting data, thus emerging as a critical asset in informing healthcare policy and strategy development.

Furthermore, our study advocates for the implementation of systematic cancer screening programs in Jordan, targeting the most prevalent cancers. Emphasizing early detection through validated screening tests, this approach aims to significantly reduce cancer morbidity and mortality. Concurrently, the study accentuates the importance of health promotion and preventive measures tailored to the Jordanian context. Initiatives such as awareness campaigns and lifestyle interventions are crucial in mitigating the rising cancer incidence and cultivating a health-conscious society.

This research not only elucidates the current state of cancer epidemiology in Jordan but also provides actionable recommendations for public health policy and healthcare delivery. By integrating advanced data visualization tools and advocating for evidence-based strategies, this study contributes significantly to the ongoing efforts in cancer prevention and control. It is hoped that these insights and recommendations will serve as a catalyst for informed decision-making and progressive action in the battle against cancer in Jordan.

REFERENCES

Abdel-Razeq, H., Attiga, F., & Mansour, A. (2015). Cancer care in Jordan. *Hematology/Oncology and Stem Cell Therapy*, *8*(2), 64–70. doi:10.1016/j.hemonc.2015.02.001 PMID:25732671

Al-Mousa, A., & Alomari, M. A. (2019). Trends in cancer incidence in Jordan, 2000-2013. *Eastern Mediterranean Health Journal*, *25*(1), 10–18.

American Cancer Society. (2020). *Cancer Facts & Figures*. American Cancer Society.

American Society of Clinical Oncology. (2020). The State of Cancer Care in America, 2020: A Report by the American Society of Clinical Oncology. *Journal of Oncology Practice / American Society of Clinical Oncology*, *16*(4), 175–203.

Bray, F., Ferlay, J., Soerjomataram, I., Siegel, R. L., Torre, L. A., & Jemal, A. (2020). Global cancer statistics 2018: GLOBOCAN estimates of incidence and mortality worldwide for 36 cancers in 185 countries. *CA: a Cancer Journal for Clinicians*, *68*(6), 394–424. doi:10.3322/caac.21492 PMID:30207593

Cancer Research UK. (2021). *Cancer statistics*. Cancer Research. https://www.cancerresearchuk.org/health-professional/cancer-statistics

Ferlay, J., Soerjomataram, I., Dikshit, R., Eser, S., Mathers, C., Rebelo, M., & Bray, F. (2015). Cancer incidence and mortality worldwide: Sources, methods and major patterns in GLOBOCAN 2012. *International Journal of Cancer*, *136*(5), 359–386. doi:10.1002/ijc.29210 PMID:25220842

Fitzmaurice, C., Allen, C., Barber, R. M., Barregard, L., Bhutta, Z. A., Brenner, H., & Fleming, T. D. (2017). Global, Regional, and National Cancer Incidence, Mortality, Years of Life Lost, Years Lived with Disability, and Disability-Adjusted Life-years for 32 Cancer Groups, 1990 to 2015. *JAMA Oncology*, *3*(4), 524–548. doi:10.1001/jamaoncol.2016.5688 PMID:27918777

Harford, J. B. (2021). Current status and future directions of breast cancer prevention and early detection in Jordan. *Breast Cancer: Targets and Therapy*, *13*, 25–33.

Hussein, A. A., Haddad, F. H., & Al-Fayyadh, M. J. (2018). Cancer trends and incidence and mortality patterns in Jordan. *Asian Pacific Journal of Cancer Prevention*, *19*(3), 735–740.

Jemal, A., Bray, F., Center, M. M., Ferlay, J., Ward, E., & Forman, D. (2011). Global cancer statistics. *CA: a Cancer Journal for Clinicians*, *61*(2), 69–90. doi:10.3322/caac.20107 PMID:21296855

Jordan Ministry of Health. (Annual Reports). Annual health statistics. Amman, Jordan: Ministry of Health.

KHCC.jo - King Hussein Cancer Foundation and Center: Reference for the comprehensive care and skilled oncologists at King Hussein Cancer Center.

National Cancer Institute. (2018). Surveillance, Epidemiology, and End Results Program. *SEER Cancer Statistics Review*. Bethesda, MD: National Cancer Institute.

Siegel, R. L., Miller, K. D., & Jemal, A. (2020). Cancer statistics, 2020. *CA: a Cancer Journal for Clinicians*, *70*(1), 7–30. doi:10.3322/caac.21590 PMID:31912902

Siegel, R. L., Miller, K. D., & Jemal, A. (2021). Cancer statistics, 2021. *CA: a Cancer Journal for Clinicians*, *71*(1), 7–33. doi:10.3322/caac.21654 PMID:33433946

Sung, H., Ferlay, J., Siegel, R. L., Laversanne, M., Soerjomataram, I., Jemal, A., & Bray, F. (2021). Global cancer statistics 2020: GLOBOCAN estimates of incidence and mortality worldwide for 36 cancers in 185 countries. *CA: a Cancer Journal for Clinicians*, *71*(3), 209–249. doi:10.3322/caac.21660 PMID:33538338

Torre, L. A., Bray, F., Siegel, R. L., Ferlay, J., Lortet-Tieulent, J., & Jemal, A. (2015). Global cancer statistics, 2012. *CA: a Cancer Journal for Clinicians*, *65*(2), 87–108. doi:10.3322/caac.21262 PMID:25651787

World Cancer Research Fund International. (2021). *Cancer prevention*. WCRF. https://www.wcrf.org/dietandcancer/cancer-prevention

World Health Organization. (2019). *Cancer*. WHO. https://www.who.int/news-room/fact-sheets/detail/cancer

Compilation of References

Abdel-Razeq, H., Attiga, F., & Mansour, A. (2015). Cancer care in Jordan. *Hematology/Oncology and Stem Cell Therapy*, *8*(2), 64–70. doi:10.1016/j.hemonc.2015.02.001 PMID:25732671

Abdullah, M., & Akhbar, T. (2020). Capacity building for SMEs: Realising training gap amongst SMEs in Malaysia, In M.A.Abdullah, R.Yayla, & D.Abdulrazak (Eds.) Cross Border SMEs: Malaysia & Indonesia (pp.107-131), UMY Press.

Abina, A., Batkovič, T., Cestnik, B., Kikaj, A., Kovačič Lukman, R., Kurbus, M., & Zidanšek, A. (2022). Decision Support Concept for Improvement of Sustainability-Related Competences. *Sustainability (Basel)*, *14*(14), 8539. doi:10.3390/su14148539

Abu-Taieh, E. M., AlHadid, I., Abu-Tayeh, S., Masa'deh, R., Alkhawaldeh, R. S., Khwaldeh, S., & Alrowwad, A. (2022). Continued Intention to Use of M-Banking in Jordan by Integrating UTAUT, TPB, TAM and Service Quality with ML. *Journal of Open Innovation*, *8*(3), 120. doi:10.3390/joitmc8030120

Achillas, C. (2019). *Green supply chain management*. Routledge, Taylor & Francis Group.

Ackerman, D., & Chung, C. (2018). Is RateMyProfessors. com unbiased? A look at the impact of social modelling on student online reviews of marketing classes. *Journal of Marketing Education*, *40*(3), 188–195. doi:10.1177/0273475317735654

Adedeji, B. S., Popoola, O. M. J., & Tze, S. O. (2017). National culture and sustainability disclosure practices: A literature review. [IPJAF]. *Indian-Pacific Journal of Accounting and Finance*, *1*(1), 26–50. doi:10.52962/ipjaf.2017.1.1.6

Adi, A., Crowther, D., & Grigore, G. (2015). Introduction to Corporate Social Responsibility in the Digital Age. In Corporate Social Responsibility in the Digital Age (pp. ix-xvi). Emerald Group Publishing Limited. doi:10.1108/S2043-052320150000007028

Afesorgbor, S. K., & Demena, B. A. (2022). Trade openness and environmental emissions: Evidence from a meta-analysis. *Environmental and Resource Economics*, *81*(2), 287–321. doi:10.1007/s10640-021-00627-0

Aghakhani, N., Oh, O., Gregg, D., & Jain, H. (2023). How review quality and source credibility interacts to affect review usefulness: An expansion of the elaboration likelihood model. *Information Systems Frontiers: A Journal of Research and Innovation, 25*(4), 1513–1531. doi:10.1007/s10796-022-10299-w

Ahmedov, I. (2020). The Impact Of Digital Economy On International Trade. *European Journal of Business and Management Research*, *5*(4). doi:10.24018/ejbmr.2020.5.4.389

Ahvenniemi, H., Huovila, A., Pinto-Seppä, I., & Airaksinen, M. (2017). What are the differences between sustainable and smart cities? *Cities (London, England)*, *60*, 234–245. doi:10.1016/j.cities.2016.09.009

Akcali, S., & Ispalar Cahantimur, A. (2023). How socio-spatial aspects of urban space influence social sustainability: A case study. *Journal of Housing and the Built Environment*, *38*(4), 1–33. doi:10.1007/s10901-023-10052-y

Akter, S., Michael, K., Uddin, M. R., McCarthy, G., & Rahman, M. (2022). Transforming business using digital innovations: The application of AI, blockchain, cloud and data analytics. *Annals of Operations Research, 308*(1-2), 1–33. doi:10.1007/s10479-020-03620-w PMID:35935743

Al Mashalah, H., Hassini, E., Gunasekaran, A., & Bhatt, D. (2022). The impact of digital transformation on supply chains through e-commerce: Literature review and a conceptual framework. *Transportation Research Part E, Logistics and Transportation Review, 165*, 102837. doi:10.1016/j.tre.2022.102837

Alabdali, M. A., Salam, M. A., Mangla, S., Li, G., Sun, J., Wu, H., Alabdali, M. A., & Salam, M. A. (2022). The Impact of Digital Transformation on Supply Chain Procurement for Creating Competitive Advantage: An Empirical Study. *Sustainability, 14*(19), 12269. https://doi. doi:org/10.3390/SU141912269

Alba, J. W., & Hutchinson, J. W. (1987). Dimensions of Consumer Expertise. *The Journal of Consumer Research, 13*(4), 411–454. doi:10.1086/209080

Albashrawi, M., & Motiwalla, L. (2019). Privacy and Personalization in Continued Usage Intention of Mobile Banking: An Integrative Perspective. *Information Systems Frontiers, 21*(5), 1031–1043. doi:10.1007/s10796-017-9814-7

Albino, V., Berardi, U., & Dangelico, R. M. (2015). Smart cities: Definitions, dimensions, performance, and initiatives. *Journal of Urban Technology, 22*(1), 3–21. doi:10.1080/10630732.2014.942092

Al-Debei, M. M., & Avison, D. (2010). Developing a unified framework of the business model concept. *European Journal of Information Systems, 19*(3), 359–376. doi:10.1057/ejis.2010.21

Aleksic, S. (2014, May). Green ICT for sustainability: A holistic approach. In *2014 37th International Convention on Information and Communication Technology, Electronics and Microelectronics (MIPRO)* (pp. 426-431). IEEE. 10.1109/MIPRO.2014.6859604

Alexander, B., Hubers, C., Schwanen, T., Dijst, M., & Ettema, D. (2011). Anything, anywhere, anytime? Developing indicators to assess the spatial and temporal fragmentation of activities. *Environment and Planning. B, Planning & Design, 38*(4), 678–705. doi:10.1068/b35132

Alghareeb, S. (2022). Mobile banking adoption among undergraduate students in Kuwait university. *OAlib, 09*(06), 1–13. doi:10.4236/oalib.1106458

Aljowder, T., Ali, M., & Kurnia, S. (2019, September). Systematic literature review of the smart city maturity model. In *2019 International Conference on Innovation and Intelligence for Informatics, Computing, and Technologies (3ICT)* (pp. 1-9). IEEE. 10.1109/3ICT.2019.8910321

Al-Laheebi, G. A. J. (2022). Continuous Intention to Use Mobile Banking Apps: Empirical Study in Iraq. *THEORY METHODOLOGY PRACTICE-REVIEW OF BUSINESS AND MANAGEMENT, 18*(1), 61–74. http://real.mtak.hu/144917/1/5_k.pdf

Allam, Z., & Newman, P. (2018). Redefining the smart city: Culture, metabolism and governance. *Smart Cities, 1*(1), 4–25. doi:10.3390/smartcities1010002

Allweins, M. M., Proesch, M., & Ladd, T. (2021). The platform canvas—Conceptualization of a design framework for multi-sided platform businesses. *Entrepreneurship Education and Pedagogy, 4*(3), 455–477. doi:10.1177/2515127420959051

Al-Mousa, A., & Alomari, M. A. (2019). Trends in cancer incidence in Jordan, 2000-2013. *Eastern Mediterranean Health Journal, 25*(1), 10–18.

Al-Shuaibi, K. M. (2016). A structural equation model of CSR and performance: Mediation by innovation and productivity. *Journal of Management and Sustainability, 6*(2), 139–153. doi:10.5539/jms.v6n2p139

Altin Gumussoy, C., Kaya, A., & Ozlu, E. (2018). Determinants of Mobile Banking Use: An Extended TAM with Perceived Risk, Mobility Access, Compatibility, Perceived Self-efficacy and Subjective Norms. In *Industrial Engineering in the Industry 4.0 Era* (pp. 225–238). Springer International Publishing. doi:10.1007/978-3-319-71225-3_20

Alusi, A., Eccles, R. G., Edmondson, A. C., & Zuzul, T. (2011). Sustainable cities: oxymoron or the shape of the future? *Harvard Business School Organizational Behavior Unit Working Paper*, (11-062), 11-062.

Aly, H. (2022). Digital transformation, development and productivity in developing countries: Is artificial intelligence a curse or a blessing? *Review of Economics and Political Science*, *7*(4), 238–256. doi:10.1108/REPS-11-2019-0145

American Cancer Society. (2020). *Cancer Facts & Figures*. American Cancer Society.

American Society of Clinical Oncology. (2020). The State of Cancer Care in America, 2020: A Report by the American Society of Clinical Oncology. *Journal of Oncology Practice / American Society of Clinical Oncology*, *16*(4), 175–203.

Amoako, G. K., & Dartey-Baah, K. (2020). *Corporate social responsibility: strategy for boosting brand perception and competitive advantage. CSR and Socially Responsible Investing Strategies in Transitioning and Emerging Economies.* IGI Global. doi:10.4018/978-1-7998-2193-9.ch004

Amrutha, V. N., & Geetha, S. N. (2020). A systematic review on green human resource management: Implications for social sustainability. *Journal of Cleaner Production*, *247*, 119131. doi:10.1016/j.jclepro.2019.119131

Ancillai, C., Sabatini, A., Gatti, M., & Perna, A. (2023). Digital technology and business model innovation: A systematic literature review and future research agenda. *Technological Forecasting and Social Change*, *188* (September 2022), 122307. doi:10.1016/j.techfore.2022.122307

Anderson, C., & Ellerby, W. (2018). Digital maturity model. *Achieving digital maturity to drive growth.* Deloitte. https://www2.deloitte.com/content/dam/Deloitte/global/Documents/ Technology-Media-Telecommunications/deloitte-digital-maturity-model.pdf

Androniceanu, A., Georgescu, I., & Sabie, O. M. (2022). The impact of digitalization on public administration, economic development, and well-being in the EU countries. *Central European Public Administration Review*, *20*(2), 9–31. doi:10.17573/cepar.2022.2.01

Angelidou, M. (2016). Four European smart city strategies. *International Journal of Social Science Studies*, *4*(4), 18. doi:10.11114/ijsss.v4i4.1364

Anthopoulos, L. G. (2015). Understanding the smart city domain: A literature review. *Transforming city governments for successful smart cities*, 9-21.

Antioco, M., & Coussement, K. (2018). Misreading of consumer dissatisfaction in online product reviews: Writing style as a cause for bias. *International Journal of Information Management*, *38*(1), 301–310. doi:10.1016/j.ijinfomgt.2017.10.009

Antonijević, M. S., Ljumović, I., & Ivanović, Đ. (2022). Is there a Gender Gap in Financial Inclusion across Countries? *JWEE*, (1-2), 79–96. doi:10.28934/jwee22.12.pp79-96

Antonijević, M., Ivanović, Đ., & Simović, V. (2021). Adoption of Mobile Banking in the Republic of Serbia. In *Finance, Innovation and Technology: new models and structures* (p. 197). Institute of Economics - Ss. Cyril & Methodius University. http://ebooks.ien.bg.ac.rs/1594/

Anuradha, J., & Samy, G. (2014). The role of foreign direct investment in India. *International Journal of Current Research*, *6*(9), 8897–8901.

Apostu, S. A., Vasile, V., Vasile, R., & Rosak-Szyrocka, J. (2022). Do Smart Cities Represent the Key to Urban Resilience? Rethinking Urban Resilience. *International Journal of Environmental Research and Public Health, 19*(22), 15410. doi:10.3390/ijerph192215410 PMID:36430131

Aral, S., Ipeirotis, P., & Taylor, S. J. (2011). Content and context: Identifying the impact of qualitative information on consumer choice. *International Conference on Information Systems 2011*. SSRN. 10.2139/ssrn.1784376

Arcand, M., PromTep, S., Brun, I., & Rajaobelina, L. (2017). Mobile banking service quality and customer relationships. *International Journal of Bank Marketing, 35*(7), 1068–1089. doi:10.1108/IJBM-10-2015-0150

Arora, N. K. (2018). Environmental Sustainability—Necessary for survival. *Environmental Sustainability, 1*(1), 1–2. doi:10.1007/s42398-018-0013-3

Arora, N. K., Fatima, T., Mishra, I., Verma, M., Mishra, J., & Mishra, V. (2018). Environmental sustainability: Challenges and viable solutions. *Environmental Sustainability, 1*(4), 309–340. doi:10.1007/s42398-018-00038-w

Aruldoss, M., Lakshmi, T. M., & Venkatesan, V. P. (2013). A survey on multi criteria decision making methods and its applications. *The African Journal of Information Systems, 1*(1), 31–43. doi:10.12691/ajis-1-1-5

Ashby, A., Leat, M., & Hudson-Smith, M. (2012). Making connections: A review of supply chain management and sustainability literature. *Supply Chain Management, 17*(5), 497–516. doi:10.1108/13598541211258573

Ashrafi, R., & Murtaza, M. (2008). Use and impact of ICT on SMEs in Oman. *Electronic Journal of Information Systems Evaluation, 11*(3).

Ashrafi, M., Magnan, G. M., Adams, M., & Walker, T. R. (2020). Understanding the Conceptual Evolutionary Path and Theoretical Underpinnings of Corporate Social Responsibility and Corporate Sustainability. *Sustainability (Basel), 12*(3), 760. doi:10.3390/su12030760

Askalidis, G., Kim, S. J., & Malthouse, E. C. (2017). Understanding and overcoming biases in online review systems. *Decision Support Systems, 97*, 23–30. doi:10.1016/j.dss.2017.03.002

Askay, D. A. (2015). Silence in the crowd: The spiral of silence contributing to the positive bias of opinions in an online review system. *New Media & Society, 17*(11), 1811–1829. doi:10.1177/1461444814535190

Aslanova, I. V., & Kulichkina, A. I. (2020, May). Digital maturity: Definition and model. In *2nd International Scientific and Practical Conference "Modern Management Trends and the Digital Economy: from Regional Development to Global Economic Growth" (MTDE 2020)* (pp. 443-449). Atlantis Press.

Asnakew, Z. S. (2020). Customers' continuance intention to use mobile banking: Development and testing of an integrated model. *The Review of Socionetwork Strategies, 14*(1), 123–146. doi:10.1007/s12626-020-00060-7

Asongu, S. A., Le Roux, S., & Biekpe, N. (2018). Enhancing ICT for environmental sustainability in sub-Saharan Africa. *Technological Forecasting and Social Change, 127*, 209–216. doi:10.1016/j.techfore.2017.09.022

Atanasov, A., Chipriyanova, G., & Krasteva-Hristova, R. (2023). Integration of Digital Technologies in Corporate Social Responsibility (CSR) Activities: A Systematic Literature Review and Bibliometric Analysis. *Journal of Risk and Financial Management, 16*(8), 373. doi:10.3390/jrfm16080373

Avornyo, P., Fang, J., Odai, R. O., Vondee, J. B., & Nartey, M. N. (2019). Factors affecting continuous usage intention of mobile banking in Tema and Kumasi. *International Journal of Business and Social Science, 10*(3). doi:10.30845/ijbss.v10n3p11

Awan, U., Sroufe, R., & Kraslawski, A. (2019). Creativity Enables Sustainable Development: Supplier Engagement as a Boundary Condition for the Positive Effect on Green Innovation. *Journal of Cleaner Production*, *226*, 172–185. doi:10.1016/j.jclepro.2019.03.308

Awawdeh, A. E., Ananzeh, M., El-khateeb, A. I., & Aljumah, A. (2022). Role of green financing and corporate social responsibility (CSR) in technological innovation and corporate environmental performance: A COVID-19 perspective. *China Finance Review International*, *12*(2), 297–316. doi:10.1108/CFRI-03-2021-0048

Bacak, S., & Aydin, Y. (2018). Üretim İşletmelerindeki Lojistik Faaliyetlerin Finansal Performansa Etkisinin İşletme Yetkilileri Algısı: Sivas İlinde Bir Araştırma. *Kahramanmaraş Sütçü İmam Üniversitesi Sosyal Bilimler Dergisi*, *15*(1), 1.

Baeza-Yates, R. (2018). Bias on the web. *Communications of the ACM*, *61*(6), 54–61. doi:10.1145/3209581

Bag, S., Telukdarie, A., Pretorius, J. H. C., & Gupta, S. (2018). Industry 4.0 and supply chain sustainability: Framework and future research directions. *Benchmarking: An International Journal*, BIJ-03-2018-0056. doi:10.1108/BIJ-03-2018-0056

Bahta, D., Yun, J., Islam, M. R., & Ashfaq, M. (2021). Corporate social responsibility, innovation capability, and firm performance: Evidence from SME. *Social Responsibility Journal*, *17*(6), 840–860. doi:10.1108/SRJ-12-2019-0401

Bai, F., Huang, Y., Shang, M., & Ahmad, M. (2022). Modeling the impact of digital economy on urban environmental pollution: Empirical evidence from 277 prefecture-level cities in China. *Frontiers in Environmental Science*, *10*, 991022. doi:10.3389/fenvs.2022.991022

Baig, U., Hussain, B. M., Meidute-Kavaliauskiene, I., & Davidavicius, S. (2022). Digital entrepreneurship: Future research directions and opportunities for new business model. *Sustainability (Basel)*, *14*(9), 5004. doi:10.3390/su14095004

Bakari, S., & El Weriemmi, M. (2022). The Impact of Digitalization and Trade Openness on Economic Growth: New Evidence from Richest Asian Countries. *Journal of Research. Innovation and Technologies*, *1*(2(2)), 95–106. doi:10.57017/jorit.v1.2(2).01

Balkan, D., & Akyuz, G. A. (2023). Logistics Sector Turnover: Forecasting for Turkey, EU27 and EA19 under Effects of COVID-19. *Logistics*, *7*(2), 23. doi:10.3390/logistics7020023

Balogun, A. L., Marks, D., Sharma, R., Shekhar, H., Balmes, C., Maheng, D., Arshad, A., & Salehi, P. (2020). Assessing the potentials of digitalization as a tool for climate change adaptation and sustainable development in urban centres. *Sustainable Cities and Society*, *53*, 101888. doi:10.1016/j.scs.2019.101888

Baluch, A. (2023). E-Commerce Statistics of 2023. *Forbes Advisor*. www.forbes.com/advisor/business/ecommerce-statistics/

Bangor, A., Kortum, P., & Miller, J. (2009). Determining What Individual SUS Scores Mean: Adding an Adjective Rating Scale. *Journal of Usability Studies*, *4*(3), 114–123.

Bao, Z., & Chau, M. (2016). *The effect of collective rating on the perception of online reviews.*

Bao, Z., Li, W., Yin, P., & Chau, M. (2018). How does the review tag function benefit highly-rated popular products in online markets? In *Lecture Notes in Business Information Processing* (pp. 47–63). Lecture Notes in Business Information Processing. doi:10.1007/978-3-319-99936-4_5

Bao, Z., Li, W., Yin, P., & Chau, M. (2021). Examining the impact of review tag function on product evaluation and information perception of popular products. *Information Systems and e-Business Management*, *19*(2), 517–539. doi:10.1007/s10257-021-00532-5

Barnett, M. L., Henriques, I., & Husted, B. W. (2020). Beyond Good Intentions: Designing CSR Initiatives for Greater Social Impact. *Journal of Management*, *46*(6), 937–964. doi:10.1177/0149206319900539

BasuS. (2017). Beyond Agenda: Digital Divide and Corporate Social Responsibility. ResearchGate. DOI: doi:10.13140/RG.2.2.32149.63206

Battaglia, M., Testa, F., Bianchi, L., Iraldo, F., & Frey, M. (2014). Corporate Social Responsibility and Competitiveness within SMEs of the Fashion Industry: Evidence from Italy and France. *Sustainability (Basel)*, *6*(2), 872–893. doi:10.3390/su6020872

Baumgartner, R. J., & Rauter, R. (2017). Strategic perspectives of corporate sustainability management to develop a sustainable organization. *Journal of Cleaner Production*, *140*, 81–92. doi:10.1016/j.jclepro.2016.04.146

Bazerman, M. H., & Moore, D. A. (2013). *Judgement in Managerial Decision Making*. John Wiley & Sons, Inc.

Bednarčíková, D., & Repiská, R. (2021). Digital Transformation in the Context of the European Union and the Use of Digital Technologies as a Tool for Business Sustainability. *SHS Web of Conferences*. 10.1051/shsconf/202111501001

Beerepoot, I., Di Ciccio, C., Reijers, H. A., Rinderle-Ma, S., Bandara, W., Burattin, A., … Zerbato, F. (2023). The biggest business process management problems to solve before we die. *Computers in Industry*, *146* (October 2022). doi:10.1016/j.compind.2022.103837

Bekaroo, G., Bokhoree, C., & Pattinson, C. (2016). Impacts of ICT on the natural ecosystem: A grassroot analysis for promoting socio-environmental sustainability. *Renewable & Sustainable Energy Reviews*, *57*, 1580–1595. doi:10.1016/j.rser.2015.12.147

Bekele, S. (2023). *The Role of Transparency and Accountability in Digital Transformation*. ISACA https://www.isaca.org/resources/news-and-trends/industry-news/2023/the-role-of-transparency-and-accountability-in-digital-transformation

Benayoun, R., Roy, B., & Sussman, N. (1966). Manual de reference du programme electre. *Note de synthese et Formation, 25*(79).

Berghaus, S., Back, A., & Kaltenrieder, B. (2017). *Digital Maturity & Transformation Report 2017*. St.Gallen. Crosswlk. www.crosswalk.ch/dmcheck

Betz, M. R., Partridge, M. D., & Fallah, B. (2016). Smart cities and attracting knowledge workers: Which cities attract highly-educated workers in the 21st century? *Papers in Regional Science*, *95*(4), 819–841. doi:10.1111/pirs.12163

Bhola, P., Chronis, A. G., Kotsampopoulos, P., & Hatziargyriou, N. (2023). Business Model Selection for Community Energy Storage: A Multi Criteria Decision Making Approach. *Energies*, *16*(18), 6753. doi:10.3390/en16186753

Bhole, B., & Hanna, B. (2017). The effectiveness of online reviews in the presence of self-selection bias. *Simulation Modelling Practice and Theory*, *77*, 108–123. doi:10.1016/j.simpat.2017.05.005

Bibri, S. E., & Krogstie, J. (2017). Smart sustainable cities of the future: An extensive interdisciplinary literature review. *Sustainable Cities and Society*, *31*, 183–212. doi:10.1016/j.scs.2017.02.016

Bican, P. M., & Brem, A. (2020). Digital Business Model, Digital Transformation, Digital Entrepreneurship: Is There A Sustainable "Digital"? *Sustainability (Basel)*, *12*(5239), 5239. doi:10.3390/su12135239

Billon, M., Lera-Lopez, F., & Marco, R. (2010). Differences in digitalization levels: A multivariate analysis studying the global digital divide. *Review of World Economics*, *146*(1), 39–73. doi:10.1007/s10290-009-0045-y

Bing, X., & Yang, Z. (2020). Study of two-period pricing strategies for experiential products based onpraise cash-back' and negativity bias. *Journal of Industrial Engineering and Engineering Management*, *34*(2), 21–29.

Bohnsack, R., Bidmon, C. M., & Pinkse, J. (2022). Sustainability in the digital age: Intended and unintended consequences of digital technologies for sustainable development. *Business Strategy and the Environment, 31*(2), 599–602. https://doi-org.proxy.library.nyu.edu/10.1002/bse.2938. doi:10.1002/bse.2938

Bokhari, S. A. A., & Myeong, S. (2022). Use of Artificial Intelligence in Smart Cities for Smart Decision-Making: A Social Innovation Perspective. *Sustainability (Basel), 14*(2), 620. doi:10.3390/su14020620

Bouwman, H., Faber, E., & Van der Spek, J. (2005). *Connecting future scenarios to business models of insurance intermediaries.* AIS. https://aisel.aisnet.org/bled2005/16

Bouzguenda, I., Alalouch, C., & Fava, N. (2019). Towards smart sustainable cities: A review of the role digital citizen participation could play in advancing social sustainability. *Sustainable Cities and Society, 50*, 101627. doi:10.1016/j.scs.2019.101627

Brandes, L., Godes, D., & Mayzlin, D. (2022). Extremity Bias in Online Reviews: The Role of Attrition. *JMR, Journal of Marketing Research, 59*(4), 675–695. doi:10.1177/00222437211073579

Branstad, A., & Solem, B. A. (2020). Emerging theories of consumer-driven market innovation, adoption, and diffusion: A selective review of consumer-oriented studies. *Journal of Business Research, 116*, 561–571. doi:10.1016/j.jbusres.2020.01.028

Bray, F., Ferlay, J., Soerjomataram, I., Siegel, R. L., Torre, L. A., & Jemal, A. (2020). Global cancer statistics 2018: GLOBOCAN estimates of incidence and mortality worldwide for 36 cancers in 185 countries. *CA: a Cancer Journal for Clinicians, 68*(6), 394–424. doi:10.3322/caac.21492 PMID:30207593

Breukelman, H., Krikke, H., & Löhr, A. (2019). Failing services on urban waste management in developing countries: A review on symptoms, diagnoses, and interventions. *Sustainability (Basel), 11*(24), 6977. doi:10.3390/su11246977

Bridges, J., & Vásquez, C. (2018). If nearly all Airbnb reviews are positive, does that make them meaningless? *Current Issues in Tourism, 21*(18), 2065–2083. doi:10.1080/13683500.2016.1267113

Broccardo, L., Zicari, A., Jabeen, F., & Bhatti, Z. A. (2023). How digitalization supports a sustainable business model: A literature review. *Technological Forecasting and Social Change, 187*(October 2022). doi:10.1016/j.techfore.2022.122146

Broccardo, L., Truant, E., & Dana, L. P. (2023). The interlink between digitalization, sustainability, and performance: An Italian context. *Journal of Business Research, 158*, 113621. doi:10.1016/j.jbusres.2022.113621

Browne, G. J., & Parsons, J. (2012). More enduring questions in cognitive is research. *Journal of the Association for Information Systems, 13*(12), 1000–1011. doi:10.17705/1jais.00318

Budler, M., Župič, I., & Trkman, P. (2021). The development of business model research: A bibliometric review. *Journal of Business Research, 135*, 480-495.

Bulgurcu, B., & Nakiboglu, G. (2018). An extent analysis of 3PL provider selection criteria: A case on Turkey cement sector. *Cogent Business & Management, 5*(1), 1469183. doi:10.1080/23311975.2018.1469183

Bumann, J., & Peter, M. (2019). Action fields of digital transformation–a review and comparative analysis of digital transformation maturity models and frameworks. *Digitalisierung und andere Innovationsformen im Management. Innovation und Unternehmertum, 2*, 13–40.

Burhanudin, B., Ronny, R., & Sihotang, E. T. (2019). Connecting Intention to Use Online Banking, Commitment to Environmental Sustainability, and Happiness: The Role of Nature Relatedness. *Procedia Computer Science, 161*, 341–349. doi:10.1016/j.procs.2019.11.132

Businesspostbd.com (2023). *Bangladesh's potential as a manufacturing hub*. Business Post BD. businesspostbd.com/editorial/2023-03-12/bangladeshs-potential-as-a-manufacturing-hub-2023-03-12.

Caetano, L., Crespo, J., & Paraizo, R. (2020). Digital Governance and Digital Literacy: examining the Portuguese case. *Emergent technologies, New media and the Cities: Shifting Paradigms in Urban Communication. Capítulo, 9*, 135–152.

Camodeca, R., & Almici, A. (2021). Digital Transformation and Convergence toward the 2030 Agenda's Sustainability Development Goals: Evidence from Italian Listed Firms. *Sustainability (Basel), 13*(21), 11831. doi:10.3390/su132111831

Campos, A. L. N., & Oliveira, T. C. (2011). Modeling work processes and software development: Notation and tool. *ICEIS 2011 - Proceedings of the 13th International Conference on Enterprise Information Systems, 3 ISAS*(January), (pp. 337–343). ACM. 10.5220/0003581403370343

Cancer Research UK. (2021). *Cancer statistics*. Cancer Research. https://www.cancerresearchuk.org/health-professional/cancer-statistics

Caputo, A., Pizzi, S., Pellegrini, M. M., & Dabić, M. (2021). Digitalization and business models: Where are we going? A science map of the field. *Journal of Business Research, 123*, 489–501. doi:10.1016/j.jbusres.2020.09.053

Carmo, C., Correia, I., Leite, J., & Carvalho, A. (2023). Towards the Voluntary Adoption of Integrated Reporting: Drivers, Barriers, and Practices. *Administrative Sciences, 13*(6), 148. https://doi-org.proxy.library.nyu.edu/10.3390/admsci13060148. doi:10.3390/admsci13060148

Carroll, A. B. (1991). The pyramid of corporate social responsibility: Toward the moral management of organizational stakeholders. *Business Horizons, 34*(4), 39–48. doi:10.1016/0007-6813(91)90005-G

Carroll, A. B. (1999). Corporate Social Responsibility: Evolution of a Definitional Construct. *Business & Society, 38*(3), 268–295. doi:10.1177/000765039903800303

Carter, C. R., & Rogers, D. S. (2008). A framework of sustainable supply chain management: Moving toward new theory. *International Journal of Physical Distribution & Logistics Management, 38*(5), 360–387. doi:10.1108/09600030810882816

Carter, M., & Carter, C. (2020). The creative business model canvas. *Social Enterprise Journal, 16*(2), 141–158. doi:10.1108/SEJ-03-2019-0018

CASBEE. (2023). *Index*. CASBE. https://www.ibec.or.jp/CASBEE/english/index.htm.

Cenamor, J., Sjödin, D. R., & Parida, V. (2017). Adopting a platform approach in servitization: Leveraging the value of digitalization. *International Journal of Production Economics, 192*, 54–65. doi:10.1016/j.ijpe.2016.12.033

Ceniga, P., & Sukalova, V. (2020). Sustainable Business Development in the Context of Logistics in the Globalization Process. *SHS Web of Conferences, 74*, 04003. 10.1051/shsconf/20207404003

Centobelli, P., & Ndou, V. (2019). Managing customer knowledge through the use of big data analytics in tourism research. *Current Issues in Tourism, 22*(15), 1862–1882. doi:10.1080/13683500.2018.1564739

Chang, H. H., & Sokol, D. D. (2022). How incumbents respond to competition from innovative disruptors in the sharing economy— The impact of Airbnb on hotel performance. *Strategic Management Journal, 43*(3), 425–446. doi:10.1002/smj.3201

Chaouali, W., Imene, B. Y., Lunardo, R., & Triki, A. (2019). Reconsidering the "what is beautiful is good" effect: When and how design aesthetics affect intentions towards mobile banking applications. *International Journal of Bank Marketing, 37*(7), 1525–1546. doi:10.1108/IJBM-12-2018-0337

Charamba, K. (2022). Beyond the Corporate Responsibility to Respect Human Rights in the Dawn of a Metaverse. *International & Comparative Law Review*, *30*(1), 110–149.

Chatterjee, S. (2019). Explaining customer ratings and recommendations by combining qualitative and quantitative user generated contents. *Decision Support Systems*, *119*(February), 14–22. doi:10.1016/j.dss.2019.02.008

Chaudhary, P., Aeron, A., & Vijay, S. (2020). Quantify The Reviewer Genunity Based On Behavior Metrics And Past Trust Analysis. *International Journal of Scientific and Technology Research*, *8*(8), 1116-1121.

Chauhan, S., Singh, R., Gehlot, A., Akram, S. V., Twala, B., & Priyadarshi, N. (2022). Digitalization of Supply Chain Management with Industry 4.0 Enabling Technologies: A Sustainable Perspective. *Processes (Basel, Switzerland)*, *11*(1), 96. doi:10.3390/pr11010096

Chen, C., Lin, Y., Chen, W., Chao, C., & Pandia, H. (2021). Role of government to enhance digital transformation in small service business. *Sustainability (Basel)*, *13*(3), 1028. doi:10.3390/su13031028

Chen, H., Zheng, Z., & Ceran, Y. (2016). De-biasing the reporting bias in social media analytics. *Production and Operations Management*, *25*(5), 849–865. doi:10.1111/poms.12509

Chen, P., & Kim, S. (2023). The impact of digital transformation on innovation performance – The mediating role of innovation factors. *Heliyon*, *9*(3), e13916. doi:10.1016/j.heliyon.2023.e13916 PMID:36895347

Chen, Z., & Lurie, N. H. (2013). Temporal contiguity and negativity bias in the impact of online word of mouth. *JMR, Journal of Marketing Research*, *50*(4), 463–476. doi:10.1509/jmr.12.0063

Chesbrough, H., & Rosenbloom, R. S. (2002). The role of the business model in capturing value from innovation: Evidence from Xerox Corporation's technology spin-off companies. *Industrial and Corporate Change*, *11*(3), 529–555. doi:10.1093/icc/11.3.529

Choi, H. S. (2022). Do extraordinary claims require extraordinary evidence? Differential effect of trust cues on helpfulness by review extremity: An empirical study using big data. *European Journal of Information Systems*, 1–22. doi:10.1080/0960085X.2022.2104665

Chong, A. Y.-L. (2013). A two-staged SEM-neural network approach for understanding and predicting the determinants of m-commerce adoption. *Expert Systems with Applications*, *40*(4), 1240–1247. doi:10.1016/j.eswa.2012.08.067

Chung, N., Tyan, I., & Lee, S. J. (2019). Eco-Innovative Museums and Visitors' Perceptions of Corporate Social Responsibility. *Sustainability (Basel)*, *11*(20), 5744. doi:10.3390/su11205744

Cicognani, S., Figini, P., & Magnani, M. (2022). Social influence bias in ratings: A field experiment in the hospitality sector. *Tourism Economics*, *28*(8), 2197–2218. doi:10.1177/13548166211034645

Cisco. (2023). *Digital readiness index: World distribution for 2021*. Cisco. https://www.cisco.com/c/m/en_us/about/corporate-social-responsibility/research-resources/digital-readiness-index.html#/

Ciulli, F., & Kolk, A. (2023). International Business, Digital Technologies, and Sustainable Development: Connecting the Dots. *Journal of World Business*, *58*(4), 101445. doi:10.1016/j.jwb.2023.101445

Ciurea, C., & Filip, F. G. (2015). Multi-Criteria Analysis in Choosing IT&C Platforms for Creative Digital Works. *Uncommon Culture*, 20-27.

Ciuriak, D., & Ptashkina, M. (2018). *The Digital Transformation and the Transformation of International Trade*. SSRN. https://papers.ssrn.com/abstract=3107811

Clarkson, M. E. (1995). A stakeholder framework for analyzing and evaluating corporate social performance. *Academy of Management Review*, *20*(1), 92–117. doi:10.2307/258888

Clayton, S., Litchfield, C., & Geller, E. S. (2013). Psychological science, conservation, and environmental sustainability. *Frontiers in Ecology and the Environment*, *11*(7), 377–382. doi:10.1890/120351

Compagnucci, I., Corradini, F., Fornari, F., & Re, B. (2023). A Study on the Usage of the BPMN Notation for Designing Process Collaboration, Choreography, and Conversation Models. *Business & Information Systems Engineering*, (March). doi:10.1007/s12599-023-00818-7

Cong, X., Wang, S., Wang, L., Qi, Z., & Skibniewski, M. J. (2023). New smart city clusters' construction level evaluation under economic circles: The case of Shandong, China. *Technological and Economic Development of Economy*, *29*(3), 949–980. doi:10.3846/tede.2023.18792

Cook, K. A., Romi, A. M., Sánchez, D., & Sánchez, J. M. (2019). The influence of corporate social responsibility on investment efficiency and innovation. *Journal of Business Finance & Accounting*, *46*(3-4), 494–537. doi:10.1111/jbfa.12360

Coppola, D. (2020) Global e-commerce share of retail sales 2026. *Statista*. https://www.statista.com/statistics/534123/e-commerce-share-of-retail-sales-worldwide/#statisticContainer

Cortimiglia, M. N., Ghezzi, A., & Frank, A. G. (2016). Business model innovation and strategy making nexus: Evidence from a cross-industry mixed-methods study. *R & D Management*, *46*(3), 414–432. doi:10.1111/radm.12113

Coşkun, A. A., & Turker, O. (2011). Analysis of environmental impact assessment (EIA) system in Turkey. *Environmental Monitoring and Assessment*, *175*(1–4), 213–226. doi:10.1007/s10661-010-1507-3 PMID:20521100

Cox, B. (2023). *Ecommerce statistics to get you ahead in 2022*. Dash. dash.app/blog/ecommerce-statistics.

Currie, G., Truong, L., & De Gruyter, C. (2018). Regulatory structures and their impact on the sustainability performance of public transport in world cities. *Research in Transportation Economics*, *69*, 494–500. doi:10.1016/j.retrec.2018.02.001

Currie, W. L. (2004). Value creation from the application service provider e-business model: The experience of four firms. *Journal of Enterprise Information Management*, *17*(2), 117–130. doi:10.1108/17410390410518763

Cusumano, M. A. (2014). How traditional firms must compete in the sharing economy. *Communications of the ACM*, *58*(1), 32–34. doi:10.1145/2688487

Daly, J. C., & Cohen, J. (1978). Statistical power analysis for the behavioral sciences. Journal of the American Statistical Association, 73(363), 680. doi:10.2307/2286629

Daragmeh, A., Lentner, C., & Sági, J. (2021). FinTech payments in the era of COVID-19: Factors influencing behavioral intentions of "Generation X" in Hungary to use mobile payment. *Journal of Behavioral and Experimental Finance*, *32*, 100574. doi:10.1016/j.jbef.2021.100574 PMID:34540592

Daugherty, P. J., Chen, H., & Ferrin, B. G. (2011). Organizational Structure and Logistics Service Innovation. *International Journal of Logistics Management*, *22*(1), 26–51. doi:10.1108/09574091111127543

Dau, L., Chacar, A., Lyles, M., & Li, J. (2022). Informal institutions and international business: Toward an integrative research agenda. *Journal of International Business Studies*, *53*(6), 985–1010. doi:10.1057/s41267-022-00527-5

Davis, F. D. (1989). Perceived Usefulness, Perceived Ease of Use, and User Acceptance of Information Technology. *Management Information Systems Quarterly*, *13*(3), 319. doi:10.2307/249008

De Andres Gonzalez, O., Koivisto, H., Mustonen, J. M., & Keinänen-Toivola, M. M. (2021). Digitalization in Just-In-Time Approach as a Sustainable Solution for Maritime Logistics in the Baltic Sea Region. *Sustainability (Basel), 13*(3), 1173. doi:10.3390/su13031173

de Barra, M. (2017). Reporting bias inflates the reputation of medical treatments: A comparison of outcomes in clinical trials and online product reviews. *Social Science & Medicine (1982), 177,* 248–255. doi:10.1016/j.socscimed.2017.01.033

de Fine Licht, K., & de Fine Licht, J. (2020). Artificial intelligence, transparency, and public decision-making. *AI & Society, 35*(4), 917–926. doi:10.1007/s00146-020-00960-w

Denktaş Şakar, G., Yıldırım, E., & Mansuroğlu, E. (2018). Value Creation in Project Cargo Logistics: A Delphi Study. *Journal of ETA Maritime Science, 6*(3), 255–274. doi:10.5505/jems.2018.48343

Department of Revenue and Customs. (2021). Bhutan Trade Statistics 2021. Department of Revenue and Customs. [https://www.mof.gov.bt/wp-content/uploads/2022/04/BhutanTradeStatistics2021.pdf]

Dethine, B., Enjolras, M., & Monticolo, D. (2020). Digitalization and SMEs' export management: Impacts on resources and capabilities. *Technology Innovation Management Review, 10*(4), 18–34. doi:10.22215/timreview/1344

DeVellis, R. F. (2003). *Scale Development: Theory and Applications.* SAGE. https://play.google.com/store/books/details?id=BYGxL6xLokUC

Dewan, S., & Kraemer, K. (2000). Information technology and productivity: Evidence from country-level data. *Management Science, 46*(4), 548–562. doi:10.1287/mnsc.46.4.548.12057

Díaz, S., Settele, J., Brondízio, E., Ngo, H., Guèze, M., Agard, J., & Chan, K. (2020). *Summary for policymakers of the global assessment report on biodiversity and ecosystem services of the Intergovernmental Science-Policy Platform on Biodiversity and Ecosystem Services.*

Digital skills gap index. (2021, June 1). Wiley. https://dsgi.wiley.com/.

Dintrans, P., Anand, A., Ponnuveetil, M., Acharya, A., & Chardukian, A. (2017). Why Banks Must Become Smart Aggregators in the Financial Services Digital Ecosystem. Technology Solutions, Cognizant. Retrieved from Bumann, J., & Peter, M. (2019). Action fields of digital transformation–a review and comparative analysis of digital transformation maturity models and frameworks. Digitalisierung und andere Innovationsformen im Management. *Innovation und Unternehmertum, 2,* 13–40.

Dionisio, M. (2021). Corporate social innovation in practice : People with disabilities project in Brazil. *International Journal of Business and Globalisation, 1*(1), 1–18. https://www.researchgate.net/publication/348131612_Corporate_Social_Innovation_CSI_in_practice_People_with_disabilities_project_in_Brazil. doi:10.1504/IJBG.2021.10034457

Dionisio, M., de Souza Junior, S. J., Paula, F., & Pellanda, P. C. (2023). The role of digital social innovations to address SDGs: A systematic review. *Environment, Development and Sustainability, 34,* 100442. doi:10.1007/s10668-023-03038-x PMID:36855437

Di, Q., Wang, Y., Zanobetti, A., Wang, Y., Koutrakis, P., Choirat, C., Dominici, F., & Schwartz, J. D. (2017). Air pollution and mortality in the Medicare population. *The New England Journal of Medicine, 376*(26), 2513–2522. doi:10.1056/NEJMoa1702747 PMID:28657878

DLA. (n.d.). Law in Kuwait - *DLA Piper global data protection laws of the world.* DLA. https://www.dlapiperdataprotection.com/index.html?t=law&c=KW

Dolkar, D. (2023). GoI to facilitate Bhutan-Bangladesh electricity trade." *Kuensel Online.* kuenselonline.com/goi-to-facilitate-bhutan-bangladesh-electricity-trade/.

Domazet, I. S., Marjanović, D., Ahmetagić, D., & Stantić, J. (2023). Innovation and ICT: Key Factors of Successful Business. In Innovation, Strategy, and Transformation Frameworks for the Modern Enterprise (pp. 327-345). IGI Global. doi:10.4018/979-8-3693-0458-7.ch014

Dorin, M. (2018). Product and process innovation: A new perspective on organizational development. *International Journal of Advanced Engineering and Management Research, 3*(6), 132–138.

Dragana, R. P., Nedeljković, I., & Marinković, V. (2022). The role of the hedonistic and utilitarian quality dimensions in enhancing user satisfaction in mobile banking. *International Journal of Bank Marketing, 40*(7), 1610–1631. doi:10.1108/IJBM-03-2022-0112

Du, J., Rong, J., Wang, H., & Zhang, Y. (2021). Neighbor-aware review helpfulness prediction. *Decision Support Systems, 148*, 113581. doi:10.1016/j.dss.2021.113581

Dumas, M., Rosa, M., La, Mendling, J., & Hajo, A. Reijers. (2018). Fundamental Business Process Management. *Lecture Notes in Business Information Processing, 168.*

Dwivedi, P., Chaturvedi, V., & Vashist, J. K. (2021). Innovation for Organizational Sustainability: The Role of HR Practices and Theories. *The International Journal of Organizational Analysis*. Advance online publication. doi:10.1108/IJOA-07-2021-2859

Dykes, T. (2022). *China E-Commerce: Is it time to look beyond regulatory pressures?* Schroders. www.schroders.com/en-us/us/individual/insights/china-e-commerce-is-it-time-to-look-beyond-regulatory-pressures/

Dženopoljac, V., Georgievski, B., Cavagnetto, S., & Abidi, O. (2022). National intellectual capital: A comparative longitudinal study. *Ekonomika Preduzeca, 70*(3–4), 147–160. doi:10.5937/EKOPRE2204147D

Ebinger, F., & Omondi, B. (2020). Leveraging digital approaches for transparency in sustainable supply chains: A conceptual paper. *Sustainability (Basel), 12*(15), 6129. https://doi-org.proxy.library.nyu.edu/10.3390/su12156129. doi:10.3390/su12156129

Economy data . (n.d.). World Bank. https://rulemaking.worldbank.org/en/data/explorecountries/serbia

e-estonia.com. (2023). *Government cloud.* e-estonia. https://e-estonia.com/solutions/e-governance/government-cloud/

Eichler, G. M., & Schwarz, E. J. (2019). What Sustainable Development Goals Do Social Innovations Address? A Systematic Review and Content Analysis of Social Innovation Literature. *Sustainability (Basel), 11*(2), 522. doi:10.3390/su11020522

Einar, B., Havro, L. J., & Moen, O. (2015). An Empirical Investigation of Self-Selection Bias and Factors Influencing Review Helpfulness. *International Journal of Business and Management, 10*(7), 16–30. doi:10.5539/ijbm.v10n7p16

EisapeD. (2020). Comparing platform business models: A balanced scorecard approach based on the platform business model canvas. *Nordic Journal of Media Management, 1*(3), 401-432. doi:10.5278/njmm.2597-0445.5842

Eisenmann, T., Parker, G., & Van Alstyne, M. W. (2006). Strategies for two-sided markets. *Harvard Business Review, 84*(10), 92. https://www.binhphuongnguyen.com/wp-content/uploads/2021/07/HBR-Strategy-for-2-side-market-Egg-and-Chicken-Dilemma-Startup.pdf

Eizenberg, E., & Jabareen, Y. (2017). Social sustainability: A new conceptual framework. *Sustainability (Basel), 9*(1), 68. doi:10.3390/su9010068

Elia, S., Petruzzelli, A. M., & Piscitello, L. (2019). The impact of cultural diversity on innovation performance of MNC subsidiaries in strategic alliances. *Journal of Business Research, 98*, 204–213. doi:10.1016/j.jbusres.2019.01.062

Elkington, J. (1998). *Cannibals with Forks: The Triple Bottom Line of Sustainability*. New Society Publishers.

Elliot, S. (2011). Transdisciplinary perspectives on environmental sustainability: A resource base and framework for IT-enabled business transformation. *Management Information Systems Quarterly*, *35*(1), 197–236. doi:10.2307/23043495

ElMassah, S., & Mohieldin, M. (2020). Digital transformation and localizing the Sustainable Development Goals (SDGs). *Ecological Economics*, *169*, 106490. doi:10.1016/j.ecolecon.2019.106490

ENCORE. (2021). Status-Quo Analysis of the Status of Entrepreneurship Efforts in Bhutan, Nepal and Lao PDR. ENCORE. ENCORE. https://encore.fh-joanneum.at/wp-content/uploads/2022/08/ENCORE_Status-Quo_WEB.pdf

Epstein, M. J., Buhovac, A. R., & Yuthas, K. (2010). Implementing sustainability: The role of leadership and organizational culture. *Strategic finance*, *91*(10), 41.

Erevelles, S., Fukawa, N., & Swayne, L. (2016). Big Data consumer analytics and the transformation of marketing. *Journal of Business Research*, *69*(2), 897–904. doi:10.1016/j.jbusres.2015.07.001

Eslami, S. P., Ghasemaghaei, M., & Hassanein, K. (2018). Which online reviews do consumers find most helpful? A multi-method investigation. *Decision Support Systems*, *113*, 32–42. doi:10.1016/j.dss.2018.06.012

Etezadzadeh, C. (2016). Digitalization. *Smart City–Future City? Smart City 2.0 as a Livable City and Future Market*, 37-45.

European Commission. (2019). *Corporate Social Responsibility, Responsible Business Conduct, and Business and Human Rights: Overview of Progress, Commission Staff Working Document No. 143*. EC. https://ec.europa.eu/docsroom/documents/34963

European Commission. (2020). Directorate General for Communications Networks, Content and Technology. In *Shaping Europe's Digital Future*. Publications Office of the European Union.

European Commission. (n.d.). *Sustainable Development*. EC. https://ec.europa.eu/environment/eussd/

Evangelista, P., Santoro, L., & Thomas, A. (2018). Environmental Sustainability in Third-Party Logistics Service Providers: A Systematic Literature Review from 2000–2016. *Sustainability (Basel)*, *10*(5), 1627. doi:10.3390/su10051627

Evans, D. S., & Schmalensee, R. (2016). *Matchmakers: The new economics of multisided platforms*. Harvard Business Review Press.

Falcon, E. (2023). *Why Is South Korea a Global Broadband Leader?* Electronic Frontier Foundation. https://www.eff.org/deeplinks/2020/02/why-south-korea-global-broadband-leader

Fallah, S. N., Mohabbati-Kalejahi, N., Alavi, S., & Zahed, M. A. (2022). Sustainable Development Goals (SDGs) as a Framework for Corporate Social Responsibility (CSR). *Sustainability (Basel)*, *14*(3), 1222. doi:10.3390/su14031222

Fang, J., Hu, L., Hossin, M. A., Yang, J., & Shao, Y. (2019). Polluted online reviews: The effect of air pollution on reviewer behavior. *International Journal of Electronic Commerce*, *23*(4), 557–594. doi:10.1080/10864415.2019.1655206

Farias-Gaytan, S., Aguaded, I., & Ramirez-Montoya, M. S. (2022). Transformation and digital literacy: Systematic literature mapping. *Education and Information Technologies*, *27*(2), 1417–1437. doi:10.1007/s10639-021-10624-x

Farzin, M., Sadeghi, M., Yahyayi Kharkeshi, F., Ruholahpur, H., & Fattahi, M. (2021). Extending UTAUT2 in M-banking adoption and actual use behavior: Does WOM communication matter? *Asian Journal of Economics and Banking*, *5*(2), 136–157. doi:10.1108/AJEB-10-2020-0085

Fassio, C. (2018). Export-led innovation: The role of export destinations. *Industrial and Corporate Change*, *27*(1), 149–171. doi:10.1093/icc/dtx028

Faur, M., & Bungau, C. (2019). Outsourcing Towards Greater Agility Through Investigating Decoupling Points in Leagile Supply Chains. *MATEC Web of Conferences, 290*, 07006. 10.1051/matecconf/201929007006

Feng, H., Wang, F., Song, G., & Liu, L. (2022). Digital Transformation on Enterprise Green Innovation: Effect and Transmission Mechanism. *International Journal of Environmental Research and Public Health, 19*(17), 10614. https:// doi. doi:org/10.3390/IJERPH191710614

Ferlay, J., Soerjomataram, I., Dikshit, R., Eser, S., Mathers, C., Rebelo, M., & Bray, F. (2015). Cancer incidence and mortality worldwide: Sources, methods and major patterns in GLOBOCAN 2012. *International Journal of Cancer, 136*(5), 359–386. doi:10.1002/ijc.29210 PMID:25220842

Feroz, A. K., Zo, H., & Chiravuri, A. (2021). Digital Transformation and Environmental Sustainability: A Review and Research Agenda. *Sustainability (Basel), 13*(3), 1530. doi:10.3390/su13031530

Fertner, C., Christensen, A. A., Andersen, P. S., Olafsson, A. S., Caspersen, S. P. O. H., & Grunfelder, J. (2019). Emerging digital plan data – New research perspectives on planning practice and evaluation. *Geografisk Tidskrift, 119*(1), 6–16. doi:10.1080/00167223.2018.1528555

Fesenko, T., & Fesenko, G. (2017). City-Governance: Conceptualizing digital maturity model. *SOCRATES, 5*(2), 106–122. doi:10.5958/2347-6869.2017.00016.4

Filieri, R., Raguseo, E., & Vitari, C. (2021). Extremely negative ratings and online consumer review helpfulness: The moderating role of product quality signals. *Journal of Travel Research, 60*(4), 699–717. doi:10.1177/0047287520916785

Fitzmaurice, C., Allen, C., Barber, R. M., Barregard, L., Bhutta, Z. A., Brenner, H., & Fleming, T. D. (2017). Global, Regional, and National Cancer Incidence, Mortality, Years of Life Lost, Years Lived with Disability, and Disability-Adjusted Life-years for 32 Cancer Groups, 1990 to 2015. *JAMA Oncology, 3*(4), 524–548. doi:10.1001/jamaoncol.2016.5688 PMID:27918777

Fleischmann, M., Amirpur, M., Benlian, A., & Hess, T. (2014). Cognitive biases in information systems research: A scientometric analysis. *ECIS 2014 Proceedings - 22nd European Conference on Information Systems.*

Flint, D. J., Larsson, E., Gammelgaard, B., & Mentzer, J. T. (2005). Logistics Innovation: A Customer Value-Oriented Social Process. *Journal of Business Logistics, 26*(1), 113–147. doi:10.1002/j.2158-1592.2005.tb00196.x

Foroughi, B., Iranmanesh, M., & Sean, H. S. (2019). Understanding the determinants of mobile banking continuance usage intention. *Journal of Enterprise Information Management, 32*(6), 1015–1033. doi:10.1108/JEIM-10-2018-0237

Fosso Wamba, S., Akter, S., Edwards, A., Chopin, G., & Gnanzou, D. (2015). How 'big data' can make big impact: Findings from a systematic review and a longitudinal case study. *International Journal of Production Economics, 165*, 234–246. doi:10.1016/j.ijpe.2014.12.031

Freeman, E. R. (1984). *Strategic Management: A Stakeholder Approach.* Harpercollins College Div: Pitman.

Fujita, A., Lhendup, J., & Thinley, S. (2022). *Promoting Entrepreneurship in Bhutan.* Asian Development Bank Institute. doi:10.56506/USDA5186

Galbreath, J. (2019). Drivers of Green Innovations: The Impact of Export Intensity, Women Leaders, and Absorptive Capacity. *Journal of Business Ethics, 158*(1), 47–61. doi:10.1007/s10551-017-3715-z

Gao, B. J., & Katrompas, A. (2020, December 10). A preliminary experimental analysis on RateMyProfessors. *2020 IEEE International Conference on Big Data (Big Data).* IEEE. 10.1109/BigData50022.2020.9378446

Gao, B., Hu, N., & Bose, I. (2017). Follow the herd or be myself? An analysis of consistency in behavior of reviewers and helpfulness of their reviews. *Decision Support Systems*, *95*, 1–11. doi:10.1016/j.dss.2016.11.005

Gao, J., Zhang, W., Guan, T., Feng, Q., & Mardani, A. (2023). The effect of manufacturing agent heterogeneity on enterprise innovation performance and competitive advantage in the era of digital transformation. *Journal of Business Research*, *155*, 113387. doi:10.1016/j.jbusres.2022.113387

Gartner. (2023). *Business Process Management (BPM)*. Gartner. https://www.gartner.com/en/information-technology/glossary/business-process-management-bpm

Gasser, U., Gassmann, O., Hens, T., Leifer, L., Puschmann, T., & Zhao, L. (2018). Digital Banking 2025. FinTech. https://www.fintech.uzh.ch/dam/jcr: 2ef31105-1a60-43da-a657-8b140e47b3b4/Digital Banking 2025 FINAL.pdf

Gawer, A. (2014). 'Bridging differing perspectives on technological platforms: Toward an integrative framework'. *Research Policy*, *43*(7), 1239–1249. doi:10.1016/j.respol.2014.03.006

GDP per capita (current US $). (n.d.). World Bank Open Data. https://data.worldbank.org/indicator/NY.GDP.PCAP.CD?name_desc=true.

Ge, Y., & Li, J. (2015). Measure and Mitigate the Dimensional Bias in Online Reviews and Ratings. In ICIS 2015.

Gebert, H., Geib, M., Kolbe, L., & Brenner, W. (2003). Knowledge-enabled customer relationship management: Integrating customer relationship management and knowledge management concepts [1]. *Journal of Knowledge Management*, *7*(5), 107–123. doi:10.1108/13673270310505421

Gefen, D., Karahanna, E., & Straub, D. W. (2003). Trust and TAM in Online Shopping: An Integrated Model. *Management Information Systems Quarterly*, *27*(1), 51–90. doi:10.2307/30036519

George, J. F., Duffy, K., & Ahuja, M. (2000). Countering the anchoring and adjustment bias with decision support systems. *Decision Support Systems*, *29*(2), 195–206. doi:10.1016/S0167-9236(00)00074-9

Ghazinoory, S., Roshandel, J., Parvin, F., Nasri, S., & Fatemi, M. (2023). Smart city maturity models: A multidimensional synthesized approach. *Wiley Interdisciplinary Reviews. Data Mining and Knowledge Discovery*, 1516.

Gibbert, M., Leibold, M., & Probst, G. (2002). Five styles of customer knowledge management, and how smart companies use them to create value. *European Management Journal*, *20*(5), 459–469. doi:10.1016/S0263-2373(02)00101-9

Gilster, P., & Glister, P. (1997). *Digital literacy*. Wiley Computer Pub.

Gimpel, H., Hosseini, S., Xaver, R., Huber, R., Probst, L., Röglinger, M., & Faisst, U. (2018). Structuring Digital Transformation: A Framework of Action Fields and its Application at ZEISS. *Journal of Information Technology, 19*(1), 31–54. https://aisel.aisnet.org/cgi/viewcontent.cgi?article =1726&context=jitta

Giovanis, A., Athanasopoulou, P., Assimakopoulos, C., & Sarmaniotis, C. (2019). Adoption of mobile banking services: A comparative analysis of four competing theoretical models. *International Journal of Bank Marketing*, *37*(5), 1165–1189. doi:10.1108/IJBM-08-2018-0200

Godina, R., Ribeiro, I., Matos, F. T., Ferreira, B., Carvalho, H., & Peças, P. (2020). Impact assessment of additive manufacturing on sustainable business models in industry 4.0 context. *Sustainability*, *12*(17), 7066. doi:10.3390/su12177066

Gollhardt, T. (2022). *Towards Business Model Tools for SMEs–Knowledge Boundaries in Business Model Innovation Projects*.

Gond, J., Augustine, G., Shin, H., Tirapani, A., & Mosonyi, S. (2022). *How corporate social responsibility and sustainable development functions impact the workplace: A review of the literature.* (ILO Working Paper 71). Geneva, ILO. https://www.ilo.org/wcmsp5/groups/public/---dgreports/---inst/documents/publication/wcms_850856.pdf

Gong, C., & Ribiere, V. (2021). Developing a unified definition of digital transformation. *Technovation, 102*, 102217. doi:10.1016/j.technovation.2020.102217

González, J. L., & Ferencz, J. (2018, October 29). *Digital Trade and Market Openness | Documents de travail de l'OCDE sur la politique commercial.* (OECD Trade Policy Papers). OECD. https://www.oecd-ilibrary.org/trade/digital-trade-and-market-openness_1bd89c9a-en

González-Fernández, M., & González-Velasco, C. (2018). Innovation and Corporate Performance in the Spanish Regions. *Journal of Policy Modeling, 40*(5), 998–1021. doi:10.1016/j.jpolmod.2018.05.005

Goodland, R. (1995). The concept of environmental sustainability. *Annual Review of Ecology and Systematics, 26*(1), 1–24. doi:10.1146/annurev.es.26.110195.000245

Goodwin, P., & Wright, G. (2014). *Decision analysis for management judgment.* John Wiley & Sons.

Gracias, J. S., Parnell, G. S., Specking, E., Pohl, E. A., & Buchanan, R. (2023). Smart Cities—A Structured Literature Review. *Smart Cities, 6*(4), 1719–1743. doi:10.3390/smartcities6040080

Grawe, S. J. (2009). Logistics Innovation: A Literature-based Conceptual Framework. *International Journal of Logistics Management, 20*(3), 360–377. Advance online publication. doi:10.1108/09574090911002823

Gritsenko, S., Karpun, Oi., & Kolisnichenko, A. (2022). Digitalization of logistics company business process in conditions of industry 4.0. *Electronic Scientific Journal Intellectualization of Logistics and Supply Chain Management, 11*, 46–56. doi:10.46783/smart-scm/2022-11-4

Gruchmann, T., Melkonyan, A., & Krumme, K. (2018). Logistics Business Transformation for Sustainability: Assessing the Role of the Lead Sustainability Service Provider (6PL). *Logistics, 2*(4), 25. doi:10.3390/logistics2040025

Guerrero-Villegas, J., Sierra-García, L., & Palacios-Florencio, B. (2018). The role of sustainable development and innovation on firm performance. *Corporate Social Responsibility and Environmental Management, 25*(6), 1350–1362. doi:10.1002/csr.1644

Gu, J.-C., Lee, S.-C., & Suh, Y.-H. (2009). Determinants of behavioral intention to mobile banking. *Expert Systems with Applications, 36*(9), 11605–11616. doi:10.1016/j.eswa.2009.03.024

Guo, D., Zhao, Y., Zhang, L., Wen, X., & Yin, C. (2019). Conformity feedback in an online review helpfulness evaluation task leads to less negative feedback-related negativity amplitudes and more positive P300 amplitudes. *Journal of Neuroscience, Psychology, and Economics, 12*(2), 73–87. doi:10.1037/npe0000102

Gupta, J., Hurley, F., Grobicki, A., Keating, T., Stoett, P., Baker, E., Guhl, A., Davies, J., & Ekins, P. (2019). Communicating the health of the planet and its links to human health. *The Lancet. Planetary Health, 3*(5), e204–e206. doi:10.1016/S2542-5196(19)30040-3 PMID:30876842

Gupta, P., Prashar, S., Vijay, T. S., & Parsad, C. (2021). Examining the influence of antecedents of continuous intention to use an informational app: The role of perceived usefulness and perceived ease of use. *International Journal of Business Information Systems, 36*(2), 270–287. doi:10.1504/IJBIS.2021.112829

Gurbaxani, V., & Dunkle, D. (2018). *Gearing Up for Successful Digital Transformation Center for Digital Transformation.* Center for Digital Transformations. http://www.centerfordigitaltransformation.org/assets/APC-Report-Digital-Transformation_18_r2-merged.pdf

Habibi, F., & Zabardast, M. A. (2020). Digitalization, education and economic growth: A comparative analysis of Middle East and OECD countries. *Technology in Society*, *63*, 101370. doi:10.1016/j.techsoc.2020.101370

Hägg, J., & Sandhu, S. (2017). *Do or Die: How large organizations can reach a higher level of digital maturity.*

Hagiu, A., & Wright, J. (2015). Marketplace or reseller? *Management Science*, *61*(1), 184–203. doi:10.1287/mnsc.2014.2042

Hagiu, A., & Wright, J. (2019). The status of workers and platforms in the sharing economy. *Journal of Economics & Management Strategy*, *28*(1), 97–108. doi:10.1111/jems.12299

Hair, J. F., Black, W. C., Babin, B. J., & Anderson, R. E. (2014). *Multivariate data analysis: Pearson new international edition*. Pearson Education Limited.

Haley, U. C. V., & Stumpf, S. A. (1989). Cognitive Trails in Strategic Decision-Making: Linking Theories of Personalities and Cognitions. *Journal of Management Studies*, *26*(5), 477–497. doi:10.1111/j.1467-6486.1989.tb00740.x

Hanafizadeh, P., Behboudi, M., Koshksaray, A. A., & Tabar, M. J. S. (2014). Mobile-banking adoption by Iranian bank clients. *Telematics and Informatics*, *31*(1), 62–78. doi:10.1016/j.tele.2012.11.001

Han, S., & Anderson, C. K. (2020). Customer motivation and response bias in online reviews. *Cornell Hospitality Quarterly*, *61*(2), 142–153. doi:10.1177/1938965520902012

Harford, J. B. (2021). Current status and future directions of breast cancer prevention and early detection in Jordan. *Breast Cancer: Targets and Therapy*, *13*, 25–33.

Harindranath, G., Dyerson, R., & Barnes, D. (2008). ICT adoption and use in UK SMEs: a failure of initiatives? *Electronic Journal of Information Systems Evaluation, 11*(2).

Harmon, P. (2015). The State of Business Process Management. *BP Trends.* https://www.bptrends.com/bpt/wp-content/uploads/2015-bpt-survey-report.pdf

Härting, R.-C., Reichstein, C., Sandkuhl, K., Hoppe, N., & Yesilay, H. (2020). *Potential Benefits of Enterprise Architecture Management in the Digital Transformation Process*. Complex Systems Informatics and Modeling Quarterly., doi:10.7250/csimq.2020-24.04

Hart, S. L. (1995). A natural-resource-based view of the firm. *Academy of Management Review*, *20*(4), 986–1014. doi:10.2307/258963

Hart, S. L. (1997). Beyond greening: Strategies for a sustainable world. *Harvard Business Review*, *75*, 66–77.

Haryanti, T., Rakhmawati, N. A., & Subriadi, A. P. (2023). The extended digital maturity model. *Big Data and Cognitive Computing*, *7*(1), 17. doi:10.3390/bdcc7010017

Hayes, B. K., Wisken, A., & Cruz, N. (2021). Explaining the popularity bias in online consumer choice. *Journal of Experimental Psychology. General*, *150*(10), 2185–2191. doi:10.1037/xge0001031 PMID:33734776

Heck, D. W., Seiling, L., & Bröder, A. (2020). The love of large numbers revisited: A coherence model of the popularity bias. *Cognition*, *195*(104069), 104069. doi:10.1016/j.cognition.2019.104069 PMID:31877503

Heemsbergen, L. (2016). From radical transparency to radical disclosure: Reconfiguring (in) voluntary transparency through the management of visibilities. *International Journal of Communication*, *10*, 138–151.

He, G., Boas, I., Mol, A. P., & Lu, Y. (2016). E-participation for environmental sustainability in transitional urban China. *Sustainability Science*, *12*(2), 187–202. doi:10.1007/s11625-016-0403-3

Helbing, D. (2012). Introduction: The FuturICT knowledge accelerator towards a more resilient and sustainable future. In P. Ball (Ed.), *Why society is a complex matter* (pp. 55–60). Springer. doi:10.1007/978-3-642-29000-8_12

Helmke, G., & Levitsky, S. (2004). Informal institutions and comparative politics: A research agenda. *Perspectives on Politics*, *2*(4), 725–740. doi:10.1017/S1537592704040472

Hermundsdottir, F., & Aspelund, A. (2022). Competitive sustainable manufacturing-Sustainability strategies, environmental and social innovations, and their effects on firm performance. *Journal of Cleaner Production*, *370*, 133474. doi:10.1016/j.jclepro.2022.133474

Hervé, A., Schmitt, C., & Baldegger, R. (2020). Digitalization, entrepreneurial orientation and internationalization of micro-, small- And medium-sized enterprises. *Technology Innovation Management Review*, *10*(4), 5–17. doi:10.22215/timreview/1343

Hervé, A., Schmitt, C., & Baldegger, R. (2020). Internationalization and digitalization: Applying digital technologies to the internationalization process of small and medium-sized enterprises. *Technology Innovation Management Review*, *10*(7), 28–40. doi:10.22215/timreview/1373

Hess, T., Matt, C., Benlian, A., & Wiesböck, F. (2016). Options for Formulating a Digital Transformation Strategy. *MIS Quarterly Executive*, *15*(2), 123139.

Hidayat-ur-Rehman, I., Ahmad, A., Khan, M. N., & Mokhtar, S. A. (2021). Investigating Mobile Banking Continuance Intention: A Mixed-Methods Approach. *Mobile Information Systems*, *2021*, 1–17. doi:10.1155/2021/9994990

Higón, D. A., Gholami, R., & Shirazi, F. (2017). ICT and environmental sustainability: A global perspective. *Telematics and Informatics*, *34*(4), 85–95. doi:10.1016/j.tele.2017.01.001

Hillman, A. J., & Keim, G. D. (2001). Shareholder Value, Stakeholder Management, and Social Issues: What's the Bottom Line? *Strategic Management Journal*, *22*(2), 125–139. doi:10.1002/1097-0266(200101)22:2<125::AID-SMJ150>3.0.CO;2-H

Hilty, L., Lohmann, W., & Huang, E. M. (2011). Sustainability and ICT-an overview of the field. *Notizie di Politeia*, *27*(104), 13–28.

Hitt, M. A., Worthington, W. J. IV, & Li, H. (2005). Emerging Markets as Learning Laboratories: Learning Behaviors ofLocal Firms and Foreign Entrants in Different InstitutionalContexts. *Management and Organization Review*, *1*(3), 353–380. doi:10.1111/j.1740-8784.2005.0019a.x

Ho, Y.-C., Wu, J., & Tan, Y. (2017). Disconfirmation effect on online rating behavior: A structural model. *Information Systems Research : ISR*, *28*(3), 626–642. doi:10.1287/isre.2017.0694

Hoffmann, S. C., Junior, L. W., & De Oliveira, S. F. (2017). Apps for mobile banking and customer satisfaction: A cross-cultural study. *International Journal of Bank Marketing*, *35*(7), 1133–1153. doi:10.1108/IJBM-09-2015-0146

Hofstede, G. (2010). Geert hofstede. *National cultural dimensions*, 2-7.

Holmström, J., Liotta, G., & Chaudhuri, A. (2017). Sustainability outcomes through direct digital manufacturing-based operational practices: A design theory approach. *Journal of Cleaner Production*, *167*, 951–961. doi:10.1016/j.jclepro.2017.03.092

Holzer, M., Manoharan, A., & Van Ryzin, G. (2010). Global cities on the web: An empirical typology of municipal websites. *International Public Management Review*, *11*(3), 104–121.

Ho, M. H. C. (2022). Evolutionary network of business model studies and applications in emerging economies. *The Singapore Economic Review*, *67*(03), 1005–1028. doi:10.1142/S0217590820550012

Hong, S., Thong, J. Y. L., & Tam, K. Y. (2006). Understanding continued information technology usage behavior: A comparison of three models in the context of mobile internet. *Decision Support Systems*, *42*(3), 1819–1834. doi:10.1016/j.dss.2006.03.009

Hoorens, V. (2014). Positive Bias. Encyclopedia of Quality of Life and Well-Being Research, 4938-4941. Springer. doi:10.1007/978-94-007-0753-5

Horani, L. F. (2023). Sustainable design concepts and their definitions: An inductive content-analysis-based literature review. *Technological Sustainability*, *2*(3), 225–243. doi:10.1108/TECHS-10-2022-0041

Hortovanyi, L., Morgan, R. E., Herceg, I. V., Djuricin, D., Hanak, R., Horvath, D., Mocan, M. L., Romanova, A., & Szabo, R. Z. (2023). Assessment of digital maturity: The role of resources and capabilities in digital transformation in B2B firms. *International Journal of Production Research*, *61*(23), 1–19. doi:10.1080/00207543.2022.2164087

Houy, C., Fettke, P., & Loos, P. (2010). Empirical research in business process management – analysis of an emerging field of research. *Business Process Management Journal*, *16*(4), 619–661. doi:10.1108/14637151011065946

Hu, N. (2017). On self-selection biases in online product reviews. MIS Quarterly: Management Information Systems, 41(2), 449–471. doi:10.25300/MISQ/2017/41.2.06

Huang, H. H., Hsu, J. S. C., & Ku, C. Y. (2012). Understanding the role of computer-mediated counter-argument in countering confirmation bias. *Decision Support Systems*, *53*(3), 438–447. doi:10.1016/j.dss.2012.03.009

Huang, Y., Li, K., & Li, P. (2023). Innovation ecosystems and national talent competitiveness: A country-based comparison using fsQCA. *Technological Forecasting and Social Change*, *194*, 122733. doi:10.1016/j.techfore.2023.122733

Huckstep, R. (2016). Insurance of Things–How IoT shows prevention is better than cure for insurers. *InsurTech Weekly*, *39*. https://www.the-digital-insurer.com/blog/insurtech-insurance-of-things-how-iot-shows-prevention-isbetter-than-cure-for-insurers/.

Hughes, L. (2003). Climate change and Australia: Trends, projections and impacts. *Austral Ecology*, *28*(4), 423–443. doi:10.1046/j.1442-9993.2003.01300.x

Humbani, M., & Wiese, M. (2019). An integrated framework for the adoption and continuance intention to use mobile payment apps. *International Journal of Bank Marketing*, *37*(2), 646–664. doi:10.1108/IJBM-03-2018-0072

Hussein, A. A., Haddad, F. H., & Al-Fayyadh, M. J. (2018). Cancer trends and incidence and mortality patterns in Jordan. *Asian Pacific Journal of Cancer Prevention*, *19*(3), 735–740.

Husted, B. W. (2005). Culture and ecology: A cross-national study of the determinants of environmental sustainability. *MIR. Management International Review*, 349–371.

Hu, X., He, L., & Liu, J. (2022). Status reinforcing: Unintended rating bias on online shopping platforms. *Journal of Retailing and Consumer Services*, *67*(102995), 102995. doi:10.1016/j.jretconser.2022.102995

Hu, X., He, L., & Liu, J. (2022). The power of beauty: Be your ideal self in online reviews—an empirical study based on face detection. *Journal of Retailing and Consumer Services*, *67*, 102975. doi:10.1016/j.jretconser.2022.102975

Hu, Y., & Liu, Q. (2023). Local Digital Economy and Corporate Social Responsibility. *Sustainability (Basel)*, *15*(11), 8487. https://doi-org.proxy.library.nyu.edu/10.3390/su15118487. doi:10.3390/su15118487

Hu, Y., & Zhou, S. (2023). Will reviewer recommendation source and cured status bias review helpfulness in online health community? *Online Information Review*, *47*(4), 680–696. doi:10.1108/OIR-05-2021-0248

Hwang, C. L., Yoon, K., Hwang, C. L., & Yoon, K. (1981). Methods for multiple attribute decision making. Multiple attribute decision making: methods and applications a state-of-the-art survey, 58-191. doi:10.1007/978-3-642-48318-9_3

Inan, D. I., Hidayanto, A. N., Juita, R., Soemawilaga, F. F., Melinda, F., Puspacinantya, P., & Amalia, Y. (2023). Service quality and self-determination theory towards continuance usage intention of mobile banking. *Journal of science and technology policy management, 14*(2), 303–328. doi:10.1108/JSTPM-01-2021-0005

Iñiguez de Onzoño, S., & Carmona, S. (2007). The changing business model of B-schools. *Journal of Management Development*, *26*(1), 22–32. doi:10.1108/02621710710720059

Intisar, R. A., Yaseen, M. R., Kousar, R., Usman, M., & Amjad Makhdum, M. S. (2020). Impact of Trade Openness and Human Capital on Economic Growth: A Comparative Investigation of Asian Countries. *Sustainability, 12*(7), 2930. https://doi. doi:org/10.3390/SU12072930

Ionaşcu, I., Ionaşcu, M., Nechita, E., Săcărin, M., & Minu, M. (2022). Digital transformation, financial performance and sustainability: Evidence for European Union listed companies. *Amfiteatru Economic*, *24*(59), 94–109. doi:10.24818/EA/2022/59/94

Irshad, A. U. R., Safdar, N., Younas, Z. I., & Manzoor, W. (2023). Impact of Corporate Governance on Firms' Environmental Performance: Case Study of Environmental Sustainability-Based Business Scenarios. *Sustainability (Basel)*, *15*(10), 7775. doi:10.3390/su15107775

Isensee, C., Teuteberg, F., Griese, K. M., & Topi, C. (2020). The relationship between organizational culture, sustainability, and digitalization in SMEs: A systematic review. *Journal of Cleaner Production*, *275*, 122944. doi:10.1016/j.jclepro.2020.122944

Ismayil, N., & Karagulle, O. A. (2023). *The Effect of Digitalization Process and Green Logistics Applications on Logistics Performance: Measuring Azerbaijan Logistics Companies* [Preprint]. SOCIAL SCIENCES. doi:10.20944/preprints202301.0189.v1

Ivanovic, D., Simovic, V., Domazet, I., & Antonijevic, M. (2021). Average Matching Levels for Two DigComp Competence Areas of the Female Entrepreneurs in Serbia. *JWEE*, (3-4), 42–60. doi:10.28934/jwee21.34.pp42-60

Jabr, W., Lohtia, R., Zhao, Y., & Guillory, M. D. (2022). Hidden power: Impact of the "snippet" on online consumer engagement. *Electronic Commerce Research and Applications*, *55*(101196), 101196. doi:10.1016/j.elerap.2022.101196

Jafari-Sadeghi, V., Garcia-Perez, A., Candelo, E., & Couturier, J. (2021). Exploring the impact of digital transformation on technology entrepreneurship and technological market expansion: The role of technology readiness, exploration and exploitation. *Journal of Business Research*, *124*, 100–111. doi:10.1016/j.jbusres.2020.11.020

Janurova, M., Chaloupkova, M., & Kunc, J. (2020). Smart city strategy and its implementation barriers: Czech experience. *Theoretical and Empirical Researches in Urban Management*, *15*(2), 5–21.

Jayarathna, C. P., Agdas, D., & Dawes, L. (2023). Exploring sustainable logistics practices toward a circular economy: A value creation perspective. *Business Strategy and the Environment*, *32*(1), 704–720. doi:10.1002/bse.3170

Jemal, A., Bray, F., Center, M. M., Ferlay, J., Ward, E., & Forman, D. (2011). Global cancer statistics. *CA: a Cancer Journal for Clinicians*, *61*(2), 69–90. doi:10.3322/caac.20107 PMID:21296855

Jenks, M., & Jones, C. (Eds.). (2010). *Dimensions of the sustainable city* (Vol. 2). Springer Science & Business Media.

Jeong, B. K., & Yoon, T. E. (2013). An Empirical Investigation on Consumer Acceptance of Mobile Banking Services. *Business and Management Research, 2*(1), 31–40. https://ideas.repec.org/a/jfr/bmr111/v2y2013i1p31-40.html

Jerene, W., & Sharma, D. (2020). The adoption of financial technology in Ethiopia: A study of bank customers perspective. *Journal of Banking and Financial Technology*, *4*(1), 53–63. doi:10.1007/s42786-020-00015-0

Jia, Q., Guo, Y., & Barnes, S. (2020). Understanding information bias: The perspective of online review component: An abstract. In Marketing Opportunities and Challenges in a Changing Global Marketplace (pp. 157–158). Springer. doi:10.1007/978-3-030-39165-2_69

Jiang, M., & Jia, P. (2022). Does the level of digitalized service drive the global export of digital service trade? Evidence from global perspective. *Telematics and Informatics*, *72*, 101853. doi:10.1016/j.tele.2022.101853

Jiao, H., Wang, L., & Shi, Y. (2022). How does institutional environment in the digital context affect technology entrepreneurship? The moderating roles of government digitalization and gender. *Journal of Organizational Change Management*, *35*(7), 1089–1112. doi:10.1108/JOCM-10-2021-0321

João, B., Nascimento, D., Souza, C. L. D., & Serralvo, F. A. (2020). A systematic review of smart cities and the internet of things as a research topic. *Cadernos EBAPE.BR*, *17*(4), 1115–1130. doi:10.1590/1679-395174442x

Jones, M. D., Hutcheson, S., & Camba, J. D. (2021). Past, present, and future barriers to digital transformation in manufacturing: A review. *Journal of Manufacturing Systems*, *60*, 936–948. doi:10.1016/j.jmsy.2021.03.006

Jordan Ministry of Health. (Annual Reports). Annual health statistics. Amman, Jordan: Ministry of Health.

Joseph, C. M. (2007). India-Bhutan relations: An overview. *Indian Foreign Affairs Journal*, *2*(1), 88–101. https://www.jstor.org/stable/45340648

Joyce, A., & Paquin, R. L. (2016). The triple layered business model canvas: A tool to design more sustainable business models. *Journal of Cleaner Production*, *135*, 1474–1486. doi:10.1016/j.jclepro.2016.06.067

Jurca, R., Garcin, F., Talwar, A., & Faltings, B. (2010). Reporting incentives and biases in online review forums. [TWEB]. *ACM Transactions on the Web*, *4*(2), 1–27. doi:10.1145/1734200.1734202

Kabakuş, A. K., & Küçükoğlu, H. (2022). THE EFFECT OF TRUST ON MOBILE BANKING USAGE: THE MEDIATING ROLES OF PERCEIVED USEFULNESS AND PERCEIVED EASE OF USE. *Ekonomski vjesnik/Econviews - Review of Contemporary Business. Entrepreneurship and Economic Issues*, *35*(2), 231–246. doi:10.51680/ev.35.2.1

Kache, F., & Seuring, S. (2017). Challenges and opportunities of digital information at the intersection of Big Data Analytics and supply chain management. *International Journal of Operations & Production Management*, *37*(1), 10–36. doi:10.1108/IJOPM-02-2015-0078

Kahneman, D., Lovallo, D., & Sibony, O. (2011). Before you make that big decision. *Harvard Business Review*, *89*(6), 50–60, 137. https://www.ncbi.nlm.nih.gov/pubmed/21714386 PMID:21714386

Kaklauskas, A., & Kaklauskiene, L. (2022). Analysis of the impact of success on three dimensions of sustainability in 173 countries. *Scientific Reports*, *12*(1), 14719. doi:10.1038/s41598-022-19131-6 PMID:36042278

Kalling, T. (2003). The business model concept: Theoretical underpinnings and empirical illustrations. *European Journal of Information Systems*, *12*(1), 49–59. doi:10.1057/palgrave.ejis.3000446

Kamal, N., Imran, M., & Tripati, N. K. (2017). Greening the Urban Environment Using Geospatial Techniques, A Case Study of Bangkok, Thailand. *Procedia Environmental Sciences*, *37*, 141–152. doi:10.1016/j.proenv.2017.03.030

Kamble, S. S., Mor, R. S., & Belhadi, A. (2023). Big Data Analytics for Supply Chain Transformation: A Systematic Literature Review Using SCOR Framework. In S. S. Kamble, R. S. Mor, & A. Belhadi (Eds.), *Digital Transformation and Industry 4.0 for Sustainable Supply Chain Performance* (pp. 1–50). Springer International Publishing., doi:10.1007/978-3-031-19711-6_1

Kane, G. C., Palmer, D., & Phillips, A. N. (2017). Achieving digital maturity. *MIT Sloan Management Review*.

Kang, Y., Zhao, C., & Battisti, M. (2022). Organizational learning in SMEs' internationalization: A moderated mediating effect of absorptive capacity. *Long Range Planning*, *55*(4), 102220. doi:10.1016/j.lrp.2022.102220

Kapkaev, Y., & Kadyrov, P. (2021). Digital maturity of territories during digital transformation. In *E3S Web of Conferences* (Vol. 258, p. 01001). EDP Sciences. doi:10.1051/e3sconf/202125801001

Karakuş, İ., & Kılıç, F. (2022). 'digital'Overview At The Profiles Of Pre-Service Teachers: Digital Awareness, Competence And Fluency. *Problems of Education in the 21st Century*, *80*(2), 324.

Karaman Kabadurmuş, F. N. (2019). The Relationship Between Logistics Performance and Innovation: An Empirical Study of Turkish Firms. *Alphanumeric Journal*, *7*(2), 157–172. doi:10.17093/alphanumeric.614170

Karaman, H. (2021). Online review solicitations reduce extremity bias in online review distributions and increase their representativeness. *Management Science*, *67*(7), 4420–4445. doi:10.1287/mnsc.2020.3758

Kariuki, D. W. (2021). ICT for Sustainability or Sustainability in ICT? A Review of the Role of ICT in Enhancing Sustainability versus the Need to Enhance Sustainability in ICT. *East African Journal of Information Technology*, *3*(1), 7–21. doi:10.37284/eajit.3.1.333

Kashima, Y. (2020). Cultural dynamics for sustainability: How can humanity craft cultures of sustainability? *Current Directions in Psychological Science*, *29*(6), 538–544. doi:10.1177/0963721420949516

Kastelli, I., Dimas, P., Stamopoulos, D., & Tsakanikas, A. (2022). Linking Digital Capacity to Innovation Performance: The Mediating Role of Absorptive Capacity. *Journal of the Knowledge Economy*. doi:10.1007/s13132-022-01092-w

Khan, F. N., Sana, A., & Arif, U. (2020). Information and communication technology (ICT) and environmental sustainability: A panel data analysis. *Environmental Science and Pollution Research International*, *27*(29), 36718–36731. doi:10.1007/s11356-020-09704-1 PMID:32566985

KHCC.jo - King Hussein Cancer Foundation and Center: Reference for the comprehensive care and skilled oncologists at King Hussein Cancer Center.

Kiiski, S., & Pohjola, M. (2002). Cross-country diffusion of the Internet. *Information Economics and Policy*, *14*(2), 297–310. doi:10.1016/S0167-6245(01)00071-3

Kim, H. M., Sabri, S., & Kent, A. (2021). Smart cities as a platform for technological and social innovation in productivity, sustainability, and livability: A conceptual framework. In *Smart cities for technological and social innovation* (pp. 9–28). Academic Press. doi:10.1016/B978-0-12-818886-6.00002-2

Kim, J. M., Kim, M., & Key, S. (2020). When profile photos matter: The roles of reviewer profile photos in the online review generation and consumption processes. *Journal of Research in Interactive Marketing*, *14*(4), 391–412. doi:10.1108/JRIM-10-2019-0163

Kleindorfer, P. R., Singhal, K., & Van Wassenhove, L. N. (2005). Sustainable operations management. *Production and Operations Management*, *14*(4), 482–492. doi:10.1111/j.1937-5956.2005.tb00235.x

Kobayashi, T., Ohshima, H., Oyama, S., & Tanaka, K. (2009, March). Modeling and analyzing review information on the web focusing on credibility. In *Proceedings of the 2009 ACM symposium on Applied Computing* (pp. 1316-1317). ACM. 10.1145/1529282.1529577

Köcher, S., Paluch, S., & Küsgen, S. (2016). The recommendation bias: The effects of social influence on individual rating behavior. In Marketing Challenges in a Turbulent Business Environment (pp. 353–354). Springer. doi:10.1007/978-3-319-19428-8_93

Koh, N. S., Hu, N., & Clemons, E. K. (2010). Do Online Reviews Reflect a Product's True Perceived Quality? - An Investigation of Online Movie Reviews Across Cultures. *2010 43rd Hawaii International Conference on System Sciences*, (pp. 1–10). IEEE. 10.1109/HICSS.2010.154

Kokkodis, M., & Lappas, T. (2020). Your hometown matters: Popularity-difference bias in online reputation platforms. *Information Systems Research*, *31*(2), 412–430. doi:10.1287/isre.2019.0895

Köksal, Y. A. D. P. (2015). An Investigation of the Important Factors Influence Web Trust in Online Shopping, *6*(1), 28–40. https://search.proquest.com/openview/39b4398d3c177cf881a6467140794ba7/1?pq-origsite=gscholar&cbl=2032031

Kong, Q., Peng, D., Ni, Y., Jiang, X., & Wang, Z. (2021). Trade openness and economic growth quality of China: Empirical analysis using ARDL model. *Finance Research Letters*, *38*, 101488. doi:10.1016/j.frl.2020.101488

Korachi, Z., & Bounabat, B. (2018, October). Data driven maturity model for assessing smart cities. In *Proceedings of the 2nd International Conference on Smart Digital Environment* (pp. 140-147). ACM. 10.1145/3289100.3289123

Kordzadeh, N. (2019). Investigating bias in the online physician reviews published on healthcare organizations' websites. *Decision Support Systems*, *118*, 70–82. doi:10.1016/j.dss.2018.12.007

Korucuk, S., Aytekin, A., Ecer, F., Pamucar, D. S. S., & Karamaşa, Ç. (2023). Assessment of ideal smart network strategies for logistics companies using an integrated picture fuzzy LBWA–CoCoSo framework. *Management Decision*, *61*(5), 1434–1462. doi:10.1108/MD-12-2021-1621

Kuan, K. (2015). What makes a review voted? An empirical investigation of review voting in online review systems. Journal of the Association for Information Systems, 16(1), 48–71. doi:10.17705/1jais.00386

Kuhlman, T., & Farrington, J. (2010). What is sustainability? *Sustainability (Basel)*, *2*(11), 3436–3448. doi:10.3390/su2113436

Kumar, A., Sah, B., Singh, A. R., Deng, Y., He, X., Kumar, P., & Bansal, R. C. (2017). A review of multi criteria decision making (MCDM) towards sustainable renewable energy development. *Renewable & Sustainable Energy Reviews*, *69*, 596–609. doi:10.1016/j.rser.2016.11.191

Kumar, R. R., Israel, D., & Malik, G. (2018). Explaining customer's continuance intention to use mobile banking apps with an integrative perspective of ECT and Self-determination theory. *Editorial Introduction*, *10*(2), 79–112. doi:10.17705/1pais.10204

Kummitha, R. K. R., & Crutzen, N. (2017). How do we understand smart cities? An evolutionary perspective. *Cities (London, England)*, *67*, 43–52. doi:10.1016/j.cities.2017.04.010

Kunkel, S., & Matthess, M. (2020). Digital transformation and environmental sustainability in industry: Putting expectations in Asian and African policies into perspective. *Environmental Science & Policy*, *112*, 318–329. doi:10.1016/j.envsci.2020.06.022

Kupilas, K. J., Montequin, V. R., González, J. G., & Iglesias, G. A. (2023). Digital maturity model for research and development organization with the aspect of sustainability. *Procedia Computer Science, 219*, 1583–1590. doi:10.1016/j.procs.2023.01.450

Kutnjak, A. (2021). Covid-19 Accelerates Digital Transformation in Industries: Challenges, Issues, Barriers and Problems in Transformation. *Ieee Access*. doi:10.1109/ACCESS.2021.3084801

Kwilinski, A., Vyshnevskyi, O., & Dzwigol, H. (2020). Digitalization of the EU Economies and People at Risk of Poverty or Social Exclusion. *Journal of Risk and Financial Management, 13*(7), 142. https://doi. doi:org/10.3390/JRFM13070142

Kwilinski, A., Lyulyov, O., & Pimonenko, T. (2023). Environmental Sustainability within Attaining Sustainable Development Goals: The Role of Digitalization and the Transport Sector. *Sustainability (Basel), 15*(14), 11282. doi:10.3390/su151411282

Kwon, H. B., & Lee, J. (2019). Exploring the differential impact of environmental sustainability, operational efficiency, and corporate reputation on market valuation in high-tech-oriented firms. *International Journal of Production Economics, 211*, 1–14. doi:10.1016/j.ijpe.2019.01.034

Lambert, D. M., Cooper, M., & Pagh, J. D. (1998). Supply Chain Management: Implementation Issues and Research Opportunities. *International Journal of Logistics Management, 9*(2), 1–20. doi:10.1108/09574099810805807

Lara, A. P., Da Costa, E. M., Furlani, T. Z., & Yigitcanlar, T. (2016). Smartness that matters: Towards a comprehensive and human-centred characterisation of smart cities. *Journal of Open Innovation, 2*(2), 1–13. doi:10.1186/s40852-016-0034-z

Latora, A. G., Compagno, L., & Trapani, N. (2018). A decision support tool for business model analysis. International. *Journal of the Analytic Hierarchy Process, 10*(2). doi:10.13033/ijahp.v10i2.516

Laukkanen, T. (2017). Mobile banking. *International Journal of Bank Marketing, 35*(7), 1042–1043. doi:10.1108/IJBM-10-2017-0218

Laursen, K., & Salter, A. (2006). Open for innovation: The role of openness in explaining innovation performance among UK manufacturing firms. *Strategic Management Journal, 27*(2), 131–150. doi:10.1002/smj.507

Leão, P., & da Silva, M. M. (2021). Impacts of digital transformation on firms' competitive advantages: A systematic literature review. *Strategic Change, 30*(5), 421–441. doi:10.1002/jsc.2459

Lee-Geiller, S., & Lee, T. (2022). How Does Digital Governance Contribute to Effective Crisis Management? A Case Study of Korea's Response to COVID-19. *Public Performance & Management Review, 45*(4), 860–893. doi:10.1080/15309576.2022.2054434

Lee, H., & Lee, K. (2021). The Effects of Technology Innovation Activity on CSR: Emphasizing the Nonlinear and Heterogeneous Effects. *Sustainability (Basel), 13*(19), 10893. doi:10.3390/su131910893

Lee, K. (2021). A systematic review on social sustainability of artificial intelligence in product design. *Sustainability (Basel), 13*(5), 2668. doi:10.3390/su13052668

Lee, P., Hu, Y., & Lu, K. (2018). Assessing the helpfulness of online hotel reviews: A classification-based approach. *Telematics and Informatics, 35*(2), 436–445. doi:10.1016/j.tele.2018.01.001

Le, H. B. H., Ngo, C. T., Trinh, T. T. H., & Nguyen, T. T. P. (2020). Factor affecting customers' decision to use mobile banking service: A case of Thanh Hoa province, Vietnam. *Journal of Asian Finance Economics and Business, 7*(2), 205–212. doi:10.13106/jafeb.2020.vol7.no2.205

Lei, Z., Yin, D., & Zhang, H. (2023). Positive or Negative Reviews? Consumers' Selective Exposure in Seeking and Evaluating Online Reviews. *Journal of the Association for Information Systems*, *24*(4), 1162–1183. doi:10.17705/1jais.00823

Lekan, M., & Rogers, H. A. (2020). Digitally enabled diverse economies: Exploring socially inclusive access to the circular economy in the city. *Urban Geography*, *41*(6), 898–901. doi:10.1080/02723638.2020.1796097

Lema, A. (2017). Factors influencing the adoption of mobile financial services in the unbanked population. Inkanyiso. *Journal of the Humanities and Social Sciences*, *9*(1), 37–51.

Lennerfors, T. T., Fors, P., & van Rooijen, J. (2015). ICT and environmental sustainability in a changing society: The view of ecological World Systems Theory. *Information Technology & People*, *28*(4), 758–774. doi:10.1108/ITP-09-2014-0219

Liang, S., Chu, Y., Wang, Y., Zhang, Z., Wu, Y., & Chang, Y. (2021). 'scapegoat' for offline consumption: Online review response to social exclusion. *Frontiers in Psychology*, *12*, 783483. doi:10.3389/fpsyg.2021.783483 PMID:34925186

Li, C.-Y., & Fang, Y.-H. (2019). Predicting continuance intention toward mobile branded apps through satisfaction and attachment. *Telematics and Informatics*, *43*, 101248. doi:10.1016/j.tele.2019.101248

Li, H., Meng, F., & Pan, B. (2020). How does review disconfirmation influence customer online review behavior? A mixed-method investigation. *International Journal of Contemporary Hospitality Management*, *32*(11), 3685–3703. doi:10.1108/IJCHM-03-2020-0234

Li, H., Zhang, Z., Meng, F., & Janakiraman, R. (2017). Is peer evaluation of consumer online reviews socially embedded? – An examination combining reviewer's social network and social identity. *International Journal of Hospitality Management*, *67*, 143–153. doi:10.1016/j.ijhm.2017.08.003

Lim, A. J., Village, J., Salustri, F. A., & Neumann, W. P. (2014). Process mapping as a tool for participative integration of human factors into work system design. *European Journal of Industrial Engineering*, *8*(2), 273–290. doi:10.1504/EJIE.2014.060477

Lim, S., & Tucker, C. S. (2017). Mitigating Online Product Rating Biases Through the Discovery of Optimistic, Pessimistic, and Realistic Reviewers. *Journal of Mechanical Design*, *139*(11), 111409. doi:10.1115/1.4037612

Lin, C., & Ho, Y. (2009). RFID technology adoption and supply chain performance: An empirical study in China's logistics industry. *Supply Chain Management*, *14*(5), 369–378. doi:10.1108/13598540910980288

Lindkvist, C., Temeljotov Salaj, A., Collins, D., Bjørberg, S., & Haugen, T. B. (2021). Exploring urban facilities management approaches to increase connectivity in smart cities. *Facilities*, *39*(1/2), 96–112. doi:10.1108/F-08-2019-0095

Linkov, I., Trump, B., Poinsatte-Jones, K., & Florin, M.-V. (2018). Governance Strategies for a Sustainable Digital World. *Sustainability (Basel)*, *10*(2), 440. doi:10.3390/su10020440

Linnenluecke, M. K., & Griffiths, A. (2010). Corporate sustainability and organizational culture. *Journal of World Business*, *45*(4), 357–366. doi:10.1016/j.jwb.2009.08.006

Li, R., Rao, J., & Wan, L. (2022). The digital economy, enterprise digital transformation, and enterprise innovation. *MDE. Managerial and Decision Economics*, *43*(7), 2875–2886. doi:10.1002/mde.3569

Li, R., Xin, Y., Sotnyk, I., Kubatko, O., Almashaqbeh, I., Fedyna, S., & Prokopenko, O. (2022). Energy poverty and energy efficiency in emerging economies. *International Journal of Environment and Pollution*, *69*(1/2), 1–21. doi:10.1504/IJEP.2021.125188

Liu, Q. B., & Karahanna, E. (2017). The dark side of reviews: The swaying effects of online product reviews on attribute preference construction. MIS Quarterly: Management. *Management Information Systems Quarterly, 41*(2), 427–448. doi:10.25300/MISQ/2017/41.2.05

Liu, Y., & Hu, H. (2021). Online review helpfulness: The moderating effects of review comprehensiveness. *International Journal of Contemporary Hospitality Management, 33*(2), 534–556. doi:10.1108/IJCHM-08-2020-0856

Liu, Y., Song, Y., Sun, J., Sun, C., Liu, C., & Chen, X. (2020). Understanding the relationship between food experiential quality and customer dining satisfaction: A perspective on negative bias. *International Journal of Hospitality Management, 87*(102381), 102381. doi:10.1016/j.ijhm.2019.102381

Li, Y., Shi, C., Zhao, H., Zhuang, F., & Wu, B. (2016). Aspect mining with rating bias. In Machine Learning and Knowledge Discovery in Databases: European Conference. *Proceedings, 16*(Part II), 458–474.

Lobacz, K., & Szanter, R. (2022). Measuring innovation process digitalisation in SMEs - a methodological approach. *Procedia Computer Science, 207*, 3520–3529. doi:10.1016/j.procs.2022.09.411

Longoni, A., & Cagliano, R. (2015). Environmental and social sustainability priorities: Their integration in operations strategies. *International Journal of Operations & Production Management, 35*(2), 216–245. doi:10.1108/IJOPM-04-2013-0182

Lucidchart. (2023a). *What is a data flow diagram?* Lucidchart. https://www.lucidchart.com/pages/data-flow-diagram

Lucidchart. (2023b). *What is a Flowchart.* Lucidchart. https://www.lucidchart.com/pages/what-is-a-flowchart-tutorial

Lukić, V., Čolić, L., & Prica, I. (2019). Perspectives and adoption of mobile banking in Serbia: The case of young adults. *Ekonomika preduzeca, 67*(5-6), 334–344. doi:10.5937/EKOPRE1906334L

Lyons, G., Mokhtarian, P., Dijst, M., & Böcker, L. (2018). The dynamics of urban metabolism in the face of digitalization and changing lifestyles: Understanding and influencing our cities. *Resources, Conservation and Recycling, 132*, 246–257. doi:10.1016/j.resconrec.2017.07.032

Macedo de Morais, R., Kazan, S., de Pádua, S. I. D., & Costa, A. L. (2014). An analysis of BPM lifecycles: From a literature review to a framework proposal. *Business Process Management Journal, 20*(3), 412–432. doi:10.1108/BPMJ-03-2013-0035

Magon, R. B., Thomé, A. M. T., Ferrer, A. L. C., & Scavarda, L. F. (2018). Sustainability and performance in operations management research. *Journal of Cleaner Production, 190*, 104–117. doi:10.1016/j.jclepro.2018.04.140

Majeed, M. T. (2018). Information and communication technology (ICT) and environmental sustainability in developed and developing countries. *Pakistan Journal of Commerce and Social Sciences, 12*(3), 758–783.

Majumder, M., & Majumder, M. (2015*). Multi criteria decision making. Impact of urbanization on water shortage in face of climatic aberrations*, 35-47. doi:10.1007/978-981-4560-73-3_2

Malaquias, R. F., & Hwang, Y. (2019). Mobile banking use: A comparative study with Brazilian and U.S. participants. *International Journal of Information Management, 44*, 132–140. doi:10.1016/j.ijinfomgt.2018.10.004

Malkawi, B. H. (2019). Digitalization of International Trade. *The Journal of Law and Technology, 23*. https://philpapers.org/rec/MALDOI

Marans, R. W. (2015). Quality of urban life & environmental sustainability studies: Future linkage opportunities. *Habitat International, 45*, 47–52. doi:10.1016/j.habitatint.2014.06.019

Marinescu, I., Chamberlain, A., Smart, M., & Klein, N. (2021). Incentives can reduce bias in online employer reviews. *Journal of Experimental Psychology. Applied, 27*(2), 393–407. doi:10.1037/xap0000342 PMID:33764122

Marinković, V., Đorđević, A., & Kalinić, Z. (2020). The moderating effects of gender on customer satisfaction and continuance intention in mobile commerce: A UTAUT-based perspective. *Technology Analysis and Strategic Management, 32*(3), 306–318. doi:10.1080/09537325.2019.1655537

Market Analysis Division, Office of Consumer Protection, Department of Trade. (2022). Econpmic Research. Market Analysis Division, Office of Consumer Protection. [https://www.moice.gov.bt/wp-content/uploads/2023/04/Ecommerce-Research-MAD.pdf]

Martin, C. J., Evans, J., & Karvonen, A. (2018). Smart and sustainable? Five tensions in the visions and practices of the smart-sustainable city in Europe and North America. *Technological Forecasting and Social Change, 133*, 269–278. doi:10.1016/j.techfore.2018.01.005

Martínez-Bravo, M., & Martínez-del-Río, J. (2019). Urban pollution and emission reduction. Sustainable Cities and Communities. Encyclopedia of the UN Sustainable Development Goals, 1-11.

Martínez-Jurado, P. J., & Moyano-Fuentes, J. (2014). Lean Management, Supply Chain Management and Sustainability: A Literature Review. *Journal of Cleaner Production, 85*, 134–150. doi:10.1016/j.jclepro.2013.09.042

Marzban, S., & Asutay, M. (2015). Alternative ways of developing GCC Islamic funds industry: Entrepreneurial development. In M. Asutay & A. Turkistani (Eds.), *Islamic Finance: Political Economy Perspectives*. Gerlach.

Mason-Jones, R., & Towill, D. R. (1999). Using the Information Decoupling Point to Improve Supply Chain Performance. *International Journal of Logistics Management, 10*(2), 13–26. doi:10.1108/09574099910805969

Mathison, S. (2005). *Increasing the outreach and sustainability of microfinance through ICT innovation*. Electronic Banking with the Poor, The Foundation for Development Cooperation.

Matthess, M., & Kunkel, S. (2020). Structural change and digitalization in developing countries: Conceptually linking the two transformations. *Technology in Society, 63*, 101428. doi:10.1016/j.techsoc.2020.101428

McCarthy, B. (2008). Case study of an artists' retreat in Ireland: An exploration of its business model. *Social Enterprise Journal, 4*(2), 136–148. doi:10.1108/17508610810902020

Mehraliyev, F., Kirilenko, A. P., & Choi, Y. (2020). From measurement scale to sentiment scale: Examining the effect of sensory experiences on online review rating behavior. *Tourism Management, 79*, 104096. doi:10.1016/j.tourman.2020.104096

Melkonyan, A., & Gottschalk, D., & VP, V. K. (. (2017). Sustainability assessments and their implementation possibilities within the business models of companies. *Sustainable Production and Consumption, 12*, 1–15. doi:10.1016/j.spc.2017.04.001

Melnyk, S. A., Sroufe, R., & Calantone, R. J. (2002). Assessing the Impact of Environmental Management Systems on Corporate and Environmental Performance. *Journal of Operations Management*. doi:10.1016/S0272-6963(02)00109-2

Melville, N. P. (2010). Information systems innovation for environmental sustainability. *Management Information Systems Quarterly, 34*(1), 1–21. doi:10.2307/20721412

Mergel, I., Edelmann, N., & Haug, N. (2019). Defining digital transformation: Results from expert interviews. *Government Information Quarterly, 36*(4), 101385. doi:10.1016/j.giq.2019.06.002

Merhi, M., Hone, K., & Tarhini, A. (2019). A cross-cultural study of the intention to use mobile banking between Lebanese and British consumers: Extending UTAUT2 with security, privacy and trust. *Technology in Society, 59*, 101151. doi:10.1016/j.techsoc.2019.101151

Methlie, L. B., & Pedersen, P. E. (2007). Business model choices for value creation of mobile services. *info, 9*(5), 70-85. doi:10.1108/14636690710816462

Meyer, K., Li, J., Brouthers, K. D., & Jean, R. B. (2023). International business in the digital age: Global strategies in a World of National Institutions. *Journal of International Business Studies, 54*(4), 577–598. doi:10.1057/s41267-023-00618-x PMID:37305175

Miethlich, B., Belotserkovich, D., Abasova, S., Zatsarinnaya, E., & Veselitsky, O. (2020). Digital economy and its influence on competitiveness of countries and regions. *Revista espacios, 41*(12). http://ww.revistaespacios.com/a20v41n12/20411220.html

Millwood, A. (2015). *How star ratings influence customers' behavior.* Yotpo. https://www. yotpo.com/blog/star-ratings-influence-customers

Mini, T., & Widjaja, T. (2019). *Tensions in Digital Platform Business Models: A Literature Review.* ICIS.

Missimer, M. (2015). *Social sustainability within the framework for strategic sustainable development* [Doctoral dissertation, Blekinge Tekniska Högskola].

Missimer, M., Robèrt, K. H., & Broman, G. (2017). A strategic approach to social sustainability–Part 1: Exploring the social system. *Journal of Cleaner Production, 140*, 32–41. doi:10.1016/j.jclepro.2016.03.170

Modgil, S., Dwivedi, Y. K., Rana, N., Gupta, S., & Kamble, S. (2021). Has Covid-19 accelerated opportunities for digital entrepreneurship? An Indian perspective. *Technological Forecasting and Social Change, 175*(6), 121415. doi:10.1016/j.techfore.2021.121415 PMID:36536802

Moeini Gharagozloo, M. M., Askarzadeh, F., & Moeini Gharagozloo, A. (2021). More power for international entrepreneurs: The effect of digital readiness of economies on channeling national R&D resources to entrepreneurship. *Journal of International Entrepreneurship, 20*(3), 474–502. doi:10.1007/s10843-021-00296-6

Moktan, S. (2007). Development of small and medium enterprises in Bhutan: Analysing constraints to growth. *South Asian Survey, 14*(2), 251–282. doi:10.1177/097152310701400205

Moldabekova, A., Philipp, R., Reimers, H.-E., & Alikozhayev, B. (2021). Digital Technologies for Improving Logistics Performance of Countries. *Transport and Telecommunication Journal, 22*(2), 207–216. doi:10.2478/ttj-2021-0016

Monzon, A. (2015, May). Smart cities concept and challenges: Bases for the assessment of smart city projects. In 2015 international conference on smart cities and green ICT systems (SMARTGREENS) (pp. 1-11). IEEE.

Moore, K. R. (1998). Trust and Relationship Commitment in Logistics Alliances: A Buyer Perspective. *International Journal of Purchasing and Materials Management, 34*(4), 24–37. doi:10.1111/j.1745-493X.1998.tb00039.x

Morais, P., & Camanho, A. S. (2011). Evaluation of performance of European cities with the aim to promote quality of life improvements. [Elsevier.]. *Omega, 39*(4), 398–409. doi:10.1016/j.omega.2010.09.003

Munim, Z. H., & Schramm, H.-J. (2018). The impacts of port infrastructure and logistics performance on economic growth: The mediating role of seaborne trade. *Journal of Shipping and Trade, 3*(1), 1. doi:10.1186/s41072-018-0027-0

Muthuraman, S. (2020). Digital business models for sustainability. *Gedrag Organizational Review, 33*, 1095–1102.

Myovella, G., Karacuka, M., & Haucap, J. (2020). Digitalization and economic growth: A comparative analysis of Sub-Saharan Africa and OECD economies. *Telecommunications Policy, 44*(2), 101856. doi:10.1016/j.telpol.2019.101856

N'dri, L. M., Islam, M., & Kakinaka, M. (2021). ICT and environmental sustainability: Any differences in developing countries? *Journal of Cleaner Production, 297*, 126642. doi:10.1016/j.jclepro.2021.126642

Nadeem, A., Abedin, B., Cerpa, N., & Chew, E. (2018). Editorial: Digital Transformation &Amp;amp; Digital Business Strategy in Electronic Commerce—The Role of Organizational Capabilities. *Journal of Theoretical and Applied Electronic Commerce Research*, *13*(2), I–VIII. Advance online publication. doi:10.4067/S0718-18762018000200101

Nakayama, M., & Wan, Y. (2019). Cross-cultural examination on content bias and helpfulness of online reviews: Sentiment balance at the aspect level for a subjective good. *Proceedings of the 52nd Hawaii International Conference on System Sciences*. HDL. http://hdl.handle.net/10125/59555

Nambisan, S., Lyytinen, K., Majchrzak, A., & Song, M. (2017). Digital innovation management: Reinventing innovation management research in a digital world. *Management Information Systems Quarterly*, *41*(1), 223–238. doi:10.25300/MISQ/2017/41:1.03

Nam, T., & Pardo, T. A. (2011, June). Conceptualizing smart city with dimensions of technology, people, and institutions. In *Proceedings of the 12th annual international digital government research conference: digital government innovation in challenging times* (pp. 282-291). ACM. 10.1145/2037556.2037602

National Cancer Institute. (2018). Surveillance, Epidemiology, and End Results Program. *SEER Cancer Statistics Review*. Bethesda, MD: National Cancer Institute.

National Statistical Bureau. (2022). *Bhutan Living Standard Survey-2022*. NSB. https://www.nsb.gov.bt/wp-content/uploads/ dlm_uploads/2022/12/Updated-BLSS-2022.pdf

National Statistics Bureau. (2020a). *2020 Labour Force Survey Report*. NSB. https://www.nsb.gov.bt/wp-content/uploads/dlm_uploads/2021/04/2020-Labour-Force-Survey-Report.pdf

Navarro-Galera, A., Rodríguez-Bolívar, M. P., Alcaide-Muñoz, L., & López-Subires, M. D. (2016). Measuring the financial sustainability and its influential factors in local governments. *Applied Economics*, *48*(41), 3961–3975. doi:10.1080/00036846.2016.1148260

Naylor, R. W., Lamberton, C. P., & Norton, D. A. (2011). Seeing ourselves in others: Reviewer ambiguity, egocentric anchoring, and persuasion. *JMR, Journal of Marketing Research*, *48*(3), 617–631. doi:10.1509/jmkr.48.3.617

Nesdoly, N., Tulk, C., & Mantler, J. (2020). The effects of perceived professor competence, warmth and gender on students' likelihood to register for a course. *Assessment & Evaluation in Higher Education*, *45*(5), 666–679. doi:10.1080/02602938.2019.1689381

Nguyen, T. T. P., Van Nguyen, A., & Han, S.-L. (2021). The Role of Trust Factors Toward Technological Innovation in Explaining the Effects of CSR Concerns on Mobile Banking Adoption: A Comparative Study Between Vietnam and South Korea. *Academy of Asian Business Review*, *7*(1). https://repository.hanyang.ac.kr/handle/20.500.11754/176357

Nguyen, N. M., Hoai, T. T., Vo, H. V., & Nguyen, N. P. (2023). Digital approach toward environmental sustainability in supply chains: Evidence from Vietnamese firms. *Sustainable Development (Bradford)*, *31*(5), 3303–3317. doi:10.1002/sd.2586

Nicolau, J. L., de Carlos Villamarín, P., Alén, E., & González, A. P. (2022). Asymmetric effects of extreme-moderate online reviews in the language-satisfaction relationship. *Tourism Management*, *91*, 104524. doi:10.1016/j.tourman.2022.104524

Nidumolu, R., Prahalad, C. K., & Rangaswami, M. R. (2013). Why Sustainability is now the key driver of innovation. *IEEE Engineering Management Review*, *41*(2), 30–38. doi:10.1109/EMR.2013.6601104

Nikou, S., Mark, D. R., & Matin, M. K. (2022). Workplace literacy skills—How information and digital literacy affect adoption of digital technology. *The Journal of Documentation*, *78*(7), 371–391. doi:10.1108/JD-12-2021-0241

Niu, Y., Wen, W., Wang, S., & Li, S. (2023). Breaking barriers to innovation: The power of digital transformation. *Finance Research Letters*, *51*, 103457. doi:10.1016/j.frl.2022.103457

Nosratabadi, S., Pinter, G., Mosavi, A., & Semperger, S. (2020). Sustainable banking; evaluation of the European business models. *Sustainability (Basel)*, *12*(6), 2314. doi:10.3390/su12062314

Novitasari, D., Juliana, J., Asbari, M., & Purwanto, A. (2021). The Effect of Financial Literacy, Parents' Social Economic and Student Lifestyle on Students Personal Financial Management. *Economic Education Analysis Journal, 10*(3), 522–531. https://journal.unnes.ac.id/sju/index.php/eeaj/article/view/50721

Nüesch, R., Alt, R., & Puschmann, T. (2015). Hybrid customer interaction. *Business & Information Systems Engineering*, *57*(1), 73–78. doi:10.1007/s12599-014-0366-9

Nur, Y. A., & Wahyuni, Rr. E., Saidah, D., & Octaviani, R. D. (2018). *INFORMATION TECHNOLOGY, GREEN INITIATIVES AND ORGANIZATIONAL PERFORMANCE: CONTINGENCY MODELS.* Global Research on Sustainable Transport (GROST 2017), Jakarta, Indonesia. 10.2991/grost-17.2018.26

Object Management Group. (2012). *Business Process Model and Notation. Lecture Notes in Business Information Processing* (*Vol. 125 LNBIP*). doi:10.1007/978-3-642-33155-8

Ochara, N. M., & Mawela, T. (2015). Enabling social sustainability of e-participation through mobile technology. *Information Technology for Development*, *21*(2), 205–228. doi:10.1080/02681102.2013.833888

Ochoa-Urrego, R. L., & Peña-Reyes, J. I. (2021). Digital maturity models: a systematic literature review. *Digitalization: Approaches, Case Studies, and Tools for Strategy, Transformation and Implementation*, 71-85.

Ode, E., & Avavoo, R. (2020). The mediating role of knowledge application in the relationship between knowledge management practices and firm innovations. *Journal of Innovation & Knowledge*, *5*(3), 210–218. doi:10.1016/j.jik.2019.08.002

OECD. (2012). Redefining urban: A new way to measure metropolitan areas. Organisation for Economic Cooperation and Development (OECD).

Okorie, O., Russell, J., Cherrington, R., Fisher, O., & Charnley, F. (2023). Digital transformation and the circular economy: Creating a competitive advantage from the transition towards Net Zero Manufacturing. *Resources, Conservation and Recycling*, *189*, 106756. doi:10.1016/j.resconrec.2022.106756

Oláh, J., Popp, J., Khan, M. A., & Kitukutha, N. (2023). Sustainable E-Commerce and Environmental Impact on Sustainability. *Economics & Sociology (Ternopil)*, *16*(1), 85–105. doi:10.14254/2071-789X.2023/16-1/6

Olhager, J. (2010). The role of the customer order decoupling point in production and supply chain management. *Computers in Industry*, *61*(9), 863–868. doi:10.1016/j.compind.2010.07.011

Opening of Cottage and Small Industry (CSI) Market. (2023). *Paro | MoICE* | བཟོ་གྲྭ་ཚོང་ལས་དང་ལཱ་གཡོག་ལྷན་ཁག།. Ministry of Industry, Commerce and Employment. www.moice.gov.bt/?p=265901. Accessed 16 Sept. 2023.

Ordieres-Meré, J., Prieto Remón, T., & Rubio, J. (2020). Digitalization: An Opportunity for Contributing to Sustainability From Knowledge Creation. *Sustainability (Basel)*, *12*(4), 1460. doi:10.3390/su12041460

Ortiz-Martínez, E., Marín-Hernández, S., & Santos-Jaén, J.-M. (2023). Sustainability, corporate social responsibility, non-financial reporting and company performance: Relationships and mediating effects in Spanish small and medium sized enterprises. *Sustainable Production and Consumption*, *35*, 349–364. doi:10.1016/j.spc.2022.11.015

Osiyevskyy, O., & Dewald, J. (2015). Explorative versus exploitative business model change: The cognitive antecedents of firm-level responses to disruptive innovation. *Strategic Entrepreneurship Journal*, *9*(1), 58–78. doi:10.1002/sej.1192

Osman, H., D'Acunto, D., & Johns, N. (2019). Home and away: Why do consumers shy away from reporting negative experiences in the peer-to-peer realms? *Psychology and Marketing*, *36*(12), 1162–1175. doi:10.1002/mar.21264

Osterwalder, A., & Pigneur, Y. (2002). *An eBusiness model ontology for modeling eBusiness*. AIS. https://aisel.aisnet.org/bled2002/2

Osterwalder, A., Pigneur, Y., & Tucci, C. L. (2005). Clarifying business models: Origins, present, and future of the concept. *Communications of the Association for Information Systems*, *16*(1), 1. doi:10.17705/1CAIS.01601

Ourzik, V. Y. (2022). Customer Knowledge Management: A Systematic Literature Review and Agenda for Future Research. *Proceedings of the European Conference on Knowledge Management, ECKM*, *23*(2), 1384–1394. 10.34190/eckm.23.2.780

Ozcan, T., Hair, M., & Hattat, A. M. (2022). Eric is bad, but Erica is worse: Greater negativity bias toward female brands. *Journal of Marketing Theory and Practice*, 1–16. doi:10.1080/10696679.2022.2067066

Pagell, M., & Wu, Z. (2009). Building a More Complete Theory of Sustainable Supply Chain Management Using Case Studies of 10 Exemplars. *The Journal of Supply Chain Management*, *45*(2), 37–56. Advance online publication. doi:10.1111/j.1745-493X.2009.03162.x

Paiva Vianna, K. M., Cardoso, M. R. A., & Rodrigues, R. M. C. (2015). Noise pollution and annoyance: An urban soundscapes study. *Noise & Health*, *17*(76), 125. doi:10.4103/1463-1741.155833 PMID:25913551

Pallant, J. (2020). *SPSS Survival Manual: A Step by Step Guide to Data Analysis using IBM SPSS*. McGraw-Hill Education (UK). https://play.google.com/store/books/details?id=CxUsEAAAQBAJ

Panagariya, A. (2023, July). How India's economy will overtake the US.'s. *Time*, *28*. time.com/6297539/how-india-economy-will-surpass-us/

Pan, X., Sinha, P., & Chen, X. (2020). Corporate social responsibility and eco-innovation: The triple bottom line perspective. *Corporate Social Responsibility and Environmental Management*, *28*(1), 214–228. doi:10.1002/csr.2043

Paris, B., Michas, D., Balafoutis, A. T., Nibbi, L., Skvaril, J., Li, H., Pimentel, D., da Silva, C., Athanasopoulou, E., Petropoulos, D., & Apostolopoulos, N. (2023). A Review of the Current Practices of Bioeconomy Education and Training in the EU. *Sustainability (Basel)*, *15*(2), 954. doi:10.3390/su15020954

Park, C., & Jun, J. (2003). A cross-cultural comparison of Internet buying behavior: Effects of Internet usage, perceived risks, and innovativeness. *International Marketing Review*, *20*(5), 534–553. doi:10.1108/02651330310498771

Parker, G. G., Van Alstyne, M. W., & Choudary, S. P. (2016). *Platform Revolution: How Networked Markets Are Transforming the Economy—And How to Make Them Work for You*. W. W. Norton & Company.https://www.injaplus.ir/wp-content/uploads/2023/05/Platform_Revolution_Previewinjaplus.ir_.pdf

Pawlewski, P. (2010). *Petri Nets: Applications*.

Peeters, G., & Czapinski, J. (1990). Positive-negative asymmetry in evaluations: The dis- tinction between affective and informational negativity effects. *European Review of Social Psychology*, *1*(1), 33–60. doi:10.1080/14792779108401856

Peng, Y., & Tao, C. (2022). Can digital transformation promote enterprise performance?—From the perspective of public policy and innovation. *Journal of Innovation & Knowledge*, *7*(3), 100198. doi:10.1016/j.jik.2022.100198

Pereira, C. S., Durão, N., Moreira, F., & Veloso, B. (2022). The Importance of Digital Transformation in International Business. *Sustainability*, *14*(2), 834. https://doi. doi:org/10.3390/SU14020834

Pereira, C. S., Durão, N., Moreira, F., & Veloso, B. (2022). The importance of digital transformation in international business. *Sustainability (Basel)*, *14*(2), 834. doi:10.3390/su14020834

Pérez González, D., & Díaz Díaz, R. (2015). *Public services provided with ICT in the smart city environment: the case of spanish cities.*

Peter, M. K. (Ed.). (2017). *SME transformation. Successfully implement digital transformation as an SME. Research results and practical guidelines.* Olten: FHNW. https://kmu-transformation.ch/digitale-nachrichten/

Petrović, M., Rajin, D., Milenković, D., & Marić, D. (2021). The influence of eWOM on the use of mobile banking. *Ekonomika preduzeca, 69*(3-4), 95–104. doi:10.5937/EKOPRE2102095P

Pfajfar, G., Shoham, A., Małecka, A., & Zalaznik, M. (2022). Value of Corporate Social Responsibility for Multiple Stakeholders and Social Impact – Relationship Marketing Perspective. *Journal of Business Research, 143*, 46–61. doi:10.1016/j.jbusres.2022.01.051

Piccarozzi, M., Silvestri, C., Aquilani, B., & Silvestri, L. (2022). Is this a new story of the 'Two Giants'? A systematic literature review of the relationship between industry 4.0, sustainability and its pillars. *Technological Forecasting and Social Change, 177*, 121511. doi:10.1016/j.techfore.2022.121511

Piecyk, M. I., & Björklund, M. (2015). Logistics service providers and corporate social responsibility: Sustainability reporting in the logistics industry. *International Journal of Physical Distribution & Logistics Management, 45*(5), 459–485. doi:10.1108/IJPDLM-08-2013-0228

Pinzone, M., Albè, F., Orlandelli, D., Barletta, I., Berlin, C., Johansson, B., & Taisch, M. (2020). A framework for operative and social sustainability functionalities in Human-Centric Cyber-Physical Production Systems. *Computers & Industrial Engineering, 139*, 105132. doi:10.1016/j.cie.2018.03.028

Piramuthu, S., Kapoor, G., Zhou, W., & Mauw, S. (2012). Input online review data and related bias in recommender systems. *Decision Support Systems, 53*(3), 418–424. doi:10.1016/j.dss.2012.02.006

Plotkina, D., Munzel, A., & Pallud, J. (2020). Illusions of truth—Experimental insights into human and algorithmic detections of fake online reviews. *Journal of Business Research, 109*, 511–523. doi:10.1016/j.jbusres.2018.12.009

Polančič, G., & Jošt, G. (2016). The impact of the representatives of three types of process modeling tools on modeler's perceptions and performance. *Journal of Software (Malden, MA), 28*(12), 27–56. doi:10.1002/smr.1764

Poromatikul, C., Peter, D. M., Leelapanyalert, K., & Zaby, S. (2019). Drivers of continuance intention with mobile banking apps. *International Journal of Bank Marketing, 38*(1), 242–262. doi:10.1108/IJBM-08-2018-0224

Porter, M. E., & Heppelmann, J. E. (2015). How smart, connected products are transforming companies. *Harvard Business Review, 93(*10), 96-114. http://www.knowledgesol.com/uploads/2/4/3/9/24393270/hbr-how-smart-connected-products-are-transforming-companies.pdf

Portney, K. E. (2015). *Sustainability*. MIT Press.

Pousttchi, K., Schiessler, M., & Wiedemann, D. G. (2007, July). Analyzing the elements of the business model for mobile payment service provision. In *International Conference on the Management of Mobile Business (ICMB 2007)* (pp. 44-44). IEEE. DOI: 10.1109/ICMB.2007.16

Powell, D., Yu, J., DeWolf, M., & Holyoak, K. J. (2017). The love of large numbers: A popularity bias in consumer choice. *Psychological Science, 28*(10), 1432–1442. doi:10.1177/0956797617711291 PMID:28825874

Prastiawan, D. I., Aisjah, S., & Rofiaty, R. (2021). The Effect of Perceived Usefulness, Perceived Ease of Use, and Social Influence on the Use of Mobile Banking through the Mediation of Attitude Toward Use. [Asia Pacific Management and Business Application]. *APMBA, 9*(3), 243–260. doi:10.21776/ub.apmba.2021.009.03.4

Priya, R., Vikas, G. A., & Shaikh, A. (2018). Mobile banking adoption in an emerging economy: An empirical analysis of young Indian consumers. *Benchmarking, 25*(2), 743–762. doi:10.1108/BIJ-01-2016-0009

Purnawirawan, N., Dens, N., & De Pelsmacker, P. (2012). Balance and sequence in online reviews: The wrap effect. *International Journal of Electronic Commerce, 17*(2), 71–98. doi:10.2753/JEC1086-4415170203

Puron-Cid, G., & Gil-Garcia, J. R. (2022). Are smart cities too expensive in the long term? Analyzing the effects of ICT infrastructure on municipal financial sustainability. *Sustainability (Basel), 14*(10), 6055. doi:10.3390/su14106055

Puschmann, T. (2017). Fintech. *Business & Information Systems Engineering, 59*(1), 69–76. doi:10.1007/s12599-017-0464-6

Pyun, J., & Rha, J. S. (2021). Review of Research on Digital Supply Chain Management Using Network Text Analysis. *Sustainability (Basel), 13*(17), 9929. doi:10.3390/su13179929

Qahri-Saremi, H., & Montazemi, A. R. (2019). Factors affecting the adoption of an electronic word of mouth message: A meta-analysis. *Journal of Management Information Systems, 36*(3), 969–1001. doi:10.1080/07421222.2019.1628936

Qahri-Saremi, H., & Montazemi, A. R. (2023). Negativity bias in the diagnosticity of online review content: The effects of consumers' prior experience and need for cognition. *European Journal of Information Systems, 32*(4), 717–734. doi:10.1080/0960085X.2022.2041372

Qiu, Y., Shaukat, A., & Tharyan, R. (2016). Environmental and social disclosures: Link with corporate financial performance. *The British Accounting Review, 48*(1), 102–116. doi:10.1016/j.bar.2014.10.007

Quach, S., Thaichon, P., Martin, K. D., Weaven, S., & Palmatier, R. W. (2022). Digital technologies: Tensions in privacy and data. *Journal of the Academy of Marketing Science, 50*(6), 1299–1323. doi:10.1007/s11747-022-00845-y PMID:35281634

Quan, W., Li, Z., & Kim, W. (2022, December 17). *Implicit Discriminatory Bias Reflected in Yelp Reviews - A case study.* 2022 IEEE International Conference on Big Data (Big Data), Osaka, Japan. 10.1109/BigData55660.2022.10020592

Rabaa'i, A. A., & AlMaati, S. (2021). Exploring the determinants of users' continuance intention to use mobile banking services in Kuwait: Extending the expectation-confirmation model. *Asia Pacific Journal of Information Systems, 31*(2), 141–184. https://www.researchgate.net/profile/Ahmad-Rabaai-2/publication/353175206_Exploring_the_Determinants_of_Users'_Continuance_Intention_to_Use_Mobile_Banking_Services_in_Kuwait_Extending_the_Expectation-Confirmation_Model/links/60ebf0eab8c0d5588cee77cf/Exploring-the-Determinants-of-Users-Continuance-Intention-to-Use-Mobile-Banking-Services-in-Kuwait-Extending-the-Expectation-Confirmation-Model.pdf

Rachinger, M., Rauter, R., Müller, C., Vorraber, W., & Schirgi, E. (2019). Digitalization and its influence on business model innovation. *Journal of Manufacturing Technology Management, 30*(8), 1143–1160. doi:10.1108/JMTM-01-2018-0020

Ractham, P., Abrahams, A., Gruss, R., Kim, E., Davis, Z., & Kaewkitipong, L. (2021). A Comparative Evaluation of Airline Service Quality Using Online Content Analysis: A Case Study of Korean vs. International Airlines. *Asia Pacific Journal of Information Systems, 31*(4), 491–526. doi:10.14329/apjis.2021.31.4.491

Raj, A., Dwivedi, G., Sharma, A., de Sousa Jabbour, A. B. L., & Rajak, S. (2020). Barriers to the adoption of industry 4.0 technologies in the manufacturing sector: An inter-country comparative perspective. *International Journal of Production Economics, 224*, 107546. doi:10.1016/j.ijpe.2019.107546

Raza, S. A., Umer, A., & Shah, N. (2017). New determinants of ease of use and perceived usefulness for mobile banking adoption. *International Journal of Electronic Customer Relationship Management, 11*(1), 44–65. doi:10.1504/IJECRM.2017.086751

Reijers, H. A., Vanderfeesten, I., & Aalst, W. (2016). The effectiveness of workflow management systems: A longitudinal study. *International Journal of Information Management*, *36*(1), 126–141. doi:10.1016/j.ijinfomgt.2015.08.003

Report on Bhutan's External Trade. (2021). Royal Government of Bhutan.

Rigby, D. K. (2013). Management Tools 2013: An executive guide. *Bain & Company*, 1–68.

Rinzin, Y. (2021). A cursed year for the tourism sector. *Kuensel Online*. https://kuenselonline.com/a-cursed-year-for-the-tourism-sector/

Ritter, T., & Pedersen, C. L. (2020). Digitization capability and the digitalization of business models in business-to-business firms: Past, present, and future. *Industrial Marketing Management*, *86*, 180–190. doi:10.1016/j.indmarman.2019.11.019

Roca-Puig, V. (2019). The circular path of social sustainability: An empirical analysis. *Journal of Cleaner Production*, *212*, 916–924. doi:10.1016/j.jclepro.2018.12.078

Rochet, J. C., & Tirole, J. (2003). Platform competition in two-sided markets. *Journal of the European Economic Association*, *1*(4), 990–1029. doi:10.1162/154247603322493212

Rogers, D. S., Duraiappah, A. K., Antons, D. C., Munoz, P., Bai, X., Fragkias, M., & Gutscher, H. (2012). A vision for human well-being: Transition to social sustainability. *Current Opinion in Environmental Sustainability*, *4*(1), 61–73. doi:10.1016/j.cosust.2012.01.013

Rohn, D., Bican, P. M., Brem, A., Kraus, S., & Clauss, T. (2021). Digital platform-based business models–An exploration of critical success factors. *Journal of Engineering and Technology Management*, *60*, 101625. doi:10.1016/j.jengtecman.2021.101625

Royal Monetary Authority. (2022). *Annual Payment System Report 2022*. RMA. https://www.rma.org.bt/RMA%20Publication/DPSS/2023%20Q2.pdf

Roy, G., Datta, B., & Basu, R. (2017). Effect of eWOM valence on online retail sales. *Global Business Review*, *18*(1), 198–209. doi:10.1177/0972150916666966

Saaty, T. L. (1995). Transport planning with multiple criteria: The analytic hierarchy process applications and progress review. *Journal of Advanced Transportation*, *29*(1), 81–126. doi:10.1002/atr.5670290109

Sala, S., Ciuffo, B., & Nijkamp, P. (2015). A systemic framework for sustainability assessment. *Ecological Economics*, *119*, 314–325. doi:10.1016/j.ecolecon.2015.09.015

Salomon, M. F. B., Mello, C. H. P., & Salgado, E. G. (2019). Prioritization of product-service business model elements at aerospace industry using analytical hierarchy process. *Acta Scientiarum. Technology*, *41*(1), e37934. doi:10.4025/actascitechnol.v41i1.37934

Salvioni, D. M., & Almici, A. (2020). Transitioning toward a circular economy: The impact of stakeholder engagement on sustainability culture. *Sustainability (Basel)*, *12*(20), 8641. doi:10.3390/su12208641

Sanders, N. R., Boone, T., Ganeshan, R., & Wood, J. D. (2019). Sustainable Supply Chains in the Age of AI and Digitization: Research Challenges and Opportunities. *Journal of Business Logistics*, *40*(3), 229–240. doi:10.1111/jbl.12224

Saparudin, M., Rahayu, A., Hurriyati, R., & Sultan, M. A. (2020). Exploring the role of trust in mobile-banking use by Indonesian customer using unified theory of acceptance and usage technology. *International journal of financial research*, *11*(2), 51. doi:10.5430/ijfr.v11n2p51

Sarkodie, S. A., Adams, S., Owusu, P. A., Leirvik, T., & Ozturk, I. (2020). Mitigating degradation and emissions in China: The role of environmental sustainability, human capital and renewable energy. *The Science of the Total Environment, 719*, 137530. doi:10.1016/j.scitotenv.2020.137530 PMID:32143100

Sauro, J. (2011). Measuring Usability with the System Usability Scale (SUS). *MeasuringU*. https://www.measuringu.com/sus.php

Schallmo, D., Williams, C. A., & Boardman, L. (2017). DIGITAL TRANSFORMATION OF BUSINESS MODELS — BEST PRACTICE, ENABLERS, AND ROADMAP. *International Journal of Innovation Management, 21*(08), 1740014. doi:10.1142/S136391961740014X

Schlaepfer, R., Von Radowitz, K., Koch, M., & Merkofer, P. (2017). *Digital future readiness - How do companies prepare for the opportunities and challenges of digitalisation?* Deloitte. https://www2.deloitte.com/content/dam/Deloitte /ch/Documents/consumer-business/ch-cip-en-swiss-transformation.pdf

Schmietendorf, A. (2008). Assessment of business process modeling tools under consideration of business process management activities. Lecture Notes in Computer Science (Including Subseries Lecture Notes in Artificial Intelligence and Lecture Notes in Bioinformatics), 5338 LNCS, 141–154. doi:10.1007/978-3-540-89403-2_13

Schneider, C., Weinmann, M., & vom Brocke, J. (2015). Choice architecture: Using fixation patterns to analyze the effects of form design on cognitive biases. In *Lecture Notes in Information Systems and Organisation* (pp. 91–97). Information Systems and Neuroscience. doi:10.1007/978-3-319-18702-0_12

Schönborn, G., Berlin, C., Pinzone, M., Hanisch, C., Georgoulias, K., & Lanz, M. (2019). Why social sustainability counts: The impact of corporate social sustainability culture on financial success. *Sustainable Production and Consumption, 17*, 1–10. doi:10.1016/j.spc.2018.08.008

Schuchmann, D., & Seufert, S. (2015). Corporate learning in times of digital transformation: A conceptual framework and service portfolio for the learning function in banking organisations. [iJAC]. *International Journal of Advanced Corporate Learning, 8*(1), 31. doi:10.3991/ijac.v8i1.4440

Schumacher, A., Erol, S., & Sihn, W. (2016). A maturity model for assessing Industry 4.0 readiness and maturity of manufacturing enterprises. *Procedia CIRP, 52*, 161–166. doi:10.1016/j.procir.2016.07.040

Scoones, I. (2007). Sustainability. *Development in Practice, 17*(4-5), 589–596. doi:10.1080/09614520701469609

Secundo, G., Mele, G., Del Vecchio, P., Elia, G., Margherita, A., & Ndou, V. (2021). Threat or opportunity? A case study of digital-enabled redesign of entrepreneurship education in the COVID-19 emergency. *Technological Forecasting and Social Change, 166*, 120565. doi:10.1016/j.techfore.2020.120565 PMID:33518821

Seele, P. (2014). Unified reporting: integrating XBRL data repositories into sustainability reporting. *EMAN 2014.4. Presented at the 17th Environmental and Sustainability Management Accounting Network (EMAN): from sustainability reporting to sustainability management control*. EMAN.

Seele, P., & Lock, I. (2017). The game-changing potential of digitalization for sustainability: Possibilities, perils, and pathways. *Sustainability Science, 12*(2), 183–185. doi:10.1007/s11625-017-0426-4

Segatto, M., Pádua, S., & Martinelli, D. (2013). Business process management: A systemic approach? *Business Process Management Journal, 19*(4), 698–714. doi:10.1108/BPMJ-Jun-2012-0064

Sengo Furtado, F., Reutterer, T., & Schröder, N. (2022). The carrot and the stick in online reviews: Determinants of un-/helpfulness voting choices. *Journal of Business Economics, 92*(4), 565–590. doi:10.1007/s11573-021-01044-x

Senna, P. P., Roca, J. B., & Barros, A. C. (2023). Overcoming barriers to manufacturing digitalization: Policies across EU countries. *Technological Forecasting and Social Change*, *196*, 122822. doi:10.1016/j.techfore.2023.122822

Serabian, D. (2015). Consumer Protection and Cybersecurity: The Consumer Education Gap (pp. 1–16). Digital Scholarship. https://digitalscholarship.unlv.edu/brookings_pubs/33 (accessed on November 26, 2023).

Seroka-Stolka, O., Tomski, P., & Pabian, A. (2015). Environmental strategies in the management of transport & logistics sector companies. *2015 4th International Conference on Advanced Logistics and Transport (ICALT)*, (pp. 122–127). IEEE. 10.1109/ICAdLT.2015.7136607

Shahin, A., Gunasekaran, A., Khalili, A., & Shirouyehzad, H. (2016). A new approach for estimating leagile decoupling point using data envelopment analysis. *Assembly Automation*, *36*(3), 233–245. doi:10.1108/AA-07-2015-063

Sharma, S. K. (2019). Integrating cognitive antecedents into TAM to explain mobile banking behavioral intention: A SEM-neural network modeling. *Information Systems Frontiers*, *21*(4), 815–827. doi:10.1007/s10796-017-9775-x

Shen, L., Zhang, X., & Liu, H. (2022). Digital technology adoption, digital dynamic capability, and digital transformation performance of textile industry: Moderating role of digital innovation orientation. *MDE. Managerial and Decision Economics*, *43*(6), 2038–2054. doi:10.1002/mde.3507

Shen, X., Pan, B., Hu, T., Chen, K., Qiao, L., & Zhu, J. (2020). Beyond self-selection: The multilayered online review biases at the intersection of users, platforms and culture. *Journal of Hospitality and Tourism Insights*, *4*(1), 77–97. doi:10.1108/JHTI-02-2020-0012

Shetu, S. N., Islam, M. M., & Promi, S. I. (2022). An Empirical Investigation of the Continued Usage Intention of Digital Wallets: The Moderating Role of Perceived Technological Innovativeness. *Future Business Journal*, *8*(1), 1–17. doi:10.1186/s43093-022-00158-0

Shi, Z., Zhang, C., & Wu, L. (2020). Sales or reviews, which matters more to consumer preference and online advertising? – evidence from eye-tracking and self-reporting. *International Journal of Advertising*, *39*(8), 1274–1300. doi:10.1080/02650487.2020.1755181

Shreyasee, K., & Varun, R. T. (2023). Effect of Digital Readiness on the Export Preparedness in India. *Prajnan (Pune)*, *51*(4), 323–339.

Siegel, R. L., Miller, K. D., & Jemal, A. (2020). Cancer statistics, 2020. *CA: a Cancer Journal for Clinicians*, *70*(1), 7–30. doi:10.3322/caac.21590 PMID:31912902

Siegel, R. L., Miller, K. D., & Jemal, A. (2021). Cancer statistics, 2021. *CA: a Cancer Journal for Clinicians*, *71*(1), 7–33. doi:10.3322/caac.21654 PMID:33433946

Siering, M. (2021). Leveraging online review platforms to support public policy: Predicting restaurant health violations based on online reviews. *Decision Support Systems*, *143*(113474), 113474. doi:10.1016/j.dss.2020.113474

Sikora, R. T., & Chauhan, K. (2012). Estimating sequential bias in online reviews: A Kalman filtering approach. *Knowledge-Based Systems*, *27*, 314–321. doi:10.1016/j.knosys.2011.10.011

Silva, D. S., Yamashita, G. H., Cortimiglia, M. N., Brust-Renck, P. G., & ten Caten, C. S. (2022). Are we ready to assess digital readiness? Exploring digital implications for social progress from the Network Readiness Index. *Technology in Society*, *68*, 101875. doi:10.1016/j.techsoc.2022.101875

Silveira, C., Luo, J., Reis, L., & Mamede, H. S. (2022). CRESustain: Approach to Include Sustainability and Creativity in Requirements Engineering. *Journal of Engineering Research and Sciences*. doi:10.55708/js0108004

Simović, V. M., & Domazet, I. S. (2021). An Overview of the Frameworks for Measuring the Digital Competencies of College Students: A European Perspective. In *Stagnancy Issues and Change Initiatives for Global Education in the Digital Age* (pp. 259–282). IGI Global. doi:10.4018/978-1-7998-4993-3.ch012

Simovic, V., Domazet, I., Bhagat, R., Sarhan, H., & Ivanovic, D. (2022). Identification of Opportunities as the Component of Digital Entrepreneurial Competences of University Students: A pilot study in Kuwait and Serbia. In *Proceedings of the 6th International Conference on E-Commerce, E-Business and E-Government* (pp. 85–90). New York, NY, USA: Association for Computing Machinery. 10.1145/3537693.3537724

Simovic, V., Domazet, I., Bugarcic, M., Safi, M., Sarhan, H., Bhagat, R., & Bradic Martinovic, A. (2023). The association of socio-demographic characteristics of university students and the levels of their digital entrepreneurial competences. *Heliyon*, *9*(10), e20897. doi:10.1016/j.heliyon.2023.e20897 PMID:37867828

Singh, N., & Hong, P. (2023). CSR, Risk Management Practices, and Performance Outcomes: An Empirical Investigation of Firms in Different Industries. *Journal of Risk and Financial Management*, *16*(69), 69. doi:10.3390/jrfm16020069

Singh, R. K., Murty, H. R., Gupta, S. K., & Dikshit, A. K. (2012). An overview of sustainability assessment methodologies. *Ecological Indicators*, *15*(1), 281–299. doi:10.1016/j.ecolind.2011.01.007

Skotis, A., Morfaki, C., & Livas, C. (2023). Identifying drivers of evaluation bias in online reviews of city destinations. *International Journal of Information Management Data Insights*, *3*(2), 100184. doi:10.1016/j.jjimei.2023.100184

Šlaus, I., & Jacobs, G. (2011). Human capital and sustainability. *Sustainability (Basel)*, *3*(1), 97–154. doi:10.3390/su3010097

Smedlund, A. (2012). Value cocreation in service platform business models. *Service Science*, *4*(1), 79–88. doi:10.1287/serv.1110.0001

Sodiq, A., Baloch, A. A., Khan, S. A., Sezer, N., Mahmoud, S., Jama, M., & Abdelaal, A. (2019). Towards modern sustainable cities: Review of sustainability principles and trends. *Journal of Cleaner Production*, *227*, 972–1001. doi:10.1016/j.jclepro.2019.04.106

Soini, K., & Dessein, J. (2016). Culture-sustainability relation: Towards a conceptual framework. *Sustainability (Basel)*, *8*(2), 167. doi:10.3390/su8020167

Song, B., Shi, H., Wang, M., & Gu, R. (2022). The research on the effect of digital economy development on urban air quality. *Frontiers in Environmental Science*, *10*, 993353. doi:10.3389/fenvs.2022.993353

Song, M., Zheng, C., & Wang, J. (2022). The role of digital economy in China's sustainable development in a post-pandemic environment. *Journal of Enterprise Information Management*, *35*(1), 58–77. doi:10.1108/JEIM-03-2021-0153

Song, W., Ma, Y., Fan, X., & Peng, X. (2023). Corporate Environmental Ethics and Employee's Green Creativity? The Perspective of Environmental Commitment. *Corporate Social Responsibility and Environmental Management*, *30*(4), 1856–1868. doi:10.1002/csr.2459

Sorri, K., Seppänen, M., Still, K., & Valkokari, K. (2019). Business model innovation with platform canvas. *Journal of Business Models*, *7*(2), 1–13. https://cris.vtt.fi/ws/portalfiles/portal/26015079/JOBM_2019_Sorri_et_al_business_model_innovation_with_platform_canvas.pdf

Strange, R., Chen, L., & Fleury, M. T. L. (2022). Digital Transformation and International Strategies. *Journal of International Management*, *28*(4), 100968. doi:10.1016/j.intman.2022.100968

Stuermer, M., Abu-Tayeh, G., & Myrach, T. (2017). Digital sustainability: Basic conditions for sustainable digital artifacts and their ecosystems. *Sustainability Science*, *12*(2), 247–262. doi:10.1007/s11625-016-0412-2 PMID:30174752

Sultan, M., & Khan, S. A. (2023). FDI, disinvestment and growth: An appraisal of Bhutanese economy. *Journal of Chinese Economic and Foreign Trade Studies*, *16*(1), 64–82. doi:10.1108/JCEFTS-05-2022-0031

Sung, H., Ferlay, J., Siegel, R. L., Laversanne, M., Soerjomataram, I., Jemal, A., & Bray, F. (2021). Global cancer statistics 2020: GLOBOCAN estimates of incidence and mortality worldwide for 36 cancers in 185 countries. *CA: a Cancer Journal for Clinicians*, *71*(3), 209–249. doi:10.3322/caac.21660 PMID:33538338

Sun, X., Yu, H., Solvang, W. D., Wang, Y., & Wang, K. (2022). The application of Industry 4.0 technologies in sustainable logistics: A systematic literature review (2012–2020) to explore future research opportunities. *Environmental Science and Pollution Research International*, *29*(7), 9560–9591. doi:10.1007/s11356-021-17693-y PMID:34893953

Suomala, J. (2020). The Consumer Contextual Decision-Making Model. *Frontiers in Psychology*, *11*(September), 570430. doi:10.3389/fpsyg.2020.570430 PMID:33117237

Süß, A., Höse, K., & Götze, U. (2021). Sustainability-oriented business model evaluation—a literature review. *Sustainability, 13*(19), 10908. https://doi.org/ 131910908 doi:10.3390/su

Sussan, F., & Acs, Z. J. (2017). The digital entrepreneurial ecosystem. *Small Business Economics*, *49*(1), 55–73. doi:10.1007/s11187-017-9867-5

Sutton, P. (2004). A perspective on environmental sustainability. *Paper on the Victorian Commissioner for Environmental Sustainability*, *1*, 32.

Švarc, J., Lažnjak, J., & Dabić, M. (2021). The role of national intellectual capital in the digital transformation of EU countries. Another digital divide? *Journal of Intellectual Capital*, *22*(4), 768–791. doi:10.1108/JIC-02-2020-0024

Swetha, N., & Murthy, H. V. (2019). Indian heritage tourism—A netnographic approach. *International Journal of Innovative Technology and Exploring Engineering, 8*(7C2), 272-279.

Székely, F., & Knirsch, M. (2005). Responsible leadership and corporate social responsibility: Metrics for sustainable performance. *European Management Journal*, *23*(6), 628–647. doi:10.1016/j.emj.2005.10.009

Taherdoost, H., & Madanchian, M. (2023). Multi-criteria decision making (MCDM) methods and concepts. *Encyclopedia*, *3*(1), 77–87. doi:10.3390/encyclopedia3010006

Taneja, S., & Ali, L. (2021). Determinants of customers' intentions towards environmentally sustainable banking: Testing the structural model. *Journal of Retailing and Consumer Services*, *59*(102418), 102418. doi:10.1016/j.jretconser.2020.102418

Tarhan, A., Turetken, O., & Reijers, H. A. (2016). Business process maturity models: A systematic literature review. *Information and Software Technology*, *75*, 122–134. doi:10.1016/j.infsof.2016.01.010

Tata, S. V., Prashar, S., & Gupta, S. (2020). An examination of the role of review valence and review source in varying consumption contexts on purchase decision. *Journal of Retailing and Consumer Services*, *52*(101734), 101734. doi:10.1016/j.jretconser.2019.01.003

Taufani, M., & Widjaja, A. W. (2022). Digital transformation for enhancing LSP (Logistic Service Provider) performance. *Proceeding of the International Conference on Family Business and Entrepreneurship, 2*(1). 10.33021/icfbe.v2i1.3518

Tay, W. (2019, July). Not all reviews are equal: Towards addressing reviewer biases for opinion summarization. In *Proceedings of the 57th Annual Meeting of the Association for Computational Linguistics: Student Research Workshop* (pp. 34-42). ACM. 10.18653/v1/P19-2005

Tehulu, T. A. (2013). Determinants of financial sustainability of microfinance institutions in East Africa. *European Journal of Business and Management*, *5*(17), 152–158.

Teichert, R. (2019). Digital transformation maturity: A systematic review of literature. *Acta Universitatis Agriculturae et Silviculturae Mendelianae Brunensis*, *67*(6), 1673–1687. doi:10.11118/actaun201967061673

The World Bank. (2016). *Digital Adoption Index*. World Bank. https://www.worldbank.org/en/publication/wdr2016/Digital-Adoption-Index

The World Bank. (2021). *Gross Domestic Product by country*. Databank: World Development Indicators. https://databank.worldbank.org/reports.aspx?source=2&series=NY.GDP.MKTP.CD&country

The World Intellectual Property Organization. (2022). *Global innovation index 2022: What is the future of innovation-driven growth?* Global Innovation Index. https://www.globalinnovationindex.org/gii-2022-report

Thite, M. (2011). Smart cities: Implications of urban planning for human resource development. *Human Resource Development International*, *14*(5), 623–631. doi:10.1080/13678868.2011.618349

Timmers, P. (1998). Business models for electronic markets. *Electronic Markets*, *8*(2), 3–8. doi:10.1080/10196789800000016

Tiwari, P., Tiwari, S. K., & Gupta, A. (2021). Examining the impact of customers' awareness, risk and trust in M-banking adoption. *FIIB business review*, *10*(4), 413–423. doi:10.1177/23197145211019924

Tiwari, V., & Thakur, S. (2021). Environment sustainability through sustainability innovations. *Environment, Development and Sustainability*, *23*(5), 6941–6965. doi:10.1007/s10668-020-00899-4

Torre, L. A., Bray, F., Siegel, R. L., Ferlay, J., Lortet-Tieulent, J., & Jemal, A. (2015). Global cancer statistics, 2012. *CA: a Cancer Journal for Clinicians*, *65*(2), 87–108. doi:10.3322/caac.21262 PMID:25651787

Truong, B. Q., & Nguyen-Duc, A. (2023). A Quantitative Review of the Research on Business Process Management in Digital Transformation: A Bibliometric Approach. *Software*, (2), 377–399. https://doi.org/https://www.mdpi.com/2674-113X/2/3/18

Truong, T. C. (2022). The Impact of Digital Transformation on Environmental Sustainability. *Advances in Multimedia*, *2022*, 1–12. doi:10.1155/2022/6324325

Tsai, H.-T., Chien, J.-L., & Tsai, M.-T. (2014). The influences of system usability and user satisfaction on continued Internet banking services usage intention: Empirical evidence from Taiwan. *Electronic Commerce Research*, *14*(2), 137–169. doi:10.1007/s10660-014-9136-5

Tseng, M.-L., Bui, T.-D., Lim, M. K., & Lewi, S. (2021). A Cause and Effect Model for Digital Sustainable Supply Chain Competitiveness under Uncertainties: Enhancing Digital Platform. *Sustainability (Basel)*, *13*(18), 10150. doi:10.3390/su131810150

Tshering Cigay, D. (2022). *Which are the main FDI companies in the IT Sector, and how have they brought socio-economic benefits to Bhutan?* Wordpress. https://tcdorji.wordpress.com/2021/11/24/the-role-of-fdi-in-technological-and-economic-advancement-of-a-country-a-brief-look-at-fdi-in-bhutan/

Turienzo, J., & Lampón, J. F. (2023). New mobility technologies as incentive to location decisions: Relocation strategy in the automotive industry. *Kybernetes*, *52*(11), 5444–5459. doi:10.1108/K-03-2022-0317

Uludag, O., Hefele, S., & Matthes, F. (2016). Platform and ecosystem governance. *Digital Mobility Platforms and State of the Art Report*, 1-24.

UN (United Nations). (2019). *The Age of Digital Interdependence*. UN. https://www.un.org/en/pdfs/DigitalCooperation-report-for%20web.pdf

UNCTAD. (2019). *Digital Economy Report 2019: Value Creation and Capture - Implications for Developing Countries*. UNCTAD. https://unctad.org/publication/digital-economy-report-2019.

Urbinati, A., Chiaroni, D., & Chiesa, V. (2017). Towards a New Taxonomy of Circular Economy Business Models. *Journal of Cleaner Production*, *168*, 487–498. doi:10.1016/j.jclepro.2017.09.047

Valdez-de-Leon, O. (2016). A digital maturity model for telecommunications service providers. *Technology Innovation Management Review*, *6*(8), 19–32. doi:10.22215/timreview/1008

Vali, H., Xu, D., & Yildirim, B. (2015). *The effects of repeating purchase cues and mixed reviews on product attribution. Thirty-Sixth International Conference on Information Systems*, Fort Worth.

Vallance, S., Perkins, H. C., & Dixon, J. E. (2011). What is social sustainability? A clarification of concepts. *Geoforum*, *42*(3), 342–348. doi:10.1016/j.geoforum.2011.01.002

Van Looy, A., De Backer, M., Poels, G., & Snoeck, M. (2013). Choosing the right business process maturity model. *Information & Management*, *50*(7), 466–488. doi:10.1016/j.im.2013.06.002

VanBoskirk, S., Gill, M., Green, D., Berman, A., Swire, J., & Birrell, R. (2017). *The digital maturity model 5.0*. Forrester Research. https://foloop.in/uploads/images/stock/The-Digital-Maturity-Model-5.0-1.pdf

Van, H. N., Pham, L., Williamson, S., Chan, C.-Y., Thang, T. D., & Nam, V. X. (2021). Explaining intention to use mobile banking: Integrating perceived risk and trust into the technology acceptance model. *International Journal of Applied Decision Sciences*, *14*(1), 55–80. doi:10.1504/IJADS.2021.112933

Vardoulakis, S., & Kinney, P. (2019). Grand challenges in sustainable cities and health. *Frontiers in Sustainable Cities*, *1*, 7. doi:10.3389/frsc.2019.00007

Vedadi, A., & Warkentin, M. (2016). Continuance Intention on Using Mobile Banking Applications: A Replication Study of Information Systems Continuance Model. *AIS Transactions on Replication Research*, *2*(1), 7. doi:10.17705/1atrr.00014

Vial, G. (2021). Understanding digital transformation: A review and a research agenda. *Managing Digital Transformation*, 13–66. doi:10.4324/9781003008637-4

Vial, G. (2019). Understanding digital transformation: A review and a research agenda. *The Journal of Strategic Information Systems*, *28*(2), 118–144. doi:10.1016/j.jsis.2019.01.003

Vieira, E. S., Cerdeira, J., & Teixeira, A. A. (2022). Which distance dimensions matter in international research collaboration? A cross-country analysis by scientific domain. *Journal of Informetrics*, *16*(2), 101259. doi:10.1016/j.joi.2022.101259

Vijayvargiya, A., & Dey, A. K. (2010). An analytical approach for selection of a logistics provider. *Management Decision*, *48*(3), 403–418. doi:10.1108/00251741011037774

Vinson, D. W., Dale, R., & Jones, M. N. (2019). Decision contamination in the wild: Sequential dependencies in online review ratings. *Behavior Research Methods*, *51*(4), 1477–1484. doi:10.3758/s13428-018-1175-8 PMID:30604037

Visual Paradigm. (2023). *What is Unified Modeling Language (UML)?* Visual Paradigm. https://www.visual-paradigm.com/guide/uml-unified-modeling-language/what-is-uml/

Vivek, H., Gajjar, K. M., & Daruwala, S. B. (2023). A RESEARCH PAPER STUDY ON IMPLICATION OF GREEN LOGISTICS IN CHEMICAL INDUSTRIES. *International Research Journal of Modernization in Engineering Technology and Science*, *5*(3). doi:10.56726/IRJMETS33989

Vogelsang, K., Liere-Netheler, K., Packmohr, S., & Hoppe, U. (2019, January 8). Barriers to Digital Transformation in Manufacturing: Development of a Research Agenda. *Hawaii International Conference on System Sciences 2019 (HICSS-52)*. AISEL. https://aisel.aisnet.org/hicss-52/in/digital_transformation/3

Vogler, D., & Eisenegger, M. (2021). CSR Communication, Corporate Reputation, and the Role of the News Media as an Agenda-Setter in the Digital Age. *Business & Society*, *60*(8), 1957–1986. https://doi-org.proxy.library.nyu.edu/10.1177/0007650320928969. doi:10.1177/0007650320928969

Wagner, S. M. (2013). Partners for Business-to-Business Service Innovation. *IEEE Transactions on Engineering Management*, *60*(1), 113–123. doi:10.1109/TEM.2012.2198066

Waheed, S. A., Ding, D., & Siyal, S. (2019). M-banking barriers in Pakistan: A customer perspective of adoption and continuity intention. *Data Technologies and Applications*, *53*(1), 58–84. doi:10.1108/DTA-04-2018-0022

Wan, Y., & Nakayama, M. (2012). Are Amazon.com online review helpfulness ratings biased or not? In Lecture Notes in Business Information Processing (pp. 46–54). Springer. doi:10.1007/978-3-642-29873-8_5

Wang, K., & Guo, F. (2022). Towards Sustainable Development through the Perspective of Construction 4.0: Systematic Literature Review and Bibliometric Analysis. *Buildings, 12*(10). https://doi-org.proxy.library.nyu.edu/10.3390/buildings12101708

Wang, D., Tarasov, A., & Zhang, H. (2022). Environmental Regulation, Innovation Capability, and Green Total Factor Productivity of the Logistics Industry. *Kybernetes*. Advance online publication. doi:10.1108/K-04-2022-0591

Wang, J., Wang, W., Ran, Q., Irfan, M., Ren, S., Yang, X., Wu, H., & Ahmad, M. (2022). Analysis of the mechanism of the impact of internet development on green economic growth: Evidence from 269 prefecture cities in China. *Environmental Science and Pollution Research International*, *29*(7), 1–15. doi:10.1007/s11356-021-16381-1 PMID:34510353

Wangmo, C. (2023). *CSI aims to be part of global supply chain*. Kuensel Online. kuenselonline.com/csi-aims-to-be-part-of-global-supply-chain.

Warner, K. S., & Wäger, M. (2019). Building dynamic capabilities for digital transformation: An ongoing process of strategic renewal. *Long Range Planning*, *52*(3), 326–349. doi:10.1016/j.lrp.2018.12.001

Watson, R. T., Corbett, J., Boudreau, M. C., & Webster, J. (2012). An information strategy for environmental sustainability. *Communications of the ACM*, *55*(7), 28–30. doi:10.1145/2209249.2209261

Wen, J., Lin, Z., Liu, X., Xiao, S. H., & Li, Y. (2021). The interaction effects of online reviews, brand, and price on consumer hotel booking decision making. *Journal of Travel Research*, *60*(4), 846–859. doi:10.1177/0047287520912330

Westerman, G., Bonnet, D., & McAfee, A. (2014). The nine elements of digital transformation. *MIT Sloan Management Review*, *55*(3), 1–6.

Westerman, G., Calméjane, C., Bonnet, D., Ferraris, P., McAfee, A., & ... (2011). Digital Transformation: A roadmap for billion-dollar organizations. *MIT Center for Digital Business and Capgemini Consulting*, *1*, 1–68.

WHO. (2020). *Q&A on Climate Change and COVID-19*. WHO. https://www.who.int/news-room/q-a-detail/q-a-on-climate-change-and-covid-19.

Wilke, A., & Mata, R. (2012). Cognitive Bias. In Encyclopedia of Human Behavior (2nd ed., Vol. 1, pp. 531–535). Elsevier. doi:10.1016/B978-0-12-375000-6.00094-X

Williams, C., Schalimo, D. and Lang, K. (2019). Digital Maturity Models for Small and Medium-sized Enterprises: A Systematic Literature Review. ISPIM Innovation Conference – Celebrating Innovation: 500 Years Since daVinci, Florence, Italy on 16-19 June 2019.

Wolf, M. J., Emerson, J. W., Esty, D. C., de Sherbinin, A., & Wendling, Z. A. (2022). *2022 Environmental Performance Index (EPI) results.* BVEARNB. https://bvearmb.do/handle/123456789/2828.

Wood, D. J., Mitchell, R. K., Agle, B. R., & Bryan, L. M. (2021). Stakeholder Identification and Salience after 20 Years: Progress, Problems, and Prospects. *Business & Society*, *60*(1), 196–245. doi:10.1177/0007650318816522

World Bank. (2019). *Bhutan's Integration with the Global Economy: International Investment Treaties and Conventions.* World Bank.

World Cancer Research Fund International. (2021). *Cancer prevention.* WCRF. https://www.wcrf.org/dietandcancer/cancer-prevention

World Commission on Environment and Development. (1987). *Our Common Future.* Oxford University Press.

World Health Organization. (2019). *Cancer.* WHO. https://www.who.int/news-room/fact-sheets/detail/cancer

Wu, D., Guo, X., & Chen, G. (2017). *Mitigating the Dependence Bias in Online Ratings: A "Consider-the-Opposite".* Strategy for Scale Prompting.

Wu, D., Guo, X., Wang, Y., & Chen, G. (2023). A Warning Approach to Mitigating Bandwagon Bias in Online Ratings: Theoretical Analysis and Experimental Investigations. *Journal of the Association for Information Systems*, *24*(4), 1132–1161. doi:10.17705/1jais.00817

Wujarso, R. (2023). Effect of Digital Transformation on Company Operational Efficiency. *Central European Management Journal*, *31*(2), 2. doi:10.57030/23364890.cemj.31.2.16

Wu, P. F. (2013). In search of negativity bias: An empirical study of perceived helpfulness of online reviews. *Psychology and Marketing*, *30*(11), 971–984. doi:10.1002/mar.20660

Yaakub, S., Subhan, M., Abdullah, N. A. H. N., & Gapar, N. (2015, August). Environmental sustainability strategies and impacts. In *2015 International Symposium on Technology Management and Emerging Technologies (ISTMET)* (pp. 401-406). IEEE. 10.1109/ISTMET.2015.7359067

Yeewong Magazine. (2018, December). Read the stories of 50 entrepreneurs in Bhutan. *Yeewong Magazine.*

Yeh, H. (2017). The effects of successful ICT-based smart city services: From citizens' perspectives. *Government Information Quarterly*, *34*(3), 556–565. doi:10.1016/j.giq.2017.05.001

Yeo, A. D., & Deng, A. (2020). Logistics performance as a mediator of the relationship between trade facilitation and international trade: A mediation analysis. *Suid-Afrikaanse Tydskrif vir Ekonomiese en Bestuurswetenskappe*, *23*(1). doi:10.4102/sajems.v23i1.3453

Yeo, A. D., Deng, A., & Nadiedjoa, T. Y. (2020). The Effect of Infrastructure and Logistics Performance on Economic Performance: The Mediation Role of International Trade. *Foreign Trade Review*, *55*(4), 450–465. doi:10.1177/0015732520947676

Yigitcanlar, T., Kamruzzaman, M., Foth, M., Sabatini-Marques, J., Da Costa, E., & Ioppolo, G. (2019). Can cities become smart without being sustainable? A systematic review of the literature. *Sustainable Cities and Society*, *45*, 348–365. doi:10.1016/j.scs.2018.11.033

Yildiz, K., & Tabak, Ç. (2019). LPI Based Comparison of Turkey And Mexican Logistics Sector. *Politeknik Dergisi*, *22*(4), 4. doi:10.2339/politeknik.479410

Yin, D., Mitra, S., & Zhang, H. (2016). Research note—When do consumers value positive vs. negative reviews? An empirical investigation of confirmation bias in online word of mouth. *Information Systems Research, 27*(1), 131–144. doi:10.1287/isre.2015.0617

Yin, L.-X., & Lin, H.-C. (2022). Predictors of customers' continuance intention of mobile banking from the perspective of the interactivity theory. *Ekonomska Istrazivanja, 35*(1), 6820–6849. doi:10.1080/1331677X.2022.2053782

Yongrok, C., & Ning, Z. (2011). Does proactive green logistics management improve business performance? A case of Chinese logistics enterprises. *African Journal of Business Management, 5*(17), 7564–7574. doi:10.5897/AJBM11.613

Yu, J., & Moon, T. (2021). Impact of Digital Strategic Orientation on Organizational Performance through Digital Competence. *Sustainability, 13*(17), 9766. doi:10.3390/su13179766

Yuan, W., Hong, Y., & Pavlou, P. A. (2012, December). The informational role of online product review distributions: An experimental study of biases in online product reviews. In *18th Americas Conference on Information Systems 2012, AMCIS 2012* (pp. 3780-3790). IEEE.

Yuan, S., Liu, Y., Yao, R., & Liu, J. (2014). An investigation of users' continuance intention towards mobile banking in China. *Information Development.* doi:10.1177/0266666914522140

Yu, C., & Liao, W. (2023). Professionalism and homophily bias: A study of Airbnb stay choice and review positivity. *International Journal of Hospitality Management, 110*, 103433. doi:10.1016/j.ijhm.2023.103433

Yu, D., & Zhao, P. (2022). Global Value Chain Governance of the Apparel Design Industry under the Background of Global Sustainable Economic Development. *Journal of Environmental and Public Health, 2022*, 1–11. doi:10.1155/2022/5178301 PMID:36507463

Zahid, M., Naeem, H., Aftab, I., & Mughal, S. A. (2021). From corporate social responsibility activities to financial performance: Role of innovation and competitive advantage. *Asia Pacific Journal of Innovation and Entrepreneurship, 15*(1), 2–13. doi:10.1108/APJIE-04-2020-0046

Zapf, B., Hütter, M., & Sassenberg, K. (2021). Are minority opinions shared less? *Zeitschrift für Psychologie, 229*(4), 251–256. doi:10.1027/2151-2604/a000471

Zavadskas, E. K., Turskis, Z., & Kildienė, S. (2014). State of art surveys of overviews on MCDM/MADM methods. *Technological and Economic Development of Economy, 20*(1), 165–179. doi:10.3846/20294913.2014.892037

Zen Flowchart. (2023). *EPC Diagram: A Complete Guide.* Zen Flowchart. https://www.zenflowchart.com/guides/epc-diagram

Zhang, M. (2002). *Measuring urban sustainability in China.* Thela Thesis.

Zhang, J., & Chen, Z. (2023). Exploring Human Resource Management Digital Transformation in the Digital Age. *Journal of the Knowledge Economy.* doi:10.1007/s13132-023-01214-y

Zhang, Y., Feng, X., Wu, Y., & Xiao, J. (2018). The dynamics of online ratings with heterogeneous preferences in online review platform. *Chaos, Solitons, and Fractals, 109*, 26–30. doi:10.1016/j.chaos.2018.02.003

Zhao, F., Fashola, O. I., Olarewaju, T. I., & Onwumere, I. (2021). Smart city research: A holistic and state-of-the-art literature review. *Cities (London, England), 119*, 103406. doi:10.1016/j.cities.2021.103406

Zhao, M., Shen, X., Liao, H., & Cai, M. (2022). Selecting products through text reviews: An MCDM method incorporating personalized heuristic judgments in the prospect theory. *Fuzzy Optimization and Decision Making, 21*(1), 1–24. doi:10.1007/s10700-021-09359-8

Zhao, Y., Von Delft, S., Morgan-Thomas, A., & Buck, T. (2020). The evolution of platform business models: Exploring competitive battles in the world of platforms. *Long Range Planning*, *53*(4), 101892. doi:10.1016/j.lrp.2019.101892

Zheng, L. J., Zhang, J. Z., Au, A. K. M., Wang, H., & Yang, Y. (2023). Leveraging technology-driven applications to promote sustainability in the shipping industry: The impact of digitalization on corporate social responsibility. *Transportation Research Part E, Logistics and Transportation Review*, *176*, 103201. doi:10.1016/j.tre.2023.103201

Zhu, F., Li, K. J., & Liu, H. (2016). Incentive alignment and resource allocation in innovation platforms: Evidence from the IT service market. *Management Science*, *62*(4), 1040–1059.

Zhuhadar, L., Thrasher, E., Marklin, S., & de Pablos, P. O. (2017). The next wave of innovation—Review of smart cities intelligent operation systems. *Computers in Human Behavior*, *66*, 273–281. doi:10.1016/j.chb.2016.09.030

Zhu, K., Kraemer, K. L., & Xu, S. (2006). The Process of Innovation Assimilation by Firms in Different Countries: A Technology Diffusion Perspective on E-Business. *Management Science*, *52*(10), 1557–1576. doi:10.1287/mnsc.1050.0487

Zink, K. J. (2013). Social sustainability and quality of working life: a human factors perspective on sustainable HRM. In *Sustainability and Human Resource Management: Developing Sustainable Business Organizations* (pp. 35–55). Springer Berlin Heidelberg.

Zondervan, N. A., Tolentino-Zondervan, F., & Moeke, D. (2022). Logistics Trends and Innovations in Response to COVID-19 Pandemic: An Analysis Using Text Mining. *Processes (Basel, Switzerland)*, *10*(12), 2667. doi:10.3390/pr10122667

Zott, C., & Amit, R. (2007). Business model design and the performance of entrepreneurial firms. *Organization Science*, *18*(2), 181–199. doi:10.1287/orsc.1060.0232

Zuhaira, B., & Ahmad, N. (2021). Business process modeling, implementation, analysis, and management: The case of business process management tools. *Business Process Management Journal*, *27*(1), 145–183. doi:10.1108/BPMJ-06-2018-0168

About the Contributors

Alper Erturk is a professor working on business management, data science and digital transformation with more than 20 years of academic and industry experience. He is currently working as Full Professor of Management & MIS and Chair of Management Department at Australian University - Kuwait. Furthermore, he is also affiliated with Istanbul Topkapi University as Professor of MIS (Management Information Systems) and delivering lectures on Masters and Doctoral level (I am also the former Dean of Economics, Administrative and Social Sciences Faculty at Istanbul Topkapi University). Previously, he worked as Professor of Management at Rabat Business School, Morocco, and as Professor of HR Analytics at GISMA Business School, Hannover, Germany. Before that, he conducted research as Fulbright Scholar (Visiting Professor) at Portland State University, OR, USA. He also worked as the Head of Department of MIS at Duzce University, Turkey for more than 4 years. He has more than 50 publications, including journal articles, conference presentations, edited books and book chapters, as well as more than 15 years of teaching & research experience.

Faidon Theofanidis is an Associate Professor of Marketing at Australian University – Kuwait. He holds a PhD in Advertising from the University of Piraeus, an MBA in Marketing from Cardiff University, and a BSc in Business Administration from University of Piraeus. From 2003-2010 he was representing the Research Center of Piraeus University at the Board of Directors of the European Network for Social and Economic Research (ENSR), implementing over 30 European research projects. His research interests include Marketing Research, Advertising Research, Consumer Behavior, Digital Marketing and European social and economic policies. He published more than 35 marketing and business articles in peer review international journals and conferences.

Oualid Abidi is an Associate Professor of Management at Australian University of Kuwait specializing in Strategic Management, Business Organization and Management, Organizational Behavior, Leadership, Human Resources Management and Strategic Human Resources Management.

* * *

Saqr Suleiman Abushattal embarked on his academic journey by earning a master's degree from Mutah University /Jordan in 2014. He subsequently pursued his doctoral studies in the microbiology and parasitology department at the University of Santiago de Compostela/Spain, successfully completing his Ph.D. in 2021. Dr. Abushattal's research interests also extend to the fields of plasmids, mobile elements, and antimicrobial resistance genes, demonstrating his comprehensive knowledge in these critical areas.

His latest research endeavors have revolved around understanding the health implications of various types of bacterial pathogens, particularly Photobacterium damselae.

Abedalrhman Alkhateeb earned his MSc and Ph.D. in Computer Science from the University of Windsor in 2011 and 2018, respectively. His research interests include machine learning, deep learning, bioinformatics, and health informatics. His recent research focuses on the health outcomes of various types of cancers.

Abdullah Al-Refai, Ph.D. is currently an Assistant Professor in the Department of Software Engineering at Princess Sumaya University for Technology (PSUT). Dr. Al-Refai has worked in the Automotive Industry. He worked as a Senior Controls Software Engineer in the Powertrain Controls Department at Fiat Chrysler Automobiles, Michigan USA. He received his Ph.D. in Electrical and Computer Engineering from Oakland University in 2018 after obtaining his Master's in Electrical and Computer Engineering from the same university in 2012. He received his Bachelor's in Computer Engineering from Yarmouk University (Irbid, Jordan) in 2010. He worked as a research assistant in the Chrysler Lab and in the Embedded Systems Lab at Oakland University as well as a teacher assistant of a course in a Design and Analysis of Electromechanical Systems. He had two internships, one in EMC testing at Continental Automotive Company in 2012, and the other in Java programming at Petra Solar Company in 2009. He served as the president of Aerial System Club at Oakland University which successfully competed in the Collegiate Aerial Robotics Demonstration (CARD) Competition, St. Louis, MO April 2011. The team ranked 2nd place and won the "Aerial Vehicle Innovative Design Award". Dr. Abdullah has extensive experience in Software Engineering, embedded systems design, control algorithm design, and software development with applications related to Gasoline Engine Controls and Intelligent Battery Sensor Diagnostics.His main research areas are artificial intelligence, Lithium-Ion battery models, Lithium-Ion battery charging Methods,embedded systems, control systems, robotics, and UAV development

Marija Antonijević is a Research Assistant at the Institute of Economic Sciences in Belgrade, Serbia. She is a Ph.D. candidate at the Faculty of Economics (University of Belgrade). Her research interests include banking, digital skills, and foreign direct investments. Marija has published numerous scientific papers in mentioned research areas. She contributed as an interviewer to projects like HORIZON 2020 - Strength2Food (European Commission) and the Inclusion of Roma and marginalized groups in Serbia (GIZ). Currently, Marija is a participant of the COST Action CA19130 - Fintech and Artificial Intelligence in Finance. Since 2022, she has been the secretary of the Journal of Women's Entrepreneurship and Education.

Korhan Arun is a professor in Faculty of Economics and Administrative Sciences at Tekirdag Namik Kemal University since 2010. He received his BA degree in Business Administration and Organization; MA and PhD degrees in Management and Organization from Atatürk University. His research interests include management and strategic management.

Mohammad Majed Asad is a dedicated and results-driven Public Health Technology Specialist hailing from Amman, Jordan. With over 7 years of experience in the field, he has demonstrated a remarkable track record of enhancing health systems through innovative data analysis, management, and visualization. Mohammad holds a bachelor's degree in computer science from the Hashemite University and is currently pursuing a master's degree in health information technology at Princess Sumaya University for Technology. Throughout his career, Mohammad has been recognized for his exceptional contributions to high-impact projects, including critical initiatives such as the COVID-19 response and real-time disease surveillance. He has a strong background in managing health information systems, providing technical support, and implementing emerging technologies. In his current role as a Technology and Innovative Solutions Specialist at GHD|EMPHNET, Mohammad applies advanced data analysis techniques to extract meaningful insights from complex datasets, enabling data-driven decision-making. He is known for maintaining a proactive approach to staying updated on emerging technologies and implementing innovative solutions to optimize processes. His expertise extends to effective data visualization, project leadership, process automation, and regulatory compliance. Prior to this, Mohammad served as an Information and Communications Technology (ICT) Officer at GHD|EMPHNET, where he managed software deployment and updates, ensuring compliance with licensing agreements and usage policies. He also played a key role in leading software implementation projects and monitoring software performance. In his earlier role as a Website & Information Systems Admin at GHD|EMPHNET, Mohammad excelled in maintaining websites and information systems, troubleshooting technical problems, ensuring security and data protection, and implementing new features and functionalities. He also provided valuable user training and support to enhance the overall user experience. Currently pursuing a master's degree in Health Information Technology at Princess Sumaya University for Technology, Mohammad's educational background is complemented by his extensive project experience. Notable projects he has been involved in include training on Acute Flaccid Paralysis Surveillance in Iraq, developing internal dashboards for GHD|EMPHNET's internal systems, and his significant contributions to the COVID-19 response efforts in Jordan. Outside of his professional achievements, Mohammad has earned several certifications in project management, business analysis, data analysis, and IT. He has also authored publications in the field of health and safety surveillance and has received awards for his contributions, including the Best Business Plan award in 2016 and the Philadelphia University Prize for the Best Computer Software in 2018. Mohammad Majed Asad is not only a professional with a strong commitment to the healthcare sector but also a proactive and innovative individual who consistently seeks to make meaningful contributions to public health through the integration of technology and data analysis.

Sumita Dave is presently Professor and Dean at Amity University, Raipur. Her research works have been published in journals of repute that are listed in Web of Science, Scopus and UGC Care. Her areas of research interest include Change Management, EI, Supply Chain Management and Retail Management. She has more than 90 publications to her credit .She is also a reviewer for national and international journals. She has also authored 02 books. She has worked on collaborative projects with UNICEF as Project Director. She has a notable record of establishing Centers of Excellence for Tribal Studies and Gender studies .She has delivered invited talks, and guest lectures at various management institutes and keynote addresses at national and International Conferences. Her expertise in administration, teaching, and research positions her as a prominent figure in the field of management education

Antonio Duran (he/him/él) is an assistant professor in higher and postsecondary education at Arizona State University. Dr. Duran's research examines how historical and contemporary legacies of oppression influence college student development, experiences, and success. In particular, he is passionate about uplifting queer and trans individuals with multiple minoritized identities in higher education.

Laksitha M. Herath earned her Master of Science in Accounting degree at New York University's Stern School of Business and works at Pricewaterhouse Coopers (PwC). Prior to her current endeavor, she gained valuable experience as a program accountant at Enstar Group Limited, a well-known global insurance company, and at Deloitte, a Big Four accounting firm, in Atlanta and New York. Laksitha holds a Bachelor of Arts degree in Accounting from Clark Atlanta University, where she held executive positions in its Toastmasters Club and she and a team of selected classmates won the Deloitte Regional Case Study Competition. She also published two book chapters and an article in a reputable journal. In her leisure time, she enjoys photography, cooking, and quality time with her family and friends.

Siriyama Kanthi Herath is an Associate Professor of Accounting at Clark Atlanta University's School of Business (CAU) and was a Renwick Faculty Fellow at New York University's Stern School of Business in 2022. She earned a Bachelor of Commerce Honors and an MBA from the University of Colombo in Sri Lanka, as well as a Ph.D. and a Master of Commerce Honors in Accounting from the University of Wollongong in Australia. She worked at the University of Lynchburg, Georgia State University and Georgia Institute of Technology before joining CAU. Prior to relocating to the United States, Dr. Herath worked in Australia at the University of Wollongong and Western Sydney University and in Sri Lanka at the University of Ruhuna and the University of Colombo. She holds positions on the editorial boards of multiple academic journals and has contributed over 70 publications to a diverse range of journals. Her research areas include Accounting Education, Management Control and Outsourcing, Cost Management, Corporate Governance, Data Analytics, and Sustainability Accounting. She is a Distinguished Toastmaster and served as the President and Treasurer of the Georgia Institute of Technology Toastmasters International Club from 2019 to 2020, the Treasurer of the Emory University Toastmasters International Club from 2019 to 2020, and as an Area Director from 2020 to 2021 in Georgia, United States. Additionally, she possesses the TESOL Professional Certificate from Arizona State University and the Professional Certificate in Google Data Analytics. In her leisure time, she enjoys traveling and gardening.

Ana Labella Fernández is an Assistant Professor at the University of Almería. She joined the Department of Economics and Business in 2018, where she has been teaching both at the undergraduate and master's levels in the Area of Business Organization. Currently, her research focuses on studying the relationship between the environmental entrepreneurial orientation of companies and organization performance, as well as greem human resource management and organization performance.

Christos Livas is an Assistant Professor of Marketing in the Department of Business Administration at the University of Patras, Greece. His current research interests include advertising, digital marketing, social and macro-marketing, tourism, and entrepreneurial orientation.

María del Mar Martínez-Bravo is an Interim Professor at the University of Almería (Spain). She joined the Economics and Business Department in 2018, where she has been teaching both at the undergraduate and master's levels. Her research focuses on studying urban dynamics in topics such as urban sustainability, urban pollution, city livability or urban digitalization.

Yamen Nissi is an Assistant Professor in the Australian University, Kuwait (AU) and is also an active researcher in topics under Operations Management, Entrepreneurship and Digital Business Transformation, Strategy and Leadership. He has extensive Corporate Experience of more than 13 years, in the field banking & investment management where he managed teams in operations and Customer Relationship Management, product development and service design.

Gregor Polančič is an associate professor in Informatics at the University of Maribor. He received his PhD in 2008 in the fields of software engineering and information systems. He has almost two decades of experience in BPM, starting to investigate BPMN since its first version in 2004. In 2008, he was one of the first authors who published an article dedicated to the experiences and practical use of BPMN. The article was published in the "BPM and Workflow Handbook" with the Workflow Management Coalition (WfMC). In 2013 he published a business process modeling-related article in the high impact journal Empirical Software Engineering (Article title: An Experimental Investigation Comparing Individual and collaborative work productivity when using desktop and Cloud Modeling Tools). His bibliography comprises almost 300 works, out of them more than thirty journal articles. He has been teaching BPM since 2005 in several undergraduate and postgraduate courses (e.g., Business Process Modeling, Business Process Management, Advanced Business Process Management, IT Governance) and has been an invited BPM/BPMN lecturer on several Universities. In 2019, he has been a visiting professor at Vienna University of economics and business, lecturing Business process implementation course. He has participated in several BPMN-related local and international workshops and projects and is currently researching BPM from different technological and user aspects. In recent years, Gregor Polančič has been periodically authoring for Orbus Software and Good e-learning companies, located in the UK. In 2019, he got the BPM best CEE forum paper award.

Kaity Prieto's research centers the experiences of LGBTQIA+ students, with a focus on plurisexual student communities. Her dissertation, "Bisexual College Students' Identity Negotiation Narratives, challenged deficit perspectives and binary understandings of sexuality and gender. Her recent work explores plurisexual graduate student and plurisexual Christian student experiences. Dr. Prieto earned her B.A. in a self-designed honors major and M.A. in Higher Education and Student Affairs, both from New York University. She received her Ph.D. in Educational Studies with a concentration in Higher Education and Student Affairs from The Ohio State University.

Massouma Rahat is an instructor at Australian University, Kuwait (AU). She holds a masters degree in Education for Change from Lakehead University, MBA from Maastricht School of Management and Bsc in Computer Science from Arab Open University. During 2003-2011, she was actively involved in teaching corporate sector topics related to computer programming and database administration. She joined AU in 2012 to take part in IT related professional development plans of numerous corporations in Kuwait both as a teacher and as an advisor. She then joined the faculty team of the school of business at AU in 2018 till the current date. Her research interests include technology and business.

Bhuwan Shrivastava has diverse background in entrepreneurship and academics. He holds an MBA degree with a specialization in International Business from Institute of Management, Banaras Hindu University, Varanasi, India and an Executive Certificate in Strategic Management from the Indian Institute of Management, Kashipur, India. He has also completed an Advanced Diploma in HRM from the Centre for Management Education, All India Management Association, New Delhi, India. Currently, he is pursuing his Ph.D. from Amity University, Raipur, India. He has over 17 years of entrepreneurship experience in the field of printing and publication. In addition to his entrepreneurship experience, Bhuwan has over 13 years of experience in academics as Visiting and Adjunct Faculty with various Management Institutions. He has taught courses in the areas of Entrepreneurship, Strategic Management, International Business and Organizational Behavior.

Vladimir Simovic is a researcher at the Scientific Research Center of the Australian University, Kuwait (AU) and the head of Digital Economics Department at the Institute of Economic Sciences, Serbia. His professional interests are in digital marketing, digital entrepreneurship, digital competencies, and information systems in business. He is project manager of the European ESF+ project on digital marketing competencies and participant of the European COST Action on artificial intelligence in business with over 15 years of research and teaching experience. He is the founder of several digital startups in Serbia and a think tank dedicated to innovative learning practices.

Apostolos Skotis is an Adjunct Lecturer of Management Information Systems in the Department of Business Administration at the University of Piraeus, Greece. He has an extensive experience in the field of customer-centered Business Analytics in many sectors. His current research interests focus on customer knowledge management and analytics, unstructured content analysis with NLP methods and knowledge creation in virtual communities.

Madhav Verma holds a Master's Degree in Business from Jamia Millia Islamia, New Delhi, India and has done his Post Graduate Certificate in Higher Education Course from Samtse College of Education, Bhutan. He is currently serving as the BCom Program leader and as an Associate Professor in Business. He is also actively involved in EU-funded projects related to entrepreneurship ENCORE and RECALL. He also works closely with entrepreneurs to prepare them for various Pitch decks.

Saniye Yildirim Özmutlu is a lecturer in Vocational School of Social Sciences at Tekirdag Namik Kemal University since 2011. She received her BA degree from Suleyman Demirel University in 2007, her MA degree from Suleyman Demirel University in 2011 and PhD degrees in Management and Organization from Yildiz Technical University. Her research interests include management and strategic management.

Index

M

O

P

R

S

T

U

V

www.ingramcontent.com/pod-product-compliance
Lightning Source LLC
LaVergne TN
LVHW062145300926
849161LV00010B/2632
* 9 7 9 8 3 6 9 3 0 7 9 8 4 *